MW01269047

The Emergence of Public Opinion

Nineteenth-century Ottoman politics was filled with casual references to public opinion. Having been popularised as a term in the 1860s, the following decades witnessed a deluge of issues being brought into 'the tribune of public opinion'. Murat R. Şiviloğlu explains how this concept emerged, and how such an abstract phenomenon embedded itself so deeply into the political discourse that even sultans had to consider its power. Through looking at the bureaucratic and educational institutions of the time, this book offers an analysis of the society and culture of the Ottomans, as well as providing an interesting application of theoretical ideas concerning common political identity and public opinion. The result is a more balanced and nuanced understanding of public opinion as a whole.

MURAT R. ŞIVILOĞLU is an assistant professor at Trinity College Dublin, Ireland. He has published several articles in books and journals and his main research interests focus on the social and intellectual history of the Ottoman Empire during the nineteenth century.

The Emergence of Public Opinion

State and Society in the Late Ottoman Empire

MURAT R. ŞIVILOĞLU
Trinity College, Dublin

CAMBRIDGE
UNIVERSITY PRESS

University Printing House, Cambridge CB2 8BS, United Kingdom

One Liberty Plaza, 20th Floor, New York, NY 10006, USA

477 Williamstown Road, Port Melbourne, VIC 3207, Australia

314–321, 3rd Floor, Plot 3, Splendor Forum, Jasola District Centre, New Delhi – 110025, India

79 Anson Road, #06–04/06, Singapore 079906

Cambridge University Press is part of the University of Cambridge.

It furthers the University's mission by disseminating knowledge in the pursuit of education, learning, and research at the highest international levels of excellence.

www.cambridge.org
Information on this title: www.cambridge.org/9781107190924
DOI: 10.1017/9781108120371

First published 2018

Printed in the United Kingdom by TJ International Ltd. Padstow Cornwall

A catalogue record for this publication is available from the British Library.

Library of Congress Cataloging-in-Publication Data
Names: Şiviloğlu, Murat R., author.
Title: The emergence of public opinion : state and society in the late Ottoman empire / Murat R. Şiviloğlu, University of Cambridge.
Description: Cambridge ; New York, NY : Cambridge University Press, 2018.
Identifiers: LCCN 2018009840 | ISBN 9781107190924 (hardback)
Subjects: LCSH: Turkey–History–Ottoman Empire, 1288-1918. | Turkey–Intellectual life–19th century. | Turkey–Social life and customs–19th century. | Turkey–Social conditions–1288-1918. | Turkey–Politics and government–1829-1878. | Public opinion–Turkey | State, The. | BISAC: HISTORY / Middle East / General.
Classification: LCC DR568 .S58 2018 | DDC 956/.015–dc23
LC record available at https://lccn.loc.gov/2018009840

ISBN 978-1-107-19092-4 Hardback

Front cover image reproduction: Bahadır Taşkın.

Canım annem Nesrin Deniz Acar'ın aziz hatırasına.

It is evident in history that rulers can assert themselves at will against any individual and only public opinion can restrain them. In some countries, public opinion is always open and declared, but in others it is latent, and emerges only when provoked to the extreme. In every state, consequently, rulers are acutely apprehensive of its power.

— Cevdet Pasha (From a report written to Sultan Abdülhamid in 1892)

Contents

List of Figures		*page* viii
Note on Transliteration, Place Names, and Dates		x
Acknowledgements		xi
	Introduction	1
1	Historical Background	23
2	A Bureaucratic Public Sphere	72
3	The World of İsmail Ferruh Efendi	110
4	The Schooling of the Public	134
5	The Emergence of a Reading Public after c. 1860	174
6	'The Turkish Revolution'	222
	Conclusion	250
Bibliography		255
Index		313

Figures

I.1 An Ottoman Newspaper titled *Efkâr-i Umumiye* (Public Opinion) from the late nineteenth century. *page* 16
1.1 A *hatt* of Abdülhamid I on the disturbance of peace with Russia. 32
1.2 Mustafa IV's *hatt* warning about the government bluster taking place in different coffeehouses of Istanbul and demanding the restraint and detention of those responsible. 34
1.3 The cover of *Eşek* (Donkey), a humour magazine. 36
1.4 Mahmud II's *hatt* demanding punishment for janissary supporters. 52
2.1 A photo of Scaliari Bey (Kleanti Skalyeri) in his full masonic costume in 1878. 94
3.1 A 1853 depiction of Keçecizade Mehmet İzzet Molla, one of the pioneers of Ottoman realism. 117
3.2 The inventory of books left by İsmail Ferruh Efendi. 121
4.1 A view of the Ottoman *Darülfünun* positioned between Hagia Sophia and Blue Mosque. 145
4.2 Ahmed Vefik Pasha, one of the lecturers of *Darülfünun* and the first translator of Molière to Ottoman Turkish. 150
5.1 A page from a statistics register prepared by Mehmed Behiç Bey. 176
5.2 The private secretary of Midhat Pasha, reading him daily newspapers. 189
5.3 An image of Bihruz Bey, the hero of *Araba Sevdası*. 206
5.4 Namık Kemal when he was the editor-in-chief of *İbret*, c. 1872–1873. 211

6.1 A contemporary picture showing the demonstrations of madrasa students. 231
6.2 The cover of *Vakit* a day after the deposition of Sultan Abdülaziz. 234
6.3 A contemporary image of Murad V. 236
6.4 A rather disturbing image of ex-Sultan Abdülaziz just before he committed 'suicide' on 4 June 1876. 238
6.5 The Deposition Fetva of Sultan Abdülaziz. 239
6.6 A scene from the unsuccessful raid organised by a secret society under the leadership of Ali Suavi. 249

Note on Transliteration, Place Names, and Dates

Terms in Ottoman Turkish rendered in the Arabic script are transliterated according to the orthographical conventions. Modern conventions in the transliteration of personal and place names are retained. Gregorian equivalents of both Muslim *Hicrî* and the *Rumî* dates are provided either in parentheses or after a solidus.

Acknowledgements

I do not know if it is the same with all authors. Long before the completion of this book, I thought about the title, cover, and various other, and what one might call, tangential aspects of this publication. Of course, they all changed dramatically over the time and now looking back, I see that I was naïve in supposing many things I supposed back then. For one, I was sure that writing acknowledgements would be the most entertaining part of this process. How little I knew.

My supervisor, Sir Chris Bayly, was unfortunately not able to see this book in print. He was not only one of the kindest people I have ever known but also a wonderful supervisor, and needless to say a great historian, whose comments and observations tremendously contributed to the formulation of this book. He was a constant source of guidance and encouragement throughout my years in Cambridge and I will remain indebted to him for the rest of my life. In the same vein, I cannot possibly thank Norman Stone properly for his mentorship throughout all these years. Without him, it would have been impossible to write this book. Edhem Eldem has been an inspiration to me since my years as an undergraduate, and I am deeply grateful for his unceasing and unstinting support. Cemal Kafadar, with his publications and through our meetings, enriched my whole understanding of history. Kemal Beydilli kept an open-door policy with me and whenever I felt baffled with an intricate source, I was sure of his sympathetic interest and generous erudition. In the most vexing problems I came across, I was lucky to benefit from Şahin Uçar's great understanding and unique perspective. During the writing of this book, Derin Terzioğlu's teachings were always at the back of my mind, as it were, and kept me in line and focused.

I would also like to thank the Gates Cambridge Trust for funding my doctoral research. My college, Peterhouse, has provided me with support in the way of grants, as well as a happy home. After the completion of my dissertation, Ömer Koç generously subsidised the final research of this book. I thank the directorates and staff of the ISAM library and the Archives of Prime Ministry for their assistance in my years of research in Istanbul. I have also had the good fortune to work with Maria Marsh, my editor at Cambridge University Press. She was reassuring, patient, and always very generous with her time.

My friends Fatmanil Döner, Paula Haas, Kutluhan Soyubol, Amrita Dhar, Astrid Norén-Nilsson, David Motadel, Amanda Dennis, and Cumhur Bekar have all helped in countless ways throughout the process of writing. Elisabeth Leake proofread the entire manuscript and spared me some embarrassing mistakes. Yavuz Sezer was a constant intellectual companion and always a great friend with whom I could talk for hours on my little findings. I thank my wife, Gülfem Pamuk, not just for her love and inspiration but for how much good advice she has given me along the way. Finally, I would like to express my endless gratitude to my parents for their constant support. My mother, like Sir Chris, will not be able to read this book. I know that she would have been very proud and I dedicate this book to her memory. Without her love and confidence in me, I would never have the courage to follow my heart's desire.

Introduction

The theme of this book can be presented quite simply. In 1837, the second most powerful person in the Ottoman Empire, Pertev Pasha, was executed without any formal charge under Mahmud II. It was as simple as that.[1] Less than fifty years later, however, in 1881, when Abdülhamid II was resolved to get rid of his archenemy, Midhat Pasha, two-time grand vizier and great reformer, this formerly easy task proved immensely difficult. First, the Sultan staged a special tribunal in his palace to establish Midhat's guilt before the law for the 'murder' of Abdülaziz, his deposed uncle. This was relatively easy. The court did find the Pasha guilty and sentenced him to death. There were the expected procedures to follow. Midhat appealed to the court of cassation, which only ratified the original decision. But, as Abdülhamid would find out, passing a sentence was one thing, carrying it into execution was quite another. The Sultan was immediately warned by his close advisors about the 'possible adverse effect of this decision on public opinion/*efkâr-ı umûmîyeye sû-i te'siri*'.[2] The sentence could not be imposed and Midhat was sent to prison in Ta'if.[3] *The Times* reported that Abdülhamid was 'greatly disappointed with the result of the State trial. He expected that the proceedings would have received the approval of *public opinion*, both

[1] Because of his influence and power, people called him *tuğsuz padişâh* (crownless king). See İbnülemin Mahmud Kemal İnal, *Son Asır Türk Şâirleri*, 3 vols., vol. II (İstanbul: Orhaniye Matbaası, 1930), 1317. The details of his rather romantically portrayed execution can be found in Lamartine's account. See Alphonse de la Lamartine, *Œuvres complètes de Lamartine: Histoire de la Turquie*, 8 vols., vol. VI (Paris: Chez l'auteur, 1863), 418–20.

[2] Başbakanlık Osmanlı Arşivi, (the Prime Ministry's Ottoman Archives, hereafter BOA), Y..PRK.HH.. 8/21, 8 Şaban 1298 (6 July 1881).

[3] This did not appease the wrath of Abdülhamid who tried to poison the prisoner there. But not having succeeded, he eventually had Midhat Pasha strangled in secret in 1884 and declared that he died of a malignant abscess.

in Turkey and in Western Europe, and he finds that the reverse has been the case.'[4] Yet there was nothing he could do. From his uncle's experiences, Abdülhamid knew only too well that it was very dangerous to swim against the current of public opinion.[5]

But for an independent-minded ruler, the worst was still to come. Just a few months before World War I, Enver Pasha, by far the most powerful man in the Empire,[6] arranged the court-martial and execution of a 'simple major' on the General Staff, Aziz Ali Bey (later famous as Aziz Ali al-Misri).[7] To the great frustration of the Pasha, however, this scheme caused quite a stir in Istanbul. Cemal Pasha, another member of the triumvirate that deposed Abdülhamid in 1909, after recognizing that, in his own words, '*public opinion* condemned Enver Pasha more severely than Asis Ali Bey', wrote to him: 'My dear Enver, notwithstanding all the evidence which the court martial has accumulated against Asis Ali Bey, and the fact that sentence has been passed upon him; it is you whom *public opinion* condemns. Your condemnation in this way will do you a thousand times more harm than anything Asis Ali Bey will suffer.'[8]

How should we explain this? Or to put it more precisely, how should we explain this emphasis on public opinion? One immediately thinks of the effect of media technologies such as newspapers to

4 Anonymous, 'Turkey, Constantinople, July 30', *The Times*, 1 August 1881, 5.

5 See the deposition of Sultan Abdülaziz, see Chapter 6, esp. 222–235.

6 During World War I, military shipments from Germany 'arrived addressed to "Enverland" . . . a name that Kaiser Wilhelm attached to Turkey after being charmed by Enver during his stay in Germany as a military attaché.' See Charles D. Haley, 'The Desperate Ottoman: Enver Paşa and the German Empire - I', *Middle Eastern Studies* 30, no. 1 (1994): 26. For the details of the Young Turk Revolution, see Feroz Ahmad, *The Young Turks: The Committee of Union and Progress in Turkish Politics, 1908–1914* (Oxford: Clarendon Press, 1969), passim.

7 Djemal Pasha, *Memories of a Turkish Statesman 1913–1919* (New York: George H. Doran Company, 1922), 63, emphasis mine. About his trial, also see BOA, DH.KMS. 19/16, 6 Cemaziyelevvel 1332 (2 April 1914). Aziz Ali Bey, surviving Enver Pasha's fury, lived to be one of the most important names of the independent Egyptian state and died as an octogenarian in Cairo in 1965. About him, see Eliezer Tauber, *The Emergence of the Arab Movements* (London: Frank Cass, 1993), 99–326, passim; Albert Hourani, *Arabic Thought in the Liberal Age 1798 – 1939* (Cambridge: Cambridge University Press, 1962), 285.

8 Cemal Pasha, *Memories of a Turkish Statesman 1913 – 1919*, 64, emphasis mine. In the Turkish edition, the term used for public opinion was *efkâr-ı umûmîye*. See Cemal Paşa, *Hâtırat: 1913 – 1922* (Istanbul: Ahmed İhsan ve Şürekası, 1922), 51.

account for this increasing awareness. But the reality, as usual, is more complicated than that. When Pertev Pasha was executed, the Ottomans had a newspaper, albeit an official one, which published the 'sudden death' of the unfortunate pasha without any hesitation.[9] In 1881, on the other hand, Abdülhamid knew that it was actually quite easy to control the media for something specific. He sent an ordinance to reporters for not publishing a word about Midhat's trials and there were no consequences.[10] For the case of Aziz Ali Bey, that was not less true. The Ottoman authorities were not only concerned with the domestic publications but were also trying to control what was being written in Egypt as Aziz was Egyptian.[11] Was it the increasing standards of the public education behind this mutual awareness then? Again, it is difficult to say. The Ottomans have not generally been considered to be a learned society until the very end, though this is something that this book challenges, and the conventional wisdom describes them, at best, as a 'literacy aware' society, to borrow C. A. Bayly's phrase on pre-colonial India.[12] Then how can we account for this changing picture? Did the society feel more responsible for the government's actions? How did such an abstract concept as public opinion become so important in a short period of time? How did it turn into such a source of authority to which even iron-fisted monarchs were obliged to conform? How did it function, and how did it dictate? And perhaps most importantly, how did public opinion emerge in the Ottoman Empire? For a preliminary answer to these questions, it might be a good idea to follow the trail of the term throughout the nineteenth century.

A Short History of Public Opinion in the Ottoman Empire

Public opinion, or as the Ottomans called it *efkâr-ı umûmîye*, is a sociological concept which became especially popular among European academics after the disillusioning days of World War II.

9 Anonymous, '[Edirne'de ikâmete me'mûr Pertev Paşa]', *Takvîm-i Vekâyi*, 5 Ramazan/3 December 1253/1837, 3.

10 See BOA, Y..EE.. 17/68, 5 Ramazan 1298 (1 August 1881).

11 See BOA, A.}MTZ.(05) 28/63, 26 Rebiülahir 1332 (24 March 1914).

12 C. A. Bayly, *Empire and Information: Intelligence Gathering and Social Communication in India, 1780–1870* (Cambridge: Cambridge University Press, 2000), 39.

New School sociologists such as Hans Speier analysed it to understand why Germany, the cradle of Enlightenment, fell under the influence of the Nazi regime, which was not at all enlightened.[13] It was implicitly suggested that an understanding of its mechanisms could help, in the future, to avoid similar unpleasant experiences. Alongside other theoretical engagements, the concept had fallen into disuse by the 1970s and was rediscovered by Anglo-American scholars only after the English translation of Habermas's 1962 book, *Strukturwandel der Öffentlichkeit* in 1989.[14] Since then, the term public opinion has become fashionable in the social sciences and its existence in certain societies or cultures is frequently presented as a sign of political development.

Modern Ottoman historians, by contrast, have been strangely uninterested in this popular concept, and public opinion has been mentioned alongside political and social issues without really questioning its applicability.[15] This is strange because public opinion, and its emergence, was something that early republican historians were very much aware. In 1939, İbrahim Alâettin Gövsa wrote a detailed article in *Yedigün* about its development in the Ottoman Empire.[16] One of the

[13] See Hans Speier, 'Historical Development of Public Opinion', *The American Journal of Sociology* 55, no. 4 (1950): 376–88.

[14] Jürgen Habermas, *Strukturwandel der Öffentlichkeit; Untersuchungen zu einer Kategorie der bürgerlichen Gesellscahft* (Neuwied: H. Luchterhand, 1962). The English translation is Jürgen Habermas, *The Structural Transformation of the Public Sphere: An Inquiry into a Category of Bourgeois Society* trans. Thomas Burger with the assistance of Frederick Lawrence, Studies in Contemporary German Social Thought (Cambridge, MA: MIT Press, 1993; reprint, Fifth). The French translation is slightly earlier, Jürgen Habermas, *L'Espace public: Archéologie de la publicité comme dimension constitutive de la société bourgeoise*, trans. Marc B. de Launay (Paris: Payot, 1986).

[15] Leslie Peirce, for instance, referring to the sixteenth-century Ottoman Empire, wrote: 'The Ottoman sultanate was not an unlimited despotism; while the sultan enjoyed the power of summary punishment, he had to operate within the parameters of *public opinion*.' Leslie P. Peirce, *The Imperial Harem: Women and Sovereignty in the Ottoman Empire* (Oxford: Oxford University Press, 1993), 267, emphasis mine. Cengiz Kırlı must be mentioned as an exception, even though he is more interested in popular opinion than public opinion *per se*. See Cengiz Kırlı, 'The Struggle Over Space: Coffeehouses of Ottoman Istanbul, 1780–1845' (PhD diss., State University of New York, 2000). For the difference between public opinion and popular opinion, see Robert Nisbet, 'Public Opinion versus Popular Opinion', *Public Interest* 41 (1975): 166–92.

[16] İbrahim Alaettin Gövsa, 'Efkârı Umûmîye', *Yedigün Dergisi* 313, no. 13 (1939): 7–8.

first historians of journalism, Servet İskit, published a pamphlet in which he distinguished two different types of public opinion, namely static and dynamic.[17] Writing in the 1940s, Ahmet Hamdi Tanpınar, probably the most sophisticated intellectual of the era, also used the concept as a primary explanatory tool, something omnipotent and omnipresent, in his *History of the Nineteenth Century Turkish Literature*.[18]

The Republican writers' early cognizance should not be surprising for those who are familiar with the canonical texts of the nineteenth-century Ottoman Empire. Especially after the 1860s, Ottoman politics was filled with casual references to public opinion. Naturally, chroniclers always used similar phrases to express people's content or discontent through the centuries. Mustafa Naîmâ (d. 1716) for instance, referred to *âmme-i nâs* (general people) quite often as something to take into consideration in daily politics.[19] *Halkın lisânı* (language of the people) or later in the period *ezhân-ı nâs* (minds of the people) were used by different Ottoman historians to express similar feelings.[20] But none of these terms, one needs to add, had the strength or intensity of the term 'public opinion', and were mostly used with negative connotations.

[17] According to İskit, the Ottomans had a static public opinion until the 1860s and only with the establishment of private newspapers; they were able to turn it into a dynamic force. See Server İskit, *Âmme Efkârımız* (İstanbul: Gazeteciler Cemiyeti, 1959), 12. This idea, static and dynamic public opinions, is probably taken from Wilhelm Bauer, *Public Opinion*, ed. Edwin R. A. Seligman, 15 vols., vol. XII, Encylopaedia of the Social Sciences (London: Macmillan Publishers, 1934), 669–70.

[18] See, for instance, Ahmet Hamdi Tanpınar, *XIX. Asır Türk Edebiyâtı Târîhi*, ed. Abdullah Uçman (İstanbul: Yapı Kredi Yayınları, 2006), 73, 110, 29, 44, 46, 48, 50, 57, 64, 65, 203, 04, 15.

[19] See Naîmâ Mustafa Efendi, *Târîh-i Naîmâ (Ravzâtü'l-Hüseyn fi Hulâsati Ahbari'l-Hafîkayn)*, ed. Mustafa İpşirli, 4 vols., vol. II (Ankara: Türk Târîh Kurumu, 2007), 356, 797, 899.

[20] See, respectively, Şem'dânî-zâde Fındıklılı Süleyman Efendi, *Şem'dânî-zâde Fındıklılı Süleyman Efendi Târîhi Mür'i't-Tevârih*, 4 vols., vol. I (İstanbul: Edebiyât Fakültesi Matbaası, 1976), 124; Şânîzâde Mehmed 'Atâ'ullah Efendi, *Târîh-i Şânîzâde*, 4 vols., vol. II (İstanbul: Cerîde-i Havâdis 1291/1874–1875), 220. There is an excellent modern edition of Şânîzâde's history. But because this was not available during the early phases of this research, the Ottoman edition is used throughout this book. See Şânî-zâde Mehmed 'Atâ'ullah Efendi, *Şânî-zâde Târîhi*, ed. Ziyâ Yılmazer, 2 vols. (İstanbul: Çamlıca, 2008).

As in Europe, the term *efkâr-ı umûmîye*, or its equivalent *efkâr-i âmme*, had a relatively short history in the Ottoman context.[21] Gövsa in his above-mentioned article asserted that the 'pen which invented the term *efkâr-i umûmîye* to explain French *opinion publique* in our language in all probability belonged to Şinâsi', then wrote the following:

But neither Şinâsi nor Nâmık Kemal, probably being carried away with the excitement of the term, paid any attention to the flaw of the expression. Because *efkâr-ı umûmîye* in today's Turkish means general opinions and expresses the opposite of private opinions. Its equivalent in French had to be *les opinions générales*. The real expression, according to the language of the day, needed to be *efkâr-ı âmme*. As a matter of fact, some writers who, figuratively speaking, knew how to hold their pen used the term *efkâr-ı âmme* instead of *efkâr-ı umûmîye*. Having said that the old *cliché* continued to preponderate in writing and saying until the very end.[22]

Similar to many other political and philosophical terms in the Ottoman language, both *efkâr-i umûmîye* and *efkâr-i âmme* are actually Arabic loanwords, which are connected to each other with a Persian linker (*izâfe*), indicating subject–predicate inversion. *Efkâr* is the plural of *fikr* and translated by the famous nineteenth-century lexicographer, James Redhouse, as 'ideas, thoughts'.[23] *Umûm* is also very straightforward and translated, again by Redhouse, as 'the generality or universality of anything'.[24] The word *umûm* or *umûmî* is rarely used today in modern Turkish, as a relic of an older world, to denote something 'public', as in *umûmî tuvalet* (public toilet). The word *efkâr* is, on the

[21] Keith Baker attributes to the appearance of the term in Rousseau's *First Discourse* in 1750 a special significance in the French context. See Keith Michael Baker, *Inventing the French Revolution: Essays on French Political Culture in the Eighteenth Century* (Cambridge: Cambridge University Press, 1990), 186. But the term was employed much earlier. As far as one can see the first use of the term in French was through a translation, in the 1555 rendition of famous *Orlando furioso*. See Arioste, *Le premier volume de Roland furieux ... par Loys Arioste ... maintenant mys en rime françoise par Jan Fornier ... avec les arguments au commencement de chacun chant ... et avec les allégories des chants à la fin d'un chacun*, trans. Jean Fornier (Anvers: Christofle Plantin, 1555), 53b. The English usage of the term seems to be much later but these are deep waters.

[22] Gövsa, 'Efkârı Umûmîye', 8.

[23] James W. Redhouse, *An English and Turkish Dictionary in Two Parts: English and Turkish and Turkish and English* (London: Bernard Quaritch, 1856), 474.

[24] Ibid., 830–31.

other hand, used only as an adjective with the Turkish suffix *–lı* and means someone 'depressed' (literally 'with thoughts').

Rendering the word *âmme* into English can be slightly difficult as the word is historically more loaded. This time Redhouse is not very helpful as there is no description of the word in his 1856 dictionary. Cleary both words (*umûm* and *âmme*) share a mutual Arabic root, *âmm*, meaning 'common, or general, or universal'.[25] In modern Arabic, this very word is used in the phrase (*er-re'yü'l-'âmm*) to give the expression public opinion today.[26] In the classical Islamic state system, *âmme* was one of the social classes, corresponding roughly, according to Évariste Lévi-Provençal, to 'plebs' and used in opposition to *khassa* (notable or royal).[27] Toru Miura reports similar views describing *âmme* as 'common people', in Baghdad around the tenth century, covering nearly everyone from artisans to thieves.[28] The term, however, seems to have gained a more negative connotation in the following centuries. Ira Lapidus, for instance, stresses that the 'term *al-'âmma* is preferred for situations involving violent protests and demonstrations' in the later Middle Ages.[29] Some popular uprisings, it should be noted, which took place in the 1830s in the Arab hinterland, were also called *âmmiyya* (literally, *âmme* related) by Arabic-speaking

25 Edward William Lane, *An Arabic-English Lexicon*, 8 vols., vol. V (Beirut: Librarie du Liban, 1968), 2148. Hans Wehr translates it as something 'universal, common, prevalent'. Hans Wehr, *A Dictionary of Modern Written Arabic: Arabic-English*, ed. J. M. Cowan (London: Macdonald & Evans Ltd., 1991), 640.

26 See, for instance, Muhyiddin Abdülhalim, *er-Re'yü'l-amm fi'l-İslâm* (Kahire: Mektebetü'l-Hanci, 1982). In classical dictionaries, one does not come across this expression. However, in a Latin-Italian-Arabic Dictionary, published in 1639, *re'yü'l-'âmm* was translated as *comune opinione*. See Dominicus Germanus, *Fabrica linguae arabicae, cum interpretatione Latina, & Italica, accomodata ad vsum linguae vulgaris, & scripturalis* (Rome: Typis. Sac. Congreg. de Prop. Fide, 1639), 722. In classical Islamic terminology, the concept of *as-Sawad al-'Âzam* (great majority) can be considered similar to the notion of public opinion. Unfortunately, to the best of my knowledge, there is no scholarly work on this interesting topic.

27 See Évariste Lévi-Provençal, *Histoire de l'Espagne musulmane: Le siècle du califat de Cordoue*, 3 vols., vol. III (Paris: Éditions G.-P. Maisonneuve et Larose, 1944), 196–98.

28 Toru Miura, 'Mashriq', in *Islamic Urban Studies*, ed. Masashi Haneda and Toru Miura (Oxon: Routledge, 2010), 102. Also see Michael Cook, *Forbidding Wrong in Islam* (Cambridge: Cambridge University Press, 2003), 17.

29 Ira M. Lapidus, *Muslim Cities in the Later Middle Ages* (Cambridge: Cambridge University Press, 1984), 175.

people.[30] Hence maybe there is also a deliberate choice made by some Ottoman authors, to distinguish between *âmme* and *umûm*. It is difficult to imagine that a linguist like Şinâsi would do such a mistake as Gövsa claims.[31] But it is not unusual, one needs to note, to see both expressions used interchangeably, sometimes on the same page.[32]

Gövsa's assertion, later supported by other scholars such as Mehmet Kaplan, that the term was invented by Şinâsi is not really true either. It is rather difficult to talk about firsts with absolute certainty when it comes to a subject like this. And there is always a chance of another researcher finding out an earlier application of the term, if one is lucky like Gövsa more than sixty years later. But 'in all probability', the expression was used for the first time by Sadık Rifat Pasha (d. 1857) in his pamphlet entitled, 'Containing Some Fundamental Laws of the Administration of the Government', posthumously published by his son in 1857. In his treatise written for the Sultan, Rifat Pasha warned him of the dangers of the modern politics: 'the temperament of the century and the spirit of the age', Rifat Pasha wrote:

> is like a rampant river. In the universe there are two things, which are difficult to cope with. One is religious belief and the other is public opinion (*efkâr-i âmme*). Opposing these two is surrounded with great difficulty and danger. In time of agitation and turbulence of public opinion, the best thing to do for governments is to follow the current.[33]

Rifat Pasha's comparison of public opinion to a river with its agitations and currents seems rather exaggerated for the time and might suggest an external influence, especially if this is the first use of the term in literature. His expression is similar to the one used by Jean-François Marmontel (d. 1799), a French historian and a member of the *Encyclopediste* movement. Marmontel, writing on literary criticism in the

[30] See Joel Beinin, *Workers and Peasants in the Modern Middle East* (Cambridge: Cambridge University Press, 2001), xi; Albert Hourani, *The Emergence of the Modern Middle East* (Berkeley: University of California Press, 1981), 161. In a related note, colloquial Arabic is also called *'ammiyya*.

[31] Here I am referring to Gövsa's assertion, cited above, which argued that 'the real expression, according to the language of the day, needed to be *efkâr-ı âmme*.'

[32] See Anonymous, 'Ferah Tiyatrosu Vakası', *Mîzân*, 15 Safer/8 March 1327/1909, 368.

[33] Mehmed Sadık Rıfat Paşa, *Müntahabât-ı Asâr-ı Rifat Paşa: İdâre-i Hükümetin Ba'zı Kavâid-i Esâsiyesine Mutazammın Rifat Paşa Merhumun Kaleme Aldığı Risâledir*, 12 vols., vol. XII (İstanbul: Takvîmhâne-i Amire, 1275/1859), 47.

late eighteenth century, similarly argued that '*l'opinion publique est comme un fleuve qui coule sans cesse*'.[34] It is possible that his work was familiar to Rifat Pasha, who served as the Ottoman ambassador in Vienna during the time of Metternich. The Austrian statesman was supposedly an admirer of Marmontel,[35] and it is known that Metternich greatly influenced Rifat Pasha's political formation.[36] The French writer also had a vague interest in the Ottoman Empire, and this might have aroused the Pasha's curiosity.[37] Even though there are reports about Rifat Pasha's poor knowledge of French, this does not necessarily exclude the possibility of such a connection.[38]

Unfortunately, the Pasha's report is not dated. Since he died in 1857, it is probably safe to say that his *lâyıha* was written in the 1840s or 1850s. In any case, it is clear that the expression 'public opinion' found its way into the government documents relating to foreign relations around this time.[39] In 1852, a report written in French by the Ottoman envoy in Paris, Kallimaki Bey, mentions the favourable '*opinion publique*' in France for the Ottoman borrowings, and this was duly translated by an Ottoman clerk as '*efkâr-ı umûmîye*'.[40] Only eleven months

[34] Jean-François Marmontel, *Oeuvres complettes de M. Marmontel, historiographe de France*, 13 vols., vol. VI (Paris: Née de la Rochelle, 1787), 262.

[35] Anonymous, 'The Salons of Vienna and Berlin', *Bentley's Miscellany* 50, no. 1 (1861): 153.

[36] Şerif Mardin, *The Genesis of Young Ottoman Thought: A Study in the Modernization of Turkish Political Ideas* (Syracuse, NY: Syracuse University Press, 2000), 177.

[37] Marmontel wrote a short piece recounting a French woman, 'who remarks on Soleiman's resemblance to a Frenchman, becomes his wife, and thereupon reforms the Ottoman Empire on the French mode'. See Thomas Kaiser, 'The Evil Empire? The Debate on Turkish Despotism in Eighteenth-Century French Political Culture', in *Early Modern Europe*, ed. James B. Collins and Karen L. Taylor (Padstow, UK: Blackwell Publishing, 2006), 74.

[38] Ali Rıza Bey and Mehmed Gâlib, *Geçen Asırda Devlet Adamlarımız: XIII. Asr-ı Hicride Osmanlı Ricâli*, ed. Fahri Çetin Derin, 2 vols., vol. I (İstanbul: Tercüman Gazetesi, 1977), 55.

[39] For instance, a letter written by Reşid Pasha in the summer of 1845 referred to the French *efkâr-ı âmme*. See Reşat Kaynar, *Mustafa Reşit Paşa ve Tanzimat* (Ankara: Türk Târîh Kurumu, 1985), 600.

[40] BOA, Y..EE.. 137/6, 8 September 1852. Alexander Kallimaki was a member of the famous Kallimaki family, a Romanian-speaking dynasty which Hellenized into the phanariot elite in the seventeenth century. See Christine M. Philliou, *Biography of An Empire: Governing Ottomans in an Age Revolution* (Berkeley: University of California Press, 2011), 16; Zeynep Sözen, *Fenerli Beyler 110 Yılın Öyküsü (1711–1821)* (Istanbul: Aybay Yayıncılık, 2000), 113–16.

later, another document written by Grand Vizier Mustafa Naili Pasha to Sultan Abdülmecid interestingly and clearly shows how fast the Ottomans had accepted the importance of this abstract notion:

His merciful highness, even though the *public opinion* in England is favourable to the Sublime State [i.e., Ottoman Empire], it will be beneficial to the present affair [the Crimean War] to make it even stronger since this will oblige English cabinet secretaries to act on our behalf. In this regard, it might be wise to dispatch a secret message to Ambassador Kostaki Bey [Kostaki Musurus Pasha] who, by making the necessary arrangements, can organize assemblies, called *miting* [meeting], and sent papers, known as *adres* [address], to the cabinet secretaries without giving any suspicion and clue. It will be also most beneficial to give him permission to spend some money for this cause if need be.[41]

Suggestively enough in the holdings of the Ottoman archives, public opinion appears as a phenomenon belonging to Europe, and with a few exceptions is always employed in connection with the Western powers until the very end.[42] But the Ottoman application of the term should not be taken as a mere mimicking of the Western practice. As it will be shown in this book, there was a tendency to emphasise the power of the public in domestic affairs for various reasons, especially after the reign of Mahmud II. One can see Ottoman writers, such as Şânîzâde or Esad Efendi, circling around the term, without using it, for some time in the 1820s and 1830s. It was not through ignorance that Esad Efendi's French translator, Armand-Pierre Caussin de Perceval, chose to translate his *ittihâd-ı kulûb* (union of hearts) as '*opinion publique*' in 1833.[43] The feeling was there.[44]

41 BOA, HR.SYS. 903/2–26 4 Zilkade 1269 (9 August 1853).

42 See, for instance, BOA, Y..EE.. 84/88, 1 Muharrem 1294 (16 January 1877), BOA, Y..PRK.HR.. 1/73, 11 Ramazan 1294 (19 September 1877), BOA, Y..EE.. 76/10, 25 Receb 1295 (28 July 1878), BOA, Y..PRK.AZJ. 2/49, 29 Zilhicce 1295 (24 December 1878), BOA, Y..EE.. 79/119, 17 Şaban 1297 (25 July 1880), BOA, Y..EE.. 127/47, 10 Rebiülahir 1300 (18 February 1883).

43 Mohammad As'ad Efendi, *Précis Historique de la destruction du corps des Janissaires par le Sultan Mahmoud: en 1826*, trans. A. P. Caussin de Perceval (Paris: F. Didot frères, 1833), 18. Actually, the original expression is slightly longer: '*ittihâd-ı kulûbe merhûn ve ittifâk-ı ârâ-i hulus-ı mashûba makrûn*.' Sahaflar Şeyhizâde Esad Efendi, *Üss-i Zafer* (İstanbul: Matbaa-i Âmire, 1243/1828), 10.

44 Contemporary dictionaries are not very helpful to pinpoint exactly when the term began to be used. The 'public opinion' or *efkâr-ı umûmîye* does not appear in the dictionaries of Redhouse, Mallouf, Ahmed Vefik, or Mehmed Salahi. See Redhouse, *An English and Turkish Dictionary in Two Parts*, 474;

Perhaps one also needs to make a distinction between the appearance of the term in government documents, including Rifat Pasha's report, and the adoption of the term by other segments of society such as newspapers. In this case, one needs to wait for another decade, until April 1863, which is still a year earlier than Şinâsi's famous article on stray dogs of Istanbul.[45] This time the person in question is someone quite obscure. Ali Haydar Bey (d. 1914) produced the first examples of rather unsuccessful Ottoman tragedies in the 1860s and published a 'scientific journal', the main interest for this study. In the second issue of his *Mecmuâ-i İber-i İntibah*, or *Collection of Lessons of Vigilance*, he announced that they would accept political articles only if they were not composed 'with the deliberate intention of spoiling the public opinion'.[46] This is the first documented occurrence of the term in the public sphere, and as it will be explained in the following chapters, the timing was not coincidental. After this, one sees many

J. W. Redhouse, *A Lexicon English and Turkish; Shewing, in Turkish, the Literal, Incidental, Figurative, Colloquial, and Technical Significations of the English Terms* (London: B. Quaritch, 1861), 608; N. Mallouf, *Dictionnaire Turc-Français avec la pronanciation figuré*, 2 vols., vol. I (Paris: Maisonneuve, 1863), 89; Ahmed Vefik Paşa, *Lehçe-i Osmani*, 2 vols., vol. I (İstanbul: Matbaa-i Amire, 1293/1876), 92; Mehmed Salahi, *Kamûs-i Osmani* (İstanbul: Mahmud Bey Matbaası, 1313/1895), 415. Şemseddin Sâmî in his encyclopaedia mentions '*Efkâr*' only as a poet from Samarkand and not as a concept. Şemseddin Sâmî, *Kamus-ül Âlem*, 4 vols., vol. II (İstanbul: Mihran Matbaası, 1306/1889), 1003. Again, it is not possible to find it in his Turkish-French dictionary, but in his dictionary from French to Turkish, *l'opinion public* was translated as *efkâr-ı umûmîye*. See Şemseddin Sâmî, *Kamûs-ı Fransevî: Fransızca'dan Türkçe'ye Lügat* (İstanbul: Mihran Matbaası, 1299/1882), 1109; Şemseddin Sâmî, *Kamûs-ı Türki*, 2 vols., vol. I (İstanbul: İkdam Matbaası, 1317/1899), 138. It should be noted that in 1841, Alexandre Handjéri had translated *opinion publique* as *itikad-ı nâs* (the conviction of people). See Alexandre Handjéri, *Dictionnaire Français-Arabe-Persan et Turc*, 3 vols., vol. II (Moscow: L'Imprimerie de l'université impériale, 1841), 632. A notable exception is the dictionary of Barbier de Meynard, who had a separate entry for *efkâr-ı umûmîye*. See Barbier de Meynard, *Dictionnaire turc-français: supplément aux dictionnaires publiés jusqu'à ce jour*, 2 vols., vol. I (Paris: Ernest Leroux, 1881), 82.

45 İbrahim Şinâsi, 'Bend-i Mahsûs: İstanbul Sokakları Tenvîr ve Tathîri Hakkındadır', *Tasvîr-i Efkâr*, 28 Zilkade/5 May 1280/1864, 1–2.

46 [Ali Haydar Bey], 'Mecmûanın Nizâmı', *Mecmûa-ı İber-i İntibah* I, no. 2 (1279/1863): 29. A few months earlier, Refik in his journal *Mir'ât* also used the term *efkâr-ı umûmîye*, but he was referring to Spanish Muslims (Al-Andalus) and not to the Ottoman Empire. See [Mustafa Refik], 'Esbab-ı Servet', *Mir'ât* I, no. 1 (1279/1863): 6.

other writers from different backgrounds using the expression to denote a political nation.[47]

This fashion, as it were, continued until 1876 and the overthrow of Abdülaziz in May that year can be seen in many ways as its culmination point. A day after the event, *Vakit*, a popular newspaper, announced Aziz's removal from the throne as the beginning of a new era. This was, the paper argued, thanks to the power of public opinion:

> *Public opinion*, that is the title of our article, is a part of the essential laws established by the sharia, pure and celestial justice. Our whole society is in fact built on this principle. It was public opinion, which founded the Ottoman State (*Devlet-i Âliye-i Osmaniye te'sîs eden efkâr-ı umûmîyedir*). It was *public opinion*, which led all the great triumphs of the Ottoman nation. The regulations, which were in force in the early days of the Sublime State, were all based on *public opinion*. It was *public opinion*, which had legitimized the laws of the Exalted Sultanate. Here the *public opinion* has struck again and eliminated the crisis disconcerting the Ottoman nation for some time. One cannot doubt that *public opinion* exists in Turkey as it exists in other refined countries if one just looks at the unmistakable fate suffered by first Mahmud Nedim Pasha and then later his guardian and protector, Sultan Abdülaziz. *Public opinion in Turkey by elevating His Highness Murad V, adorned with virtue and intelligence, to the throne*, has renewed the hope of the people and assured our future. *Public opinion* has showed that when it comes to searching and securing our legitimate rights, we are equal with Europe.[48]

47 See, for instance, a fine example from a play co-written by a woman writer in October 1908 in which heroes went to arrest a corrupt pasha after the Revolution of 1908:

'[Kâzım] Pasha:	Who gave you orders to arrest me?
Necib Bey:	Real ruler of the country.
Pasha:	What does that mean? Who is that real ruler?
Necib Bey:	Nation!
Pasha:	Nation?
Asım Bey:	That is to say public opinion [*efkâr-ı umûmîye*].
Pasha:	Who is the prosecutor?
Asım Bey:	Everyone.'

See Ruhsan Nevvare and Tahsîn Nahid, *Jön Türk: Üç Perdelik Milli Temâşâ* (İstanbul: Kitâbhâne-i Leon Lütfi, 1325/1908), 63–64.

48 Anonymous, 'Türkistan'da Efkâr-ı Umûmîye', *Vakit*, 31 May 1876, 1.

An Indigenous Public Opinion

The question thus is very simple. Is it possible to take these ideas seriously today? Were all these references to public opinion just rhetorical flourishes to obscure something else? In other words, was the *Vakit* 's cover story just a cover story to legitimise the acts of ambitious pashas? Were the pashas, as declared by Ahmed Lûtfî Efendi (d. 1907), 'a few lowlifes who committed a devilish deed [the deposition of Sultan Aziz] in the name of *public opinion* '?[49] Or was there really a public opinion in the Ottoman Empire?

Unfortunately, there is no measuring device to ascertain the authenticity of any public and very often one needs to rely on circumstantial evidences. One does not really think of the Ottomans as a politically engaged society. Even though historians like Şerif Mardin or İlber Ortaylı have shown that the seeds of Republican modernity had already taken root during the Tanzimat era (1839–1876), this often has been presented as an elite phenomenon, furthered and carried on by a few intellectuals and enlightened pashas.[50]

The trouble is simply that it is very difficult to look at the nineteenth century without remembering that the Empire collapsed at the end. This, by seriously muddling our understanding of the Empire, makes every Ottoman political movement look naïve, divorced from the people, and ultimately unsuccessful. If one can remove teleological spectacles, which oblige the observer to see an inexorable march towards destruction, the depth and extent of the success that the Ottomans had in adapting themselves to changing circumstances prove quite surprising.

Throughout the second half of the nineteenth century, members of the Ottoman public, with their political and scientific societies or their journals and newspapers began to question the contemporary social and political issues that affected their lives and came up with their own solutions. As the idea of serving the dynasty was gradually supplanted with the idea of serving the motherland (*vatan*),[51] nineteenth-century

49 İsmail Hakkı Uzunçarşılı, 'Sultan Abdülaziz Vak'asına Dair Vak'anüvis Lütfi Efendi'nin Bir Risâlesi', *Belleten* VII, no. 28 (1943): 351. For details, see Chapter 6.

50 See Mardin, *The Genesis of Young Ottoman Thought*; İlber Ortaylı, *İmparatorluğun En Uzun Yüzyılı* (İstanbul: İletişim Yayınları, 2003).

51 In the first issue of his newspaper *Asır* (Century), Mehmed Tevfik wrote 'our century is the century of serving the motherland.' See [Mehmed Tevfik]

Ottoman reformers made considerable achievements in the areas of education and culture. The historians of the Tanzimat era, however, while narrating the story of education or scientific societies as separate phenomena, neglected what these reformers created and targeted.

To a certain extent, this is a result of the different trajectories that the Ottoman modernity, and its public, followed. As mentioned at the beginning, in the Western historiography, the discussions of 'publicness' generally follow the blueprint that German philosopher Jürgen Habermas has outlined. Habermas conceptualises this public sphere as something completely separated from the state and coextensive with public authority. The state, in his opinion, functioned as 'the executor of the political public sphere', but 'not a part of it'.[52] It was, Habermas argues:

> a domain of our social life in which such a thing as public opinion could be formed. Access to the public sphere is open in principle to all citizens. A portion of the public sphere is constituted in every conversation in which private persons come together to form a public ... Citizens act as a public when they deal matters of general interest without being subject to coercion; thus with guarantee that they may assemble and unite freely, and express and publicize their opinions freely.[53]

This ideal picture, Habermas posits, was attained in England, France, and to a lesser extent Germany after the Enlightenment, and gradually deteriorated with the expansion of the public sphere. Even though an increasing number of historians has criticised the normative nature of his design, a civil society nourished by the Enlightenment culture and a bourgeois class created by early capitalist formation are still presented as indispensable and unassailable diagnostic terms of a 'true public sphere'.[54]

Asır: Mevâd-ı politikiyye ve mebâhis-i ilmiyye dair Osmanlı Gazetesidir 1287/1870: Sâhibi: [Çaylak] Tevfik, ed. Ali Emre Özyıldırım (Ankara: Türk Târîh Kurumu, 2014), 2.

52 Jürgen Habermas, 'The Public Sphere: An Encyclopedia Article (1964)', *New German Critique*, no. 3 (1974): 49.

53 Jürgen Habermas, 'The Public Sphere', in *Jürgen Habermas on Society and Politics: A Reader*, ed. Steven Seidman (Boston: Beacon Press, 1989), 231.

54 Jon Cowans, *To Speak for the People: Public Opinion and the Problem of Legitimacy in the French Revolution* (London: Routledge, 2001), 142. Habermas prefers the term 'authentic public sphere'. See Habermas, *The Structural Transformation of the Public Sphere*, 30.

The Ottomans, on the other hand, aside from not having these historical conditions, had a political culture constructed out of completely different discursive practices and sources. Although the state, by granting privileges to Ottoman merchants, supported the creation of domestic mercantile organisations, such as *Avrupa Tüccarı* or *Hayriye Tüccarı*, to help them compete with their European counterparts, it is very difficult to argue that this amounted to any serious proportion or was sufficient to maintain an enlightened culture, like the bourgeois class in Europe.[55] Yet, Ottoman policymaking succeeded in forming, what this book calls, a 'cultural public sphere' from its members, which eventually spread to other layers of the Ottoman society. That is to say, the Ottoman public sphere was not created, as one sees in other examples, out of a clear delineation between the state and society, but rather out of their union, out of modernising reforms aimed at regenerating the failing structure of the Empire.

Despite the different trajectories however, the end result is not very different. With the expansion of the public sphere throughout the nineteenth century, the palace and *sharia* increasingly found their spheres of influence curtailed, and the Ottoman public emerged as a central influence on the politics of the century. To repeat the main point here more succinctly, this book asserts that even though the Ottoman Empire followed a distinctly different path from the Western European powers, it still managed to create a realm of social life where public opinion could be formed. But before analysing the historical conditions which paved the way to the formation of a public opinion, it might be better to answer who was the public in the modern Ottoman state.

An Ottoman Public

Until the reforms of the nineteenth century, Ottoman society was heavily segregated, with vertical and horizontal societal boundaries separating subjects. While the ruling class (*askeri*) was separated with

[55] This led, at best, 'a temporary reversal in the trend toward Western economic control'. See Bruce Masters, 'The Sultan's Entrepreneurs: The Avrupa tuccaris and the Hayriye tuccaris in Syria', *International Journal of Middle East Studies* 24, no. 4 (1992): 580. Also see Ali İhsan Bağış, *Osmanlı Ticâretinde Gayrî Müslimler: Kapitülasyonlar, Avrupa Tüccarları, Beratlı Tüccarlar, Hayriye Tüccarları (1750–1839)* (Ankara: Turhan Kitâbevi, 1983).

افکار عمومیه

صلح مرخصلرمز

قونفرانسه کیدرکن

ائتلافجیلر نظرنده

Figure I.1 An Ottoman Newspaper titled *Efkâr-i Umûmîye* (Public Opinion) from the early twentieth century. Mehmed Safa, *Êfkar-ı Umûmîye*, 6 Ramazan/5 June 1317/1919. There were quite a few newspapers with the same name. One prominent example was published by a dissident medical student, Mustafa Ragıp in Bulgaria in bilingual editions in 1909.

See, BOA, A.}MTZ.(04) 127/38, 18 Muharrem 1323 (March 25, 1909). Interestingly enough, the Bulgarian edition was also entitled ЕФКЯРИ-УМУМИЕ *(Efkâr-i Umûmîye).*

certain prerogatives from the rest of the population,[56] and had few conspicuous internal divisions,[57] the subjects (*reâya*) were appropriated into a myriad of subcategories under two main headings: Muslims and non-Muslims. Here, different layers of wealth and prestige also mattered a great deal, and the society as a whole functioned on the premise of gender separation. Ottoman writers, with references to Galenic and Aristotelian traditions, employed certain metaphors and figurative allusions, such as the Circle of Justice (*Dâire-i Adâlet*) or Four Pillars (*Erkân-ı Erbaa*), to perpetuate this graded society.[58] More often than not, the state was likened to a human body where each limb and organ had a certain function – something that is also evident in Medieval European Literature.[59] Residential segregation, another mutual feature in early modern societies,[60] was accentuated with religious overtones.[61]

56 See, for instance, Linda T. Darling, *Revenue-Raising and Legitimacy: Tax Collection and Finance Administration in the Ottoman Empire, 1560–1660* (Leiden: E. J. Brill, 1996), 89, especially fn. 22.

57 See Cornell H. Fleischer, *Bureaucrat and Intellectual in the Ottoman Empire: The Historian Mustafa Âli (1541–1600)* (Princeton, NJ: Princeton University Press, 1986), 201–13. Cornell H. Fleischer, 'Preliminaries to the Study of the Ottoman Bureaucracy', *Journal of Turkish Studies*, no. 10 (1986): 135–40. Rifa'at 'Ali Abou-El-Haj, 'The Ottoman Nâsihatname as a Discourse over 'Morality', in *Mélanges Professeur Robert Mantran*, ed. Abdeljelil Temimi (Zaghouan: Centre d'études et de recherches ottomanes, 1988), 20.

58 Kâtip Çelebi, *Düsturü'l-Amel li-Islâhi'l-Halel* (İstanbul: Tasvîr-i Efkâr Matbaası, 1280/1863–1864), 134–35; Mustafa Naîmâ, *Târîh-i Naîmâ: Ravzâtü'l-Hüseyn fi Hulâsati Ahbari'l-Hafîkayn*, 6 vols., vol. I (İstanbul: Matbaa-i Âmire, 1280/1863–64), 28–30; Kınalızâde Ali Çelebi, *Ahlâk-i Alâ'î*, 3 vols., vol. I (Kahire: Matba'a-'i Bulak, 1248/1832), 7–8. Also see Huneyn b. Ishak, *Kitâbu Calinus ila Tavsirun fi'n-Nabzi li'l-Müteallimin*, ed. Muhammed Selim Salim (Kahire: El-Hey'etü'l-Mısriyyetü'l-Âmme li'l-Kitâb, 1986), 115–21.

59 Andreas Musolff, 'The Embodiment of Europe: How do Metaphors Evolve?', in *Body, Language, and Mind: Sociocultural Situatedness*, ed. Roslyn M. Frank, et al. (Berlin: Mouton de Gruyter, 2008), 302–04; Helena M. Paavilainen, *Medieval Pharmacotherapy, Continuity and Change: Case Studies from Ibn Sīnā and Some of His Late Medieval Commentators* (Leiden: Brill, 2009), 42. Gibbon also mentions the Circle of Justice as an ancient Persian maxim. See Edward Gibbon, *The Decline and Fall of the Roman Empire*, 6 vols., vol. I (New York: Modern Library, 1943), 183.

60 See Adrian Johns, *The Nature of the Book: Print and Knowledge in the Making* (Chicago: University of Chicago Press, 1998), 64.

61 A seventeenth-century Armenian writer, Eremya Çelebi, mentioned many different Jewish bazaars and Greek quarters where Turks did not mingle. Eremya Çelebi Kömürcüyan, *İstanbul Târîhi: XVII. Asırda İstanbul*, ed. Hrand

This system was sustained and visualised through the state's interventions into clothing laws, which designated the garments of each denomination down to the minute details.[62] The Islamic law, by favouring the Muslims disproportionately over the other fractions of the population, prompted Christians and Jews to avoid any confrontations, if not any encounters, with Muslims, a meeting from which the formers had too little to obtain.[63] Although sporadic business transactions and guild connections made complete isolation impossible, and probably undesirable in terms of market flexibility, the *ulemâ* (Ottoman religious and legal scholars) advised the pious to abstain from socialising with non-Muslims; a recommendation which was duly repeated by priests and rabbis to their corresponding communities.[64]

The legal equalisation of the population as imperial subjects in 1839 and the official disestablishment of religious differences in 1856 not only laid the foundation of imperial citizenship but also

D. Andreasyan (İstanbul: İstanbul Üniversitesi Edebiyât Fakültesi Yayınları, 1952), 36, 45. In the diary of Seyyid Hasan, another seventeenth-century figure who was 'most diligent in recording such seemingly insignificant details from his daily life and the names or nicknames of every person with whom he associated during those activities ... there is not a single non-Muslim mentioned'. See Cemal Kafadar, 'Self and Others: The Diary of a Dervish in Seventeenth Century Istanbul and First-Person Narratives in Ottoman Literature', *Studia Islamica*, no. 69 (1989): 138, 45. Even in the early nineteenth century, Şânîzâde 'Atâ'ullah Efendi could not help bringing up, in his usual derisive tone, the shocking effect of the sight of a British fleet on the entire Muslim population of Istanbul who 'had not seen any infidel except the local grocer.' Şânîzâde Mehmed 'Atâ'ullah Efendi, *Târîh-i Şânîzâde*, 4 vols., vol. I (İstanbul: Cerîde-i Havâdis, 1291/1874–1875), 47.

62 Ahmet Refik, *Hicri On Birinci Asırda İstanbul Hayâtı (1000–1100)* (İstanbul: Devlet Matbaası, 1931), 20, 52. Ahmet Refik, *On Altıncı Asırda İstanbul Hayâtı (1553–1591)* (İstanbul: Devlet Basımevi, 1935), 47–52.

63 If one goes through the religious rulings of Ebu's-su'ud Efendi (d. 1574), probably the most honoured and venerated Chief Mufti of all times, from the legal point of view it is quite clear that the non-Muslims were better off if they could avoid any contacts with Muslims whatsoever. Their testimony, for instance, was not accepted in criminal cases even at proportions as one village to one person. See *Şeyhülislam Ebusuud Efendi Fetvâları Işığında 16. Asır Türk Hayâtı*, ed. Mehmet Ertuğrul Düzdağ (İstanbul: Enderun Kitâbevi, 1972), 89–105, especially rulings 410, 24, 47, 60, 61. Cf. Haim Gerber, *State, Society, and Law in Islam: Ottoman Law in Comparative Perspective* (Albany, New York: State University of New York Press, 1994), 56.

64 Suraiya Faroqhi, *The Ottoman Empire and the World Around It* (London: I. B. Tauris, 2004), 17.

prepared the legal ground for an Ottoman public.[65] Even though the nineteenth century is often presented as the end of the multinational Ottoman project, for the first time in its half-millennium history, people came to believe that such a venture, a multicultural Ottoman society, was possible.[66]

This book, as the title suggests, follows the trails of the Ottoman public whose sole criterion for admission was the ability to speak and write the Ottoman language. It would have been rather interesting to survey the Greek or Armenian publics as examples of counterpublics, which were coterminous, and contemporaneous, with the official public sphere. It should be noted that there were similar 'public' tendencies among the minorities of the Empire.[67] Learned societies of different communities, for instance, started their public reading rooms in Istanbul almost simultaneously. The Ottoman [speaking] *Cemiyet-i İlmiye* in 1861, the Greek *Syllogos* in 1862, and the Bulgarian *Chitalishte* in 1866 opened their doors for their respective communities in Istanbul.[68] But in this book, the members of non-Muslim communities will be mentioned, such as Alexander Karatheodori Pasha (d. 1906), only as a part of the Ottoman 'suprapublic'. This is, it should be added, due to a lack of necessary linguistic skills and not because of lack of interest.

65 Cevdet Pasha mockingly noted that when, finally, the legal equality was established in 1856, certain 'Westernized gentlemen/*alafranga çelebi*' were overjoyed saying 'non-Muslims would spread among the people of Islam so neighbourhoods would be mixed. Our properties would raise in value and civilization would be widespread'. Cevdet Paşa, *Tezâkir 1–12*, ed. Cavid Baysun, 4 vols., vol. I (Ankara: Türk Târîh Kurumu Basımevi, 1991), 68. For the type of 'westernized gentleman', see Chapter 5, 202–213.

66 Kemal Karpat, for instance, sees the nineteenth century bundled with perpetual struggle and in a strident contrast with the age of 'Pax Ottomanica, which prevailed from the 15th to 18th century'. Kemal H. Karpat, *Studies on Ottoman Social and Political History: Selected Articles and Essays* (Leiden: Brill, 2002), 604.

67 Nancy Fraser refers to 'subaltern counterpublics in order to signal that they are parallel discursive arenas where members of subordinated social groups invent and circulate counterdiscourses to formulate oppositional interpretations of their identities, interests, and needs'. Nancy Fraser, 'Rethinking the Public Sphere: A Contribution to the Critique of Actually Existing Democracy', in *Habermas and the Public Sphere*, ed. Craig Calhoun (Cambridge, MA: MIT Press, 1992), 123.

68 See Johann Strauss, 'Kütüp ve Resail-i Mevkute: Printing and Publishing in a Multi-Ethnic Society', in *Late Ottoman Society – The Intellectual Legacy*, ed. Elisabeth Özdalga (Oxford: RoutledgeCurzon, 2005), 233.

The societies and the groups that this book addresses were all Istanbul based; and provincial organisations founded in the other cities and centres of the Empire are beyond the scope of this work. Again, one can see similar patterns developing in other geographies as well,[69] but they are, to keep the focus clear, left out of this research. The scope is also limited in terms of its gender sensitivity. This was not a deliberate choice. The Ottoman societies and associations did not explicitly prohibit women from membership in their constitutions, but this was implicitly assumed to be the case. There were prominent female writers, especially later in the century, and some of them, as will be mentioned, became celebrated *salonnières*. But they seldom appeared in the sources used for this work and the Ottoman public developed as a site of masculine camaraderie.

Objectives and Outline

To explain the development of the Ottoman public, this book focuses on different moments and ruptures, which took place during the nineteenth century. First, it reviews the historical background of the Ottoman public. The economic crisis of the 1780s and the subsequent large domestic borrowings of the Ottoman government are discussed with specific reference to public formation. The effects of modern state-making on public identity are analysed here with a particular focus on the reforms of Mahmud II. It is mainly argued that Mahmud II's centralisation policies and the abolition of the janissaries created favourable social and political conditions for the emergence of an Ottoman public.

The second chapter attempts to locate the bureaucratic phase, a transitionary period, of the Ottoman public. It examines the new forms of sociability and solidarity, which developed among the members of the Ottoman elite as a result of increasing bureaucratisation. Here particular attention is paid to the emergence of secret societies, such as freemasonry, as they are considered crucial in the development of a political criticism of the regime. In this chapter, after discussing various

[69] Such as a public reading room established by twin brothers, local Muslims, in Vidin at the end of the nineteenth century. See Hüseyin Memişoğlu, 'Bulgaristan'ın Vidin Şehrinde Halil ve İbrahim İkiz Kardeşlerin Kurdukları Kültür Vakfı ve Onun "Şefkat" Kırâathânesi', *Türk Dünyası Araştırmaları*, no. 169 (2007): 205–20.

examples, a taxonomy for classifying different types of house gatherings (*meclis*) is proposed. The influence of changing political culture on the formation of such sociability is also surveyed with a particular focus on *münâzara* (debate). The main argument is that through the institution of *meclis*, the Tanzimat bureaucracy created a critical intellectual and social space for a new public discourse.

The third chapter explores the connection between the reading material and discursive practices. Through an analysis of probate records, it proves that the reading habits of the Ottoman elite changed dramatically over the course of the nineteenth century. This was, it is argued, a result of the paradigm shift that the Empire went through during the Tanzimat era. By examining social and political reasons, which gave rise to this profound transformation, the chapter also advances the idea that the emergence of notions like public or public opinion was not mere adaptations of Western practices but arose from tremendous changes that had taken place since the beginning of the nineteenth century.

The fourth chapter advances the argument made in the previous chapters by examining the Ottoman Empire's reforms to state education. It has a selective approach and deals only with one dimension of this complex phenomenon: the schooling of the public (*terbiye-i âmme*), an imperial policy first emerged during the reign of Sultan Abdülmecid (r. 1839–1861). The chapter gives a short account of the introduction of modern education into the Ottoman Empire and briefly discusses how this changed the perceptions of mass education. Next it investigates the construction of the first Ottoman University, *Dârülfünun*, as an example of this changing attitude in governmental circles. This chapter then analyses the emergence of new type of societies, which began developing around the beginning of the 1860s while the pasha houses were slowly losing their public character and monopoly over the opinion-making process. Here it is argued that these 'epistemic communities', by establishing the Empire's sense of cultural identity helped the development of new participatory spheres, civic awareness, and citizenship in the burgeoning Ottoman public sphere.

The fifth chapter deals with the emergence of a cultural public sphere in the Ottoman Empire. It begins with a discussion of *Cerîde-i Havâdis* (1840) as the first example of private newspapers in the Ottoman Empire. Here the chapter emphasises the importance of printing houses as political spaces and analyses the commodification of discourse through the birth of the professional author. By focusing on Nâmık Kemal as the prime example, it proposes that a new relationship between public and intellectuals was established during this period. Through a close reading of Kemal's articles, the chapter shows the increasing importance of the term 'public opinion' in daily political language in the 1860s and 1870s. By focusing on the writings of Kemal and other contemporary authors, the chapter also investigates the significance of unofficial spaces in providing intellectual communication, including discussions of transparently political questions. The book ends with an account of Sultan Abdülaziz's deposition in 1876. Here it is argued that unfavourable public opinion was the main motivation behind the event and this represents the culmination point of public formation in the Ottoman Empire.

1 Historical Background

Introduction

Throughout the ages, Ottoman authors have often used words related to the public in the Ottoman language, such as *âmm, âmme, umûm*, and *avâm*, with a negative connotation. In one of the most popular books of all time, *Muhammediye*, Yazıcıoğlu Mehmed Efendi (d. 1451), after dividing the population into three classes, described the common people (*âmm*) as having negligible religious beliefs and being very much lost to earthly affairs.[1] A century later, Kınalızâde Ali (d. 1572), in his *Ahlâk-ı Alâ'î*, called it a calamity (*âfet*), when the *avâm* began questioning serious matters.[2] Perhaps the most sophisticated and prolific writer of Ottoman history, Kâtib Çelebi (d. 1657) took this elitist view somewhat further and portrayed the common people as vermin (*el-'avâm ke'l-hevâmm*),[3] an idea which found widespread approval among later generations.[4]

While Islamic concepts such as *maslahah*, the common good; *istihsân*, the promotion of the common good over strict legal reasoning through exceptions; and *istislâh*, the public interest, were very much parts of Ottoman legal discourse, they had little or no impact on the lives of ordinary people in conflicts with authority. In fact, these concepts, rather than providing legal refuge, more often than not

1 Yazıcıoğlu Mehmed Efendi, *Muhammediye: Kitâb-ı Muhammediyye*, ed. Amil Çelebioğlu, 4 vols., vol. I (İstanbul: Tercüman Gazetesi, 1975), 115.

2 Kınalızâde Ali Çelebi, *Ahlâk-ı Alâ'î: Kınalızâde'nin Ahlâk Kitâbı*, ed. Mustafa Koç (İstanbul: Türkiye Yazma Eserler Kurumu Başkanlığı, 2014), 590.

3 Kâtip Çelebi, *Mîzânü'l-Hakk Fi İhtiyari'l-Ehakk* (İstanbul: Ebuzziyâ Matbaası, 1306/1888–1889), 15. In the Turkish edition, this Arabic phrase was translated as '*the rabble are like animals/ayak takımı hayvan gibidir*'. In the English translation, it becomes 'masses are asses'. Kâtip Çelebi, *Mîzânü'l-Hakk Fi İhtiyari'l-Ehakk (En Doğruyu Sevmek İçin Hak Terazisi)*, ed. Orhan Şaik Gökyay (İstanbul: Milli Eğitim Basımevi, 1972), 12. Kâtip Çelebi, *The Balance of Truth*, trans. Geoffrey L. Lewis (London: George Allen and Unwin, 1957), 29.

4 Naîmâ Efendi, *Târîh-i Naîmâ II*, 931–32.

served as discursive tools of the political and economic domination of the ruling classes.[5] In a similar vein, Ottoman advice writers and chroniclers, under the intricate rhetoric of *adl*/justice, often recommended a firm approach towards the commoners to keep them in their stations in every sense of the word.[6] According to Mustafa Naîmâ (d. 1716) even the ban on tobacco, the enforcement of which terrorised Istanbul residents through on-the-spot executions during the reign of Murad IV (r. 1623–1640) was 'clearly just an excuse to leave the common people terrified' (*avâm-ı nâsı terhîb maslahatı için bir bahâne idüği bedîhîdir*).[7] Looking back, he unequivocally approved of this ban, which helped to deter members of the public from meeting to discuss governmental affairs in coffeehouses, barbershops, and residences.[8]

This policy of deliberate contempt and (when the centre had enough power) control remained more or less the norm up until the transformations, which form the theme of this book. So much so, in fact, that even at the beginning of the nineteenth century (in 1803), a book of advice presented to Selim III, with the very suggestive title, *A Brief for Speaking in Response to the Common People* (*Hulâsatü'l- kelâm fi reddi'l-avâm*), advocated the complete abstinence of the *avâm* from public affairs on pain of death.[9] Accordingly, this chapter will give a background of how the Ottoman public transformed itself from a rabble not given the time of day by authorities to the ultimate source of political legitimacy. It will be mainly suggested that only the complete breakdown of the old system allowed something akin to a

[5] Engin Deniz Akarlı, 'Maslaha: From "Common Good" to "Raison d'état" in the Experience of Istanbul Artisans, 1730–1840', in *Hoca, 'Allame, Puits De Science: Essays in Honor of Kemal Karpat*, eds. Kaan Durukan, Robert Zens, and A. Zorlu-Durukan (Istanbul: The Isis Press, 2010), 66–67. Also see Frederick F. Anscombe, *State, Faith, and Nation in Ottoman and Post-Ottoman Lands* (Cambridge: Cambridge University Press, 2014), 29.

[6] Lütfi Paşa, *Âsafnâme* (İstanbul: Matbaa-i Amedi, 1326/1908–1909), 25.

[7] Naîmâ Efendi, *Târîh-i Naîmâ II*, 757.

[8] Ibid.

[9] Koca Sekbanbaşı [Ahmed Vasıf Efendi], *Hulâsatü'l-kelâm fi reddi'l-avâm* (İstanbul: Hilal Matbaası, 1332/1916), 7. On the identity of Ahmed Vasıf and for more information on this interesting text, see Kemal Beydilli, 'Sekbanbaşı Risâlesinin Müellifi Hakkında', *Türk Kültürü İnceleme Dergisi* 12 (2005): 221–24, Ethan L. Menchinger, *The First of the Modern Ottomans: The Intellectual History of Ahmed Vasif* (Cambridge: Cambridge University Press, 2017), 268–276.

modern public sphere and an endogenous public opinion, as understood by Habermas and others, to develop.

To this end, this chapter starts with the beginning of the famous Eastern Question. Here it is discussed that the *Great Divergence*, as Kenneth Pomeranz has shown, did not really take place, at least for the Ottomans, until the last quarter of the eighteenth century, and the Empire more or less remained competitive with Europe through its extensive artisanal industries. Next, the question of public debt is examined through specific references to the public and the makeup of the public. It is suggested that public debt created a new type of awareness between the state and society. This is followed by an account of the elimination of rival power centres as a crucial step towards the construction of a disciplinary space. Thanks to the transfer of their authority to the state, it is shown here how a discursive sphere emerged where public discussion was possible. The chapter then surveys the question of janissaries and their relationship with society. Here the main argument is that they were the most important component of the *Ancien Régime* and that only with their removal from the Ottoman system could an Ottoman public in its fullest sense be formed. Finally, the chapter concludes with a short account of the first Ottoman newspaper, *Takvîm-i Vekâyi*.

Beginning of the Eastern Question

By the early nineteenth century, the Ottoman Empire looked like feudal Europe at its worst.[10] Perhaps it was still colossal in size – stretching from Bosnia to Algeria to Basra – but the old political structure was crumbling at every corner. As early as 1802 the *chargé d'affaires* of the British Embassy in Constantinople was expecting an imminent end, which would turn the Empire into 'numberless, petty, piratical states'.[11] Comte Auguste de Forbin, travelling through the Levant in 1816, found it difficult to believe how 'Turks' could still be

[10] 'In fact', Şükrü Hanioğlu wrote, 'the Ottoman state can only be considered an empire in the loose sense in which the term is used to refer to such medieval states as the Chinese under the late T'ang dynasty.' M. Şükrü Hanioğlu, *A Brief History of the Late Ottoman Empire* (Princeton: Princeton University Press, 2010), 6–7.

[11] Allan Cunningham, 'The Sick Man and the British Physician', *Middle Eastern Studies* 17, no. 2 (1981): 160.

present in Europe after witnessing the 'ignorance and indiscipline of their troops, [and] disorder of their finances'.[12] There were even rumours about the *Turk's* possible extinction which was seen as a historical opportunity by science-minded people like Hyde Clarke who invited the public 'to the spectacle of the extinction of a mighty and numerous people, such as took place with the ancient Greeks and Romans'.[13]

This gloomy picture was not, however, the result of an inevitable Ottoman decline begun in the late sixteenth century, as has been generally depicted.[14] The economy grew an estimated 50 per cent over the period, while some lost land was recuperated following the failure of the second siege of Vienna (1683).[15] Until the 1760s, Ottoman producers were major participants in international trade, and as Şevket Pamuk points out, the 'trend was toward balanced budgets, and surpluses were enjoyed in many years'.[16] Though the centre's political

[12] Comte Auguste de Forbin, *Voyage dans le Levant en 1817 et 1818* (Paris: de l'Imprimerie royale, 1819), 46–47. Thirteen years later, Adolphus Slade fretted over the fate of 'stately minarets' in Constantinople, as he feared that 'a mistaken zeal for religion' would remove them 'whenever the cross replaces the crescent'. Adolphus Slade, *Records of Travels in Turkey, Greece, etc. and of a Cruise in the Black Sea, with the Capitan Pasha, in the Years 1829, 1830, and 1831* (London: Saunders and Otley, 1854), 388. The Greek legends of the time also mentioned a 'Nation of Blondes', which would soon seize Istanbul from the hands of Turks. A. Ubicini, *La Turquie actuelle* (Paris: Librarie de L. Hachette, 1855), 100.

[13] Hyde Clarke, 'On the Supposed Extinction of the Turks and Increase of the Christians in Turkey', *Journal of the Statistical Society of London* 28, no. 2 (1865): 262.

[14] For the changing perspectives on the 'decline paradigm', see Cemal Kafadar, 'The Question of Ottoman Decline', *Harvard Middle Eastern and Islamic Review* 4, nos. 1–2 (1997–1998): 30–75. Rifa'at 'Ali Abou Abou-El-Haj, *Formation of the Modern State: The Ottoman Empire, Sixteenth to Eighteenth Centuries* (New York: Syracuse University Press, 2005). For its treatment from a global perspective, see C. A. Bayly, *Imperial Meridian: The British Empire and the World, 1780–1830* (London: Longman, 1997), 16–73.

[15] Mehmet Genç, 'L'Économie ottomane et la guerre au XVIIIe siècle', *Turcica* 27 (1995): 177–178. Also see Ariel Salzmann, 'An Ancien Régime Revisited: "Privatization" and Political Economy in the Eighteenth-Century Ottoman Empire', *Politics & Society* 21 (1993): 405.

[16] Şevket Pamuk, *A Monetary History of the Ottoman Empire* (Cambridge: Cambridge University Press, 2000), 161. Also see Yavuz Cezar, *Osmanlı Mâliyesinde Bunalım ve Değişim Dönemi* (İstanbul: Alan Yayıncılık, 1986), 74. Bruce McGowan, 'The Age of the Ayans, 1699–1812', in *An Economic and Social History of the Ottoman Empire*, ed. Halil Inalcik and Donald Quataert, 2 vols., vol. I (Cambridge: Cambridge University Press, 1997), 695.

power dwindled, the periphery's sway became more and more pervasive in the new production hubs, which appeared throughout the Empire under local dynasties.[17] These emerging local households represented the shifting power structure of the eighteenth century.[18] In this new arrangement, the centre, rather than being subverted by decentralisation, was rationalised, as a power broker, via an extensive economic network.

Ironically it was this prosperity which would bring the Empire to the verge of collapse. After the Treaties of Belgrade and Niš in 1739 with the Habsburg Empire and Russia, respectively, the Ottomans avoided major conflict in Europe. The reigning economic stability and the mood of optimism of the time encouraged Mustafa III in his already pronounced military predilections. In fact, contemporary histories blame the 'abundant treasury' for the Sultan's bellicose policies.[19] Especially after the death of his influential and staunchly anti-war Grand Vizier, Koca Râgıb Pasha, in April 1763, Mustafa's martial inclinations found a more suitable atmosphere in which to bloom.[20]

The Sultan knew that the janissaries, Ottoman infantry, and much of the rest of the Ottoman army, with their obsolete training and decaying infrastructure, needed to be completely overhauled before embarking upon any campaign. But as Osman II would have testified – he was brutally murdered after such an attempt in 1622 at the age of seventeen – this was easier said than done. After letting this scheme slip to a close companion, Mustafa did not feel safe until he sent him to Mosul, where the unfortunate man was eventually executed.[21] Yet ambition blinded him to the existence of any options other than war: his

[17] Genç, 'L'Économie ottomane et la guerre au XVIIIe siècle', 178. For a good study of local household and its politics, see Jane Hathaway, *The Politics of Households in Ottoman Egypt: The Rise of the Qazdaglis* (Cambridge: Cambridge University Press, 2002).

[18] Salzmann, 'An Ancien Régime Revisited', 397.

[19] Cezar, *Osmanlı Mâliyesinde Bunalım ve Değişim Dönemi*, 74. See, for instance, Ahmed Cevdet Paşa, *Târîh-i Cevdet*, 12 vols., vol. I (İstanbul: Matbaa-i Osmaniye, 1309/1891–1892), 78.

[20] The reports coming from Russia purported the terror felt there against a possible Ottoman attack. On one of them, the Sultan wrote the following: 'This Râgıb Pasha, traitor to the religion and state somewhat vitiated our desire. If, God's willing, had he been an agreeable vizier (*yek-dil*), they would have compared him to Sultan Suleyman.' Uğur Demir, '1768 Savaşı Öncesi Osmanlı Diplomasisi (1755–1768)', (PhD diss., Marmara University, 2012), 166.

[21] Cevdet Paşa, *Târîh-i Cevdet I*, 123.

nom de plume was Cihangir, which means 'conqueror of the world' in Persian. This was not an idle whim. He really wanted to conquer the world. In his private correspondence, Mustafa bitterly complained about Râgıb Pasha, calling him a 'traitor to the religion and state' for stopping him from pursuing his warring career.[22]

Fortunately for the Sultan, it was not long before Russia gave him the very excuse he was looking for. In June 1768, some Cossack units chased Polish Confederate troops into the town of Balta and massacred, among others, its Muslim population.[23] After failed negotiations between St. Petersburg and the Porte, the Russian resident, Obreskov, was arrested and put into Yedikule Fortress on 6 October.[24] A fatwa was secured from the *Şeyhülislam* (the head mufti) stating that innocent Muslim blood has been shed, and after twenty-two years of peace and prosperity, the Ottoman Empire was formally at war once more with its archenemy.[25]

At the beginning, the odds looked grim for Russia. The period following the death of Peter I (r. 1682–1725) was plagued by instability and competing forces within the country. Between 1725 and 1762, there were eight coups d'état in Russia, each bringing a new emperor to the throne and a completely different composition of the ruling elite: historians simply know this time as 'the era of palace revolutions'.[26] Catherine the Great, who seized power after ousting her husband in 1762, had in reality little or no legal claim to the Russian throne. She was born Sophie von Anhalt-Zerbst in Poland to German parents. She learnt Russian as a young girl but never mastered it, and converted to Orthodoxy just before her

22 Demir, '1768 Savaşı Öncesi Osmanlı Diplomasisi', 166.

23 Ahmed Resmi Efendi condemned the spread of warmongering bravado in the capital for Mustafa's rush act. Ahmed Resmî, *Hülasatü'l-İtibar* (Dersaâdet: Mühendisyan Matbaası, 1286/1869–1870), 4–5, 11–12.

24 Fındıklılı Şemdanizâde Süleyman Efendi, *Mür'i't-tevârih*, ed. M. Münir Aktepe, 3 vols., vol. II/A (Istanbul: İstanbul Üniversitesi Edebiyât Fakültesi, 1976), 113. Also see Virginia Aksan, 'The One-Eyed Fighting the Blind: Mobilization, Supply, and Command in the Russo-Turkish War of 1768–1774', in *International History Review*, 15, no. 2 (1993): 221–238.

25 For the text of the declaration, see Nigar Anafarta, *Osmanlı İmparatorluğu İle Lehistan (Polonya) Arasındaki Münasebetlerle İlgili Târîhi Belgeler* (Istanbul: Bilmen, 1979), 50.

26 Aleksandr Kamenskii, *The Russian Empire in the Eighteenth Century: Searching for a Place in the World*, trans. David Griffiths (London: Routledge, 2015), 122.

marriage.[27] The country she took over was practically on the verge of bankruptcy and often afflicted with rebellions.

To put it another way, Mustafa III was in this for the glory, but Catherine for her life. The Empress was involved in every aspect of the war from the very beginning. She was clever, ambitious, and knew how to marshal Russia's giant resources.[28] Moreover, while the Russian army had gained great experience in the Seven Years' War against the most up-to-date armies in Europe, the Ottoman forces, were antiquated and prone to irregularities. As a result, commanders such as Pyotr Rumyantsev, who impressed even Gibbon for his role in the war, marched across Ottoman territory without encountering any major difficulties, taking key Ottoman fortresses one after another.[29] Despite two devastating rebellions racking Russia – the Plague Riot of 1771 and Pugachev's Rebellion of 1773 – the Ottoman Empire stood debased and almost destroyed.[30] Mustafa III died a broken man at the age of fifty-six in 1774 and his successor, Abdülhamid I, had to end his brother's war with a humiliating treaty.[31]

It will be difficult to exaggerate the effects of this long war on Ottoman society. One contemporary of the events, even after the passage of forty years, lamented the 'confusion in which the world has been involved' from that time onwards.[32] Setting aside the

27 Lurana Donnels O'Malley, *The Dramatic Works of Catherine the Great: Theatre and Politics in Eighteenth-Century Russia* (Burlington, VT: Ashgate, 2006), 16.

28 She was greatly influenced by the Enlightenment ideas, so much so that her life work *Nakaz* or *Instruction with a View to the Elaboration of a Code of Laws*, was banned by the French censor as a subversive document. See Derek Beales, *Enlightenment and Reform in Eighteenth-Century Europe* (London: I.B. Tauris, 2005), 40.

29 David S. Katz, *The Shaping of Turkey in the British Imagination, 1776–1923* (London: Palgrave Macmillan, 2016), 21.

30 See Isabel De Madariaga, *Politics and Culture in Eighteenth-Century Russia* (London: Routledge, 1998), 211.

31 It should be noted that the Treaty of Küçük Kaynarca (1774), which concluded the war with the loss of Ottoman suzerainty in Crimea, is considered the beginning of the Ottoman claims to a Universal Caliphate. See Azmi Özcan, *Pan-Islamism: Indian Muslims, the Ottomans and Britain, 1877–1924* (Leiden: E. J. Brill, 1997), 30. Mustafa Kesbî Efendi calls the Sultan's death an *inhitat*/ collapse. Mustafa Kesbî Efendi, *İbretnümâ-yı Devlet (Tahlil ve Tenkitli Metin)*, ed. Ahmet Öğreten (Ankara: Türk Târîh Kurumu, 2002), 30. Also see Şemdanizâde Süleyman Efendi, *Mür'i't-tevârih*, vol. II/, 115.

32 [Vasıf Efendi], *Hulâsatü'l-kelâm fi reddi'l-avâm*, 6.

psychological trauma caused by the loss of Crimea, which had been a bulwark of the Empire, the financial strains caused by the war ended the economic boom and hit craftsmen and artisans with a blow from which they would not recover for many years.[33] The heavy war indemnity – half of projected Ottoman revenue – further burdened the administration, which was already barely coping with this new economic reality.[34] Confiscation (*müsâdere*), hitherto reserved to the ruling elite, was extended to cover all segments of the affluent to ease the pressure, but naturally proved to be detrimental to the already fragile commercial economy. The value of the Ottoman kuruş, which had been mostly stable between 1700 and 1760, lost about half its worth by the end of the century while the general level of European prices doubled over the same forty years.[35] In short, the Ottoman Empire was in the grip of an economic crisis which would last until the 1840s.

Public Debt

At the beginning of the war, the provincial administration was vested entirely in the hands of local notables. At that time this was thought to be a practical solution that allowed for micro-management and the

33 Genç, 'L'Économie ottomane et la guerre au XVIIIe siècle', 177, 183. The wars had devastating effects on the Ottoman economy. Traditionally strict guild regulations had ensured protection against monopolistic practices. But when the state was the buyer, it could impose anything as a fair price. This resulted in mass bankruptcies for already fragile tradesmen. See Yücel Özkaya, *18. Yüzyılda Osmanlı Toplumu* (İstanbul: Yapı Kredi Kültür Sanat Yayıncılık, 2008), 324–355, especially 330–332.

34 Even though the indemnity is called a 'relatively small' sum by Şevket Pamuk, it was, as Virginia Aksan pointed out, 'half of the projected Ottoman revenue'. Pamuk, *A Monetary History of the Ottoman Empire*, 170. Virginia H. Aksan, *Ottomans and Europeans: Contacts and Conflicts* (Istanbul: Isis Press, 2004), 114, fn. 2. Also see Cezar, *Osmanlı Mâliyesinde Bunalım ve Değişim Dönemi*, 76–78. The French Revolution, which severely interrupted Mediterranean trade, was especially important for the Ottoman economy. See Daniel Panzac, 'International and Domestic Maritime Trade in the Ottoman Empire during the 18th Century', *International Journal of Middle East Studies* 24, no. 2 (1992): 191–194. For trade relations between the Ottoman Empire and France, see Edhem Eldem, *French Trade in Istanbul in the Eighteenth Century* (Leiden: Brill, 1999), Edhem Eldem, 'Le commerce français d'Istanbul au XVIIIe siècle: d'une présence tolérée à une domination imposée'', *Le Négoce International XIIIe–XXe siècles*, ed. François M. Crouzet (Paris: Economica, 1989), 181–190.

35 McGowan, 'The Age of the Ayans', 725.

deployment of resources.[36] In the long run, however, it seriously undermined the centre's ability to secure taxes from the provinces. Sultan Abdülhamid cursed those responsible for the disturbance of the peace with Russia.[37] The situation was spiralling out of control: 'everybody is after personal benefit', the Sultan wrote bitterly, 'nobody cares for the State [and] there is no place to find money.'[38] The 'Circle of Justice' between the people and the authorities, if it had ever been implemented, was now completely broken. This had another important consequence: the first internal borrowing.

The palace knew that without adequate financial resources it would be impossible to curb already wilful notables. Hence, in April 1775, the Ottoman bureaucracy introduced a new system of *eshâm* (shares).[39] Other than increasing revenues, the scheme was intended to break the financial monopoly of the grandees, who dominated the previous *mâlikâne* system (long-term tax farming).[40] In contemporary histories, *eshâm* was presented as an antidote to the oppressive governing of the local elite, something that would save the Ottoman finances from ruination.[41]

The method was inclusive. Because the bonds were sold in small shares (which got smaller and smaller over time), people from every walk of life could invest in them.[42] As the state hankered for cross-societal popularity, traditional outcasts of the Ottoman polity such non-Muslims were also allowed to acquire these bonds.[43] Women especially rushed to invest their savings in *eshâm*.[44] This mutual

[36] Yuzo Nagata, *Muhsin-zâde Mehmed Paşa ve Âyânlık Müessesesi* (Tokyo: Institute for the Study of Languages and Cultures of Asia and Africa, 1976), 74.

[37] BOA, İE.HAT. 5/435, 29 Zilhicce 1190 (8 February 1777).

[38] BOA, HAT 1384/54777, 29 Zilhicce 1203 (20 September 1789).

[39] Cezar, *Osmanlı Mâliyesinde Bunalım ve Değişim Dönemi*, 79–88.

[40] Pamuk, *A Monetary History of the Ottoman Empire*, 192.

[41] Ahmed Vasıf Efendi, *Mehasinü'l-âsâr ve Hakayıkü'l-ahbar*, ed. Mücteba İlgürel (Ankara: Türk Târîh Kurumu, 1994), 290.

[42] See, for instance, Mustafa Nuri Paşa, *Netâyic ül-Vuku'ât: Kurumları ve Örgütleriyle Osmanlı Târîhi*, ed. Neşet Çağatay, 4 vols., vol. III (Ankara: Türk Târîh Kurumu Yayınları, 1980), 132. Vasıf, *Mehasinü'l-âsâr*, 193.

[43] Mehmet Genç, *Osmanlı İmparatorluğunda Devlet ve Ekonomi* (İstanbul: Ötüken Yayınları, 2000), 187.

[44] Yasemin Tümer Erdem and Halime Yiğit, *Bacıyân-ı Rûm'dan Günümüze Türk Kadınının İktisadî Hayâttaki Yeri* (İstanbul: İstanbul Ticâret Odası, 2010), 80. Câbi Ömer Efendi, *Câbi Târîhi: Târîh-i Sultan Selim-i Sâlis ve Mahmud-i Sâni Tahlil ve Tenkidli Metin*, ed. Mehmet Ali Beyhan, 2 vols., vol. II (Ankara: Türk Târîh Kurumu Basımevi, 2003), 733. Also see Yavuz Cezar, 'Osmanlı Mâli

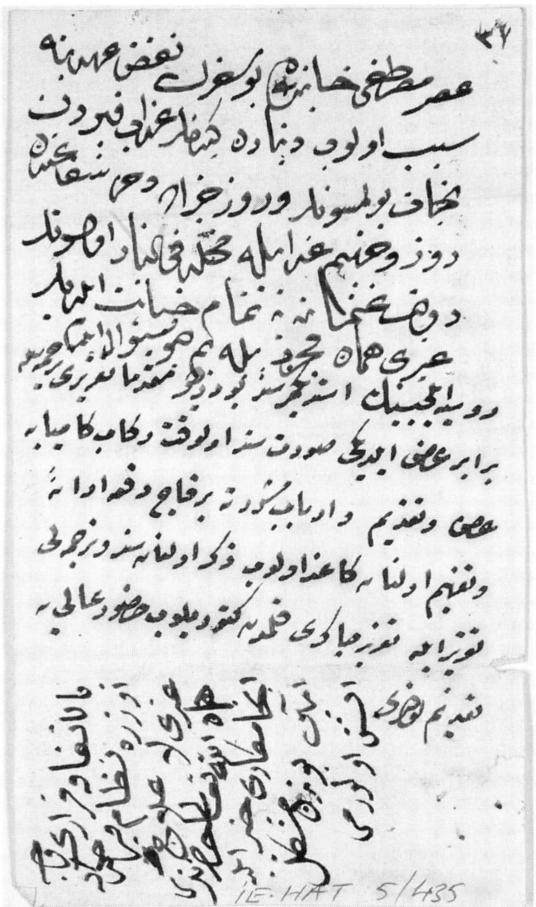

Figure 1.1 'Those who are responsible for the disturbance of the peace during the reign of Mustafa Khan and departed from this world should not find salvation from the punishment of the grave/*azab-ı kabirden necât bulmasınlar*'. BOA, İE.HAT. 5/435, 29 Zilhicce 1190 (8 February 1777).

dependence created a new reciprocal awareness between state and society. According to Ariel Salzmann, 'it was these social groups [*eshâm* holders] who would become invaluable allies in the processes

Târîhinde "Eshâm" Uygulamasının İlk Dönemlerine İlişkin Ba'zı Önemli Örnek ve Belgeler', *Toplum ve Bilim* 12 (1981): 135–137.

of administrative reorganization of the empire'.[45] In 1800, *eshâm* comprised more than 50 per cent of total tax revenues and provided the very financial resources which were necessary for the transition to a modern state.[46]

This pecuniary support, however, was conditional. The growing reliance of the state on *eshâms*[47] and the simultaneous increase in political discourse within society are by no means coincidental. In a very short period of time, there emerged in Istanbul a new class of people watching every step of the government and engaging in what came to be known as *devlet sohbeti* (government talk) in the public sphere.[48] For the Ottoman ruling elite, this was a new type of nuisance. Koca Sekbanbaşı, writing in 1803, called these people 'a rabble composed of the dregs of the populace, setting themselves up for judges of the times, and assembling in the coffee-houses, barbers' shops'.[49] 'This perverse race', he continued:

[45] Ibid.

[46] Mehmet Genç, Esham, Bekir Topaloğlu et al., eds. 19 vols., vol. XI, *Türkiye Diyanet Vakfı İslam Ansiklopedisi* (İstanbul: Türkiye Diyanet Vakfı, 1995), 378. Also see Murat Çizakça, *A Comparative Evolution of Business Partnerships: The Islamic World and Europe, with Specific Reference to the Ottoman Archives, The Ottoman Empire and Its Heritage* (Leiden: E.J. Brill, 1996), 185. Janissaries, ultimate representatives of the Ottoman *Ancien Régime*, understood this relationship very well. When their salaries were not paid, for instance, it was from the *eshâm* purse they demanded to be recompensed. *Eshâm* holders were not, they argued, poor women barely scraping a living; they were the establishment (ricâlden ve kibardandırlar). See Câbi Efendi, Câbi Târîhi II, 733

[47] See, for instance, a *Hatt-ı Hümâyun* (imperial rescript) written by Selim III in 1806 urging the sales of more *eshâms* as the 'revenues of the state do not cover the expenses'. BOA HAT 111/4423, 29 Zilhicce 1220 (3 March 1806). For the documents of the same character also see BOA, HAT, 111/4414 29 Zilhicce 1220 (20 March 1806), BOA, HAT, 110/4373 29 Zilhicce 1221 (9 March 1807), BOA, HAT, 1355/53002 29 Zilhicce 1222 (27 February 1808), BOA, HAT, 1356/53114 29 Zilhicce 1222 (27 February 1808), BOA, HAT, 1006/ 42216 29 Zilhicce 1224 (4 February 1810).

[48] Mustafa IV, Selim's immediate successor, warned of the *devlet lakırdısı* (government bluster) taking place in different coffeehouses of Istanbul and demanded the detention of those responsible, see BOA, HAT 1362/53732, 29 Zilhicce 1222 (27 February 1808). Selim's sensitivity is also attested to by contemporary histories. Câbi Ömer Efendi, for instance, mentions Sultan's orders for the demolition of a coffeehouse and a shop with the same incentive. Câbi Efendi, *Câbi Târîhi*, 220, 225, 236.

[49] Here a contemporary translation is used. Sekbanbaşı's text is given in full in an appendix in William Wilkinson, *An Account of the Principalities of Wallachia*

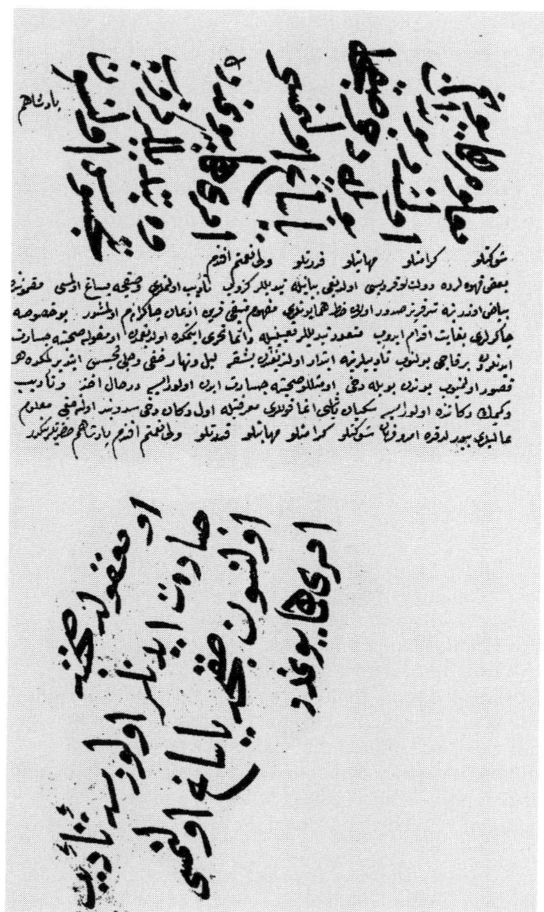

Figure 1.2 Mustafa IV's *hatt* warning about the government bluster taking place in different coffeehouses of Istanbul and demanding the restraint and detention of those responsible. BOA, HAT 1362/53732, 29 Zilhicce 1222 (27 February 1808).

are outwardly Mussulmans yet have they not the least idea of religious purity, and are indeed a collection of baccals [grocers], boatmen, fishermen, porters, coffee-house keepers, and such like persons. Although it would be

and Moldavia with Various Political Observations Relating to Them (London: Longman, 1820), 216–294.

requisite to punish many of them for opening their mouths on state matters, and to make public examples of them for the purpose of restoring order to the world, *yet the force of necessity obliges the government to overlook their faults.*[50]

As anyone familiar with chroniclers knows, routine complaints about sultans had not been unusual over the long history of the Ottoman Empire. But this was of different nature; it was persistent and frequent. Insomuch that Sekbanbaşı complained of 'men of sagacity' who 'on account of the situation of the world, and the circumstances of the times ... are obliged, in their discourse, to appear to agree with the opinions of the people at large.'[51] This overt limitation to what a proper public was, and more importantly the criticism of its influence on private reason reminds one of what John Stuart Mill described as 'collective mediocrity'.[52] To put it shortly, Mill, like Tocqueville, had a negative concept of public opinion as something, which placed 'enormous weight upon the minds of each individual'.[53] It was a tyranny, they argued, 'not over the body, but over the mind'.[54] Naturally it would be an enormous exaggeration to compare Sekbanbaşı with Mill or the early nineteenth-century Ottoman Empire with the contemporary state of America or Britain. There were, after all, big qualitative and quantitative differences. But it is interesting to note that even before the ascendancy of the newspaper age, Ottoman intellectuals expressed such concerns.

Thus, in contemporary accounts, the reign of Sultan Selim, who succeeded his royal uncle in 1789, is characterised by a constant struggle to keep a tight rein on his government's image.[55] Coffeehouses

50 Ibid., 220–221. In the Ottoman edition, see [Vasıf Efendi], *Hulâsatü'l-kelâm fi reddi'l-avâm*, 6–7.

51 Wilkinson, *An Account of the Principalities of Wallachia*, 219, [Vasıf Efendi], *Hulâsatü'l-kelâm fi reddi'l-avâm*, 6.

52 J. S. Mill, *On Liberty and Other Writings*, ed. Stefan Collini (Cambridge: Cambridge University Press, 1989), 66.

53 Alexis de Tocqueville, *The Republic of the United States of America and Its Political Institutions, Reviewed and Examined*, trans. Henry Reeves (New York: A. S. Barnes, 1855), 277.

54 J. S. Mill, *Dissertations and Discussions: Political, Philosophical, and Historical*, 3 vols., vol. II (Boston: William V. Spencer, 1864), 118.

55 Like Mustafa III, Abdülhamid also died of a massive stroke after the news of a Russian victory.

Figure 1.3 The cover of *Eşek* (Donkey), a humour magazine. The man tells the donkey in a menacing tone: 'now you can pen whatever you want. There is no court-martial. You are free and at liberty to write as much as you like.' Three other men (one restraining him with rope, and two other threatening with mace and club) represent respectively 'Press Law', 'Criminal Law', and 'public opinion/*efkâr-ı umumiye*'. Baha, *Eşek*, 20 Eylül/3 October [1]328/1912.

and barbershops were constantly demolished on accusations that the owners and patrons engaged in 'government talk' on the premises. Even women's baths were haunted by female informers who would send hapless ladies to prison for a simple 'conversation about the exalted state'.[56] It must be clear that Selim III's preoccupation with the image of his reign, extending even to women's baths, cannot be understood solely as a security concern. It was also an economic consideration.[57] If potential creditors foresaw that the government might default, either they would not invest or they would demand a high rate of return that would compensate them for the risk. For the Ottoman state, the financial creditability became something important to take into account.[58]

One should remember that in France and Britain the idea of public opinion emerged along very similar lines. In the words of Lord Acton, 'the sovereignty of public opinion was just then coming in through the rise of national debts and the increasing importance of the public creditor'.[59] Eighteenth-century English fiscal theory indeed celebrated public finance as a barrier to despotism since 'no government could risk losing public confidence by acting arbitrarily'.[60] Jacques Necker (d. 1804), finance minister for Louis XVI, considered public opinion 'a kind of national credit rating'.[61] The *eshâm* succeeded in 'mobilising the savings of small savers' in a 'massive expansion'.[62] Apart from increasing revenues, it orchestrated popular support from people who feared the 'return of monopolistic practices of provincial magnates and

[56] Câbi Ömer Efendi, *Câbi Târîhi I*, 392.

[57] He would get frustrated with the scarcity of any article however trivial that may be. In a *hatt* written to the Grand Vizier he warned him about the rumours of silk shortages in the market and asked him to inquire into the matter. See BOA, HAT 238/13198, 29 Zilhicce 1218 (10 April 1804). Also see BOA, HAT 174/7554, 29 Zilhicce 1212 (14 June 1798).

[58] Ali Yaycioglu, *Partners of the Empire: The Crisis of the Ottoman Order in the Age of Revolutions* (Stanford: Stanford University Press, 2016), 83.

[59] John Emerich Edward Dalberg-Acton, *Essays on Freedom and Power* (Boston, MA: Beacon Press, 1949), 267.

[60] James Van Horn Melton, *The Rise of the Public in Enlightenment Europe* (Cambridge: Cambridge University Press, 2001), 58.

[61] Linda Orr, 'Outspoken Women and the Rightful Daughter of the Revolution: Madame de Staël's *Considérations sur la Révolution Française* ', in *Rebel Daughters: Women and the French Revolution*, ed. Sara E. Melzer and Leslie W. Rabine (Oxford: Oxford University Press, 1992), 122.

[62] Çizakça, *A Comparative Evolution of Business Partnerships*, 183.

military elites'.[63] But this came with a price tag. The Empire was slowly but steadily going public-minded.

The Empire Strikes Back

As mentioned above, the decentralisation of the seventeenth and eighteenth centuries created a multi-layered power structure whereby the Sultan's authority was conveyed by local magnates.[64] Especially during the maelstrom of the late eighteenth century, powerful governors with their private armies emerged and assumed the public authority. 'Each of these *â'yân* households', Mustafa Cezar stated, 'lavish in expenditures on luxury and on manpower thus became a small replica of the Ottoman state'.[65] Thanks to the tax farming system, they were capable of amassing great fortunes – far beyond the reach of earlier vizier households.[66] Ali Pasha of Janina (Ioannina)[67] and Muhammed Ali Pasha of Egypt[68] are only the most famous examples. There were many others: 'Azm family of Damascus,[69] Pazvantoğlu of Vidin[70] and Çapanoğlu of Eastern Anatolia,[71] to name but a few, ruled in their respective domains effectively uninhibited and established nearly

[63] Salzmann, 'An Ancien Régime Revisited', 408. It must be mentioned that Salzmann here uses a more general term, i.e., privatisation, rather than referring to *eshâms* specifically.

[64] They are called either *â'yân*, rarely used plural Arabic word for 'eye', figuratively meaning prominent, visible person; or *derebeyi*, a Turkish phrase meaning 'lord of the valley'. Throughout the chapter, the terms 'local notables' or 'magnates' are used to denote both.

[65] Mustafa Cezar, *Osmanlı Târîhinde Levendler* (İstanbul: İstanbul Güzel Sanatlar Akademisi, 1965), 337. Cited in Mardin, 'Power, Civil Society and Culture in the Ottoman Empire', 267.

[66] Jane Hathaway and Karl K. Barbir, *The Arab Lands under Ottoman Rule, 1516–1800* (Harlow: Pearson Education, 2008), 82.

[67] Katherine E. Fleming, *The Muslim Bonaparte: Diplomacy and Orientalism in Ali Pasha 's Greece* (Princeton, NJ: Princeton University Press, 1999), passim.

[68] Khaled Fahmy, *All the Pasha's Men* (Cambridge: Cambridge University Press, 2004), passim.

[69] Philip S. Khoury, *Urban Notables and Arab Nationalism: The Politics of Damascus 1860–1920* (Cambridge: Cambridge University Press, 2003), 36–37.

[70] Osman Pazvantoğlu, if contemporary rumours are to be believed, started to mint his own coins at the beginning of the nineteenth century. See Rossitsa Gradeva, 'Osman Pazvantoğlu of Vidin: Between Old and New', in *The Ottoman Balkans, 1750–1830*, ed. Frederick F. Anscombe (Princeton, New Jersey: Markus Wiener Publishers, 2005), 126–127.

[71] İsmail Hakkı Uzunçarşılı, 'Çapanoğulları', *Belleten* XXXVIII, no. 150 (1974).

autonomous rule over much of Anatolia and the Balkans.[72] By the beginning of the nineteenth century, the French ambassador, Antoine-François Andréossy bemoaned how the Sultan's orders were overtly ignored and adroitly avoided by local powers. The real authority of the Grand-Seigneur, he explained, 'does go not out of the palace walls'.[73] Indeed, even in places like Şile, only 70 km away from Istanbul proper, there were independent *â'yân*s who blatantly disregarded the orders of the Sultan.[74]

Following the Rebellion of Kabakçı Mustafa and the murder of Selim III, another victim of the habitual distaste for reform and regulation, in 1808, the Grand Vizier, Alemdâr Mustafa Pasha, a powerful magnate himself, invited all these families for a *Meclis-i Meşveret-i Âmme* (the Assembly of Public Consultation).[75] This specific usage of '*Âmme*' here is no accident and reverberates with their public claim. On the designated date, some, like Çapanoğlu, arrived in person with their private armies, others, such as Muhammed Ali Pasha, sent representatives.[76] Cevdet Pasha, indefatigable statesman, historian, jurist, and linguist, attributed the attendance to the personal influence of the Grand Vizier and wrote:

> Even though for the order of that time, it was considered highly improbable for many local notables and dynasties to come to Istanbul, as they were praying for their independence, since Alemdâr Pasha came to the grand vizierate, *public opinion* changed so much and so fast, his guardianship

[72] Sam White, *The Climate of Rebellion in the Early Modern Ottoman Empire* (Cambridge: Cambridge University Press, 2011), 278.

[73] Antoine-François Andréossy, *Constantinople et le Bosphore de Thrace* (Paris: B. Duprat, 1841), 45.

[74] Câbi Ömer Efendi, *Câbi Târîhi II*, 726.

[75] Kâmil Paşa, *Târîh-i Siyâsiye-i Devleti Âliye-i Osmaniye*, 21. He was the *â'yân* of Rusçuk (Russe), a seat which gained, thanks to its strategic location, unprecedented importance after the Ottoman Russian Wars of 1768–1774. See Nagata, *Muhsin-zâde Mehmed Paşa ve Âyânlık Müessesesi*, 75–76. It should be noted that throughout the book, the word *â'yân* is also used as a byword to denote a semi-independent Ottoman grandee during the late eighteenth and early nineteenth centuries without taking technicalities into account. From the bureaucratic point of view, Ali and Muhammed Ali Pashas were governors (*vâli*), Çapanoğlu Mustafa Bey was a deputy governor (*mutasarrıf*), and etc. See, Ali Yaycioglu, *Partners of the Empire*, 80.

[76] A. de Juchereau de Saint-Denys, *Revolutions de Constantinople en 1807 et 1808: Précédées d'observations générales sur l'état actuel de l'empire ottoman, et de considérations sur la Grèce*, 2 vols., vol. II (Paris: Brissot-Thivars, 1819), 199–200.

and his might reach far over the lands to the horizon, and his domination in the countryside began to be as prevailing as his in Dersaâdet [Istanbul].[77]

Cevdet Pasha's reference to public opinion's sway on the notables might be just a retrospective reading of a post-Tanzimat statesman and need not to be exaggerated. The increasing power of Alemdâr Mustafa Pasha, on the other hand, must be taken seriously. Before he was killed and hanged naked on a mulberry tree by the janissaries,[78] thanks to his growing influence, Alemdâr Mustafa Pasha commenced a critical phase in the central authority's consolidation of power (he was the useful idiot of Mahmud II). Even though the Deed of Agreement in 1808 that Mahmud II had to sign with magnates for their support,[79] was perceived by the Sultan as a breach of his worldly authority and deeply resented,[80] it precipitated the defeat of local notables by incorporating them into the state system.[81] After the death of his mentor, Mahmud II adopted a permutation policy against these powerful *â'yâns* and *derebeys*.[82] This cut them off from their indigenous power

[77] Ahmed Cevdet Paşa, *Târîh-i Cevdet*, 12 vols., vol. IX (İstanbul: Matbaa-i Amire, 1292/1875–1876), 3, emphasis mine.

[78] For the details, see Fahri Ç. Derin, 'Yayla İmâmı Risâlesi', *Târîh Enstitüsü Dergisi*, no. 3 (1973): 259–260. Also see Kalost Arapyan, *Rusçuk Âyânı Mustafa Paşa'nın Hayâtı ve Kahramanlıkları*, trans. Esat Uras (Ankara: Türk Târîh Kurumu Basımevi, 1943), 19–20.

[79] It came out as a result of the *Meclis-i Meşveret-i Âmme* and limited the Sultanic authority. For an analysis of the document, see Halil İnalcık, 'Sened-i ittifâk ve Gülhâne Hatt-i Hümâyûnu', *Belleten* XXVIII, no. 112 (1964).

[80] Kâmil Paşa, *Târîh-i Siyâsiye-i Devleti Âliye-i Osmaniye*, 21. According to İlber Ortaylı when Mahmud II felt strong enough, he destroyed the original document and the text is only available from Cevdet Pasha's account. See Ortaylı, *İmparatorluğun En Uzun Yüzyılı*, 36. This cannot be, however, true as the text was also given in Şânîzâde's book. See Şânîzâde Mehmed 'Atâ'ullah Efendi, *Târîh-i Şânîzâde I*, 66–73.

[81] The idea of an alliance between the Sultan and the *â'yân* is the most important subtext of the document. There are dozens of references to this coalition in a relatively short document (such as *bi'l-ittifâk* five times or *'ale'l-ittifâk* two times and many others as in *ale'l-umûm, cümlenin ittihâd ü ittifâkı, dâire-i ittifâk, bi'l-ittihâd, bi'l-müzakere*).

[82] He created his own version of the 'Versailles Syndrome' in Istanbul. Some of the notables were 'invited' to stay in the capital such as Karaosmanoğlu who was, as a result of 'expensive employments forced on him during several years', financially ruined. Slade, *Records of Travels in Turkey*, 115. See BOA, HAT 410/21317 29 Zilhicce 1229 (12 December 1814). For the 'Versailles Syndrome', see Peter Burke, 'The Courtier', in *Renaissance Characters*, ed. Eugenio Garin (Chicago: University of Chicago Press, 1997), 102. There are other examples of the *â'yân* families being awarded official pardons under the

bases and turned the rebellion-prone magnates into tame civil servants.[83] This was not always easy. In some cases, the Sultan would find a hard nut to crack: Ali Pasha, for instance, the famous Lion of Janina, did not accept his deposition in 1820 and kept the Sultan's troops busy for more than two years.[84] Muhammed Ali of Egypt went on to be all but independent.[85] But by the beginning of 1822, the centralisation was almost complete.[86] The power of local notables was gradually subsumed by the authority of the state.[87] As a result,

condition of living in Istanbul. See, for instance, BOA, HAT 503/24750, 29 Zilhicce 1228 (23 December 1813), for Kapıcıbaşı Mehmed Ağa, former *â'yân* of Stara Zagora (Zağra-i Âtîk). Another example from Stara Zagora would be the unfortunate *â'yân* of Aydos (Aytos). After he was exiled to Stara Zagora because of his dissident tendencies, it was discovered that he had not completely given up on his 'factious deeds'. His head was sent to Istanbul. See BOA, HAT 515/25197, 3 Cemaziyelahir 1234 (30 March 1819). Through a reading of municipal records, Socrates Petmezas shows the increasing financial autonomy of Zagora during the heyday of *Â'yân* rule. See Socrates D. Petmezas, 'Christian Communities in 18th and Early 19th Century Ottoman Greece: Their Fiscal Functions', in *Minorities in the Ottoman Empire*, ed. Molly Greene (Princeton, New Jersey: Markus Wiener Publishers, 2005), 86–113.

83 Ercüment Kuran, 'Derebeys et Agas d'Anatolie orientale dans le dernier siècle de l'empire ottoman', in *Histoire économique et sociale de l'Empire ottoman et de la Turquie (1326–1960)*, ed. Daniel Panzac (Leuven: Peeters, 1995), 396. Most of the important pashas of the Tanzimat era came from these *â'yân* families as the palace incorporated them into the state system. See, for instance, Murat R. Şiviloğlu, 'Abidin Paşa', in *Abidin Dino: Bir Dünya*, ed. Zeynep Avcı (İstanbul: Sabancı Üniversitesi Yayınları, 2007), 36–45.

84 See Fleming, *The Muslim Bonaparte*, 33. In this respect, while he is retrospectively held responsible for Greek independence, Pazvantoğlu is associated with the start of Serbian revolt. See Charles Jelavich and Barbara Jelavich, *The Establishment of the Balkan National States, 1804–1920* (Seattle: University of Washington Press, 1977), 18.

85 Interestingly enough, even at the peak of his power, Muhammed Ali attached much importance to the sultanic legitimacy. See, for instance, Fahmy, *All the Pasha's Men*, 58, 72.

86 It was reported to the Sultan that with the exception of a few places 'from Rumeli to Iran, there is nobody to be called *derebeyi*' and 'all of them became subordinate'. BOA, HAT 822/37837-D, 27 Rebiülahir 1237 (21 January 1822).

87 Şerif Mardin's comment about the Ottoman power structure is very apt here: 'Turkish revolutions, which usually involved an alliance of Janissaries and craftsmen of the capital or a local outburst of notables allied with the lower classes, did not have the organizational autonomy that would permit the consolidation of victories. This is why the modernizing bureaucracy was always successful in the long run. This explains why even successful rebellious â'yâns or janissaries were eventually picked up like ripe plums by succeeding administrations and crushed, in the midst of general indifference.' Mardin, 'Power, Civil Society and Culture in the Ottoman Empire', 269–270.

the imperial subjects under this new authority, as its addressees, were brought into a new and less segregated type of public.[88] This centralisation had two significant long-term effects on the Ottoman society: the heteroglossia of political language disappeared in favour of unified discourse(s), and the concentration of political power in Istanbul led the establishment of the bureaucratic machine of the Tanzimat era.[89]

The First Public Campaign

The Ottoman Empire did not turn into 'numberless, petty, piratical states' as most people expected and went on to exist for another century.[90] Most historians would agree that this tenacity relates to Mahmud II. In so many respects, although something of a latecomer, he is an archetypical enlightened despot.[91] He came to the throne during tumultuous times. His cousin, Selim III, was murdered by the palace officials in 1808, and young Mahmud escaped death only by fleeing to the terrace of the palace.[92] After securing his position by getting Mustafa IV, his brother, executed,[93] and signing the abovementioned Deed of Agreement (*Sened-i İttifâk*) with powerful local rulers, Mahmud was still face-to-face with a formidable adversary:

88 In an article published in 1918, Ziyâ Gökalp argued that: 'when the mass called *avâm* became equal to *â'yâns*, it turned into people (*halk*)'. Ziyâ Gökalp, 'Halkçılık', *Yeni Mecmûa*, no. 32, 14 Şubat 1918, 104.

89 Here Bakhtin's term on linguistic decentralization is borrowed. The reference to Ottomanism of later years must be clear. See M. M. Bakhtin, *The Dialogic Imagination: Four Essays by M. M. Bakhtin* ed. Caryl Emerson and Michael Holquist (Austin: University of Texas Press, 2004), 272.

90 For eighty-nine different projects discussing the pros and cons of an Ottoman dismemberment, see T. G. Djuvara, *Cent Projets de Partage de la Turquie (1281–1913): Avec 18 cartes hors texte* (Paris: Librarie Félix Alcan, 1914). The first eleven projects, until page 39, actually are about the Holy Land.

91 One can cite Frederick the Great of Prussia (d. 1786), Joseph II of Austria (d. 1790), or Catherine the Great of Russia (d. 1796) as his precursor.

92 Mahmud II owed his life to the intervention of one *Harem* woman, Cevri Kalfa. See Kâmil Paşa, *Târîh-i Siyâsiye-i Devleti Âliye-i Osmaniye*, 3 vols., vol. III (İstanbul: Matbaa-i Ahmed İhsan, 1327/1909–1910), 17. In different districts of Istanbul, there are two monumental buildings dedicated to Cevri Kalfa, an elementary school in Sultanahmet and a mosque in Üsküdar.

93 Georg Oğulukyan, *Georg Oğulukyan'ın Ruznamesi: 1806–1810 İsyanları: III. Selim, IV. Mustafa, II. Mahmud ve Alemdâr Mustafa Paşa*, ed. Hrand D. Andreasyan, trans. Hrand D. Andreasyan (İstanbul: Edebiyât Fakültesi Basımevi, 1972), 43.

he must have felt the sword of Damocles – or rather those of the janissaries – constantly hanging over him.

In fact an old Ottoman saying makes this point abundantly clear: 'The Family of Osman', it warns, 'shall not reach the throne of power without passing under the sword of the janissaries.'[94] Especially after the Ottomans stopped practicing fratricide in favour of primogeniture in the early seventeenth century, the janissaries began playing a central role in Ottoman politics and became, as it were, the kingmakers of the Empire. As the Sultan's personal army, they had a full access to the dynastic pool, from which they chose, deposed, and killed according to their needs and circumstances.

But when it comes to the reign of Mahmud in the early nineteenth century, the situation was rather delicate. He was the only surviving male member of the dynasty and the janissaries, whether they liked it or not, were stuck with him. Even though there were rumours of a plotted dynastic change in favour of certain Crimean Khans then residing in Istanbul, the rumours remained rumours and there no serious attempts or plans to carry out this project were documented.[95]

Mahmud used his unique position to carry out the dream of every Ottoman sultan since Osman II, assassinated in 1622: the annihilation of the janissary corps. In order to achieve this goal, he had to display remarkable tact. First, as detailed earlier, he consolidated his power in the provinces. By doing so, he established direct control over the finances and local administration of janissary strongholds such as Aleppo and Thessaloniki.[96] Second, Mahmud focused on strengthening the artillery and cannon corps. This was, he foresaw, going to be crucial when the deciding moment came and these units indeed proved vital in the fight against the janissaries.

Perhaps most importantly, he constantly changed the officials closest to him: Between 1808 and 1826, for instance, there were twenty-four janissary commanders and sixteen grand viziers. This continuous circulation ensured that he found the right men for the key positions. Ağa

[94] *Âl-i Osman saltanat tahtına geçmez, madem ki kulun kılıcı altından geçmeye.*' Selaniki Mustafa Efendi, *Târîh-i Selaniki*, ed. Mehmet İpşirli, 2 vols., vol. I (Ankara: Türk Târîh Kurumu, 1999), 49.

[95] Tahsîn Öz, 'Selim III Mustafa IV. ve Mahmud II. Zamanlarına Ait Birkaç Vesika', *Târîh Vesikaları* 1, no. 1 (1941–1942): 23–25.

[96] Howard A. Reed, 'Destruction of the Janissary Corps by Mahmud II in June 1826', unpublished PhD thesis, Princeton University, New Jersey, 1951, 38.

Hüseyin Pasha, for one, became the janissary *agha* in 1823 and practically acted as Mahmud's agent inside the corps, banishing all the ringleaders. In a similar vein, Galib Pasha, after a grand vizierate of three years, recommended Benderli Selim Paşa for the office and excused himself, arguing that he was a literary man (*kâtiplikten gelme*) and that for the job Mahmud envisioned the Sultan needed someone courageous (*cerî' ve pek gözlü*).[97] Similar changes also took place within the high-ranking *ulemâ*. Şeyhülislam Mekkizâde was replaced with Mehmed Tahir Efendi in 1825. The argument was the same. Without a stain on his character, he was studious and not quite the man for the enterprise ahead.[98]

The increasing control of the Sultan and the political claims of the janissaries inevitably constituted a contested terrain for which open war later took place to assume what one might call 'representative authority'. While the janissaries were laying their cards on the table by covering the city's walls with posters calling the Sultan a liar,[99] Mahmud II subtly tried to create favourable public opinion. He knew that he had to create his own public to frustrate the janissaries. He, for instance, ordered the translation of an old Islamic classic, *Şerh-i Siyer-i Kebîr*, to 'remove the ignorance of people'.[100] Cevdet Pasha explained this move and the janissaries' reaction in his usual statist but illuminating tone: 'For some time', he wrote:

[97] Ahmed Cevdet Paşa, *Târîh-i Cevdet*, 12 vols., vol. XII (İstanbul: Matbaa-i Osmaniye, 1301/1883–1884), 114.

[98] Ibid., 159. [99] Câbî Efendi, *Câbî Târîhi I*, 701.

[100] Muhammed Eş-Şaybani, *Tercüme-i Şerh-i Siyer-i Kebîr*, ed. Muhammed es-Serahsi, trans. Mehmed Münîb Ayntâbî (İstanbul: Matbaa-i Amire, 1241/1825). Muhâmmed Eş-Şaybani (or al-Shaybani), together with Abu Yusuf, was one of the two most important disciples of Abu Hanifa, founder of the Hanafi School of Islamic jurisprudence. The original text of the *Siyer-i Kebîr* has been lost and the book is only known through the commentary of Es-Serahsi (El-Sarakhsi) who explains the basic premise in the following manner: 'It describes the conduct of the believers ... *with rebels (baghīs), who were not counted as unbelievers, though they were ignorant and their understanding [of Islam] was false*.' Emphasis mine. Mahmud II, of course, must have found the relevant passages about rebellion to the point. Quotation is from Majīd Khaddūrī, *The Islamic Law of Nations: Shaybani's Siyar* (Baltimore, MD: Johns Hopkins University Press, 2002), 40. The book was also distributed to all the libraries and courthouses for the 'general benefit/*menâfi'-i tamim*'. See BOA, C..MF.. 129/6446, 20 Safer 1241 (4 October 1825).

the public was beset with ignorance and impertinence and people began not to know their place. Because of their custom of debauched order, which they took as the law, the janissaries were looking at legit regulations with abhorrence. When His Highness intended to instruct and reform the military, at the outset removing the ignorance of the public, as much as possible, was seen as a necessity of the time. Hence Imam Muhammed's *Siyer-i Kebîr*, as it was a respected book containing the examples of the prophet's jihad and deemed beneficial for the public, was ordered to be published and disseminated with the exegesis of the *sun of scholars*, august imam Serahsi and with the translation of famous Münîb Efendi. Its publication began in the government printing house and when it was finished, copies were given to the libraries and corps [*ocak* in the original].[101] Free copies were also sent to the *shari'a* courts in the provinces. As reclaiming *public opinion* as such did not suit the *ocaks*' interests, they sent letters to the troops in the provinces and said in writing 'don't you dare to take heed of these books, don't go astray from the principals and laws of your *ocak*.'[102]

The fact that the state was trying to 'reclaim' public opinion with a ninth-century classic (or rather with its eleventh-century exegesis) might seem naïve. Clearly Mahmud was no Goebbels. The alarm felt by the janissaries, on the other hand, illustrates how seriously they took any sultanic attempt to gain public support.

The culmination of the competition between Mahmud and the janissaries took place through discussions in the *Meclis-i Meşveret* (Consultative Assembly). Since the troubled days following the assassination of Alemdâr Mustafa Pasha, the janissaries sought to be present in the *Meclis-i Meşveret*, an old institution with a new momentum since the reign of Selim III, who differed somewhat from his predecessors due to the liberal political ideas he entertained.[103] Mahmud II,

[101] This literally means kitchen-range, but it was the term used to designate the janissary centres. The janissaries took most of their titles and symbols from culinary terminology. See J. Hammer-Purgstall, *Histoire de l'Empire ottoman, depuis son origine jusqu'à nos jours*, trans. J. J. Hellert, 18 vols., vol. I (Paris: Bellizard Barthès, Dufour & Lowell, 1835), 124. Edward Joy Morris, *The Turkish Empire, Embracing the Religion, Manners and Customs of the People, with a Memoir of the Reigning Sultan and Omer Pacha* (Philadelphia: Lindsay and Blakiston, 1855), 52.

[102] Cevdet Paşa, *Târîh-i Cevdet XII*, 160, emphasis mine.

[103] When he was the heir apparent, he exchanged letters with Louis XVI to gain his support, asking his advice about the possible reform programmes suitable to the Ottoman Empire. Needless to say, at the time Louis XVI had more serious problems at hand. Even though he sent some French officers, his help did not

however, did not desire to bestow such a privilege out of sheer obligation. In the ideal Ottoman state tradition, the Sultan was the only source of legitimacy; and politics could only take place at his desire and in his person.[104] Should he wish, he could confer with his viziers and *ulemâ* on 'the matters of great importance', yet this was not incumbent on him; rather it was his accolade.[105] In an age characterised by decentralisation and limited technology, the absolutist claims of the Grand Seigneur were naturally more or less stylistic and most of the time fell a good deal short.[106] Yet, Mahmud's hands-on approach meant growing pressure to turn this rhetoric into reality.

During the commotion following the Greek War of Independence (1821), Mahmud II finally had to acquiesce 'to create the union of hearths' and let the janissary officers attend the meetings.[107] Robert

amount to much. See Enver Ziyâ Karal Karal, *Selim III.'ün Hatt-ı Hümâyunları*, 2 vols., vol. II (Ankara: Türk Târîh Kurumu Basımevi, 1942), 16–19. İsmail Hakkı Uzunçarşılı, 'III. Selim'ün Velihat iken Fransa Kralı XVI. Louis ile Muharabeleri', *Belleten* II, no. 5–6 (1938). For the increasing importance of consultative assemblies, see Ekmeleddin İhsanoğlu, *Osmanlı Devleti ve Medeniyeti Târîhi*, 2 vols., vol. I (İstanbul: IRCICA, 1994), 187–188. Also see Stanford. J. Shaw, *Between Old and New: the Ottoman Empire under Sultan Selim III, 1789–1807* (Cambridge, MA: Harvard University Press, 1971), passim.

104 Defterdar Sarı Mehmet Paşa, *Devlet Adamlarına Öğütler*, ed. Hüseyin Râgıb Uğural (Ankara: Türkiye ve Orta Doğu Âmme İdâresi Enstitüsü Yayınları, 1969), 17. Halil İnalcık, 'Osmanlı Padişâhı', *Ankara Üniversitesi Siyasal Bilgiler Fakültesi Dergisi* 12, no. 4 (1958): 78. The Sultans were supposed to have miraculous powers, not unlike the 'royal touch' in the Western tradition. According to a popular belief, when a sultan visited the site of a conflagration, for instance, his presence would extinguish the fire immediately. See Abdurrahman Şeref, 'Fuâd Paşa Konağı Nasıl Mâliye Dâiresi Oldu?', *Târîh-i Osmanî Encümeni* 1, no. 3 (1328–1910): 131. About the royal touch, see the classical account of March Bloch, especially its new preface written by Jacques Le Goff. Marc Bloch, *Les rois thaumaturges* (Paris: Gallimard, 1983), I–XXXVIII.

105 See, for instance, Şânîzâde Mehmed 'Atâ'ullah Efendi, *Târîh-i Şânîzâde*, 4 vols., vol. IV (İstanbul: Cerîde-i Havâdis Matbaası, 1291/1874–1875), 3.

106 See, for instance, Rhoads Murphey's article. According to Murphey, 'the imposition of the imperial will ... [was based] on negotiated settlement and compromised solution.' Rhoads Murphey, 'An Ottoman View from the Top and Rumblings from Below: The Sultanic Writs (Hatt-i Hümâyun) of Murad IV (R. 1623–1640)', *Turcica* 28(1996): 331. Also see Gilles Veinstein, 'La voix du maître à travers les firmans de Soliman le Magnifique', in *Soliman le Magnifique et son temps*, ed. Gilles Veinstein (Paris: La Documentation française, 1992), 127–144.

107 Cevdet Paşa, *Târîh-i Cevdet XII*, 62. BOA, HAT, 339/19367, 22 Zilhicce 1236 (12 September 1821). The janissaries took this right seriously as a political tool.

Walsh (d. 1852), an Irish clergyman living in Istanbul at the time, described this assembly as a creation of 'something like an approximation to a popular government'. For Walsh, as the janissaries 'included a large body of the citizens of Constantinople they were in some measure the representatives of the people'.[108] According to Şânîzâde 'Atâ'ullah Efendi (d. 1826), another contemporary, even the fellows who had this privilege were stupefied by this 'contriving'.[109] Şânîzâde, well known for his liberal tendencies, found the whole experience tantalising, as members of the assembly were not entitled to vote.[110] Hence its benefit, he wrote, amounted to little. He was not altogether comfortable with the qualifications of the people involved either. Acknowledging that there were analogous institutions in some 'orderly countries', Şânîzâde stressed that their representatives were chosen 'among those known for their learning and eloquence'. Otherwise, he added derisively, 'there is no point of redundantly hoarding and bending it into the shape of

When Haydar Baba, a Bektaşi dervish, was exiled from the capital because of his involvement in the 1808 rebellion, to protest the decision they did not attend the meeting taking place at the *konak* of Şeyhülislam. Cevdet Paşa, *Târîh-i Cevdet XII*, 61–62. It should be also mentioned that the government accused Haydar Baba of being an Iranian spy and tried to remove him from the capital many times without any success. See, for instance, BOA, HAT 284/170178, 29 Zilhicce 1230 (2 December 1815).

108 Robert Walsh, *A Residence at Constantinople During a Period Including the Commencement, Progress and Termination of the Greek and Turkish Revolutions*, 2 vols., vol. I (London: Westley & Davis, 1836), 394–395. Some sort of popular government was also established after the rebellions of 1656 (*Vak'a-i Vakvakiye*). According to Münir Aktepe, during the tumultuous days of the revolt, janissary *ağas* governed the Empire for seventy days. Münir Aktepe, *Patrona İsyanı* (İstanbul: İstanbul Üniversitesi Edebiyât Fakültesi Yayınları, 1958), VII.

109 '*Gerçi bu takrible o makulelerde dahi mûcib-i hayret . . .* ' According to him, the reason for such inclusion was the ever-increasing gossip among the population of Istanbul. The decision not only included the janissaries but also the representatives of guilds. This probably was intended to present this decision as a grace rather than an exaction. In any case, the guilds were closely associated with the janissaries. See Şânîzâde Efendi, *Târîh-i Şânîzâde IV*, 2.

110 These liberal ideas, and the Bektaşi connection, often went hand in hand in the Ottoman Empire, and caused his exile after the abolition of the janissary corps. Unfortunately, no work has been done on this fascinating character. Physician by trade, Şânîzâde mastered several European languages and singlehandedly created modern Ottoman medical terminology. See Adnan Adıvar, *Osmanlı Türklerinde İlim* (İstanbul: Maârif Vekâleti, 1943), 192–195.

republic'.[111] This dubious attribution to them of the idea of a republic was perhaps the last but indubitably the most significant political acquisition of the janissaries.

By the spring of 1826, Mahmud must have felt confident enough to begin his project. That is to say, as confident as he could ever be with such a project on the table. On 8 April, at the opening ceremony of the Nusretiye Mosque, Mahmud II saluted his artillerymen yet intentionally ignored the janissaries, his royal guard.[112] This could have no other effect than exacerbating existing irritations between him and the units. A more serious provocation would come only a month later. A new corps, the *Eşkinci Ocağı*, was raised and recruited its novices from the janissaries. The name, it seems, was chosen with great deliberation. There was an historical organisation called *Eşkinci* and probably Mahmud wanted to tone down the novelty of his soldiers through reference to it. He must have remembered the stir that the novelty of Selim III's New Model Army (*Nizâm-ı Cedîd Ordusu*) had caused among the population. In Europe, one should note, this appeal to tradition was a common practice in times of great reforms, something that Marx calls the 'awakening of the death' when 'revolutionizing themselves and things'.[113] But in the annals of the Ottoman Empire, this was seen as a novelty that Mahmud had brought about.

On 4 June the company appeared for their first drill and the next day, a large parade took place in front of principal janissary barracks. All the government officials, including the Grand Vizier in *halb europäischen Uniform*, imitating the uniform of Egyptian officers, were

[111] Şânîzâde Efendi, *Târîh-i Şânîzâde IV*, 3. The term *cumhûriyet* or *jumhuriyya* gained a new meaning after the French revolution in the Ottoman political context. Before it had been occasionally used to describe the Republic of Venice, but its full political connotation was achieved only after 1789. For the details, see Bernard Lewis, *Political Words and Ideas in Islam* (Princeton, NJ: Markus Wiener Publishers, 2007), 127–133. Also see Gilles Veinstein and Nicolas Vatin, *Le sérail ébranlé* (Paris: Fayard, 2003), 198–199. The word *cumhûr*, on the other hand, simply meant majority. For instance, in 1648, when Ibrahim I was dethroned by janissaries, all the calls of his mother, Kösem Sultan, proved inefficacious and the rebels told her that the '*decision was taken with unanimity and it is illicit to act against majority/cumhûra muhâlefet câiz değildir*'. Kâtip Çelebi, *Fezleke-i Kâtib Çelebi*, 2 vols., vol. II (Istanbul: Cerîde-i Havâdis Matbaası, 1286/1869), 328.

[112] Cevdet Paşa, *Târîh-i Cevdet XII*, 167.

[113] See Karl Marx, *The Eighteenth Brumaire of Louis Bonaparte* (Moscow: Progress Publisher, 1972), 10.

present.[114] According to Rosen, a dragoman at the Prussian embassy in Constantinople in the 1840s, the entire masquerade was orchestrated by the Sultan who 'like a physician intentionally agitating a peptic ulcer' worked the janissaries to bursting point. For the unruly soldiers of the Empire, Rosen reported, the aim was indisputably insult and humiliation (*Beleidigung und Demütigung*) and the janissaries, as the Sultan knew, were known to act brutally with much less provocation and offence.[115]

We shall never know if Mahmud intended to exacerbate tensions by enraging the janissaries as he has been portrayed as doing. This, however, is certainly the impression that one gets from [near] contemporary sources such as Rosen or Cevdet Pasha. In any case, it is certain that the janissaries wanted to end the stalemate once and for all. On the night of 12 June 1826, the Grand Vizier, Benderli Mehmed Selim Sırrı Pasha, sent a messenger to Ağa Hüseyin Pasha informing him of his fears that revolt might break out any moment. Hüseyin Pasha commanded determination and perseverance as 'public opinion was on the Sultan's side'.[116] Three days later, the janissaries rose in rebellion for the last time. They demanded the execution of certain officers whom they regarded as the enemies of their corps. In return, criers were dispatched across Istanbul inviting public to unite under the standard of Prophet Muhammad. The janissaries, using the same method, also tried to entice the population to join their ranks, or at least to open their shops as usual – with all kind of guarantees for their security.

This part is worth considering in more detail. In the past, every janissary intervention was actually a temporary power alliance with

114 Georg Rosen, *Geschichte der Türkei von dem Siege der reform im Jahre 1826 bis zum Pariser Tractat vom Jahre 1856*, 2 vols., vol. I (Leipzig: S. Hirzel, 1866), 11. I am grateful to Prof. Dr. Kemal Beydilli for this reference.

115 Ibid.

116 Howard A. Reed, 'The Destruction of the Janissaries in June 1826' (PhD, Princeton University, 1951), 186. It should be noted that here Reed makes a somewhat liberal reading of Cevdet Pasha's terminology. A verbatim translation of *ittifâk-ı umûmî* had to be 'general consensus' rather than public opinion. The passage that he is referring to can be found in Cevdet Paşa, *Târîh-i Cevdet XII*, 177. This is the edition used throughout this book. Reed is using the famous 'new-edition' of 1309/1891 where the page number is given as 153 for the same episode. Slightly different version of the same story can be also found in Slade, *Records of Travels in Turkey*, 136.

the common people (*avâm*).[117] Yet, owing to the increasing quarrels among the former collaborators the idea of common sense, as it were, had shattered since the beginning of the nineteenth century.[118] The reason for this was partly the government's deliberate attempts to alienate former allies without any doubt.[119] But it was also the recognition that janissary relations with society, due to their monopolistic tendencies, could not cope with the changing economic and social dynamics of the nineteenth century.[120] This change of 'attitude' can be considered the birth of modernity in the Ottoman context.[121]

Subsequent events indeed proved Ağa Hüseyin Pasha to be right. Public opinion was on the Sultan's side. What could have been the end of Mahmud II's reign a couple of decades previously was easily warded off.[122] In a matter of a few hours, the janissaries, one of the most

117 See, for instance, Robert Olson's articles, which depict the solidarity between *Esnaf* (shopkeepers and artisans) and the janissaries as a key factor for understanding the rebellions of 1730 and 1740. Robert W. Olson, 'The Esnaf and the Patrona Halil Rebellion of 1730: A Realignment in Ottoman Politics?', *Journal of the Economic and Social History of the Orient* 17, no. 3 (1974). Robert W. Olson, 'Jews, Janissaries, Esnaf and the Revolt of 1740 in Istanbul: Social Upheaval and Political Realignment in the Ottoman Empire', *Journal of the Economic and Social History of the Orient* 20, no. 2 (1977). Donald Quataert points out that the janissaries' commercialisation accelerated after 1740. Thus, it is also possible to argue that their increasing corporate power might have resulted in their alienation from their former 'partners in crime'. Donald Quataert, 'Workers and the State during the Late Ottoman Empire', in *The State and the Subaltern: Modernization, Society and the State in Turkey and Iran*, ed. Touraj Atabaki (London: I. B. Tauris, 2007), 23.

118 See, Câbî Efendi, *Câbî Târîhi II*, 741–749.

119 See, for instance, ibid., 728–729.

120 Donald Quataert rightly stressed that the 1826 Auspicious Event was one of the 'hallmarks of further Ottoman integration into the world market'. Quataert, 'The Age of Reforms, 1812–1914', 825. In this respect, when the government was not able to pay their wages, the fact that they threateningly asked to be compensated from the *eshâm* funds is quite symbolic. Câbî Efendi, *Câbî Târîhi II*, 733. This desire was surely not only a practicality but also imbued with criticism towards the changing economic structure.

121 Here it is referred to Michel Foucault's presentation of modernity 'as an attitude than as a period of history. And by "attitude", [Foucault continues] I mean a mode of relating to contemporary reality; a voluntary choice made by certain people; in the end, a way of thinking and feeling; a way, too, of acting and behaving that at one and the same time marks a relation of belonging and presents itself as a task.' Michel Foucault, 'What Is Enlightenment?', in *The Foucault Reader*, ed. Paul Rabinow (New York: Pantheon Books, 1984), 39.

122 For the details of the night, see the official history of the event produced by the palace chronicler. Esad Efendi, *Üss-i Zafer*, 67–88. And its contemporary

ancient Ottoman institutions, were annihilated by a coalition of imperial powers and civilians gathered around the Topkapı Palace. For Cevdet Pasha this was a clear evidence of public opinion's strength:

> Up until now, [he wrote], the janissaries lived through many episodes as such and always had the best of it. Yet in this instance they were rendered wretched with facility ... This event was a probative force of the sway of *public opinion* in the universe. For more than five hundred years, the janissaries with their perpetuity and stability weathered too many storms. But this time their corps (*ocak*) was burned to a crisp in four to five hours. This was because they became the object of public hatred.[123]

Official decrees following the 'Auspicious Event' did not confine themselves to the abolition of the corps. They also emphasised that 'their name and reputation ceased to exist',[124] 'their appellation was completely and certainly demolished',[125] 'the name janissary was removed from the face of the earth'.[126] 'There is no doubt that', Mahmud II opined grimly, 'it will be difficult to eradicate such a name so ancient and people are so used to. But even if a sudden estranging is not possible it can be done, however, by striking terror to their lips *(dudaklarına havf düşürererek)*.'[127] Five years later when there was some janissary talk in Baghdad, Istanbul warned sternly that they had to be removed at once; and it added ominously: 'the epithet of janissary should not be voiced at all'.[128] The documents belonging to the company were burnt in a public bath in the vicinity of Hagia Sophia,[129]

French translation, Efendi, *Précis Historique de la destruction du corps des Janissaires par le Sultan Mahmoud*, 108–27.

123 Cevdet Paşa, *Târîh-i Cevdet XII*, 189–90, emphasis mine.

124 BOA, C..AS.. 549/23023, 29 Zilhicce 1241 (4 August 1826).

125 BOA, HAT 1318/51356-C, 29 Zilhicce 1241 (4 August 1826).

126 BOA, C..DH.. 52/2589, 3 Muharrem 1242 (7 August 1826).

127 BOA, HAT 290/17388, 29 Zilhicce 1241 4 (4 August 1826). They made no bones about it and the heads of unfortunate janissaries kept coming to Istanbul from different parts of the Empire. BOA, C..AS..1018/44612, 29 Cemâziyelahir 1242 (28 January 1827), BOA, HAT 293/17464-F, 17 Receb 1242 (14 February 1827), BOA, HAT 293/17464-J, 24 Recep 1242 (21 February 1827), BOA, HAT 291/17402-H, 29 Şevval 1242 (26 May 1827). According to Slade, 'five thousand fell under the grand blow, and in the whole, twenty or twenty-five thousand are supposed to have perished throughout the empire'. Slade, *Records of Travels in Turkey*, 137. Cevdet Pasha, citing Esad Efendi, gives the number as six thousand. See Cevdet Paşa, *Târîh-i Cevdet XII*, 207.

128 BOA, C..DH.. 62/3056, 29 Rebiülevvel 1247 (7 September 1831).

129 BOA, C..AS.. 615/25937, 29 Safer 1243 (21 September 1827).

Figure 1.4 Mahmud II's *hatt* ordering his vizier to 'strike terror to the lips of people' so that the name 'janissary' would be forgotten. BOA, HAT 290/17388, 29 Zilhicce 1241 (4 August 1826).

and the land near the ancient Forum of Theodosius (Etmeydanı) where their barracks once stood was put on sale in great haste to 'enliven' the environment.[130] Finally, their names were erased from the ceremony books of the state.[131] 'It is not fifteen months since they filled his [Mahmud's] dominions', a Navy Chaplain, George Jones wrote, 'you may now travel all through the empire, and it is as if they had never been. Their name is never mentioned, and the memory of the Janissaries seem already fast passing into oblivion.'[132] Charles MacFarlane observed in 1828, the 'name of Janissary was ... a sound proscribed and accursed'.[133] But why was such reiteration, one cannot help feeling, almost a reminder of Orwell's Newspeak, required? In other words, what was the 'thoughtcrime' in this context?

Generally speaking, like the *â'yân* in the provinces, the janissaries at the centre gradually assumed the 'representative publicness' in the absence of any other recognised political institutions.[134] The power void created by the lack of sultanic authority was filled with their courtly ceremonies.[135] Their status was rather vague at the beginning, but they managed to establish a tangible presence with their increasing

130 BOA, HAT 294/17489, 29 Zilhicce 1242 (24 July 1827).

131 BOA, HAT 1426/58146, 29 Zilhicce 1250 (28 April 1835).

132 [George Jones] A civilian, *Sketches of Naval Life with Notices of Men, Manners and Scenery on the Shores of the Mediterranean in a Series of Letters from the Brandywine and Constitution Frigates*, 2 vols., vol. II (New Haven, CT: H. Howe, 1829), 139.

133 Charles MacFarlane, *Constantinople in 1828: A Residence of Sixteen Months in the Turkish Capital and Provinces: With an Account of the Present State of the Naval and Military Power and of the Resources of the Ottoman Empire*, 2 vols., vol. II (London: Saunders and Otley, 1829), 70.

134 Talking about the janissaries in the eighteenth century, Ali Yaycıoğlu argued that they 'had accumulated privileges and rights throughout the previous two centuries and had come to control public opinion in Istanbul and other cities'. Ali Yaycioglu, *Partners of the Empire*, 2.

135 Even the daily transportation of the meat consumed by the janissaries was a big public event. These formidable soldiers could kill unfortunate bystanders who dared to block the road during this process. For the details of the convoy of butchers as depicted by a seventeenth-century Ottoman traveller, see Evliya Çelebi, *Narrative of Travels in Europe, Asia, and Africa in the Seventeenth Century*, trans. Joseph Von Hammer-Purgstall, 2 vols., vol. I (London: Oriental Translation Fund, 1846), 144. After the 'Auspicious Event', Mahmud II immediately removed the butchers who were associated with the janissaries and exiled them to different parts of the Empire. See BOA, HAT 289/17338, 29 Zilhicce 1241 (4 August 1826). Also see Cem Behar, *A Neighborhood in Ottoman Istanbul: Fruit Vendors and Civil Servants in the Kasap İlyas Mahalle* (New York: State University of New York Press, 2003), 55–57.

level of political and economic interventions.[136] They expanded their territory at the expense of sultanic rule, as they were the only order adequately united and powerful enough to enforce their rights. They were valued as a source of liberty by certain segments of the society – if liberty is the right word here. Slade, for instance, credited them with a 'loop-hole', which helped the public escape from tyranny. As a result, they were employed by *ulemâ* and other dignitaries to regulate and control particularly troublesome rulers like Selim III or Mahmud II.[137]

Their growing commercialisation, often described as the degeneration of their warlike qualities, was a union of forces, as it were, between them and commercial classes against the arbitrary encroachments of the Sultan.[138] Victor Fontanier, a contemporary traveller, talked at length about the sense of helplessness that some felt in seeing the janissaries suppressed as such. One peasant told him disconsolately, 'Sultan Mahmud, our lord, does not want the janissaries anymore. But what will happen to us when the pashas and grandees can *get through* the country at their ease? We will have to run away and become Kurds.'[139]

136 The provincial janissaries had also emerged as important competitors in the provincial auctions of tax-farms in the eighteenth century. See, for instance, Dina Rizk Khoury, *State and Provincial Society in the Ottoman Empire: Mosul, 1540–1834* (Cambridge: Cambridge University Press, 2002), 133–34.

137 According to Cevdet Pasha, when there were preliminary talks in the State Council about declaring war on Russia, Derviş Pasha, deeply troubled because of the situation of the army, asked Halet Efendi if they should not first ameliorate the state of the janissaries. Halet Efendi, the Ottoman *éminence grise*, replied grimly, 'Today it is easy to abolish janissaries and create an orderly army but then who will tame my lion?' The lion, of course, was Mahmud II. See Cevdet Paşa, *Târîh-i Cevdet XII*, 62.

138 A classic account of this view is the highly influential work of İsmail Hakkı Uzunçarşılı. A product of Ottoman historiography, Uzunçarşılı depicts the commercialisation of the janissaries with the modernist makeup of the republic. See İsmail Hakkı Uzunçarşılı, *Osmanlı Devleti Teşkilâtından Kapıkulu Ocakları: Acemi Ocağı ve Yeniçeri Ocağı* (Ankara: Türk Târîh Kurumu, 1988), 477–479. For an analysis of the 'corruption literature', see Cemal Kafadar, 'On the Purity and Corruption of the Janissaries', *Turkish Studies Association Bulletin* 15, no. 2 (1991): 273–280. For the increasing commercialisation of the janissaries, see Andre Raymond, 'Soldiers in Trade: The Case of Ottoman Cairo', *British Journal of Middle Eastern Studies* 18, no. 1 (1991): 23–29. Gibb and Bowen, *Islamic Society and the West*, 280.

139 Victor Fontanier, *Voyages en Orient Constantinople, Grèce: événements politiques de 1827 à 1829* (Paris: Librairie Universelle de P. Mongie Aîné, 1829), emphasis in the original. 321. According to Fontanier, the janissaries turned into genuine national guards 'defending the local interest against the

As such, their legacy is of vital importance for understanding the emergence of public opinion. The history of the janissaries shows that there was a political culture where the voice of the opposition had to be heard. And perhaps more significantly by their absence they deflated the very space where the public opinion could and would blossom. On the eve of the 'Auspicious Event' when there were fervent discussions about the fate of the janissaries at the imperial council, one of the attendees said, 'since the general public is janissary, it is not permissible to act against the public/*umûm ahâlî yeniçeri olduğundan umûma karşu hareket câiz değildir*'.[140] This charting is important and in a way elucidates the post-1826 legitimacy crises of the Ottoman state. Mahmud II intuitively knew that like nature, politics also abhors a vacuum. Henceforth he endeavoured to assume this representative role in his public persona by pressing ahead with sometimes controversial measures, such as ordering his portraits be hung in public buildings in the midst of pompous ceremonies.[141] Perhaps even more to the point,

innovations of power', and 'people all instinctively felt that the only dyke against the absolute authority was overthrown, their freedom was destroyed'. Victor Fontanier, *Voyages en Orient de l'année 1821 à l'année 1829 entrepris par ordre du governement français: Turquie d'Asie* (Paris: Librairie Universelle de P. Mongie Aîné, 1829), 30, 322. They were, he wrote in another book, the 'representative of political opposition', and since 'they were wiped out, the country has been declining'. Victor Fontanier, *Voyages en Orient entrepris par ordre du gouvernement français de 1830 à 1833: Deuxième Voyage en Anatolie* (Paris: Librarie de Dumont, 1834), 216, 35.

140 Ahmed Lûtfî omits who. Ahmed Lûtfî, *Târîh-i Lûtfî*, 8 vols., vol. I (İstanbul: Matbaa-i Amire, 1290 [1873]), 154. For a similar argument also see ibid., 10. An early-eighteenth-century bureaucrat, Defterdar Sarı Mehmed Pasha was also of the same opinion. See Defterdar Sarı Mehmed Paşa, *Devlet Adamlarına Öğütler*, 67.

141 Ahmed Lûtfî Efendi also stated that people found such ostentatious ceremonies 'ugly', and after the death of Mahmud II the portraits were 'put aside'. Lûtfî, *Târîh-i Lûtfî V*, 50–52. Mahmud II used this newly found weapon extensively by not only sending it to his governors as a token of his appreciation and his surveillance but also to European monarchs probably, with a subtext of being one of them. See BOA, HAT 658/32154 3 Şevval 1247 (6 March 1832), BOA, HAT 1179/46567 29 Zilhicce 1250 (28 April 1835), BOA, HAT 714/34088 27 Cemâziyelahir 1252 (9 October 1836), BOA, HAT 367/20282 29 Zilhicce 1248 (19 May 1833). Also see Stephen Vernoit, 'The Visual Arts in Nineteenth Century Muslim Thought', in *Islamic Art in the 19th century: Tradition, Innovation, and Eclecticism*, ed. Doris Behrens-Abouseif and Stephen Vernoit (Leiden: Brill, 2006), 23. Wendy M. K. Shaw, *Ottoman Painting: Reflections of Western Art from the Ottoman Empire to the Turkish Republic* (London: I. B. Tauris, 2011), 26–30.

he went out of his palace and became publicly available by breaking away from the tradition of imperial reclusion.[142] But to mediate the tension engendered by the abolition of the janissaries, he resorted to the abstract authority of the public as well.[143] When documents reiterated that the name janissary was obliterated, they also emphasised another thing: 'their obliteration was decided by the grandees of the state and the *public* assembled in Sultanahmet'.[144] The *hatt* issued to all the provinces made this subtext even more pronounced: 'in this auspicious affair, attempted and undertaken by the public alliance (*ittifâk-ı âmme*) praise be Allah, every believer is united and unified and no way whatsoever an individual will dare to utter a dissident opinion. But if somebody does, he will be surmounted with the sword of law consistent with the judgement rendered by the *public alliance*.'[145] In other words, Mahmud wanted to emphasise that it was the sword of the public, and not his own, which would strike the fatal blow. By spreading the responsibility in this way, he sought to create the illusion of public consent for this most dramatic move.

Post-Janissary Reforms of Mahmud II

After removing the biggest obstacle from his path, Mahmud embarked upon an extensive reform programme.[146] These are not in themselves a

142 François Georgeon, 'Les usages politiques du ramadan, de l'Empire ottoman à la république de Turquie', in *Ramadan et politique*, ed. Fariba Adelkhan and François Georgeon (Paris: CNRS Éditions, 2000), 24.

143 As Selim Deringil stated for later periods, 'it was hoped in both the Russian and Ottoman cases that by forging a link of sacrality directly with the people, inconvenient intermediaries like political parties and parliaments could be avoided.' Selim Deringil, *The Well-Protected Domains: Ideology and the Legitimation of Power in the Ottoman Empire 1876–1909* (London: I. B. Tauris, 1999), 17.

144 BOA, HAT 1236/48106, 29 Zilhicce 1241 (4 August 1836). Or 'the verdict was agreed upon by a general consensus', see BOA, HAT 1137/45268-E, 21 Rebiülahir 1242 (22 November 1826).

145 Cevdet Paşa, *Târîh-i Cevdet XII*, 315. For the full text of the *hatt*, see ibid., 311–316. It seems that the formula of *ittifâk-ı âmme* was used extensively during the gruelling days following the event. The *hatt*, for instance, announcing the foundation of new corps to replace the janissaries (*Asâkir-i Mansûre-i Muhâmmediyye*/Victorious Troops of Muhammad), stated that 'because it could not be found any other solution to reform them, it was decided by the *public alliance* ...' BOA, HAT, 1438/59106, 1 Zilhicce 1241 (7 July 1826), emphasis mine.

146 After the execution of his brother, he was the only surviving male member of the dynasty. Some seriously contemplated upon starting a new ruling family

matter of concern for this book. However, there is a causal link, albeit often overlooked, between modernist projects and the emergence of public opinion across the world. It was not a coincidence that when Bulgarin in Russia warned his government to take public opinion into account 'since it is impossible to do away with [it]',[147] Sadık Rifat Pasha happened to advise his Sultan against 'religious belief and public opinion' as to oppose either one of them was 'surrounded with great difficulty and danger'.[148] While Mahmud II undertook an 'arduous journey' in 1830 just to examine the condition of his subjects 'whether Muslim or non-Muslim',[149] an unprecedented event in the then half-millennium-long history of the Ottoman Empire, young *tsarevich* Alexander II was unintentionally following his footsteps in a seven-month-long grand tour of Russia in 1837 to show 'his kindliness through the acts of charity'.[150] One would be struck by the common themes encapsulated in their narratives, both published in the official newspapers *Takvîm-i Vekâyi* and *Severnaia pchela* respectively.[151] The Sultan even took the trouble of warning the palace chronicler, Esad Efendi, who was writing the account somewhat pompously, although he said, 'there is nothing to say against its artful and delightful penning,

with the ousted Crimean Khans residing in Istanbul at the time. Even Mahmud's sister, Esma Sultan, was considered a legitimate alternative by the rebels. The absence of a serious domestic 'substitute' shows the strength of sultanic legitimacy. See Tahsîn Öz, 'Selim III Mustafa IV. ve Mahmud II. Zamanlarına Ait Birkaç Vesika', *Târîh Vesikaları*, 23–25. Probably to compensate the deficit of heir, Mahmud II fathered twenty-three children. Ahmet Akgündüz and Said Öztürk, *Yedi Yüzüncü Yılında Bilinmeyen Osmanlı* (İstanbul: Osmanlı Araştırmaları Vakfı, 1999), 240.

147 Nurit Schleifman, 'A Russian Daily Newspaper and Its New Readership: 'Severnaia Pchela', 1825–1840', *Cahiers du Monde russe et soviétique* 28, no. 2 (1987): 130.

148 Rifat Paşa, *Müntahabât-ı Asâr-ı Rifat Paşa: İdâre-i Hükümetin Ba'zı Kavâid-i Esâsiyesine Mutazammın Rifat Paşa Merhumun Kaleme Aldığı Risâledir*, 47.

149 Abdülkadir Özcan, 'II. Mahmud'un Memleket Gezileri', in *Prof. Dr. Bekir Kütükoğlu'na Armağan*, ed. Mübahat S. Kütükoğlu and et al. (İstanbul: İstanbul Üniversitesi Edebiyât Fakültesi, 1991), 372. The journeys began in 1830 but Mahmud's quotations are from his 1837 journey. For his 1830 journey, see ibid., 362–363.

150 Richard Wortman, 'Rule by Sentiment: Alexander II's Journeys through the Russian Empire', *The American Historical Review* 95, no. 3 (1990): 747, 51. This was not the first, however, ceremonial trip undertaken by a Russian monarch, yet it was the 'longest tour of the empire by a tsar or tsarevich'. Ibid., 747.

151 Özcan, 'II. Mahmud'un Memleket Gezileri', 362 fn. 2. Wortman, 'Rule by Sentiment', 748.

it is necessary for these sorts of things, which are going to be made public (*umûma neşr olunacak*), to be comprehensible by everyone'.[152] Throughout the nineteenth century, people in different parts of the world began to think about politics in similar terms as *gonglun* in China and *'anzar-i umûmî* in Iran, both meaning public opinion, emerged simultaneously as significant categories of reckoning.[153]

How can this omnipresence be accounted for without getting into bed, as it were, with modernisation theory? Such a big question cannot be answered rigorously here; but briefly considering it might be helpful for charting the specific conditions, which gave rise to new sensibilities in the Ottoman Empire. In recent years, the theory of multiple modernities has presented itself as a serious alternative. Shmuel Eisenstadt's solution is to see modernity as a 'story of continual constitution and reconstitution of a multiplicity of cultural programs'.[154] On the face of it, with its less Eurocentric and more culturally neutral perspective, it is perhaps more suitable for non-Western historiography. It does not, however, explain the simultaneity of the modern. What made these countries outside the 'West' experience similar, near simultaneous political and social tensions is a vital element in better understanding modernity.[155] The applicability of the 'hybrid talk' to the Ottoman Empire is also dubious. In the colonial context, hybridisation is meaningful as a way of thinking beyond the binary opposition of modernity. The Ottoman case, however, presents more complex power relations: the external influences were quite negligible until approximately the 1860s, and they did not create what Homi Bhabha called the 'hybrid'

[152] Ahmed Lûtfî Efendi, *Tarîh-i Devlet-i Âliyye-i Osmaniyye*, 8 vols., vol. V (Dersaâdet: Mahmud Bey Matbaası, 1302/1884–1885), 90.

[153] Murata Yūjirō, 'Dynasty, State and Society: The Case of Modern China', in *Imagining the People: Chinese Intellectuals and the Concept of Citizenship, 1890–1920*, ed. Joshua A. Fogel and Peter G. Zarrow (New York: M.E. Sharpe, 1997), 132–33. Shiva Balaghi, 'Nationalism and Cultural Production in Iran, 1848–1906' (PhD diss., the University of Michigan, 2008), 143. Actually, in modern Persian, the term *efkâr-ı umûmîye* is also commonly used. See, for instance, Masoud Kohestani Nejad, *İhtiyarat, Islâhat ve Levayih-i Kanûni-i Doktor Mohammad Mosaddegh* (Tehran: Kitaphâne-i Milli-i İran, 1383/1963–1964), 437.

[154] S. N. Eisenstadt, 'Multiple Modernities', in *Comparative Civilizations and Multiple Modernities*, ed. S. N. Eisenstadt (Leiden: E. J. Brill, 2003), 536.

[155] As Timothy Mitchel points out, it might be also too general to be truly useful. Timothy Mitchell, 'Introduction', in *Questions of Modernity*, ed. Timothy Mitchell (Minneapolis: University of Minnesota Press, 2000), xii.

moment of political change.[156] The Empire was never 'officially' colonised. This is not to say that there was not any foreign influence. Certainly there was but its importance is often exaggerated in the secondary literature and based on selective reading.[157]

Perhaps it is possible to talk of a *weltzeit* (universal time) as proposed by Reinhard Schulze, who interpreted the transformations of the Islamic world within the framework of an international context in terms of its economic, social, and political associations.[158] According to Schulze, rather than seeing the changes taking place in the East as the result of ubiquitous Western influence, a practice laden with normative political categories and implications, one can see them as global changes, which arose owing to a common world-time.[159] But despite its appeal, there are still problems to be overcome. It does not, for instance, explain the 'pioneering role' of the West. From this perspective, it is difficult to answer why all these transformations first took place in Europe and North America and later 'other' countries as far apart from each other as the Kingdom of Hawaii and the Ottoman Empire, followed them almost simultaneously.[160]

Leaving this question aside and returning to Mahmud II's modernisation efforts, one can say that the idea of change was perhaps not new.[161] But its execution proved to be immensely difficult: it had

156 Homi K. Bhabha, *The Location of Culture* (London: Routledge, 1994), 28.

157 Compare, for instance, Şerif Mardin's quotation from the *Revue des Deux Mondes* of 1840 about a 'small literary colony which is going to exploit liberal ideals in Turkey' and the original text. The sarcastic tone of the latter is difficult to miss, especially for a scholar like Mardin who preferred to translate the quotation at its face value. Mardin, *The Genesis of Young Ottoman Thought*, 194. Edouard Thouvenel, 'Constantinople sous Abdul-Medjid', *Revue des Deux Mondes* XXI, no. Seris IV (1840): 68–69.

158 See Benjamin C. Fortna, *Imperial Classroom: Islam, the State, and Education in the Late Ottoman Empire* (Oxford: Oxford University Press, 2002), 12, 40.

159 See Reinhard Schulze, *A Modern History of the Islamic World*, trans. Azizeh Azodi (London: I.B. Tauris, 2002), 3–6.

160 Here I am referring to the emergence of newspapers in native languages, which took place in 1831 in the Ottoman Empire (*Takvîm-i Vekâyi*) and in 1834 in Hawaii (*Ka Lama Hawaii*). For the Hawaiian example, see Robert W. Kirk, *Paradise Past: The Transformation of the South Pacific, 1520–1920* (Jefferson, NC: McFarland & Company, 2012), 113.

161 For an 'imbued' sense of decline in the Ottoman intellectual life, see Cemal Kafadar, 'The Myth of the Golden Age: Ottoman Historical Consciousness in the Post-Süleymânic Era', in *Süleymân the Second and His Time*, ed. Halil İnalcık and Cemal Kafadar (Istanbul: The Isis Press, 1993), 38.

cost Mustafa II his throne (r. 1695–1703) and Selim III his life (r. 1789–1807). By the time Mahmud II succeeded his cousin, it had become apparent that the band-aid approach of the Ottoman statesmen was not going to solve anything. Hence Mahmud II launched a wide-ranging reform programme, which can be best described as self-colonisation for self-empowerment. This was a defensive project and some of its elements are explicitly related to the creation of the public. The law of compulsory education, for instance, prepared by the newly established 'Council of Public Works', was vital in the commercialisation of cultural productions in the following years.[162] The Clothing Law of 1829 similarly 'removed the visible distinctions between non-Muslims and Muslims and facilitated the formation of a new elite without the distinctive markings that had long set one community apart from the other'.[163] Mahmud II also attacked the traditional privileges of Ottoman guilds (*gedik*).[164] These mediaeval institutions had sought to regulate the market until the 1830s in a strict manner and 'hindered the growth of mercantile capital'.[165] The changing market conditions of the nineteenth century, however, made their monopolistic tendencies impracticable. With the abolition of the janissaries, with whom *gediks* were traditionally associated,[166] they

[162] For a detailed account of Mahmud II's educational policies, see Selçuk Akşin Somel, *The Modernization of Public Education in the Ottoman Empire, 1839–1908: Islamization, Autocracy, and Discipline* (Leiden: E. J. Brill, 2001), 15–37.

[163] Donald Quataert, 'Clothing Laws, State, and Society in the Ottoman Empire, 1720–1829', *International Journal of Middle East Studies* 29, no. 3 (1997): 413. In a way, as Donald Quataert stated, 'Mahmud offered non-Muslims and Muslims a common subjecthood/citizenry.' Ibid.

[164] See Donald Quataert, 'The Social History of Labor in the Ottoman Empire, 1800–1914', in *The Social History of Labor in the Middle East*, ed. Ellis Goldberg (Boulder, CO: Westview Press, 1996), 23. For a literature review of Ottoman guilds, also see Eunjeong Yi, *Guild Dynamics in Seventeenth-Century Istanbul: Fluidity and Leverage* (Leiden: E. J. Brill, 2004), 1–19.

[165] Şerif Mardin, 'Power, Civil Society and Culture in the Ottoman Empire', *Comparative Studies in Society and History* 11, no. 3 (1969): 261. Also see, Sabri F. Ülgener, *İktisadi Çözülmenin Ahlak ve Zihniyet Dünyası: Fikir ve Sanat Târîhi Boyu Akisleri İle Bir Portre Denemesi* (İstanbul: Der Yayınları, 1981), 79–84.

[166] Hamilton A. R. Gibb and Harold Bowen, *Islamic Society and the West: A Study of the Impact of Western Civilization on Moslem Culture in the Near East*, 2 vols., vol. I (Oxford: Oxford University Press, 1950), 278–280. Yi, *Guild Dynamics in Seventeenth-Century Istanbul: Fluidity and Leverage*, 137.

were eradicated without too much trouble.[167] The laissez-faire tendency of Mahmud II's reign reached a peak when the Anglo-Turkish convention was signed in 1838 (Balta Limanı Treaty), which consequentially dissolved all commercial monopolies.[168]

Even though traditional historiography depicts the growing financial dependence of the Empire upon the West as the main cause of imperial decline in the nineteenth century,[169] in fact there is ground to believe that it was one of the reasons which made its survival possible. Throughout its last phase, Ottoman finances were less than perfect, to be sure. But integration with the global economy provided protection against foreign encroachments as the Crimean War would demonstrate.[170] The Empire suddenly found itself 'supported by the unanimous sympathy and public opinion of Europe'.[171] Hence in the second half of the nineteenth century, the Russian Empire was unleashed only once and it was not before the Ottoman bankruptcy following the European financial crisis of 1873.[172] The 1838 treaty

167 Donald Quataert, 'The Age of Reforms, 1812–1914', in *An Economic and Social History of the Ottoman Empire*, ed. Halil İnalcık, Suraiya Faroqhi, and Donald Quataert (Cambridge: Cambridge University Press, 1997), 768.

168 The Article II of the Treaty reads: 'The subjects of Her Britannic Majesty or their agents shall be permitted to purchase at all places in the Ottoman Dominions whether for the purposes of internal trade or exportation all articles without any exception whatsoever the produce growth or manufacture of the said Dominions and the Sublime Porte formally engages to abolish all monopolies of agricultural produce or of any other articles whatsoever as well as . . .' Foreign Office, *Treaties between Turkey and Foreign Powers 1535–1855* (London: Foreign Office, 1855), 277. For the full text of the treaty followed by the French translation of the Sultan's *firman*, see ibid., 276–283.

169 See, for instance, this book about 'Turkey's financial suicide'. Mehmet Fatih Ekinci, *Türkiye'nin Mali İntiharı: Kapitülasyonlar ve 1838 Balta Limanı Ticâret Sözleşmeleri'nden Sevres Andlaşması'na* (İstanbul: Barış Platin Kitap, 2008), 188–202.

170 Of course, this does not mean that the Empire was an economically neutral zone before the nineteenth century. The trade with India and France had a significant place in the economic scene of the Empire. See, Panzac, 'International and Domestic Maritime Trade', 191. According to Fernand Braudel, from an economical point of view, the Ottoman Empire represented an intermediate case. That is to say it was not perhaps immediately responsive to the global economic changes, yet it was not untouched. See Fernand Braudel, *Civilization and Capitalism, 15th–18th Century: The Wheels of Commerce* (Los Angeles: University of California Press, 1992), 199.

171 Slade, *Records of Travels in Turkey*, v.

172 After the first foreign loan in 1854, the Empire became more and more dependent on European financial aid and when it was unattainable after the

possibly made Ottoman merchants vulnerable, but this was a price that Ottoman statesmen were willing to pay.

Moreover, Balta Limanı was not Nanjing: it was an agreement 'involving equal treatment of foreign and Ottoman merchants'.[173] The treaty had some positive effects on the Ottoman economy. According to Şevket Pamuk 'during the three quarters of a century following the Free Trade Treaties, total Ottoman exports measured in current prices increased more than five times'.[174] The total value of Ottoman trade with Europe surpassed £15 million in the early 1850s and even with the loss of Wallachia and Moldavia reached £30 million by the early 1870s.[175] The expansion of markets for free trade helped develop an industrial economy at home and created a new commercial class, which became an important part of the newly emerging public.[176]

There were also more subtle changes, which, though less easily quantified and demonstrated, may have had greater long-term significance for the public in formation. The introduction of passports in the late 1830s, for instance,[177] during an age when identities were

crisis of 1873, debt payments fell into arrears. This led to the establishment of the Ottoman Public Debt Administration. See, for example, Charles Lipson's account giving an international perspective of the Ottoman financial situation. Charles Lipson, 'International Debt and National Security: Comparing Victorian Britain and Postwar America' in *The International Debt Crisis in Historical Perspective*, ed. Barry Eichengreen and Peter H. Lindert (Cambridge, MA: MIT Press, 1992), 193–98.

173 Giovanni Arrighi, Iftikhar Aḥmad, and Min-wen Shih, 'Western Hegemonies in World-Historical Perspective', in *Chaos and Governance in the Modern World System*, ed. Giovanni Arrighi and Beverly J. Silver (Minneapolis: University of Minnesota Press, 1999), 233.

174 Şevket Pamuk, *The Ottoman Empire and European Capitalism, 1820–1913: Trade, Investment and Production* (Cambrige: Cambridge University Press, 2010), 23.

175 Ibid., 30.

176 For the detailed statistics of the Ottoman trade between 1830 and 1913, see Şevket Pamuk, *19. Yüzyılda Osmanlı Dış Ticâreti*, 7 vols., vol. I, Târîhi istatistikler Dizisi (Ankara: TC. Başbakanlık Devlet İstatistik Enstitüsü, 1995), 25–26.

177 Even though Kemal Karpat states that 'regular Ottoman passports' were issued only after 1861 and with the adoption of modern nationality law, it seems that preparations, and its application, started some time before. In 1835, the Ottoman ambassador in London, Nuri Efendi, sent an 'exemplar passport' to Istanbul as a model. BOA, HAT 1174/46429/R, 29 Zilhicce 1250 (28 April 1835). In 1838, a cipher message from the Ottoman *chargé d'affaires* in Paris, Talat Efendi, informed the Sublime Porte that he seized the French passports of

extremely fluid, must have contributed to facilitating the public discourse. Common sense would indicate that there was always a distinction of self and the other — even in an ethnically mixed empire like the Ottomans. But before the nineteenth century, rather than state affiliation, a person's identity was based on religious affiliation.[178] Hence it was a common practice for Ottoman subjects to hold passports from other countries.[179] They could easily claim to be under Swedish protection by 'wearing yellow boots and white fur caps', as one Ottoman officer mockingly noted.[180] Selim III was deeply troubled by the ease with which identities could shift.[181] But only after 1838, did the state fight relentlessly against this.[182] In conjunction with the census of 1831, the first of its kind, the government was trying to create what Michel Foucault called a 'disciplinary space' in which the aim was to 'establish presences and absences, to know where and how to locate individuals'.[183] Naturally there were financial concerns behind this

five Ottoman students studying medicine there and replaced them with Ottoman ones. BOA, HAT 827/37465-C, 19 Şevval 1253 (16 January 1838). In 1839, all the necessary rules and regulations were ready to be published in the official newspaper. BOA, HAT 491/ 24044, 29 Zilhicce 1254 (15 March 1839). Also see Karpat, *Studies on Ottoman Social and Political History*, 110.

178 See, for instance, Cengiz Kırlı, 'The Struggle Over Space', 111.

179 Ahmed Lûtfî, *Târîh-i Lûtfî*, 8 vols., vol. V (İstanbul: Mahmud Bey Matbaası, 1302/1884–1885), 116–17. The Ottoman Ambassador to London, İsmail Ferruh Efendi, for instance, had to obtain a French passport to gain his post in 1797, BOA, HAT 144/6030, 09 Zilkade 1212 (25 April 1798).

180 BOA, A.DVNS.MHM.d 208, Hüküm 153, Fî evâil-i Receb 1213 (December 1798).

181 Once he complainingly wrote to the Grand Vizier: 'This [foreign protection] is something that we need to be extra careful about. [In fact] there is no foreign ship [around], all of them belong to our good-for-nothing infidels. Whichever country is in favour in our eyes, the ships acquire its subjecthood. Now all of them are English. How could this be?' BOA, HAT, 35/1757, 29 Zilhicce 1212 (14 June 1798).

182 See, for instance, BOA, A.}DVN.DVE. 11/26, 19 Cemaziyelevvel 1258 (29 June 1842) and BOA, İ..MSM. 2/29, 23 Muharrem 1259 (24 February 1843) where the Ottoman government asks repeatedly, imploring the fellow states not to distribute passports amongst Ottoman subjects.

183 Michel Foucault, *Discipline and Punish: the Birth of the Prison*, trans. Alan Sheridan (New York: Vintage Books, 1995), 143. See, for instance, a document sent to all provinces and dating 1829 that invited all the *tımar* (fief) holders to Istanbul to be present in person for a 'proof of existence'. BOA, HAT 300/ 17871, 3 Şaban 1244 (8 February 1829). For an earlier and similar attempt, also see Cengiz Kırlı, 'Devlet ve İstatistik: Esnaf ve Kefalet Defterleri Işığında III. Selim İktidarı', in *Nizâm-ı Kadim'den Nizâm-ı Cedîd'de III. Selim ve Dönemi*, ed. Seyfi Kenan (İstanbul: İslam Araştırmaları Merkezi, 2010), 183–212.

edifice.[184] But it also helped the construction of a discursive space where a public discourse was possible and in which an individual could relate himself or herself to the idea of an abstract state.

The introduction of official postal services in 1833 can also be considered in the same disciplinary framework. The *Hatt-ı Hümâyun*, announcing its establishment, firmly asserted that 'hereinafter no one will send a letter by oneself'.[185] The insistence is telling. But the effects of expanding communication networks will be addressed later in more detail. Here instead this chapter will end with a brief account of the first official newspaper, *Takvîm-i Vekâyi*. This development was quite significant in the history of Ottoman public, perhaps not so much for the sales figures that the newspaper ever achieved but rather for the synthesis that the *Takvîm* sought to create.

An Ottoman Newspaper

The official Ottoman gazette commenced its publication in 1831, five years after the abolishment of the janissaries. Mahmud II took a personal interest in the project from the very beginning. In a dispatch written to the Grand Vizier, he explained how he 'wished to carry out this plan for a long time and was waiting calmly since its time and season had still not arrived' (*vakit ve mesvimi henüz gelmemiş olduğundan*).[186] They recommended him a few names, avoiding anything carrying any European connotation and largely emphasising the pragmatic character of this new tool, such as the *Correction of Doubts* (*Islah-ı Zunûn*) or *Eradication of Suspicions* (*Def'i-Şübühât*).[187]

[184] As Charles Tilly pointed out, 'the transition to direct rule gave rulers access to citizens and the sources they controlled through household taxation, mass conscription, censuses, police systems, and many other invasions of small-scale social life. But it did so at the cost of widespread resistance, extensive bargaining, and the creation of rights and perquisites for citizens.' Charles Tilly, *Coercion, Capital, and European States AD 990–1990* (Cambridge, MA: Basil Blackwell, 1990), 25.

[185] For the full text, see Enver Ziyâ Karal Karal, *Osmanlı Târîhi: Nizâm-ı ve Tanzimat Devirleri (1789–1856)*, 9 vols., vol. V (Ankara: Türk Târîh Kurumu Basımevi, 1988), 157. Even though Karal gives neither the reference nor the date, the document that he refers must be BOA, HAT 489/2395, 29 Zilhicce 1249 (19 May 1833).

[186] BOA, İ..DUİT 136/28, 29 Zilhicce 1254 (15 March 1839).

[187] They also gave several European and Russian titles with their Ottoman renditions aside such as *Globe* (*Küre*), *Gazette universelle* (*Gazete-i umûmî*)

But Mahmud II, feeling more independent after the events of 1826, came up with another name: he laconically wrote that his newspaper would be called the *Takvîm-i Vekâyi* (*Calendar of Events*), a choice that Kaymakam Pasha found 'handsome, most appropriate and fine' (*yakışıklı pek enseb ve ahsen*).[188]

The chronicler Esad Efendi was appointed as the first editor-in-chief of the newspaper. He had served his master well during the troubled days of the Auspicious Event. He was the one who read out the imperial order announcing the abolishment of the janissaries from the pulpit of the Sultanahmet Mosque. Later on, he penned a rather laudatory account of this episode entitled *Üss-i Zafer* (*the Bases of Victory*).[189] Esat Efendi was Mahmud II's *de facto* Minister of Propaganda – if not, as Virginia Aksan has argued, the 'ideologue of the new order'.[190] Hence, it is no surprise that for the management of his newspaper, Mahmud II found him 'more appropriate than others' (*diğerlerinden münâsib görünmekle*).'[191] As far as the pre-Tanzimat era was concerned, Esad Efendi was also the 'first and only man who openly and adamantly declared that writing in a style which could be

and *Journal de Pétersbourg* (*Petersburg Jurnali*). One should add that local touch was not forgotten and *Constitutionnel* turned into *Nizâmi* (regular). BOA, İ..DUİT 136/28, 29 Zilhicce 1254 (15 March 1839).

188 BOA, İ..DUİT 136/30, 29 Zilhicce 1254 (15 March 1839). The name seems like a reference to its Egyptian counterpart, *Vakâyi-i Mısriye* (Egyptian Events). A few years previously, around the end of 1828, Muhammed Ali Pasha, had begun to publish the first copies of his official gazette from the citadel of Cairo. His success in general provided Mahmud II with a justification and model for his modernisation reforms and made them more acceptable for the Ottoman public. Mahmud II, for instance, appeared in Egyptian style garments, not in Western. His new army drilled under Egyptian instructors and in Egyptian style so on and so forth. For the details of the newspaper see Ami Ayalon, *The Press in the Arab Middle East: A History* (Oxford: Oxford University Press, 1995), 15–18.

189 Esat Efendi, *Üss-i Zafer* (Istanbul: Matbaa-i Âmire, 1243 [1828]). Mohammad As'ad Efendi, *Précis Historique de la destruction du corps des Janissaires par le Sultan Mahmoud: en 1826*, trans. A. P. Caussin de Perceval (Paris: F. Didot frères, 1833).

190 Virginia H. Aksan, 'Ottoman Military and Social Transformations, 1826–28: Engagement and Resistance in a Moment of Global Imperialism', in *Empires and Autonomy: Moments in the History of Globalization*, ed. Stephen M. Streeter, John C. Weaver, and William D. Coleman (Vancouver: UBC Press, 2010), 72.

191 BOA, İ..DUİT 136/28, 29 Zilhicce 1254 (15 March 1839).

understood by everybody was to be preferred'.[192] Even though Esad Efendi did not always keep to this rhetorical position,[193] such a desire was remarkable and must have had a bearing on Mahmud II's belief, which he emphasised many times, that *Takvîm* should be published in comprehensible language.[194]

In the prologue, written by Esad Efendi himself, the newspaper was presented as an appendix of Ottoman historiography (*fenn-i târîh*), figuring in the genealogy of Ottoman chroniclers such as Naîmâ, Raşid, Subhi, İzzî, and Vasıf.[195] The Ottoman words for *takvîm* (calendar) and *târîh* (history), it should be noted, are closely related in Arabic.[196] This was a carefully calculated decision aimed at making a European invention more acceptable to the public. The newspaper, in

192 M. Fuâd Köprülü, *Edebiyât Araştırmaları*, 2 vols., vol. I (İstanbul: Ötüken Yayınları, 1989), 297. Also see Nihad Sâmi Banarlı, *Resimli Türk Edebiyâtı Târîhi: Destanlar Devrinden Zamânımıza Kadar*, 2 vols., vol. II (İstanbul: M. E. B. Devlet Kitapları, 1971), 842–843.

193 Charles MacFarlane 'was curious to learn how this work (The Basis of Victory) was received by the people on having enquiries made among certain Turks who were not exactly of the lowest condition, but what we should call of the middling class ... [and] was surprised to learn that there was hardly a man among them who could understand it'. Charles MacFarlane, *Constantinople in 1828: A Residence of Sixteen Months in the Turkish Capital and Provinces with an Account of the Present State of the Naval and Military Power and of the Resources of the Ottoman Empire* (London: Saunders and Otley, 1829), 270.

194 BOA, HAT 668/32606, 29 Zilhicce 1247 (30 May 1832).

195 After talking about the necessity of writing history with examples from the early Islamic past, Esad Efendi explained how the newspaper, prudently without calling it as such, was meant to protect the public (*âmme-i ibâd-ı bilâd*) from apprehensions and delusions. 'The external and internal events related to the Sublime State are not going to be piled up anymore', he wrote, 'but rather by stating their true causes and consequences via publication, they are going to be clearly explained to people (*halka tefhim olundukta*). In this way, everybody will learn the truth (*kesb-i ıttıla*) and not suffer, like they did in the past, because of any apprehension'. This prologue was distributed before the actual publication and published without date or page number. In some collections, such as that of the National Library in Ankara, it is bound in the same volume with the newspaper. See, [Esad Efendi], 'Mukaddime-i Takvîm-i Vekâyi', *Takvîm-i Vekâyi*, 1247/1831. Esad Efendi's prologue was presented to Mahmud for his approval before its publication. See BOA, HAT 1431/59121, 29 Zilhicce 1247 (30 May 1832).

196 The word *târîh* comes from *erreha* meaning moon in Semitic languages. Lane says that the root was 'borrowed by the Muslim people from the people of the Bible.' Edward William Lane, *An Arabic-English Lexicon*, 8 vols., vol. I (Beirut: Librarie du Liban, 1968), 46.

this way, was shown as already being a part of the Ottoman tradition. In doing so, the Sultan must have hoped to prevent any reactions from conservative circles.[197] It is striking to see how much *Vakâyi-i Mısriye* (*Egyptian Events*), its Egyptian rival and counterpart, was free from such rhetorical considerations and simply presented, a few years previously, as a practical device for the use of government officials (*ekalîm-i Mısriye me'mûrları*).[198]

Some historians tend to dismiss *Takvîm* as an organ of 'bland official narrative' in which one can find nothing but the 'promotions and the demotions in the higher bureaucracy and the accomplishments of the Ottoman state from an official point of view'.[199] No doubt, this sneer has some truth in it. The government used this new tool mostly for bureaucratic purposes, and, one must add, with a rather Gogolesque efficiency.[200] This need to disseminate the official narrative is of course enough to call *Takvîm* an interesting development. For one, it proves that it was necessary to convince the public, to whatever degree, of 'the accomplishments of the Ottoman state'. But even a perfunctory reading of *Takvîm* 's pages reveals that it was more than simply a vehicle for the official narrative, at least in Mahmud's mind.

Every issue was presented to him for approval before its publication.[201] 'The first thing a Turk of any consequence is anxious to know', Robert Walsh explained, 'is, whether he has been mentioned, and what is said of him, and in this he shows a sensitiveness even superior to a Londoner or a Parisian, because, as the Sultan is the virtual editor, his opinion of a man is of some importance.'[202] The newspaper mentioned

[197] Earlier, Mahmud also wrote that 'this [*Takvîm*] has nothing misbecoming the holy law and the regime and everybody acknowledges and advocates its benefits to the land. BOA, İ..DUİT 136/28, 29 Zilhicce 1254 (15 March 1839).

[198] Anonymous, '[Cevahir-i tahmîd-i hüdâ]', *Vak'a-i Mısriye*, 25 Cemaziyelevvel (3 December) 1244/1828.

[199] Cengiz Kırlı, 'Coffeehouses: Public Opinion in the Nineteenth-century Ottoman Empire', in *Public Islam and the Common Good*, ed. Armando Salvatore and Dale F. Eickelman (Leiden: Brill, 2004), 75.

[200] The governor of Servi (Sevlievo), for instance, had to convey a letter of complaint to Istanbul for learning about his dismissal on charges of embezzlement only through the latest issue of the official gazette. BOA, A.} MKT. 63/55, 7 Safer 1253 (25 January 1847).

[201] BOA, HAT, 668/32606C, 29 Zilhicce 1247 (30 May 1832), BOA, HAT 668/ 32606A, 29 Zilhicce 1247 (30 May 1832), BOA, HAT 668/32606B, 29 Zilhicce 1247 (30 May 1832).

[202] Walsh, *A Residence at Constantinople*, 283.

the Sultan's charitable deeds in different parts of the Empire, under the rubric of 'Some Benevolent Works' (*Ba'zı Âsâr-ı Hayriye*).[203] *Takvîm* brought out Mahmud from behind his abstract identity: for the readers of the newspaper, he was not merely a venerated name but a tangible reality that one could meet and see travelling through the Empire. News like his examination of dockyard or the seasonal movement of his court to the summer palace was often printed in long and detailed articles to firmly establish his public persona.[204] His calls to convalescent state officials pictured him as the 'most merciful sultan'.[205] Caring Mahmud would even deign to inquire about what they ate or drank (*ekl ve şurbuna dikkat etmesi*) and such beneficence was extended to the lower orders without any reserve.[206]

More striking articles, however, are those, which set the newspaper almost in a hagiographical vein. In these accounts, Mahmud is endowed with divine powers. He is the *kutb* (perfect man) of the time, performing

203 See, for instance, Anonymous, 'Ba'zı Âsâr-ı Hayriye', *Takvîm-i Vekâyi*, 2 Şaban/21 October 1254/1838, 2, Anonymous, 'Ba'zı Âsâr-ı Hayriye', *Takvîm-i Vekâyi*, 4 Safer/19 April 1255/1839, 2, Anonymous, 'Ba'zı Âsâr-ı Hayriye', *Takvîm-i Vekâyi*, 3 Rebiyülevvel/17 May 1255/1839, 2. Also see, BOA, HAT, 545/26945, 29 Zilhicce 1249 (9 May 1834), BOA HAT 492/24105, 29 Zilhicce 1250 (28 April 1835).

204 In fact, the very first news that the newspaper reported was an account of the Sultan's travels, undertaken to examine the condition of his subjects 'whether Muslim or non-Muslim. '*Gerek ehl-i islam ve gerek ehl-i zimmet-i reâyasının*.' See [Esad Efendi], 'Umûr-ı Dâhiliye', *Takvîm-i Vekâyi*, 25 Cemaziyelevvel/ 1 November 1247/1831, 1. According to Engelhardt, Mahmud once said '*Je ne veux reconnaître désormais les musulmans qu'à la mosquée, les chrétiens qu'à l'église et les juifs qu'à la synagogue*.' Ed. Engelhardt, *La Turquie et le Tanzimat; ou Histoire des réformes dans l'Empire ottoman depuis 1826 jusqu'à nos jours*, 2 vols., vol. I (Paris: A. Cotillon, 1882), 33. For his examination of the dockyard, see Anonymous, 'Umûr-ı Dâhiliye', *Takvîm-i Vekâyi*, 3 Ramazan/5 February 1247/1832, 1. Also see BOA HAT 492/24109, 29 Zilhicce 1250 (28 April 1835). For the seasonal moving of his palace to Beylerbeyi, see Anonymous, '[Hamden li-vâhibi'l-'atâyâ]', *Takvîm-i Vekâyi*, 6 Rebiyülahir/19 June 1255/1839, 2. In a related note, this article was published only two weeks before Mahmud's death.

205 Anonymous, '[Serasker Paşa Hazretleri]', *Takvîm-i Vekâyi*, 6 Receb/11 December 1247/1831, 1, Anonymous, '[Reîs-ül Küttab es-Seyyid Süleyman Necib Efendi Hazretleri]', *Takvîm-i Vekâyi*, 11 Şaban/15 January 1247/ 1832, 1.

206 A Christian labourer, for instance, injured after a work accident, enjoyed the Sultan's attention while the latter was riding through the city. See Anonymous, 'Umûr-ı Dâhiliye', *Takvîm-i Vekâyi*, 10 Zilkade/11 Nisan 1247/1832, 1.

saintly miracles (*kerâmet*).[207] Those who even contemplated raising arms against the state were afflicted with death and misery.[208]

One can go through the adventures of Mahmud as if reading the miracles of a minor prophet of the Old Testament. His spiritual powers led an outlaw to die in his hiding place.[209] He cured the sick by 'his royal touch',[210] or by appearing in the dreams of deserving people; he ended the aridity in the region of Salonika.[211] Such elements of the supernatural were also employed in propaganda dissemination. Janissaries, for instance, again carefully never named through the *Takvîm*'s pages but referred as abolished corps (*ocağ-ı mülga*),[212] were claimed to have 'risen from death' and to be haunting the people of Tarnovo as evil spirits.[213] The whole episode was presented as another miracle

207 He was often depicted as *kutb* with other qualifying adjectives such as *kutb-u zaman*, perfect man of the age. See, for instance, Anonymous, '[Rumelinin ba'zı mahallerinde olduğu misillü]', *Takvîm-i Vekâyi*, 3 Zilhicce/4 May 1247/1832, 2. This language of *kutb* and *kerâmet* also shows up very often in contemporary poetry written for Mahmud. An inscription, for instance, in front of Kocamustafapaşa Mosque, described him as '*Kerâmet-pişe, hayr-endişe, kutb-ı devlet-i dünya.*'

208 A woman, for instance, fancied an objection to Mahmud's new army, saw in her dream an old man throwing her into the furnace to be burnt alive. Waking up screaming, she said: 'I believed in the good intentions of the Sultan/*sıdk-ı niyet-i Pâdişâhiye inandım.*' That was, however, too late: she found her infant child dead with burns over the body. It was not, the article pointed out, enough to obey the Sultan ostensibly (*zahiri*). One also had to obey him spiritually (*mânevi*). One, in other words, had to love the 'Big Brother'. See, Anonymous, 'Tabsıra', *Takvîm-i Vekâyi*, 1 Cemazeyilahir/26 October 1248/1832, 3. In another episode, a certain Bektaş from Ottoman Karlofça (Karlovci) planning to join the rebels, had his 'wrist swollen like a bagpipe/*bileğine kadar tulum gibi şişib.*' The limb was about to fall off and the repenting man went to the *kadi* court to seek pardon and submit himself to the authority of the Sultan. Anonymous, 'Gâribe der Suret-i Zuhûru Mücâzât', *Takvîm-i Vekâyi*, 29 Şevval/1 April 1247/1832, 3.

209 Anonymous, 'Te'sir-i nüfûz-u Padişâhi', *Takvîm-i Vekâyi*, 29 Şevval/1 April 1247/1832, 3.

210 Anonymous, '[Reîs-ül Küttab es-Seyyid Süleyman Necib Efendi Hazretleri]', *Takvîm-i Vekâyi*, 11 Şaban/15 January 1247/1832, 1.

211 Anonymous, '[Rumelinin ba'zı mahallerinde olduğu misillü]', *Takvîm-i Vekâyi*, 3 Zilhicce/4 May 1247/1832, 2.

212 Anonymous, 'Meâl-i Tercüme-i Dîbâce', *Takvîm-i Vekâyi*, 19 Şaban/1 January 1249/1834, 3. They were also referred as abolished class, *sınıf*. See, for instance, Anonymous, '[Mâlum Ola ki]', *Takvîm-i Vekâyi*, 21 Cemazeyilahir/ 27 Noveber 1247/1831, 2.

213 See, Anonymous, 'Tırnova Nâibi Müderrisin-i Kirâmdan Ahmed Şükrü Efendinin der-Âliye'ye Takdim Eylediği İbret Alınacak İlâmdır ki Aynıyla Tab

(*kerâmet*) relating to Mahmud: public naturally hated the abolished corps, but it was only the Sultan who saw the real evil (*habis*) behind them.[214]

In the other words, with its emphasis on both history and the supernatural, *Takvîm* was a continuation of classical Ottoman literature in many respects. But a careful reader, going through the pages of the *Takvîm* with patience – after all, the language was still the language of high literature – would find the signs of a new world. The 1831 Barbados–Louisiana hurricane, affecting Cuba and Haiti and thus disturbing the coffee trade, was given in detail.[215] News of technical developments on the Liverpool and Manchester Railway, or advances in terms of water rebreathers, again provided the reader with a sense of the most up-to-date achievements of the age.[216] *Takvîm* opened the gates of a world, which had never before been known, or had only been accessible to a very limited milieu. Hence it is hardly surprising that the newspaper was widely read in the coffeehouses throughout the Empire. Walsh, writing in the 1830s, noted how the *Takvîm* and what he called the 'news-rooms' became a universal attraction in a short period of time.'[217] 'Crowds assembled in the streets round any learned scribe who could spell its pages out to them', he wrote approvingly.[218]

But perhaps more importantly, a student of *Takvîm* had first-hand information on the political situation in Europe. *Takvîm*, like its counterparts, relied heavily on foreign newspapers and borrowed

Olunur', *Takvîm-i Vekâyi*, 29 Cemazeyilahir/13 November 1249/1833, 3–4. When the usual methods of dealing with these creatures (*cadı*) proved to be useless, such as wooden stakes or boiling water, they were cremated with an official permission.

214 The symbiotic relationship between magic, witchcraft, and politics was a common feature in Early Modern Europe. Rebellion to the state was often considered in terms of necromancy. See, for instance, E. J. Kent, 'Tyrannical Beasts: Male Witchcraft in Early Modern English Culture', in *Emotions in the History of Witchcraft*, ed. Laura Kounine and Michael Ostling (London: Palgrave, 2016), 82.

215 Anonymous, '[Yeni Dünya Dediğimiz Amerika'nın]', *Takvîm-i Vekâyi*, 6 Receb/11 December 1247/1831, 4.

216 See, Anonymous, '[Bu yakınlarda İngiltere memleketinde]', *Takvîm-i Vekâyi*, 1 Cemazeyilahir/26 October 1248/1832, 4.

217 See Walsh, *A Residence at Constantinople*, 283. Using government spy reports, Cengiz Kırlı also revealed how newspapers were read in coffeehouses in the 1840s. See Kırlı, 'The Struggle Over Space', 118, 219.

218 F. A. Neale, *Islamism: Its Rise and Its Progress, or the Present and Past Conditions of the Turks*, 2 vols., vol. II. (London: J. Madden, 1854), 283.

profusely from their political articles without any reserve. This immersed the reader in a whirlpool of contemporary debates and discussions. Thanks to these translations, Ottoman readers met, for the first time, concepts like public freedom (*hürriyet-i âmme*),[219] public benefit (*menâfi'-i âmme*),[220] and public security (*emniyet-i âmme*) in the pages of *Takvîm*.[221] One can immediately note the influence of this 'foreign' phraseology, coupled with domestic changes, on the contemporary political language. Next to the Sultan's classical titles such as Shadow of God (*zıllullah*)[222] or King of kings (*şehinşâh*),[223] 'merciful to the public' (*âmmeye merhametlü*) strikes one, for instance, as a new, modest, and rather meaningful addition.[224]

This use of rhetoric, as will be explained throughout this book, eventually ushered in the political agency of the public. This trend would continue – with some fluctuations – until the reign of Abdülhamid II (r. 1876–1909) who by ruling the country with an iron hand attempted to suppress it. But at the beginning, little did Mahmud II know that he was exchanging one nightmare for another. Perhaps none of his grandchildren were deposed by formidable janissaries; but public opinion was the biggest fear of Abdülhamid II as he believed that two of his predecessors were overthrown by its power.[225]

[219] Anonymous, '[Fransa Kralının verdiği cevâbın suretidir]', *Takvîm-i Vekâyi*, 25 Safer/3 July 1250/1834, 4.

[220] Anonymous, 'Montalivet Nam Umûr-ı Dâhiliye Nâzırının Keyfiyet ve Vuku'ât-ı Hâzıraya dair Fransa Kralına Arz Eylediği Bir Kıta Takrîrir Suretidir' *Takvîm-i Vekâyi*, 5 Rebiyülevvel/2 August 1248/1832, 4.

[221] Anonymous, '[Fransa Kralı Teşrinisâni yedisinde rüesa-yı devlet ve vükela-ı milletten olan iki umûmî meşveretgahın meclisini bizzât akd edip erbâb-ı meclise hitaben ber vech-i ati takrîr eylediği makalın suretidir]', *Takvîm-i Vekâyi*, 20 Ramazan/10 February 1248/1833, 3–4.

[222] See Anonymous, '[Zât-ı refet semat-ı zıllulahileri]', *Takvîm-i Vekâyi*, 29 Rebiyülahir/25 September 1248/1832, 1.

[223] Or *shahanshah* in Persian. See Anonymous, '[Bundan Akdem Vuku' Bulan]', *Takvîm-i Vekâyi*, 28 Cemazeyilahir/4 December 1247/1831, 3.

[224] Anonymous, '[Serasker Paşa Hazretleri]', *Takvîm-i Vekâyi*, 6 Receb/11 December 1247/1831, 1, Anonymous, 'Gâribe der Suret-i Zuhûru Mücâzât', *Takvîm-i Vekâyi*, 29 Şevval/1 April 1247/1832, 3.

[225] He turned out to be right, or his fear created a vicious circle, as his deposition was communicated to him as a result of the 'recent events and [unfavourable] public opinion'. Anonymous, 'Abdülhamid-i Sâniye Tebliğ-i Karar', *İkdam*, 28 April 1909, 2.

2 A Bureaucratic Public Sphere

Introduction

Following the centralisation that was achieved during the last years of Mahmud II's reign, the 1830s saw the opening up of an alternative discursive space where critical deliberations regarding governmental affairs flourished through a network of novel forms of sociability. This was a transitionary period between the 'representative publicness' of the janissaries, and the large-scale realisation of an Ottoman public. During this era, increasing bureaucratisation led to the formation of a distinctive type of public sphere, which operated through house gatherings (*meclis*), and acquired a political vocation.[1] While the traditionally opaque policymaking processes became more visible through consultative assemblies and an official newspaper, this new sociability acquired more substantial forms by offering different forums for upper-class organisation. In this setting, and under circumstances profoundly different from the ones Jürgen Habermas specified as *sine qua non* for Western Europe, the *meclis* in the Ottoman Empire assumed a similar role in cementing public opinion as the *salons* in the late eighteenth-century France.[2]

[1] *Meclis* (or *majlis*; مجلس, pl. مجالس *Mecâlis*), is an Arabic word with various meanings including 'a seat, session room, conference room, party, gathering, meeting, social gathering'. Wehr, *A Dictionary of Modern Written Arabic*, 131. Also see Edward William Lane, *An Arabic-English Lexicon*, 8 vols., vol. II (Beirut: Librarie du Liban, 1968), 444. It is commonly used to describe different types of gatherings among common interest groups in Muslim countries, be they political, social, or religious.

[2] The relationship between public opinion and *salon* culture in France is well attested in secondary literature. See Dena Goodman, *The Republic of Letters: A Cultural History of the French Enlightenment* (Ithaca, NY: Cornell University Press, 1996), 41; Daniel Gordon, '"Public Opinion" and the Civilizing Process in France: The Example of Morellet', *Eighteenth-Century Studies* 22, no. 3 (1989): 322; Baker, *Inventing the French Revolution*, 167–169; James Van Horn Melton, *The Rise of the Public in Enlightenment Europe* (Cambridge: Cambridge University Press, 2001), 207.

This chapter begins by examining İsmail Ferruh Efendi, an Ottoman diplomat, and his circle as they are considered to be harbingers of the forthcoming political gatherings of the Tanzimat era.[3] Their meetings (and their alleged connections with Freemasonry) provide a lens that allows us to see the increasing political significance of secrecy in the public sphere. Here it is argued that Ottoman political secrecy did not simply imitate European patterns, but rather embedded itself beneath indigenous practices. Following on from this, the chapter proposes a taxonomy for classifying different types of *meclis*, and analyses the impact of changing political culture on the formation of such sociability, with a particular focus on *münâzara* (debate). The main argument is that through the institution of *meclis*, the Tanzimat bureaucracy deliberately generated something akin to a critical public sphere from its members, since they were very well aware that their survival depended on free political debates and discussions.

It should be noted here that any reference to the concept of 'civil society' to refer to these meetings, or to explain later developments of the Ottoman public sphere (such as the appearance of scientific societies or voluntary associations), is consciously avoided as the notion is too loaded and frequently identified as a uniquely Western European phenomenon. Habermas again might be the most relevant example on this point. He sees civil society as something 'originating in the European High Middle Ages', and as a precursor of bourgeois public sphere which cannot be, he reports, 'transferred, idealtypically generalized, to any number of historical situations that represent formally similar constellations'.[4]

Habermas's views stem from the deeply embedded Eurocentric perspectives of his field. As Gyan Prakash rightly states, 'the scholarship in different disciplines has made us all too aware that such dichotomies reduced complex differences and interactions to the binary (self/other) logic of colonial power.'[5] Yet anything against this well-entrenched

[3] Many important figures of the subsequent years such as Midhat Pasha, Yusuf Kâmil Pasha, Safvet Pasha, and Melekpaşazâde Abdülkadir Bey all attended the meetings of this society when they were but pupils. Each one of them, in return, (and it should be added that many others followed), set up their own residences around the same premises. Mardin, *The Genesis of Young Ottoman Thought*, 231.

[4] Habermas, *The Structural Transformation of the Public Sphere*, xvii.

[5] Gyan Prakash, 'Introduction: After Colonialism', in *After Colonialism: Imperial Histories and Postcolonial Displacements*, ed. Gyan Prakash (Princeton, NJ: Princeton University Press, 1995), 3.

discourse is probably a hopeless battle. Even Şerif Mardin, one of the most prolific scholars of Ottoman historiography in recent times, has described civil society as the 'missing link' of Turkish history.[6] Although 'a new literature has taken shape that is centred less on structures than on voluntary action, on the dynamics by which democratic institutions can be made sprout on the seemingly inhospitable ground of authoritarian rule',[7] many historians still hold the view that 'the Ottoman political culture built a continuing tradition of a weak and underdeveloped civil society'.[8]

This negative view derives from both historical and historiographical realities. They are historical because the intertwining structure of the Ottoman elite with the government makes such neat distinctions (public–private or civil–state) rather difficult. And they are historiographical because we have a ubiquitous tendency to compare European norms to Ottoman normalities.[9] What is suggested here as an alternative, however, is to avoid lumping together what are often unique and particular experiences under homogenising blanket terms (such as 'the West'), when we compare Ottoman and European experiences entailing universal categories such as public opinion.[10] Any attention paid to individual ramifications of their trajectory is bound to reveal that German, French, and British routes to civil society, hence to a buoyant public, were marked by profound inconsistencies among each other and therefore should not be posited as one normative

[6] Mardin, 'Power, Civil Society and Culture in the Ottoman Empire', 279.
[7] Philip Nord, *The Republican Moment: Struggles for Democracy in Nineteenth-Century France* (Cambridge, MA: Harvard University Press, 1995), 6.
[8] Ömer Çaha and M. Lutfullah Karaman, 'Civil Society in The Ottoman Empire', *Journal of Economic and Social Research* 8, no. 2 (2006): 61.
[9] In the predominant view of the Ottoman historiography, the state is seen as an omnipotent and repressive entity, depriving its subjects of basic rights while a politically unformed and passive public was simply subjugated from above. Perhaps the Ottoman subjects did not have explicit civil rights to make an appeal. But as it was explained in the first chapter, they did have a delineated space in which their political practices could emerge, however partially and perceptually.
[10] While the differences between the Ottoman Empire and the European powers certainly have been overstated, the similarities have also been frequently overlooked. As early as 1865 Hyde Clarke pointed out that 'things and institutions, common in Europe [with the Ottoman Empire] are daily marked out for censure against the Turks and represented as in opposition to European standards'. Clarke, 'On the Supposed Extinction of the Turks and Increase of the Christians in Turkey', 262.

itinerary leading to a 'true public sphere'.[11] The German example, for instance, more germane to the Ottoman case than the others, is distinguished by its cohesion to or rather by its synchronisation with the 'reforms from above' throughout the late eighteenth and early nineteenth centuries as a result of its 'defensive modernisation'.[12]

A New Type of Publicity

In the first chapter, it was mentioned briefly how the Ottoman ambassador in London, İsmail Ferruh Efendi, had to obtain a French passport in order to assume his post in 1797.[13] This most likely turned into a rather excruciating experience for him, since only a year later France occupied Egypt and during his brief sojourn in London, he had to deal with the effects of this situation.[14] In fact at the first glance, there is nothing remarkable about him.[15] He was not a great statesman, either in his career or achievement. He moved up through the usual echelons of Ottoman bureaucracy. He was the storekeeper of the dockyards,

11 Jon Cowans, *To Speak for the People: Public Opinion and the Problem of Legitimacy in the French Revolution* (London: Routledge, 2001), 142. Habermas prefers the term 'authentic public sphere'. See Habermas, *The Structural Transformation of the Public Sphere*, 30.

12 See respectively David Blackbourn, *History of Germany, 1780–1918: The Long Nineteenth Century*, 2nd edn. (Padstow, Cornwall: Blackwell, 2003), 54; Michael Rowe, *From Reich to State: the Rhineland in the Revolutionary Age, 1780–1830* (Cambridge: Cambridge University Press, 2003), 159. About the historiographical process at work here, see Sebastian Conrad, *The Quest for the Lost Nation: Writing History in Germany and Japan in the American Century* (Los Angeles: University of California Press, 2010), 58; Konrad H. Jarausch and Michael Geyer, *Shattered Past: Reconstructing German Histories* (Princeton, NJ: Princeton University Press, 2003), 96.

13 BOA, HAT 144/6030, 09 Zilkade 1212 (25 April 1798).

14 See, for instance, BOA, C..HR..91/4501, 5 Zilkade 1213 (10 April 1799), BOA, HAT 257/14754, 20 Safer 1215 (13 July 1800). Naturally he was actively involved in the formation of an Ottoman-British alliance that routed out Napoleon's forces from Egypt. See BOA, HAT 144/6031, 29 Zilhicce 1213 (3 June 1799).

15 Some biographic information on him can be found in Mehmed Süreyya, *Sicill-i 'Osmanî, yahud, Tezkire-i Meşâhîr-i 'Osmaniyye*, 4 vols., vol. III (İstanbul: Matba'a-i Âmire, 1308/1890), 14. The modern edition of this book unfortunately contains some reading errors. (İsmail Ferruh Efendi appears to be from Crete even though at the original edition he was clearly from Crimea (قريمليدر). Mehmed Süreyya, *Sicill-i Osmani yahud Tezkire-i Meşâhir-i Osmaniye*, ed. Mustafa Keskin, Ayhan Öztürk, and Ramazan Tosun, 4 vols., vol. IV (İstanbul: Sebil Yayınevi, 1995), 15.

and later consignee of goods, before being appointed as the Ottoman ambassador to London.[16] When he left the country in 1797, Spencer Smith, the British *Chargé d'Affaires* in Istanbul described him as a 'well informed middle-aged man with some knowledge of Europeans'.[17] He served there for three years 'not with great success', according to Ercümend Kuran, but 'meticulously enough'.[18] Following his return to Istanbul in 1800, his residence became a gathering place for Ottoman liberals such as Şânîzâde Mehmet Ataullah Efendi, Kethüdâzâde Mehmet Arif Efendi, and Melekpaşazâde Abdülkadir Bey.[19] This assembly was going to be called – somewhat anachronistically – the first scientific society of the Empire by later Ottoman historians.[20]

[16] For the steps of his career, see BOA, C..BH..52/2444, 27 Cemâziyelevvel 1206 (22 January 1792). BOA, C..BH..202/9475, 5 Zilkade 1207 (14 June 1793). BOA, C..BH..103/4984, 6 Cemâziyelevvel 1208 (10 December 1793). BOA, C.. BH..103/4984, 3 Cemâziyelahir 1208 (6 January 1794). Finally for his appointment as Ottoman Ambassador to London, see BOA, HAT 206/10823, 1 Cemâziyelevvel 1211 (2 November 1796) and BOA, C..ML..714/2976, 3 Cemâziyelevvel 1211 (4 November 1796).

[17] Cited in Thomas Naff, 'Reform and the Conduct of Ottoman Diplomacy in the Reign of Selim III, 1789–1807', *Journal of the American Oriental Society* 83, no. 3 (1963): 304.

[18] About the details of his embassy, see Ercümend Kuran, *Avrupa'da Osmanlı İkamet Elçiliklerinin Kuruluşu ve İlk Elçilerin Siyâsi Faâliyetleri, 1793–1821* (Ankara: Türk Kültürünü Araştırma Enstitüsü, 1968), 35–41.

[19] Mardin, *The Genesis of Young Ottoman Thought*, 229. As Chris Bayly argues for Indian languages, there is no historic or linguistic equivalent of this loaded term, 'liberal', in Ottoman Turkish. People like Şânîzâde and İsmail Ferruh Efendi were generally described with adjectives such as *ârif-i laubâli-meşreb*, or *feylesof-i lâ-kaydi*, mostly denoting their permissive tendencies in social and religious life. For this reason, Redhouse, translating the term into the Ottoman language in 1861, seems to have had a rather difficult time. He first differentiated the political expression from other meanings by making a separate entry for the word 'liberal', corresponding to *cömert* (generous), and *sahî* (munificent). The political 'liberal', by contrast, was translated as a 'person who works to promote and advance freedom (*serbestiyet*) for his nation'. Redhouse, *A Lexicon English and Turkish*, 479. For the discussion of the term in the Indian context, see C. A. Bayly, *Recovering Liberties: Indian Thought in the Age of Liberalism and Empire* (Cambridge: Cambridge University Press, 2012), 3, 36–37.

[20] Ahmed Cevdet Paşa, *Târîh-i Cevdet*, 12 vols., vol. XII (İstanbul: Matbaa-i Amire, 1309–1891/1892), 184. The same description can be also found in Ahmed Lûtfî Efendi's account, see Ahmed Lûtfî Efendi, *Târîh-i Lûtfî*, 8 vols., vol. I (İstanbul: Matbaa-i Amire, 1290/1873–1874), 123. While İsmail Hakkı Uzunçarşılı prefers to call them 'Ortaköy Scientific Society', later scholarship anonymously referred to them as 'Beşiktaş Scientific Society'. See İsmail Hakkı Uzunçarşılı, 'Nizâm-ı Cedit Ricâlinden Vâlide Sultan Kethüdâsı Meşhûr Yusuf

It is difficult to say if İsmail Ferruh Efendi was significantly exposed to any more 'European ideas' during his time spent in England. There have been a number of suggestions about his association with Freemasonry. Allegedly, after being enrolled in London, he secretly founded the first Masonic lodge of Istanbul when he returned – a scenario that is not entirely inconceivable.[21] For instance, we know that, Mirza Abu-l-Hasan Khan Shirazi (d. 1846), Iranian ambassador to Great Britain at the same period, was recommended for membership of a London lodge by his official host, Sir Gore Ouseley (d. 1844), and was eventually initiated.[22] But even though this fact renders the assertion more plausible there is no record of İsmail Ferruh Efendi's admission to any European order. Had there been any primary evidence, this could have been interesting for obvious reasons. Habermas sees Freemasonry as an important indicator of the formation of a public.[23] Masons played a significant role in the emergence of public sphere in Russia during the late eighteenth and early nineteenth centuries.[24] They were certainly major and visible protagonists of the Ottoman public scene after the Crimean War.[25] Some lodges were regularly organising official balls where the brethren were 'requested to appear

Ağa ve Kethüdâzâde Mehmet Arif Efendi', *Belleten* XX, no. 79 (1956): 507. Ekmeleddin İhsanoğlu, *Osmanlı İlmî ve Meslekî Cemiyetleri* (İstanbul: Edebiyât Fakültesi Basımevi, 1987), 49.

21 This information stems from an article of Midhat Sertoğlu written for the Turkish edition of *The Encyclopaedia of Islam*. See Mithat Sertoğlu, *İstanbul [1520'den Cumhûriyete Kadar]*, ed. A. Adıvar, et al., 13 vols., vol. 5/2, İslam Ansiklopedisi: İslâm Ậlemi, Târîh, Coğrafya, Etnografya ve Biyografya Lugâtı (İstanbul: Milli Eğitim Basımevi, 1988), 1214/28. A semi-official history, written by a 'Worshipful Master', repeats the same assertion citing Sertoğlu. See Celil Layiktez, *Türkiye'de Masonluk Târîhi Cilt: 1 - Başlangıç 1721 – 1956* (İstanbul: Yenilik Basımevi, 1999), 14. Kemal Karpat has also reiterated the same argument a few times, but without any reference. See Karpat, *Studies on Ottoman Social and Political History*, 257. Kemal Karpat, *Ottoman Population 1890–1914: Demographic and Social Chracteristics* (Madison: University of Wisconsin Press, 1985), 91–92.

22 Hamid Algar, 'An Introduction to the History of Freemansonry in Iran', *Middle Eastern Studies* 6, no. 3 (1970): 277.

23 Habermas, *The Structural Transformation of the Public Sphere*, 35, 107.

24 Douglas Smith, 'Freemasonry and the Public in Eighteenth-Century Russia', in *Imperial Russia: New Histories for the Empire*, ed. Jane Burbank and David L. Ransel (Bloomington: Indiana University Press, 1998), 281.

25 Dumont Paul. La franc-maçonnerie ottomane et les «idées françaises» à l'époque des Tanzimat. In: *Revue du monde musulman et de la Méditerranée*, n°52–53, 1989. Les Arabes, les Turcs et la Révolution française. pp. 150–159.

in full Masonic costume'.[26] However, for the 1830s, there is no evidence to support such an assumption; primary sources do not mention any Masonic connection for İsmail Ferruh Efendi and his circle.[27] What they do mention, however, is the reticent nature of their meetings. Ahmed Lûtfî Efendi for instance, the official chronicler of the palace, probingly remarked that 'they did not accept any outsiders into their company'.[28] This sense of privacy (or maybe an early example of intellectual alienation) is completely outside of societal expectations and seems important, whether it stems from a Masonic connection or not.[29]

This displacement should be conceptualised as the centre of a new sphere in society – independent of the court of the Sultan, and one which could not be simply fitted into the available forms of sociability.[30] In the Ottoman Empire, as in the European case before the nineteenth century, 'there was no status that in terms of private law

26 See Anonymous, 'The Third Annual Ball of the Oriental Lodge', *Levant Herald*, 9 January 1861, 1034.

27 There is, of course, what one might call circumstantial evidence. An article, appeared in 1858, mentions the 'traces' of a Masonic lodge discovered by Russian soldiers after the campaign of 1829. See Anonymous, 'Freemasonry in Turkey', *The American Quarterly Review of Freemasonry and Its Kindred Sciences* 1(1858): 140. There is a widely repeated story of a lodge, which was burned down by the order of the Sultan, Mahmud I, in 1738; but this sounds highly speculative. See F. T. B. Clavel, *Histoire pittoresque de la franc-maçonnerie et des sociétés secrétes anciennes et modernes* (Paris: Pagnerre, 1843), 131. John Dove, *The Masonic Text-Book: Containing a History of Masonry and Masonic Grand Lodges from the Earliest Times: Together with the Constitution of Masonry, or Ahiman Rezon, and a Digest of the Laws, Rules and Regulations of the Grand Lodge of Virginia* (Richmond, VA: Randolph, 1854), 67. The last one gives the date of the same event as 1748, again during the reign of Mahmud I.

28 Ahmed Lûtfî Efendi, *Târîh-i Lûtfî I*, 123. İbnülemin Mahmud Kemal İnal, *Son Asır Türk Şâirleri*, 3 vols., vol. I (İstanbul: Orhaniye Matbaası, 1930), 115.

29 Franz Fanon also noted how it was necessary for a native intellectual to realize a certain level of 'estrangement' to 'go forward resolutely'. See Franz Fanon, *The Wretched of the Earth* (New York: Grove Press, 1968), 226. Reinhart Koselleck, on the other hand, assigns a twin function to secrecy in the Enlightenment Europe, that of 'uniting and protecting the society'. See Reinhart Koselleck, *Critique and Crisis: Enlightenment and the Pathogenesis of Modern Society* (Cambridge, MA: MIT Press, 1988), 80.

30 As Philippe Ariès pointed out 'the entire history of the private life comes down to a change in the forms of sociability'. Philippe Ariès, 'Introduction', in *A History of Private Life: Passions of the Renaissance*, ed. Roger Chartier (Cambridge, MA: Belknap Press of Harvard University Press, 1989), 9.

defined in some fashion the capacity in which private people could step forward into a public sphere'.[31] This clearly delineated sphere of 'good society' provided private people (in the widest possible sense of the word) with new opportunities that had been denied to them by the system during the incremental politicisation of the public sphere.[32] It is no accident that after this point we see the emergence of various underground societies, founded for a variety of purposes, developing throughout the Empire.[33] Sadık Rifat Pasha (d. 1857), for instance, warned Sultan Abdülmecid against the power of 'shrouded and hidden words'.[34] In the end, the legislator felt compelled to lay down a specific law in the Criminal Code of 1858 dealing with the *ittifâk-ı hafîs* or secret alliances.[35] In vain; according to Nâmık Kemal, the Istanbul police forces were discovering three new secret societies every day.[36] This was symptomatic of the cleft between the state and society. While these private groups, such as the Young Ottomans or Masons, were trying to problematise new arenas, hitherto left unquestioned, in the name of inchoate notions such as public benefit (*menfaat-i âmme*),[37]

31 Habermas, *The Structural Transformation of the Public Sphere*, 5.

32 Here I am mostly referring to the political struggle between the janissaries and Mahmud II. For the details, see Chapter 1, 42–56.

33 See, for instance, BOA, A.}MKT.UM.. 382/85, 9 Cemaziyelevvel 1276 (4 December 1859), BOA, A.}MKT.UM.. 442/10, 29 Cemaziyelevvel 1277 (13 December 1860), BOA, İ..ŞD.. 18/752, 4 Zilkade 1286 (5 February 1870), BOA, A.}MKT.MHM. 479/34, 20 Zilkade 1292 (18 December 1875). During the reign of Abülhamid II (r. 1876–1909), this rising trend turned into a race among university students and intellectuals. See Niyazi Berkes, *Türkiye'de Çağdaşlaşma*, ed. Ahmet Kuyaş (İstanbul: Yapı Kredi Yayınları, 2002), 389–90.

34 Mehmed Sadık Rifat Paşa, *Müntahabât-ı Âsâr*, 11 vols., vol. XI (İstanbul: Takvîmhâne-i Amire, 1275/1858), 48.

35 See article 58 of *Ceza Kanûnnâme-i Hümâyunu, Düstûr*, Tertîb-i Evvel ed., 4 vols., vol. I (İstanbul: Matbaa-i Amire, 1289 (1872/1873), 548. Though this penal code was an adaptation of the French corpus, it was not done so uncritically. This very article, for instance, was referred by public prosecutors in many instances. See the last pages of these verdicts: BOA, Y..EE.. 106/13, 18 Şevval 1296 (5 October 1879) and BOA, İ.DH. 816/65892, 27 Zilkade 1297 (31 October 1880).

36 Nâmık Kemal, 'Avrupa Şarkın Asâyişini İster', *Hürriyet*, 7 Decembre 1868, 6. One, of course, needs to leave a margin of doubt here.

37 The concept of public benefit became more and more dominant in the governmental discourse as well, especially after the 1850s. See, for instance, BOA, A.}MKT.NZD. 87/66, 20 Zilkade 1269 (25 August 1853), BOA, A.}MKT.UM.. 195/10, 23 Şaban 1271 (11 May 1855), BOA, A.}MKT.UM.. 241/58, 27 Şevval 1272 (1 July 1856).

the state, finding its authority threatened by their autonomous political activities, forced them towards greater secrecy.

When it comes to the İsmail Ferruh Efendi circle, it is clearly difficult to pass an opinion on the character of their meetings. In the French context, many of the *salons* actually published newsletters which were circulated in the countryside, and, in some cases, abroad.[38] Without doubt, they were closer to epistolary exchange than a 'real publication' and were disseminated in very small numbers. Yet, they supplied people with a sense of what was being communicated in those meetings.[39] In the case of İsmail Ferruh Efendi however there is no counterpart. Rumour had it that they were indulging in 'government talk'.[40] At any rate, in the uncertain atmosphere of the post-janissary era, Mahmud II considered them pernicious enough to banish to the different parts of the Empire, since he supposedly associated them with Bektaşis – a Sufi order with close ties with janissaries.[41] Even though

[38] Susan Herbst, *Politics at the Margin: Historical Studies of Public Expression Outside the Mainstream* (Cambridge: Cambridge University Press, 1994), 54. Goodman, *The Republic of Letters*, 154–155.

[39] Ibid., 156–157. Erica Harth, 'The Salon Woman Goes Public . . . or Does She?', in *Going Public: Women and Publishing in Early Modern France*, ed. Erica C. Goldsmith and Dena Goodman (Ithaca, NY: Cornell University Press, 1995), 187.

[40] Emin Efendi, *Menâkıb-ı Kethüdâzâde el-Hac Mehmed Ârif Efendi* (İstanbul: s.n., 1305/1887), 143.

[41] For the details of their exile, see Mehmed Esad Efendi, *Vak'anüvis Esad Efendi Târîhi*, ed. Ziyâ Yılmazer (İstanbul: OSAV Yayınları, 2000), 650. For the connection between Bektaşis and the Janissaries, see Hülya Küçük, *The Role of the Bektāshīs in Turkey's National Struggle* (Leiden: Brill, 2002), 32–40. H. A. R. Gibb and Harold Bowen, *Islamic Society and the West: A Study of the Impact of Western Civilization on Moslem Culture in the Near East*, 2 vols., vol. I (Oxford: Oxford University Press, 1969), 191–192. Hence, in the verdict of expulsion, handed down against İsmail Ferruh Efendi, there is nothing but a pious explication given by the Sultan himself. 'It is particularly necessary', Mahmud II wrote to the Grand Vizier, 'to endeavour genuinely hard to staunch, in any way possible, the conduct of things which might be deemed contrary to the Holy Law. If one remains quiescent knowingly [against the misdemeanours], God forbid, one can be considered a partner in sin. Although the aforementioned İsmail Efendi is an old and elderly person, most of his intercourse is always with infidels [here meaning with Bektaşis] and he does not have any religious principals (*akâid-i diniye*)'. See BOA, HAT, 503/24730, 29 Zilhicce 1242 (24 July 1827). The Sultan here misspells *akaid*, rather than writing عقائد, he wrote عقايد. On the very same page, the Grand Vizier, who probably did not dare to correct the Sultan's spelling, chose a different word to repeat the order and claimed that İsmail Ferruh Efendi did not have '*mübalat-i diniye*' (religious consideration, regard or deference). Such alteration might

Cevdet Pasha did his best to exculpate İsmail Ferruh Efendi posthumously from such 'crime',[42] indeed one could note that many Bektaşis joined the ranks of Freemasonry around the late nineteenth century on account of the affinity between their rites and ideologies.[43] 'Dervishes of the Bektashee Order', as an article published in 1863 put it, 'consider themselves quite the same as the Freemasons, and are disposed to fraternise with them.'[44] Such a connection, probably related to the alleged oriental origin of Masonry, is also worth noting.[45]

Another interesting aspect of İsmail Ferruh Efendi's circle was the unusual structure of their meetings – as demonstrated in their fee arrangements and somewhat regular lecture schedule.[46] Needless to say, their gatherings did not develop in a vacuum, but rather were rooted in what one might call an early modern sociability that surfaced in different parts of the world almost simultaneously, and which shared certain characteristics – such as a tendency towards a distinct leisure culture, including social drinking of alcohol, coffee, and so on.[47] At this point, it is even possible to go a step farther and posit that, as Susan Dalton does, the existence of a certain cohesion or

have also indented to soften the tone of the accusation as only a few months later the decision was revoked and Ferruh Efendi returned to Istanbul.

42 Cevdet Paşa, *Târîh-i Cevdet XII*, 184.

43 Paul Dumont, 'La franc-maçonnerie dans l'Empire ottoman: la loge grecque Prométhée à Jannina', *Revue du monde musulman et de la Méditerranée*, no. 66 (1992): 109.

44 Anonymous, 'The Dervishes and Masonry', *The Freemasons Magazine and Masonic Mirror*, no. 470 (1863): 521. But even before this article appeared, a book published during the Crimean War expounded in some detail how 'Turkish masons are called dervishes and continue to be Muslims while exercising their masonic duties and making use of special signs like their masonic counterparts in Europe.' Moreau, *Précis sur la franc-maçonnerie*, 159.

45 See, for instance, an address given by a District Grand Master, John P. Brown, on the occasion of the laying of the foundation stone of a Masonic hall at Hasseskeui (Hasköy) in Constantinople: 'as such, is destined to be mentioned in all time to come, as one wherein our brethren of Scotland took the lead here in promoting the welfare and prosperity of our beloved institution, by the erection of a lodge in *what may be truthfully called the country or empire, in which Freemasonry originated*.' See Anonymous, 'Address at the Laying the Foundation Stone of the Masonic Hall at Hassekeu', *Freemasons' Magazine and Masonic Mirror*, no. 630 (1871): 85, emphasis mine.

46 For the details, see Cevdet Paşa, *Târîh-i Cevdet XII*, 184.

47 See, for instance, Peter Clark, *British Clubs and Societies 1580–1800: The Origins of an Associational World* (Oxford: Oxford University Press, 2002), passim.

correlation between public opinion and polite conversation which often characterised these early modern gatherings.[48] Any such link, however, is but hypothetical, and it would be immensely difficult to verify or refute. What one can state with confidence here is that İsmail Ferruh Efendi's assembly proved to be different from its predecessors. If there is a rupture between conversation for the sake of conversation and politically charged discussion, in the words of Habermas, a point when bon-mot turned into argument and conversation into criticism, then Ferruh Efendi's circle emerged at that critical juncture.[49]

A Bureaucratic Public

As seen in the first chapter, by sweeping the decentralised structure away, Mahmud II (r. 1808–1839) put a bureaucratic machine together that was constructed around the principle of centralisation and built, in large part, from residual elements left over from the early modern era such as the local notables or *â'yân*. Such a concentration of vast resources in Istanbul eventually fashioned an imposing corps of well-trained public servants whose interests were inseparably linked with that of the state.[50] Throughout the course of the century, the rising power of bureaucracy, on the one hand, and the increasing depersonalised status of the state, on the other, rendered these officeholders invincible to sultanic whims. The new bureaucracy, inasmuch as the modern state machinery became liberated from the Sultan's personal sphere, increasingly detached itself from the court and became its counterpoise, as demonstrated by the Coup of 1876. With the disappearance of particular elements, such as the *â'yân*, from the political scene, a new sphere, thanks to state authority, was opened up in

48 Susan Dalton, *Engendering the Republic of Letters: Reconnecting Public and Private Spheres in Eighteenth-Century Europe* (Montreal: McGill-Queen's University Press, 2004), 47.

49 Habermas, *The Structural Transformation of the Public Sphere*, 31. One can only speculate why this differentiation emerged when it did. The French *salons*, for instance, appeared when the 'justification of noble privilege in terms of a traditional military function was under attack'. Steven Kale, *French Salons: High Society and Political Sociability from the Old Regime to the Revolution of 1848* (Baltimore, MD: Johns Hopkins University Press, 2005), 9. Considering the janissaries and the momentous events taking place in the Ottoman Empire, the similarity is striking, although perhaps not surprising.

50 About the growing dominance of the bureaucracy during this era, see Findley, *Bureaucratic Reform in the Ottoman Empire*, 151–220.

society for political deliberation. During this process, while the palace retreated into an enclave and separated itself from the rest of society, these genteel societies gradually took over its political functions.[51] Especially during the early years of 1850s, when this bureaucratic machine reached its apogee, their residences opened up hitherto unknown political spaces which enjoyed a position of civil authority between the private and the public spheres.

Later Ottoman histories are replete with anecdotal evidence about the philosophical deliberations taking place in these circles. The house of Fehim Süleyman Efendi (d. 1846), for instance, a member of the İsmail Ferruh Efendi circle, proved to be extremely popular for those wishing to discuss the questions of education and politics.[52] While in Arif Hikmet Bey's (d. 1859) residence scientific and literary inquiries were pondered,[53] in Reşid Pasha's house (d. 1858) political problems predominated over literary deliberations.[54] In his book on Ottoman

[51] What Şükrü Hanioğlu reports for the period recapitulates the degree of tension between the palace and the bureaucracy quite well: 'This [Abdülaziz's smooth succession in 1861] owed much to the progressive seepage of power from the royal court to the Sublime Porte, which continued to predominate throughout the 1860s. But as Sultan Abdülaziz matured, he began to challenge the status quo. The contest for political power between the palace and the bureaucracy intensified after the death of Âlî Pasha, the last great reforming statesman of the Tanzimat, in 1871. The Tanzimat reformers, who had laboured to construct a Weberian administrative structure founded on rational-legal authority independent of the throne, now saw the realisation of their ambition threatened. An uneasy equilibrium between court and Porte prevailed until the deposition of the Sultan in 1876.' Hanioğlu, *A Brief History of the Late Ottoman Empire*, 109.

[52] Cevdet Paşa, *Tezâkir 40 – Tetimme*, ed. Cavid Baysun, 4 vols., vol. IV (Ankara: Türk Târîh Kurumu, 1991), 13. Cevdet Pasha notes the influence of İsmail Ferruh Efendi openly in the same passage: 'because he [Fehim Süleyman Efendi] grew up in the circle of Ferruh Efendi, he was familiar with the questions of foreign affairs'. See Ibid. According to Richard Chambers 'Earnest discussions over letters, education, and politics made time pass pleasantly and rapidly for guests at the *konak* of Fehim Efendi', see Richard L. Chambers, 'The Education of a Nineteenth-Century Ottoman Alim, Ahmed Cevdet Pasa', *International Journal of Middle East Studies* 4, no. 4 (1973): 457. Cevdet Pasha gained his pseudonym *Cevdet*, meaning impeccable one, because of his brilliant performances during the discussions taking place at that house (his real name was Ahmed). See, İnal, *Son Asır Türk Şâirleri I*, 239. Fatma Âliye, *Ahmed Cevdet Paşa ve Zamanı* (İstanbul: Bedir, 1995), 35.

[53] Bilal Kemikli, '19. Yüzyılda Bir Entelektüel Muhit: Şeyhülislam Arif Hikmet Beyefendi'nin Konağı', *İlim ve Sanat*, no. 42 (1996): 92.

[54] Cevdet Paşa, *Tezâkir 13—20*, ed. Cavid Baysun, 4 vols., vol. II (Ankara: Türk Târîh Kurumu, 1991), 28.

poetry, İbnülemin Mahmud Kemal İnal wrote in some detail about how Eastern and Western savants came together at the residence of Yusuf Kâmil Pasha (d. 1876) to discuss scientific and literary questions of the time.[55] Abdurrahman Adil likened these meetings to those which took place in the Latin Quarter – a Parisian neighbourhood famous for higher educational establishments such as the Sorbonne and the École Normale Supérieure.[56] According to Midhat Cemal Kuntay, each of these assemblies had its own *public opinion* – separate and secret from that of the street.[57] Abdülhamid II (r. 1876–1909), by contrast, openly blamed these gatherings for he believed that many of them had but one aim: prejudicing domestic and foreign 'public opinion' against his late uncle Sultan Abdülaziz – who was deposed by his ministers on 30 May 1876, and committed suicide a few days later under suspicious circumstances.[58] These examples can be easily supplemented from the secondary literature. Şerif Mardin, for instance, held the view that these residences were the growing centres of 'cultural Europeanization.'[59] Cemil Meriç, in a more indigenous vein, called them 'Ottoman academies' – an assertion reiterated many times by other authors.[60]

These surrogate 'Ottoman academies' can be roughly divided into three forms in terms of their functioning in society: these were, respectively, the houses associated with the 'establishment', the houses associated with the 'opposition' and the houses associated with 'poetry recitals'. The first of these refers to the mansions and palaces of the great pashas of the Tanzimat era, such as Reşid, Âli, Fuâd, and Kâmil

55 İnal, *Son Asır Türk Şâirleri II*, 784.
56 Abdurrahman Adil, 'Yeni Osmanlılar Târîhi İnkılâbât-ı Fikriyye ve Münâkaşaları', *Hâdisât-ı Hukûkiye ve Târîhiye Mecmûası*, no. III (1341–1923): 14.
57 Mithat Cemal Kuntay, *Nâmık Kemal Devrinin İnsanları ve Olayları Arasında*, 2 vols., vol. I (İstanbul: Maârif Matbaası, 1944), 296; emphasis mine.
58 [İbnülemin] Mahmud Kemal [İnal], 'Abdülhamid-i Sâni'nin Notları', *Türk Târîh Encümeni Mecmûası* 13, no. 90 (1926): 63–64, emphasis mine.
59 Mardin, *The Genesis of Young Ottoman Thought*, 246.
60 Cemil Meriç, *Sosyoloji Notları ve Konferanslar* (İstanbul: İletişim Yayınları, 1995), 329. Dursun Gürlek, *Ayaklı Kütüphâneler* (İstanbul: Kubbealtı Neşriyâtı, 2003), 43. Hüseyin Hatemi, *Tanzimat ve Meşrûtiyet Döneminde Derneklerin Gelişimi*, ed. Vedat Çakmak, Murat Belge, and Fahri Aral, 6 vols., vol. I, Tanzimat'tan Cumhûriyet'e Türkiye Ansiklopedisi (İstanbul: İletişim Yayınları, 1985), 200. Also see Ebuzziyâ's description of Subhi Pasha's *konak* as an 'academy of science'. Ebuzziyâ Tevfik, *Yeni Osmanlılar Târîhi*, ed. Şemsettin Kutlu, 2 vols., vol. I (İstanbul: Hürriyet Yayınları, 1973), 75–76.

Pashas.[61] Their residences were deployed to create dyadic bonds through the familiar patron–client relationship of the Ottoman elite. The high bureaucracy of the Tanzimat era was diligently spawned in those spaces of political authority. Occasionally in '*soirées*' organised by viziers, thousands of guests were accommodated in these houses – with some hundreds staying overnight.[62] Cevdet Pasha, for instance, first met his future associates and comrades, Fuâd and Âli Pashas at the *konak* of Reşid Pasha.[63] Any government officer wanting to advance their career had to be present at these meetings. At one point, even a chronic opponent like Nâmık Kemal found himself attending the *meclis* of Fuâd and Kâmil Pashas every night.[64]

More specifically these households furnished a crucial space – a social crucible – for the acculturation of a new elite and the inculcation in the provincial classes of values deemed appropriate for the new Ottoman society. Here they acquired their importance in fostering cultural cohesion, or what Gramsci called 'cultural hegemony', among the upper echelons of society, all without overtly challenging the absolutist structure of the Ottoman sultanate.[65] These *meclises*

[61] This appellation, great pashas, is used throughout the text, not out of reverence, but rather as reference to the high corps of Ottoman bureaucracy. For more on its formation, see Olivier Bouquet, *Les Pachas du sultan: Essai sur les agents supérieurs de l'État ottoman (1839–1909)* (Leuven: Peters, 2007), passim.

[62] Cevdet Paşa, *Tezâkir 13—20*, 247. Wanda also points out that when Reşid Pasha was the Grand Vizier, he hosted hundreds of people [every night] for dinner. [K. C. Suchodolska], *Souvenirs anecdotiques sur la Turquie (1820–1870) par Wanda* (Paris: Firmin-Didot, 1884), 257.

[63] Fatma Âliye, *Ahmed Cevdet Paşa ve Zamanı*, 41–42. *Konak* is usually translated as mansion and a similar architectural term, *köşk*, as summer residence. *Yalı*, on the other hand, another important political space for this era, is a mansion facing the waterfront and situated around the Bosporus. For the details, see Carel Bertram, *Imagining the Turkish House: Collective Visions of Home* (Austin: University of Texas Press, 2008), 31–33; Abdülhak Şinâsi Hisar, *Boğaziçi Yalıları: Geçmiş Zaman Köşkleri* (İstanbul: Varlık Yayinevi, 1968), 119.

[64] Although, one must add that he could bring himself to attend the *meclis* of Âli Pasha who was more conservative. Cited in İnal, *Son Asır Türk Şâirleri II*, 822. When he was in Europe, Kemal criticised this system by saying that attendance to ministerial *konaks* was the only way to advance in one's career. See Nâmık Kemal, 'Bizde Adem Yetişmiyor', *Hürriyet*, 14 December 1868, 1.

[65] For the concept of 'cultural hegemony', see Antonio Gramsci, *Further Selections from the Prison Notebooks*, ed. Derek Boothman (Minneapolis: University of Minnesota Press, 1995), 474. Also see Raymond Williams, *Marxism and Literature* (Oxford: Oxford University Press, 1977), 108–114. Geoff Eley also argues that 'in Gramsci's view, a dominant class must not only impose its rule via the state, it must also demonstrate its claims to "intellectual and moral

(or *mecâlis*) represented the range of public opinion and the critical judgement at their most institutional and socially conservative state. They were completely entwined, if not identical, with the system insomuch that in 1845 an imperial decree invited the members of the rural elite, Muslim and non-Muslim alike (*vücûh ve kocabaşlar*), to be lodged in the houses of the grandees (*küberâ konaklarında*) in order to familiarise them with the reform programmes, and also to give them the opportunity to voice their opinions on public reforms (*ıslahat-ı umûmîye*).[66] This measure was most likely designed to soften the tensions that the Tanzimat had created in the provinces.[67] In this respect, as areas of debate that existed on the fringes of state authority, these *konaks* of the establishment were, to adapt Dana Goodman's formulation, the 'civil working spaces' of the Tanzimat project.[68] The members of provincial classes, again like Cevdet Pasha, were all incorporated into the system through this mechanism of social mobility and recruitment. These pasha *konaks* created a shared vision of the world that was reflected through the personification of a new Ottoman man. This *Homo bureaucratus* excelled in manners and conversational skills, and, unlike his earlier counterparts, demonstrated an increasing ability to incorporate Western values and ideals. This constituted essentially what is today referred as the Tanzimat elite.

The houses in the second category can be thought of as secret enclaves, harbouring little pockets of resistance in society. If the great pasha household served to integrate the newcomers into the system, this surreptitious network operated in exactly the opposite way – or, rather, it integrated them into a different type of system that developed independently as an alternative to that of the court. With their variegated array of ideas and political expectations, these houses are akin to what Nancy Fraser calls 'subaltern counter publics'[69] – competing, so

leadership"'. See Geoff Eley, 'Nations, Publics, and Political Cultures: Placing Habermas in the Nineteenth Century', in *Habermas and the Public Sphere*, ed. Craig Calhoun (Cambridge, MA: MIT Press, 1992), 323.

66 Ahmed Lûtfî Efendi, *Târîh-i Lûtfî*, ed. Abdurrahman Şeref, vol. VIII (İstanbul: Sabah Matbaası, 1328/1910–1911), 15. Also see BOA, HAT, 1642/14, 13 Cemaziyelevvel 1261 (20 May 1845).

67 Halil İnalcık, *Tanzimat ve Bulgar Meselesi* (Ankara Türk Târîh Kurumu, 1943), 45–57.

68 Goodman, *The Republic of Letters*, 53.

69 Nancy Fraser, *Justice Interruptus: Critical Reflections on the "Postsocialist" Condition* (New York: Routledge, 1997), 81.

to speak, with the pasha circles over the 'public interpretation of being'.[70] These places contributed immensely to the emergence of a public and private distinction in the modern sense of the dichotomy. Because of this new emphasis on *arcanum*,[71] the government viewed their progress with suspicion, as the case of İsmail Ferruh Efendi demonstrates. The Ottoman state mechanisms knew how to deal with habitual contumacy of pashas or usual mutterings of rebellious villages. Ultimately, even janissary revolts were always predictable, though they followed their own intricate logic. This pervasive culture of secretiveness, on the other hand, was tantamount to a deeper challenge, and was perceived as an attack on the existing political fabric. The fate of such an elusive group called *Meslek* (a course pursued, a path), formed in the 1860s is quite revealing as the records taken during their proceedings offer us rare and valuable insights into the structure of these gatherings:

It has come to our attention that some individuals, to stir up trouble and plot mischief against the current delegation of the state, formed a secret society (*cemiyet-i hâfîye*). As a result they have been detained one by one from the places they were located and taken into custody in the Royal Galleon of Mahmûdiyye or in Bâb-i Zabtiyye ... *Even though neither their leaders nor the genuine reason and the extent of their mutinous deeds could be completely ascertained* (*reîsi ve mevâd-i fesadiyenin mertebe ve meluf-i hakikisi doğrudan doğruya tayin edilememiş ise de*) ... *all things considered, the members of this aforesaid society confined and dedicated their efforts first to civilisation and humanity and cultivation* (*cemiyet-i mezkûrenin ibtida mesaisi medeniyet ve insâniyet ve ümrâniyete mahsur ve masruf olmak üzere*) and named themselves *Meslek* ...[72] By dint of scattering deceptive rumours to command trust and loyalty, as in the Society owns four thousand purses of

[70] Cf. Benjamin W. Redekop, *Enlightenment and Community: Lessing, Abbt, Herder, and the Quest for a German Public* (Montreal: McGill-Queen's University Press, 1999), 11.

[71] Here I am borrowing this term from Reinhart Koselleck who saw it as the 'glue' of secret societies. See Koselleck, *Critique and Crisis*, 77.

[72] One can see that both the members of this society and the bureaucrats were struggling with the available vocabulary. Although their contemporaries, the Young Ottomans had a much better political terminology. Another striking point of this early document is in its phrasing: it shows a distinct desire of the bureaucrats to understand the nature of the problem. During the reign of Abdülhamid, the 'problem' was going to be very clear and brushed aside with a simple 'to conceive some seditious thoughts' (*bir takım efkâr-i müfside ifası için*). See BOA, İ.DH. 816/65892, 27 Zilkade 1297 (31 October 1880).

gold, the members were trying to tempt and instigate those who were capable of enrolling others. At the end they succeeded in enlisting a good many neophytes whom they called *Tevfik* (success), *Kemal* (perfection), *Mukbil* (prosperous) and *Kârîn* (friend). *As for them the current governance of the state was not deemed desirable* (*idâre-i hâzıra-ı devlet derece-i matlûbede görülemediğinden*), *supposedly to find means of remedy and redress therein, they were congregating in each other's houses ...*[73]

By distilling and disseminating new political ideals, these secret hubs, or minipublics to use Lisa Wedeen's terminology, slowly became more visible throughout the Empire, and answered a deep-felt need in the society.[74] In their confrontations with authorities, these centrifugal forces resorted to an abstract public as a way of self-legitimation.[75] They were critical in the formation of a notion of a public opinion – albeit mostly to legitimise their own stance – in the paucity of extensive communication networks.[76] The most salient political opposition against the bureaucratic machinery of the Tanzimat, that of Young Ottomans, was also formed through this kind of furtive set-up and in

[73] BOA, İ..MMS. 133/5693, 5 Cemaziyelevvel 1284 (4 September 1867). During the archival work, I have stumbled across these documents, which were thought to be lost. See how they 'disappeared' from the archives in Burak Onaran, *Détrôner le sultan Deux conjurations à l'époque des réformes ottomanes: Kuleli (1859) et Meslek (1867)* (Paris: Peeters, 2013), XVIII-XXIII; M. Kaya Bilgegil, *Yakın Çag Türk Kültür ve Edebiyâti Üzerinde Araştırmalar I: Yeni Osmanlılar* (Ankara: Atatürk Universitesi, 1976), 354. Although he could not find the original document, Bilgegil published a copy of this protocol (*mazbata*) from the collection of *Mühimme-i Mektûme*. See ibid., 372–95.

[74] Lisa Wedeen, *Peripheral Visions: Publics, Power, and Performance in Yemen* (Chicago: University of Chicago Press, 2008), 113.

[75] The following line appears in the proceedings of *Meslek*: 'as this corresponded with the will of the whole nation, he participated into the society which was formed to carry out this desire (*umûm milletin dahi arzusuna muvafık olduğu idüğünden bu maksadın husûle gelmesi için teşekkül eden cemiyete suret-i duhulünü*). 'BOA, İ..MMS. 133/5693, 5 Cemaziyelevvel 1284 (4 September 1867).

[76] See the accusations of Abdülhamid against Young Ottomans: 'Every so often they were congregating in various locations, that is to say in the garden of Mustafa Fâzıl Pasha or in his *konak*, or in the garden of Köçeoğlu in Üsküdar or in his *köşk* in Nispetiye or in the *köşk* of someone called Madame Flori situated behind the *yalı* of Said Halim Pasha and frequently in the range of Kurbağlıdere to criticise maliciously the aforementioned deceased and to prejudice the local and foreign public opinion against him.' [İnal], 'Abdülhamid-i Sâni'nin Notları', 63–64.

what Cemal Kuntay called 'political *konaks*'.[77] In the alternative discursive world that these spaces provided, the dissident coteries met or rather lived – in every sense of the word – to engage in political deliberations unrestrained by the trappings of the government.[78] The private nature of a domicile gave them enough shelter to articulate new formulas designating their changing political expectations such as *Meşrûtiyet* (constitutional monarchy), *Vatan* (fatherland), or *Hürriyet* (liberty). The public sphere, whether embodied as a newspaper or as a coffeehouse was something relatively easy to monitor. The secretive nature of a *konak*, on the other hand, ordinarily out of reach of governmental investigations, consolidated an independent sphere where the criticism of the state became possible.

The line dividing these two forms of incipient public, between an oppositionary and an establishment stance was a fine one. The relationship between these two spheres became especially tenuous as the Tanzimat pashas found themselves increasingly struggling to cope with the changing political climate around the time of Abdülaziz's deposition in 1876. During this period of mutual suspicion and political obscurity, the houses of the most respected members of the ruling elite, including the five-time Grand Vizier and five-time commander-in-chief (*serasker*), Mehmed Rüşdü Pasha (d. 1882), were kept under close surveillance and heavily infiltrated by the spies of the Sultan.[79] Nor

77 'There were certain buildings', Midhat Cemal Kuntay wrote with reverence, 'where [Nâmık] Kemal spoke of revolution [*ihtilâl*]'. According to Kuntay, it was in the *konak* of Subhi Pasha a civil revolution, in the European sense of the word, was conceived for the first time. See Kuntay, *Nâmık Kemal Devrinin İnsanları I*, 293–294, 415.

78 Osman Ergin noted how 'the abodes of some viziers and dignitaries were also considered important centres of education'. Many scholars, poets and erudites', he wrote, 'were living in those places so that the viziers and his guests were able to benefit from their knowledge and experiences. These [scholars] were called *hânegi* [Persian adjective for domestic] and it was by saying "this is the *hânegi* of this or that pasha" their social and scholarly position in the society was mostly decided.' See Osman Ergin, *Türk Maârif Târîhi*, 5 vols., vol. II (İstanbul: Eser Matbaası, 1977), 376. Nâmık Kemal, indisputably the most important name of the Young Ottoman movement, was a *hânegi* of both Midhat and Süleyman Pashas in the sense that he had a permanent room in their houses. Mithat Cemal Kuntay, *Nâmık Kemal Devrinin İnsanları ve Olayları Arasında*, 2 vols., vol. II (İstanbul: Maârif Matbaası, 1956), 615.

79 BOA, Y..EE..14/125, 26 Rebiülahir 1295 (29 April 1878): 'His excellency Mehmed Rüşdü Pasha while having a private conversation in his house with the Commander in Chief, Aziz Bey used some inappropriate expressions in referring

were these types of concerns confined to Abdülhamid II. A wide range of observers and commentators predicted that the existence of these residences signalled the beginning of the end of the existing order. As their social and economic strength grew, members of the high bureaucracy increasingly began to see themselves as the legitimate guardians of the public interest, and used their residences to give expression to these claims.[80]

The house of Dâmâd Mahmud Pasha is emblematic of the overlap between this entwining structure. As the *Dâmâd* (groom) to one of Abdülmecid's daughters, Dâmâd Mahmud Pasha's royal residence operated essentially as a political cell where the Masonic committee striving to rethrone Murad V held many of its meetings.[81] When this failed, he set up another secret *komite* (committee) that gathered at his *konak* two or three times a week, in order to install Reşad Efendi, the crown prince.[82] Abdülhamid II, however, was well aware of the

to the royal personality of His Highness, the shelter of the caliphate and said "as he does not have any men in his entourage, he does not have any men among his ministers either [*kurenâsında adem olmadığı gibi vükelâsında dâhi bir âdem olmadığından*], Midhat Pasha, though heathen [*dinsiz*] and has enemies from the dynasty, could have been extremely valuable at these times as he has sagacity and capacity"'. About Rüşdü Pasha's political activities, also see Ali Fuat, 'Ricâli tanzimattan Rifat Paşa', *Türk Târîh Encümeni Mecmûası (Yeni Seri)* I, no. 2 (1929): 11.

80 BOA, Y..EE.. 79/59, 30 Receb 1295 (30 July 1879): 'Individuals who are not pleased and gratified with the sublime government often convened in one assemble. Ali Bey, who seems like has not taken any part in this affair, told me confidentially that the Grand Vizier Safvet Pasha, *aide-de-camp* of the Royal Palace, aforementioned Hasan Pasha who was the former Quarter Master, Âli Pasha, Mütercim Mehmed Rüşdü Pasha, Midhat Pasha, according to an above-mentioned program, *think about overthrowing (God Forbid) his imperial majesty and limiting the power and the glory of the new sultan (which is going to be either Sultan Murad or Reşad Efendi) so that they could rule unimpeded.*' Brackets in the original; emphasise mine.

81 BOA, Y..EE.. 23/5, 26 Safer 1296 (19 February 1879). This file includes the verbatim confessions of the masonic committee, which tried to smuggle Murad V abroad after his abdication.

82 BOA, Y..EE.. 23/13, 26 Safer 1296 (19 February 1879). The informer, a certain Yusuf Efendi, here gives interesting details about the actual recruitment process: After taking an oath, the recruit's name was registered in the roll. Then, according to the instructions, he would follow a man in a yellow jacket who led him to the *konak* of Mahmud Pasha. Later, he continued: 'then I began to go to the *konak* every two or three days. This society [*cemiyet*] was under the direction of his Excellency, Mahmud Pasha ... the above-mentioned names are the ones that I have seen coming to the *konak* regularly and also have heard from the above-mentioned Osman Bey as the members of the society.' Cavid Bey's (later

possible repercussions that these gatherings might have on public opinion, largely from his uncle's experiences. In the words of one of his closest confidants, Tahsîn Pasha, he was an 'enemy of house gatherings (*evlerde toplanmaların düşmanı idi*) and kept meetings taking place in the houses of the grandees under close surveillance'. According to Tahsîn Pasha, the Sultan:

> wished to know in whose houses these gatherings were coming about and who were going there regularly. It was his memories of the past forcing him to take such strict and severe measures as Sultan Hamid knew that the depositions of his uncle Sultan Aziz and his older brother Sultan Murad were all decided upon after the deliberations conducted in the *konaks* of grand viziers and *yalıs* of *şeyhülislams* (chief muftis). In fact he never forgot, not even for a moment, that he was also liable to such a fate.[83]

Haunted by this shadow almost to the point of obsession from the outset of his reign, Abdülhamid II used a web of informers and police officers,[84] in order to establish a political panopticon from which even the houses of relatively harmless figures such as Abidin Pasha could be subjected to close scrutiny.[85]

we learn from the document that this is the name of the man in the yellow jacket) proper *konak* was also a political centre in its own right and followed by the spies closely for suspicious activities. See, for instance, 'It has been understood from our investigations, in Beylerbeyi, on the foothill, around the top of the Bedevi Lodge, at the *konak* of Cavid Bey which is next to the house numbered 5, three or four times a week, Tayfur Ağa, from the entourage of his excellency Midhat Pasha, and his comrades [*rüfekası*] came together to utter seditious things [*bir takım tefevvuhat-ı muzırra*].' See BOA, Y..EE.. 21/7, 28 Cemaziyelevvel 1296 (20 May 1879).

83 Tahsîn Paşa, *Abdülhamit ve Yıldız Hâtıraları* (İstanbul: Muallim Ahmet Hâlit Kütüphânesi, 1931), 67.

84 At the beginning of 1880, there were only eight companies of police in Istanbul. At the end of the century the number increased to thirty-nine. See Glen W. Swanson, 'The Ottoman Police', *Journal of Contemporary History* 7, no. 1/2 (1972): 253. If the formation of the disciplinary society began in the Ottoman Empire with Mahmud II, Abdülhamid II's reign, in many respects, was its culmination and probably the modernity of his era can be fully understood only against this background. Cf. Foucault, *Discipline and Punish*, 200–218.

85 BOA, Y..PRK.AZJ. 4/6, 28 Zilkade 1297 (1 November 1880). In fact almost all of the '*jurnals*' were destroyed at the beginning of the twentieth century by the Young Turks. After the 1908 Revolution, there was a popular campaign to bring out these journals to reveal the identity of the spies. But there was a fear that this could cause so many problems for so many people who 'regret deeply their previous actions and today will sacrifice their lives without any hesitation for the sake of the constitution'. ع ل, 'Jurnaller', *Tanin*, no. 457 (27 Zilkade/10

The Masonic lodges can be also considered in this in-between category. Twenty years after İsmail Ferruh Efendi's death, there is no doubt about their presence in the Empire. If we are to believe a Washington-based journal, *The National Freemason*, around the beginning of the 1860s, thousands of members were scattered through the different parts of the Ottoman dominions – with twelve lodges functioning in Istanbul alone.[86] 'Among the Ottoman officials who are Masons', John P. Brown declared in 1865, 'I may mention N. N. Fuad Pacha, the Grand Vizier, or chief minister, the master of ceremonies of the court; Kiamil [Kâmil] Bey.'[87] The Ottoman statesmen probably found the idea of fraternity expedient during the period of rising nationalism and accordingly Freemasons took an active part in the daily life of big cities such as Izmir, Istanbul, and Alexandria.[88]

The 1860s were the apogee of Ottoman Freemasonry in many respects. The order could proudly talk of the 'education, and the light

December 1327/1909): 2. About their disposal, see Âsaf Tugay, *İbret: Abdülhamid'e Verilen Jurnaller ve Jurnalciler*, 2 vols., vol. I (İstanbul: Okat Yayınevi, 1962), 17. About Abdülhamid II's web of informers, see Süleyman Kâni İrtem, *Abdülhamid Devrinde Hafîyelik ve Sansür: Abdülhamid'e Verilen Jurnaller*, ed. Osman Selim Kocahanoğlu (İstanbul: Temel Yayınları, 1999), 21–23. About Abidin Pasha, see Murat Şiviloğlu, 'Abidin Paşa', 36–45.

86 'Turkish Freemasons', the journal claimed, 'employ[ed] as a fraternal symbol, a small brown shawl, embroidered with mystical figures, and a flat, polished, twelve-cornered piece of marble with reddish brown spots. The spots represent drops of blood, symbolic of the death of AH, the founder of the order in Turkey, who was barbarously put to death by the Sultan, at that time, for refusing to betray the secrets'. See Anonymous, 'Freemasonry in Turkey', *The National Freemason* I, no. I (1863): 13. The same information also appears in César Moreau, *Précis sur la franc-maçonnerie: son origine, ses doctrines et opinion diverses sur cette ancienne et celebre institution* (Paris: Ledoyen, 1855), 160. In his history, Asım Efendi (d. 1820) mentions one of his contemporaries, a certain Hasan Ağa, as someone who had been introduced to Freemasonry in France. Mütercim Asım Efendi, *Asım Târîhi*, 2 vols., vol. I (İstanbul: Cerîde-i Havâdis Matbaası, 1284/1867), 242. One can argue the sameness of Hasan Ağa and AH (Agha Hasan), but this is a mere speculation. The numbers given by the periodical, on the other hand, might have some truth in. At the end of the decade we know that the number of the lodges in Istanbul was about fifteen and they all had connections with the various European Orients – or Grand Lodges. Cf. Paul Dumont, 'Freemasonry in Turkey: A By-product of Western Penetration', *European Review* 13, no. 03 (2005): 482.

87 John P. Brown, 'Masonry in Turkey', *The Freemason's Monthly Magazine* 24, no. 4 (1865): 138.

88 At the end of the century, they had lodges in cities as remote as Van. See BOA, Y..PRK.ZB..13/44, 10 Muharrem 1312 (14 July 1894).

of civilization, aided by Freemasonry ... developing their blessed effects on the habits, superstitions, and morals, of the Ottoman Empire', while their organisation was flourishing 'in might, and majesty, and strength, and power, and affluence, and beauty'.[89] This was far from mere boasting. Many of the names associated with the Young Ottoman movement such as Ali Şefkati Bey, Nâmık Kemal, and even the Crown Prince Murad (later to be Murad V), were members of a Masonic lodge called *Proodos* (the Greek word for 'progress').[90] When Murad V had to abdicate, allegedly because of his 'nervous disposition' in 1877, some of his *brethren* even attempted to smuggle him abroad, relying on the support of European lodges to reinstall him to power.[91] When this failed, the Master of the lodge, Scaliari Bey, strove to bring about popular support in the public sphere by placarding the city with political posters in support of the ousted Sultan. At one point these Masons even initiated a plot to assassinate Abdülhamid II (r. 1876–1909).[92] Perhaps unsurprisingly, in return, he viewed all Masonic activities rather suspiciously throughout his long reign.[93] And one should add for good reason, as well. Virtually all the leading names of the Committee of Union and Progress, which orchestrated the Young Turk Revolution in 1908, were Freemasons.[94] The lodges in

89 Anonymous, 'Knights', *Masonic Record: A Monthly Magazine Devoted to the Interests of Fraternity and General Literature* IV(1870): 275.

90 Constantin Svolopoulos, 'L'initiation de Mourad V à la franc-maçonnerie par Cl. Scalieri: aux origines du mouvement libéral en Turquie', *Balkan Studies* 21, no. 2 (1980): 442. About Murad's low-key membership ceremony, see Ziyâ Şakir, *Çırağan Sarayında 28 Sene: Beşinci Murad'ın Hayâtı* (İstanbul: Üstün Eserler Neşriyat Evi, 1943), 56–57. Also see Edhem Eldem, 'Geç Osmanlı Döneminde Masonluk ve Siyaset Üzerine İzlenimler', *Toplumsal Târîh*, no. 33 (1996): 16–28.

91 İsmail Hakkı Uzunçarşılı, 'V. Murad'ı Tekrar Padişâh Yapmak İsteyen K. Skaliyeri-Aziz Bey Komitesi', *Belleten* VIII, no. 30 (1944): 248.

92 See BOA, Y..EE.. 106/13, 18 Şevval 1296 (5 October 1879).

93 See, for instance, a report written by Nuri Pasha for the Sultan giving the details of Masonic connection of Midhat Pasha's supporters. BOA, Y..EE.. 79/60, 28 Şevval 1295 (27 August 1878). Also see another report disclosing the meetings between the masons and Midhat Pasha, BOA, Y..EE..141/15, 6 Rebiülahir 1327 (9 November 1891). One letter, written to a Sadık Efendi in French and signed by a certain Daniel, gives the details of Masonic meetings, taking place every Wednesday. BOA, Y..EE..29/116, 12 Rebiülevvel 1283 (25 July 1866).

94 Dumont, 'Freemasonry in Turkey', 485. Şükrü Hanioğlu, on the other hand, sees this alliance as a temporary coalition. See M. Şükrü Hanioğlu, 'Notes on the Young Turks and the Freemasons, 1875–1908', *Middle Eastern Studies* 25, no. 2 (1989): 194.

Figure 2.1 A photo of Scaliari Bey (Kleanti Skalyeri) in his full masonic costume in 1878. He was the master of the Masonic lodge *Proodos* of which many Young Ottomans were members.

Bahattin Öztuncay, Dersaadet'in Fotoğrafçıları: 19. Yüzyıl İstanbul'unda Fotoğraf: Öncüler, Stüdyolar, Sanatçılar, 2 vols., vol. I (İstanbul: Aygaz, 2003), 244.

Salonika, with their close ties with various European orders, were particularly vocal opponents against his rule.[95] The constitutional monarchy, according to Ebuzziyâ Tevfik (d. 1913), famous publisher of the late nineteenth and early twentieth centuries, was only one of 'the harvests of the seeds of liberty' that the masons 'disseminated in the arable lands of opinion'.[96]

The third category might be considered, at least outwardly, not very salient for the purposes of this argument: the houses of poetry recitals where attendees occupied themselves with literary questions. Typically, the patrons of such gatherings organised assemblies once or twice a week where poems were read and discussed in detail. This provided an opportunity to poets both to join in conversations and to establish their literary fame as a critic and composer.[97] Some of these gatherings were regular, methodical, and extremely influential – such as the famous *Encümen-i Şuarâ*, the Society of Poets, founded in 1861, and presided over by Leskofçalı Galib every Tuesday at the house of Hersekli Arif Hikmet Bey.[98] Others, however, are known to us only through anecdotal evidence dispersed here and there – as in 'his place was always an assembly of virtuous and courteous',[99] or 'he was one of those elegants whose assembly was always humorous.'[100] Around the end of the century even women, latent components of the Ottoman public sphere, could form this type of circle. An accomplished poet in her own right, Nigar Hanım for instance kept her literary salon open, also on Tuesdays, between two and four o'clock

[95] Selanikli Şemseddin, *Makedonya: Târîhçe-i Devr-i İnkılab* (İstanbul: Artin Asaduryan Matbaası, 1324/1908), 124. Also see Orhan Koloğlu, *İttihatçılar ve Masonlar* (İstanbul: Gür Yayınları, 1991), 15–19.

[96] 'Even though', he felt compelled to add, 'today there can be found people who deny this [veracity]; history, which registered it in the pages of its events, is always a safeguard for the preservation of this truth.' Ebuzziyâ Tevfik, 'Farmasonluk', *Mecmûa-i Ebuzziyâ*, no. 100 (1329/1911): 682.

[97] See, for instance, Ziyâ Pasha's rise to fame through these official and unofficial circles in İbrahim Necmi Dilmen, *Târîh-i Edebiyât Dersleri*, 2 vols., vol. II (İstanbul: Matbaa-i Amire, 1922), 74.

[98] See İbnülemin Mahmud Kemal [İnal], *Kemal ül-hikme* (İstanbul: Tercüman-ı Hakikat Matbaası, 1327/1909), 14.

[99] Meşhûri, *Selanikli Meşhûri Efendinin Dîvânı* (Selanik: Selanik Vilâyet Matbaası, 1292/1875), [1].

[100] Mehmed Tevfik, *Kâfile-i Şuarâ: Meşâhir-i Şuarâ-ı Osmaniye'nin Terâcim-i Ahvâliyle Ba'zı âsâr-ı Şi'riyyelerini Câmidir* (İstanbul: s.n., 1290/1873), 118.

for women and from four to six o'clock for men – for what seems to be strictly literary discussions.[101]

These meetings can easily be appended to the tradition of early modern gatherings which characterised what Walter G. Andrews and Mehmet Kalpaklı termed the 'Age of Beloved'.[102] But there was one crucial difference. In such a highly politicised climate, there could not be any clear barrier insulating politics from literature. For poets like Figâni (d. 1532) or Taşlıcalı Yahyâ (d. 1582), such a domain of life did not exist in the modern sense of the word. They could be critical, but they were not political. However, by the second half of the nineteenth century, the difference between poetry and politics was just a matter of attitude. Before being transformed into the political cell mentioned above, Dâmâd Mahmud Pasha's *konak* also functioned as a purely literary establishment where 'the competents of poetry met regularly to discuss questions of literature'.[103] Some young members of the 'Society of Poets', including Ziyâ Pasha and Nâmık Kemal eventually formed the nucleus of what became the Young Ottoman movement. Even Nigar Hanım's circle could not be thought to be completely free of political considerations since Süleyman Nazif, one of the regular attendees of her meetings, portrayed her as 'the most patriotic person' he had ever met — whether among women or men.[104]

Münâzara as an Instrument of Change

These salons, conservative, poetic, or oppositionary, maybe did differ in substance but not so much in form. In the Ottoman *konaks*, individuals coming from various backgrounds were endowed with

[101] Süleyman Nazif, 'Nigar Hanım', *Servet-i Fünun* 62, no. 101–1575 (1926): 355–56. For the details of this 'Tuesday receptions', see Nazan Bekiroğlu, *Şâir Nigar Hanım* (İstanbul: İletişim Yayınları, 1998), 177–184.

[102] See Walter G. Andrews and Mehmet Kalpaklı, *The Age of Beloveds: Love and the Beloved in Early-Modern Ottoman and European Culture and Society* (Durham, NC: Duke University Press, 2005), 106–112. *Sohbet* or cultured conversation was an important aspect of Ottoman intellectual life. From mystic orders to literary circles, it was used as a vehicle to transfer certain values and norms embedded in the Ottoman society. Also see Osman Türer, 'Les Caractéristiques Originalles de la Pensée du Malâmat et les Transformations de Cette Pensée Avec le Temps', in *Mélamis-Bayrâmis Etudes sur trois mouvements mystiques musulmans*, ed. Nathalie Clayer, Alexandre Popovic, and Thierry Zarcone (Istanbul: Les Edition Isis, 1998), 84.

[103] İnal, *Son Asır Türk Şâirleri I*, 60.

[104] Nazif, 'Nigar Hanım', 354.

opportunities to socialise on relatively equal terms.[105] The etiquette of these gatherings was exceedingly formal and followed a very strict code of courtesy. For instance, İrfan Pasha, a poet and civil servant, was banned from the circle of Yusuf Kâmil Pasha because of what was deemed an offensive comment. Following this, Yusuf Kâmil Pasha clapped his hands and asked his butler to take the Pasha's pipe (*çubuk*) away, which meant, in accordance with the practice of the time, banishment from the *meclis*.[106] In another instance, a famous satirist such as Naili could be ostracised from the Society of Poets because of a simple altercation between him and Nâmık Kemal.[107] Nevertheless, the tone of conversation in these circles was relatively uninflected by hierarchy and presumed a readiness to suspend the sorts of social distinctions that prevailed outside.

One can find many traces of this discursive equality in contemporary literature. A prominent journalist and writer such as Şinâsi (d. 1871), for instance, could establish an aura of dignity and authority even in the salons of the most revered statesmen of the time, including those of Mustafa Fâzıl Pasha (d. 1875), the Egyptian prince, or Fuâd Pasha (d. 1868), a famous Grand Vizier. According to Ebuzziyâ, this was due to the fact that:

he would never deviate from the propriety of *münâzara* (debate) in an inquiry he engaged in and with epigrammatic yet decisive terseness he would enlighten an opinion (*tenvîr-i efkâr eyler idi*). Such trait entitled him [Ebuzziyâ continued] to a merited esteem and admiration. Even Mustafa Fâzıl Pasha who was quite loquacious and Yusuf Kâmil Pasha who constantly assumed a regal attitude before his entourage owing to his haughtiness and pride, would abstain from solemnity against him and adopt a manner of apparent humility. When Şinâsi made elegant interrogations mixed with sarcasm (*istihzâ*), the pashas could not find any answer to make. It was only

105 See, for instance, a detailed account of the guests of Münif Pasha, Metin Kayahan Özgül, *XIX. Asrın Benzersiz Bir Politekniği: Münif Paşa* (Ankara: Elips Kitap, 2005), 209–212.

106 İnal, *Son Asır Türk Şâirleri II*, 706.

107 Metin Kayahan Özgül, *Hersekli Arif Hikmet* (Ankara: Kültür ve Turizm Bakanlığı, 1987), 23. But, of course, this was not less true in the Enlightenment *salon*. Voltaire, for instance, had to flee to England after being beaten up by the servants of Chevalier de Rohan because of, again, a simple altercation between the two. See Alexander J. Nemeth, *Voltaire's Tormented Soul: A Psychobiographic Inquiry* (Cranbury, NJ: Associated University Presses, 2008), 108.

Fuâd Pasha who could have *münâzara* and argument with him uninhibitedly and without encumbrance.[108]

Ebuzziyâ's emphasis on *münâzara* here is not a coincidence. These courtly societies blended some of the ever-prevalent manners of Ottoman etiquette with newly emerging modes of society (*cemiyet*). In fact, one can easily assert the possible imprint of Islamic concepts such as *cedel* (dialectic) and *münâzara* (debate) on the very formation of a critical Ottoman public.[109]

Very early on, Islamic philosophy espoused the rules of logical discussion of the Hellenistic school through the writings of Aristotle.[110] Notions of *cedel* and *münâzara* were initially used as heuristic tools for proselytisation and religious deliberations. In due course, however, they were liberated from the confinements of theology, and were applied to diverse fields of scholarly pursuits.[111] The Ottomans received these tools of argument, possibly through Persian culture,[112] and throughout the centuries, they had a significant

108 Ebuzziyâ Tevfik, 'Şinâsi'nin Eyyâm-i Ahîre-i Hayâtı ve Vefâtı', *Mecmûa-i Ebüzziyâ*, no. 105 (1911): 839.

109 According to Ibn Khaldun, the difference between these two terms is negligible. But his translator into Ottoman, Cevdet Pasha, strongly disagrees with him in a postscript. See İbn Haldun, *Tercüme-i Mukaddime-i İbn Haldun: Mukaddime-i İbn Haldun'un Fasl-ı Sadisi'nin Tercümesidir* trans. Cevdet Paşa, 3 vols., vol. III (İstanbul: Takvîmhâne-i Amire, 1277/1860–1861), 58. For the same discussion of Ibn Khaldun, see Ibn Khaldoun, *Les Prolégomènes d'Ibn Khaldoun*, trans. M. de Slane, 3 vols., vol. III (Paris: Imprimerie Impériale, 1868), 38–39. But in the subsequent literature they were often used interchangeably. See, for instance, Serkiz Orpilyan and Seyyid Abdulzâde Mehmed Tâhir, *Mahzen ül-Ulûm* (İstanbul: A. Asaduryan Şirket-i Mürettibiye Matbaası, 1308/1890–1891), 333–334. Also see Ahmed Cevdet Paşa, *Âdâb-ı Sedad min İlmü'l-Âdâb* (İstanbul Matbaa-i Âmire, 1294/1877–1878), 3.

110 Salim Kemal, *The Philosophical Poetics of Alfarabi, Avicenna and Averroës: the Aristotelian Reception* (Oxford: RoutledgeCurzon, 2003), 5. Marta Spranzi, *The Art of Dialectic Between Dialogue and Rhetoric: The Aristotelian Tradition* (Amsterdam: John Benjamins Publishing Company, 2011), 102. Abdurrahman Badawi, 'The Way of Hellenizers: The Transmission of Greek Philosophy to Islamic Civilization', in *Culture and Learning in Islam*, ed. Ekmeleddin İhsanoğlu (Paris: UNESCO Publishing, 2003), 392. Yusuf Şevki Yavuz, *Kur'an-ı Kerim'de Tefekkür ve Tartışma Metodu* (Bursa: İlim ve Kültür Yayınları, 1983), 5–8.

111 Ibrahim Madkour, 'La logique d'Aristote chez les Mutakallimun', in *Islamic Philosophical Theology*, ed. Parviz Morewedge (New York: State University of New York Press, 1979), 66.

112 Fuâd Köprülü, by contrast, claimed that 'the *münâzara* style which is present in Arabic and Iranian literature was born under the influence of Turkish folk

normative power over Ottoman learned life as ideological templates.[113] The *münâzara* served or rather was presented as a gateway infallibly leading to truth if one complied with its precepts.[114] One hour of debate, a sixteenth-century Ottoman scholar, Taşköprülü Ahmed Efendi (d. 1561), declared, was better than one month of contemplation (*mütâlaa*).[115] In this setting, the contests of *münâzara* were the intellectual equivalent of Western duels – used specifically to build up and spread reputation.[116]

With the advent of Tanzimat, however, a renewed emphasis was placed by the Ottoman elite on this ancient art of argument. Many old classics on the rules and conventions of methodical debate, such as Lâtîfî's *Münâzara-i Lâtîfî* or Saçaklızâde's *Takrîr-u Kavanîni'l-Münâzara*, were recovered and appeared in print along with new publications on the subject.[117] Even though today these books are generally

literature'. Mehmed Fuâd Köprülü, *Türk Dili ve Edebiyâtı Hakkında Araştırmalar* (İstanbul: Kanaat Kitâbevi, 1934), 22. But of course this was the age of rising nationalism in Turkey.

113 This was, of course, a common theme in pre-modern societies. Aristotelian dialectic through a lengthy training in discussion constituted the centrepiece of French secondary education up until the end of the Old Regime. Goodman, *The Republic of Letters*, 92.

114 Cevdet Paşa, *Âdâb-ı Sedad*, 3. Arif Paşa and Hilmi Efendi, *Kanûn-ı Münâzara* (İstanbul: Muhib Matbaası, 1286/1869), 26. Taşköprüzâde Ahmed Efendi, *Risâle-i Taşköprü* (İstanbul: Arif Bey Matbaası, 1313/1895–1896), 5. Ali Rıza Ardahani, *Mi'yarü'l-Münâzara* (İstanbul Mahmud Bey Matbaası, 1307/1889–1890), 10–11.

115 Taşköprüzâde Ahmed Efendi, *Mevzuatü'l-Ulum*, trans. Kemaleddin Mehmed Efendi, 2 vols., vol. I (Dersaâdet: İkdam Matbaası, 1313/1895–1896), 63.

116 Molla Gıyaseddin, for instance, invited Allâme Devvâni to a *münâzara* to strengthen his scholarly reputation. Taşköprüzâde Ahmed Efendi, *Eş-Şakâiku'n-Nu'mâniyye fî ulemâi'd-Devleti'l-Osmâniyye*, trans. Muharrem Tan (İstanbul: İz Yayıncılık, 2007), 362. From time to time, this desire to subdue an opponent could cause what one might call today a scholarly scandal. In 1763, a famous *âlim* (erudite), Tatar Ali Efendi, for instance, was banished from Istanbul as a consequence of his unruly behaviour towards his rival, Abdülmü'min Efendi, after a particularly fervent *münâzara* over hermeneutics, which had taken place in the royal presence. Şem'dânî-zâde Fındıklılı Süleyman Efendi, *Mür'i't-Tevârih*, ed. Münir Aktepe, 4 vols., vol. II (İstanbul: Edebiyât Fakültesi Yayınları, 1978), 56.

117 These are some of the *münâzara* books published only in Istanbul. Fasih Ahmed Dede, *Münâzara-i Rūz ü Şeb* (İstanbul: Matbaa-i Dâr-üs-Saltana, 1278/1861). Fasih Ahmed Dede, *Münâzara-i Gül-ü Mül* (İstanbul: Tasvîr-i Efkâr Matbaası, 1285/1868); Arif Paşa and Hilmi Efendi, *Kanûn-ı Münâzara*; Nev'izâde Atai, *Münâzara-i Tuti ile Zag* (İstanbul: Terakki Matbaası, 1287/1870–1871); Lâtîfî, *Münâzara-i Lâtîfî* (İstanbul: Asır Matbaası, 1287/1871);

considered only a part of routine madrasa curriculum, it is clear from their content that the texts were intrinsically intended for wider circulation. In his *münâzara* book, *Âdâb-ı Sedâd*, Cevdet Pasha, for instance, explained in great detail the rules and conventions of good argument, noting that

> the presidency of the socities devoted to debate (*münâzaraya me'mûr olan meclisler*) is of the utmost significance. It has been witnessed a thousand times that these assemblies run against incongruous and ludicrous commotion simply because the presidents fall short of conducting the meeting in a proper manner and no result is obtained from the debate and discussion. At every assembly, the proceeding of debate under discipline and regularity is a binding duty.[118]

The *münâzara*, much more so than the *cedel*, became an important part of political jargon and was completely removed from its religious context. A junior officer, Abdi Efendi (d. 1884), for instance, when he committed to paper his views on the problems of local government, proudly declared that he arrived at the offered results through his 'poor reason and discourse' (*akl ve nutk-i acizanem*), and also through the use of *münâzara*.[119] Cevdet Pasha recorded in his memoirs how he had

Mahmud b. Osman Bursevi Lâmî Çelebi, *Münâzara-i Sultan Bahar ba şehriyar-ı Şita* (İstanbul: İzzet Efendi Matbaası, 1290/1873–1874); Saçaklızâde Mehmed b. Ebubekir Mar'aşi, *Takrîr u Kavânîn fi'l-Adab* (İstanbul: Matbaa-i Âmire, 1289/1872–1873); Bekir Efendizâde Mahmûd Efendi, *Lüccetü'l-münâzara* (İstanbul: Esad Efendi Matbaası, 1294/1877–1878); Ardahani, *Mi'yarü'l-Münâzara*; Cevdet Paşa, *Âdâb-ı Sedad*; Muhammed Cemaleddin b. Bekr el-İstanbuli, *Şerhü'l-Manzumeti'z-Zahire fî Kavânîni'l-Bahs ve'l-Münâzara* (İstanbul: Mahmûd Bey Matbaası, 1904); Mehmed Faik Memdûh Paşa, *Eser-i Memdûh* (İstanbul: Matbaa-i Âmire, 1289/1872). Ebü'l-Kâsım Alemülhüdâ Ali b. Hüseyin Şerif el-Murteza, *Eş-Şihab fi'ş-Şeyb ve'ş-Şebâb* (İstanbul: Matbaatü'l-Cevaib, 1302/1884–1885); Hilmi Emin, *Muhâkeme-i Yeis ü Emel* (İstanbul: Tasvîr-i Efkâr Matbaası, 1867). Bereketzâde Hakkı, *Müdâvele-i Efkâr* (İstanbul: Âlem Matbaası, 1307/1890).

118 The Pasha's views on the subject can be paraphrased in the following manner: proper discussions should be held before an audience, which is not, however, supposed to interfere by way of utterances of approval or discontent. One need not be loquacious and should not use strange expressions. During a discussion, laughing, fluttering, or raising one's voice is unseemly for a debater. And, finally, one should not discuss with those who do not know the rules of discussion, as this is, according to Pasha, a 'needless fatigue.' Cevdet Paşa, *Âdâb-ı Sedad*, 56.

119 Abdi Efendi, *Nutk-i bi-Pervâ ile Akl-i Dânâ Beyninde Muhavere* (İstanbul: Terakki Matbaası, 1287/1860–1861), 6.

many pleasant *münâzaras* over political and philosophical questions with the French ambassador, Lionel René François, marquis de Moustier (d. 1869).[120] In the heat of an ardent political discussion, Ziyâ Pasha (d. 1880), one of the forefathers of the Young Ottoman movement, reminded his friend Reşad Bey that it was, after all, his duty to adduce his proofs if he was convinced of his precision in the argument and suggested that they ought to have a *münâzara*. 'You will', he concluded, 'either accept your conviction as inconclusive or alternatively you will convince me.'[121]

The rigid rules of argument were meant to be observed even among family members. During a political debate, Ayetullah Efendi (d. 1878), another name deeply associated with the Young Ottoman movement, became irritated by his father's dismissive attitude and explained that even a father had to have respect for an individual's opinion (*sâhib-i fikr*).[122] According to Nâmık Kemal and Ziyâ Pasha, *münâzara* was the way in which the conduct of governmental deliberations had to be achieved. In Kemal's opinion, an idea not distilled through the medium of *münâzara* was bound to contain error, as it needed to be tested, developed, and strengthened by trial.[123] For Ziyâ Pasha, on the other hand, in every subject verity and veracity can be ascertained only through *münâzara* since 'over every lord of knowledge there is one more knowing'.[124]

In a contentious environment, the rules of *münâzara* in a sense, by providing the basis of a polite discourse, replicated the role of the *salonnière* in France.[125] By suspending social distinctions, its guidelines circumscribed the possibility of conflict and misunderstanding among the parties to an argument. Evidently, this rise of the *münâzara* culture should be understood against the background of political realignment

120 Cevdet Paşa, *Tezâkir 1–12*, 39.
121 Ebuzziyâ Tevfik, *Yeni Osmanlılar Târîhi*, ed. Şemsettin Kutlu, 2 vols., vol. II (İstanbul: Hürriyet Yayınları), 31.
122 Sâmî Paşazâde Hasan Bey, 'Ayetullah Bey ve Yeni Osmanlılar', *Hadisat-ı Hukukiyye ve Târîhiyye* III, no. 2 (1341/1925): 2. Cf. Cevdet Paşa, *Âdâb-ı Sedad*, 55.
123 Cited in Yusuf Tekin, 'Osmanlı'da Demokrasi Tartışmalarının Milâdı Olarak Meşrûtiyet Öncesi Tartışma Platformu', *Ankara Üniversitesi SBF Dergisi* 55, no. 3 (2000): 164–165.
124 Arabic in the original; Quran, 12: 76. Ziyâ Paşa, 'İhtilafü Ümmeti rahmetun', in *Numûne-i Edebiyât-ı Osmaniye*, ed. Ebüzziyâ Mehmed Tevfik (Kostantiniye: Matbaa-i Ebüzziyâ, 1330/1911–1912), 272.
125 Goodman, *The Republic of Letters*, 91.

away from the palace-dominated system, to the coalitional structure of bureaucratic governance. The end of Mahmud II's reign and the beginning of Abdülmecid's era coincided with the inauguration of many consultative committees and assemblies, with some of them reaching hundreds of participants at each season.[126] It is not surprising that Esad Efendi, Mahmud II's propaganda man, also happened to write a guideline for the conduct of proper *münâzara*.[127] The members of İsmail Ferruh Efendi circle, including Ferruh Efendi and Şânîzâde Ataullah Efendi all had *münâzara* books in their private libraries.[128] As a state mechanism these advice-giving bodies were not a novelty of the Tanzimat era *per se* – but rather they derived almost imperceptibly out of the old institution of *Meclis-i Meşveret*.[129] Moreover, since the late eighteenth and early nineteenth centuries, the Ottoman writers reckoned *münâzara* as something prospectively significant in governmental affairs.[130] Nevertheless, the term gained an added weight and a new significance with the mounting power of the bureaucracy and the proliferation of such assemblies.

In these consultative bodies, the Tanzimat ethos strove to achieve a sphere of political discussion where status and rank were disregarded altogether. One edict, published in the official newspaper in June

[126] Ali Akyıldız, *Tanzimat Dönemi Osmanlı Merkez Teşkilâtında Reform: 1836–1856* (İstanbul: Eren, 1993), 187.

[127] Esad Efendi, *[Fenn-i Münâzara]* (İstanbul Üniversitesi Türkçe El Yazmaları İbnülemin Mahmud Kemal İnal Kitapları, No: 2875), 13b–14a.

[128] See İstanbul Müftülüğü Şeriye Sicilleri Arşivi, Kısmet-i Askerî Mahkemesi (hereafter Ş.S.KISASKMAH). 1193, 96a-b and Ş.S.KISASKMAH. 1461, 54a.

[129] During the early days of Selim III a *Meclis-i Meşveret* met in the Topkapı Palace with more than two hundred participants representing different estates of the realm – something in the line of Imperial Diets. See Cevdet Paşa, *Târîh-i Cevdet*, 12 vols., vol. IV (İstanbul: Takvîmhâne-i Amire, 1275/1858–1859), 271–273. When he read the list of attendees, Selim III insisted that the janissaries needed to be present and represented by their senior members. Ibid., 271.

[130] Şânîzâde, for instance, pointed out the importance of *münâzara* in the making of governmental decisions: '*her bir tedbir-i umûr-i mülkiyyeleri, hademe-i devlet ve vükelâ-ı ra'iyyetden ibaret iki sınıf erbâb-ı meşveret meyanında, ber-vech-i serbesiyyet bahs ü münâzara ile karar-gir ve hükm-i agleb her ne veçhile netice-pezir olur ise*', Şânîzâde Efendi, *Târîh-i Şânîzâde IV*, 1094. In the late eighteenth century, Subhi Efendi also expressed similar ideas. See Subhi Mehmed Efendi, *Subhi Târîhi: Sâmî ve Şakir Târîhleri ile Birlikte 1730–1744 (İnceleme ve Karşılaştırma Metin)*, ed. Mesut Aydıner (İstanbul: Kitâbevi, 2007), 394–395.

1838 to regulate the rules of equity, is particularly striking for its deliberate tone:

Although the members of the recently raised and endowed High Judicial Council (*Meclis-i Ahkam-i Adliye*) and the Council of the Sublime Porte (*Dar-ı Şûrâ-ı Bâb-ı Ali)* are originally of different ranks (*rütbe-i aslileri muhtelif olub*), during the discussion of any motion, their avowing the dictates of their opinion and consideration naturally would necessitate the equality of their ranks (*rütbe-i müsâvât*). All in all, if the case requires, ministers and viziers, whatever be their excellencies, in brief all the functionaries of the state, might have to engage in consultation and arguments, perhaps even discussions, during the conduct of their proceedings. But clearly if there is a distinction between them, whichever rank they may be, inferior ones would abstain from entering into an argument with their superiors and there would not be any thoroughly conducted *münâzara*. As a result no sound judgment (*rey-i sevâb*) whatsoever will be grounded out of these discussions ... Even though the importance and significance of these members are well known in the eye of the Sultan of the sultans, with the removal of the ranks, there will be more capacity of debate between great and small, whoever they may be.[131]

It is difficult to gauge whether such a level of equality of status was ever achieved in practice. Yet the plea for rational discussion among equals as a means of reaching consensus for the common good turned into a recurring theme in the governmental lore of the Tanzimat era. Esad Pasha, former governor of Erzurum, for instance was criticised in the official newspaper, and removed from his positions, because of his scornful attitude during discussions. He was, the article emphasised, a man of older times. It went on to state that as for important matters pertaining to religion and state (*din ü devlet*), the members of the assembly should not think in terms of rank or pride (*ve rütbe davâsına ve muâmelât-ı istikbâriyeye sarf-ı zihn etmiyerek*) but rather should consider what is best for the land.[132] During a royal visit to the Supreme Council in 1839, Reşid Pasha, the Grand Vizier, read an imperial decree which urged the 'utmost liberty and impartiality in governmental deliberations (*her bir maslahat kemal-i serbestiyet ve bî-*

[131] Anonymous, 'Umûr-ı Dâhiliye', *Takvîm-i Vekâyi*, 22 Rebiülevvel/15 June 1254/1838, 1.

[132] Anonymous, '[Rabbimiz Teâlâ Hazretleri]', *Takvîm-i Vekâyi*, 6 Rebiülevvel/ 30 May 1254/1838, 3.

taraflık ile söyleşilerek)'.[133] Years later, Ahmed Rasim would describe this move as the 'first revolution (*ilk bir vakıâ-i inkılâbiyedir*)'.[134]

This principal of equity was not only recognised but also protracted in other consultative bodies, such as the *Şûrâ-ı Devlet* or the Council of State.[135] 'One should not be self-opinionated', Reîs Pasha reiterated while penning the new regulations for the High Judicial Council in 1841, 'but rather, through discussion and *münâzara*, should convince and outtalk the other by offering legitimate as well as strong evidences… since the adage that *silence gives consent* (*sükut ikrârdır*) is not valid during the proceedings of a council, members should not go without expressing their opinion on the affairs of the state and the nation.' 'In fact', the Pasha added to warn the members against the possible implications of acquiescence, 'in such case silence could only mean two things: either avoiding others for self-protection (*vikâye-i nefs*) or sidestepping because of your absence of qualification (*âdem-i liyâkat*)'.[136]

The government even created special decorations for the members of these chambers and discarded their individual ones in order to precipitate a feeling of equality between them.[137] Another memorandum, prepared for the High Judicial Council in 1839 to regulate the conduct of discussions, heavily accentuated the want of consensus on any course of action among peers before any decision thereon (there are nine references to this in a one-page document).[138] Even if the speaker was coming from the lowest rank, the document stressed (*velev ki en aşağı rütbede bulunsa bile*), members had to be all ears while he was speaking (*herkes can kulağı ile dinleyip*). The same text also asserted the inviolability of the deputies for all proceedings in consultative

133 Anonymous, 'Sûret-i Hatt-ı Hümâyun-ı Ma'adâlet-i Nümûn-Şâhâne', *Takvîm-i Vekâyi*, 11 Muharrem/15 March 1256/1840, 1. Ahmed Rasim, *İstibdaddan Hakimiyet-i Milliyeye*, 2 vols., vol. I (İstanbul: Vatan Matbaası, 1342/1923), 245. The full text of this speech is also given in ibid., 246–48; Ahmed Lûtfî Efendi, *Tarîh-i Devlet-i Âliyye-i Osmaniyye*, 8 vols., vol. VI (Dersaâdet: Mahmud Bey Matbaası, 1302/1884–1885), 92–93.

134 Rasim, *İstibdaddan Hâkimiyet-i Milliyeye*, 245.

135 See, the article 12 of '*Şûrâ-i Devlet Nizâmnâmesi.*' BOA, İ..DUİT 37–2/9, 23 Zilhicce 1285 (6 April 1869), and also *Düstûr I, Tertîb I*, 706.

136 BOA, İ..MSM. 1/19, 24 Cemaziyelevvel 1257 (14 July 1841).

137 BOA, C..ADL. 75/4520, 29 Rebiülahir 1262 (26 April 1846).

138 Eight of them is *ekseriyet-i ârâ* and one of them is *ittifâk-ı ârâ*, which is basically the same thing. In the event of a draw, the Sultan would cast the tie-breaking vote.

assemblies (*Mecâlis-i Meşveret*) and they were to debate and counsel on all affairs of state with the utmost liberty. 'There is no doubt', the document emphasised 'they shall not be responsible in any case for their opinions and judgements'.[139] In a way, the Tanzimat bureaucracy was deliberately creating what Habermas called a critical public sphere from its members; as it intuitively knew that its future survival might very well depend on it. In this sphere of political deliberation, it was not the status or rank deciding the cogency of an argument, but rather the strength of its reasoning and argumentative discourse (*kuvve-i karîha ve lisâniyesine güvenenler ve canı isteyenler söyleyerek*).[140]

Retrospectively, these rules seemed to be only valid when the interlocutors were using their public reasoning in the public sphere (i.e., within the boundaries of these state-related consultative chambers whilst discussing something pertaining to a common good or shared interest). However, as emphasised at the beginning of this chapter, the Ottoman system did not engender a contrast that paralleled the classical one between *publicus* and *privatus* (except maybe the one concerning *haremlik* and *selâmlık*, which is not particularly applicable here).[141] Some of these meetings adjourned only to resume in one of the great mansions of Istanbul.[142] A pasha's residence, or that of a *kadi*, was not simply his private sphere (i.e., pertaining to his intimate

139 See Anonymous, 'Sûret-i Lâyıha', *Takvîm-i Vekâyi*, 18 Şevval/25 December 1255/1839, 2. Cf. 'The public use of man's reason must always be free, and it alone can bring about enlightenment among men; the private use of reason may quite often be very narrowly restricted.' Immanuel Kant, *Foundations of the Metaphysics of Morals*, ed. Lewis White Beck (London: Macmillan, 1990), 85.

140 Anonymous, 'Sûret-i Lâyıha', 2. This should not be taken, however, as an originality of a few eccentric Tanzimat personas. Âli Pasha, for instance, was becoming increasingly vexed with the Public Council (*Meclis-i Umûmî*) made up of 'three hundred people' and instead wished to conduct the affairs in his inner circle and with a few trusted friends (*Cenâb-ı hak bu millet ve memleketin saâdet-i hâlini beş altı kişiye tevdi etmiş*). This disturbed Cevdet Pasha deeply as he commented 'without condescending to discuss [the important affairs] with the dignitaries of the nation (*eşraf-ı kavim*), deciding momentous matters (*mevâd-ı cesime*) all by themselves (*hod-be-hod*) was quite abusive and requiring a great deal of courage (*pek yolsuz ve büyük cesaret idi*)'. Cevdet Paşa, *Tezâkir 13–20*, 21.

141 For the analysis of this distinction in terms of public and private, see Benjamin C. Fortna, 'Reading between Public and Private in the Late Ottoman Empire and the Early Turkish Republic', *Comparative Studies of South Asia, Africa and the Middle East* XXX, no. 3 (2010): 564.

142 See Fuat, 'Ricâli tanzimattan Rifat Paşa', 9.

domestic or personal life) but in certain sense a public building that was not accessible to everyone but functioned in a governmental capacity.[143] As a result of this interwoven and intertwined character of private and public functions, in 1828, Arif Hikmet Bey, for instance, did not accept the *kadiship* of Istanbul, one of the most prestigious positions for the Ottoman *ulemâ*, by arguing that he did not have a separate *konak*.[144]

The Decrepitude of the *Münâzara*

Around the beginning of the 1860s, with the rising power of the newspaper, *münâzara* lost its former use among the Ottoman intellectuals and gave way to more comprehensive and less formal ways of political and cultural discussions, such as *münâza* (contention), *münâkaşa* (discussion), and *mübâhese* (dispute). Even though the Young Ottomans kept using the term to express their changing political expectations, particularly to denote the necessity of free political deliberations, its influence was severely impaired in high society as a discursive tool. In the end, it was confined to the palace and madrasas in its original composition (purely for religious controversies).[145] Ebuzziyâ Tevfik described a paper war that took place between Şinâsi and Said Bey in 1863 (later famous Küçük Said Pasha, nine-time Grand Vizier) as 'the epilogue of *münâzara* tradition (also known as *edeb-i bahs*) with its strict adherence to its conventions – [he added] in a way which cannot be compared to the strange arguments of our times – and the prologue of the literary discussions which were brought to the fore since the permission for unofficial newspapers.'[146]

143 See Selda Kılıç, 'Tanzimat'ın İlanından 1864 Düzenlemesinin Uygulanmasına Kadar Geçen Dönemde Osmanlı Vâlileri ve Vâlilik Kurumu', *Târîh Araştırmaları Dergisi* XXVIII, no. 45 (2009): 45–46. Also see Sâmîha Ayverdi, *İbrâhim Efendi Konağı* (İstanbul: Kubbealtı Neşriyâtı, 1999), 38.

144 Ahmed Lûtfî Efendi, *Târîh-i Lûtfî*, 8 vols., vol. II (İstanbul: Matbaa-i Amire, 1291/1874–1875), 152.

145 For *münâzaras* held in the royal presence, see Tahsîn Paşa, *Abdülhamit ve Yıldız Hâtıraları*, 129–130; Süleyman Kâni İrtem, *Sultan Abdülhamid ve Yıldız Kamarillası: Yıldız Sarayı'nda Paşalar, Beyler, Ağalar ve Şeyhler*, ed. Osman S. Kocahanoğlu (İstanbul: Temel, 2003), 118.

146 İbrahim Şinâsi, *Müntehabât-ı Tasvîr-i Efkâr* ed. Tevfik Ebüzziyâ (Kostantiniye: Matbaa-i Ebüzziyâ, 1303/1885), 104. The loss of *münâzara* etiquette was a frequent theme in subsequent literature. See, for instance, an article criticising 'those ignoramus ones whose eyes are blinded to the rule of *münâzara*'.

This strangely coincides with what Cevdet Pasha portrayed as the decline of *konaks* in his memoir. For him, Sadık Pasha's death in 1857 was the beginning of the end. 'After this point', he said to Fuâd Pasha in a rather lamenting tone, the 'time will not permit such things and the open houses available in Istanbul will be closed one by one'.[147] Şevket Rado's observation that the eclipse of ministerial *konaks* is somehow connected with the rise of literary coffee houses captures an interesting side of this shift (*münâzara* versus newspapers).[148] Although Rado omits this detail, the first and foremost of such establishments was also founded in Istanbul in the fateful year of 1857 by an Ottoman-Armenian called Sarafim and before long turned into the 'political and social club' much frequented by the city's literati.[149] Suggestively enough, in Russia, the decline of 'society' (*obshchestvo*), which served as the main locus of cultured and intellectual life, also happened around the same time, and coincided with the expansion and diversification of the readership.[150]

Although later intellectuals such as Ahmed Rasim (d. 1932) projected this change as a 'regrettable falling off' from the proper ways of the past, it was in fact a natural consequence of the sprawling character of the Ottoman public.[151] One perhaps needs to note that Rasim and others echoed the views voiced by the conservative segments of Ottoman society who had genuinely opposed the idea of an expanding public sphere. Some, living through these transformations, actually

Anonymous, 'Üdebâmızın Numûne-i İmtisalleri (Ma-Bad Elli Dokuzuncu Nüshadan)', *Mîzân*, 22 Zilhicce/30 August 1305/1888, 577.

147 Cevdet Paşa, *Tezâkir 13–20*, 18. What it is meant here was not so much that the pashas and others stopped meeting. But these meetings began to matter less. As Cevdet Pasha rightly observed, the time did not permit them to have a monopoly over governmental deliberations as politics emerged in the modern sense of the word.

148 Şevket Rado, 'Tanınmış Edebiyâtçılar İstanbul'un Nerelerinde Oturdular', *Hayât Târîh Mecmûası* I, no. I (1966): 19.

149 M. Sabri Koz, *Sarafim Kırââthânesi*, ed. İlhan Tekeli, 8 vols., vol. VI, Dünden Bugüne İstanbul Ansiklopedisi (İstanbul: Kültür Bakanlığı & Târîh Vakfı, 1993), 459. Also see Süheyl Ünver, 'Yayın Hayâtımızda Önemli Bir Yeri Olan Sarafim Kırââthânesi', *Belleten* XLIII, no. 170 (1979): 481–489.

150 See William Mills Todd III, *Fiction and Society in the Age of Pushkin: Ideology, Institutions, and Narrative* (Cambridge, MA: Harvard University Press, 1986), 69.

151 Ahmed Rasim, *Matbuat Hâtıralarından: Muharrir, Şâir, Edib* (İstanbul: Kanaat Kütübhânesi, 1342/1924), 181. Similar views also expressed in [İnal], *Kemal ül-hikme*, 15.

believed that 'public opinion' was expressed better in *salons* (*selâmlık odaları*), which were, they argued, similar to parliaments (*parlemento*) in many ways. In fact, these critics even suggested that such expansion would eventually destroy the power and influence of public opinion altogether (*bütün bütün izmihlâline kadar*).[152] It is possible to link these ideas with the Habermasian notion of the decline of the public sphere as a result of its expansion (*Verfallsgeschichte*).[153] Were some contemporaries aware of the pernicious effects of the 'democratization' at a micro level of analysis? It is a difficult argument to make without further supporting evidence. Yet one thing is certain: those who expressed their disappointment with the expansion of the Ottoman public were in the minority.

In the late 1860s, Nâmık Kemal was already mocking the house gatherings of great pashas who were postulating the impossibility of a national assembly from such a diverse population.[154] 'In such times', he argued, 'nobody can resist the [power of] public opinion'.[155] According to Kemal, even madrasas, albeit rundown, were still more purposeful than a ministerial *konak*.[156] These were superfluous places, constructed with the money of starving country folk,[157] in which ministers employed way too many people,[158] and entertained outmoded ideas.[159] The times were different now: 'the air of liberty (*hürriyet havaları*), which spread within the realm of the domain, regenerated the nature of the public. The abject condition in which the state was plunged could not be concealed or palliated any longer. Everyone acknowledged their duty of patriotism (*vatanperverlik*). Societies were formed; newspapers began to put out [and] finally the

152 See Anonymous, 'Efkâr-ı Umûmîye', *Bedir*, 27 Eylül/9 October 1288/1872, 2.

153 For an analysis of the 'decline' literature, see Jean L. Cohen and Andrew Arato, *Civil Society and Political Theory* (Cambridge, MA: MIT Press, 1993), 212.

154 Nâmık Kemal, 'Veşavirhum fi'l-Emr', *Hürriyet*, 20 July 1868, 4. Similar views are also expressed in Ali Suâvi, *Sua[v]i'nin fi 28 Desambr 1875 (Evahir zi'lkada 1292) Târîhiyle İngiltere Hâriciye Nâzırı Lord Derbi'ye Yazmış Olduğu Mektûbun Türkçe Tercümesi* (Paris: Victor Goupy, 1876), 3.

155 Kemal, 'Veşavirhum fi'l-Emr', 2.

156 Nâmık Kemal, 'Me'mûrlara Dair', *Hürriyet*, 2 November 1868, 2.

157 Nâmık Kemal, '[İngiltere Hâriciye Vekili Lord Stanley]', *Hürriyet*, 30 Novembre 1868, 2.

158 Nâmık Kemal, 'Mülkümüzün Servetine Dair Geçen Numerodaki Makaleye Zeyl', *Hürriyet*, 17 August 1868, 1.

159 Nâmık Kemal, 'Usûl-i Meşverete Dair Geçen Nümerolarda Münderic Mektûbların Altıncısı', *Hürriyet*, 26 October 1868, 7.

Party of Young Ottomans came about... from the measures aiming public liberty (*hürriyet-i âmme*), which had been obligatorily taken to alleviate the ferment of ideas (*galeyân-ı efkâr*), there yielded an unexpectedly remunerative result.'[160]

The following chapters will discuss these 'measures' in more detail. Yet it should be noted that the decade between 1855 and 1865 witnessed a plethora of innovations in the formation of the Empire's public sphere. This, in effect, rendered the first and third types of *meclis* redundant, if not superfluous. The publication of the first privately owned newspaper by an Ottoman (*Tercüman-ı Ahvâl*); the arrival of scientific societies with open lectures (*Cemiyet-i İlmiye-i Osmaniye*); the inauguration of a university (*Dârülfünun*); the legal equality between Muslims and non-Muslims (*Islahat Fermanı*); and the initiation of an Ottoman Academy of Sciences (*Encümen-i Dâniş*) were all recorded in the annals of this decade as the originalities of the Tanzimat era, and they all had an unsettling influence on the structure of the *meclis*.[161] It was no coincidence that the very expression of public opinion happened to appear during this decade and not before. The exclusive nature of *münâzara* was simply not suitable for such a booming public, who, though interested in political deliberations, had neither the patience nor the rearing to wade through a studiously conducted argument. Evidently, what they called a public was still minute; yet in the course of these years, it began to be shaped amorphously outside the governmental institutions.

[160] Nâmık Kemal, 'Hubbü'l-Vatan Mine'l-İman', *Hürriyet*, 29 June 1868, 1–2.

[161] One can also add the end of the Crimean War or the economic novelties such as the first paper note or the first foreign debt to this list. Cf. Kale, *French Salons*, 229.

3 *The World of İsmail Ferruh Efendi*

Introduction

During the early modern era, and certainly the early part of the nineteenth century, one of the favourite tropes of Western travellers was the limited nature of the Ottoman scholastic world. Sir James Porter (d. 1776), for instance, British ambassador to the Sublime Porte and great admirer of Ottoman culture, acknowledged, with some reluctance, that their knowledge system was not that 'extensive' but this was simply because 'they conceive that there is nothing superior to the Koran'.[1] The account of American zoologist, James Ellsworth De Kay who travelled in the Empire between 1831 and 1832, is another example of this widespread attitude. After praising what he called the attention of the 'Turks' to public instruction and the abundances of public libraries, De Kay wrote: 'the largest [public library] is stated to contain 6,000 volumes. This may be considered a small number, but it must be remembered that oriental literature is circumscribed in comparison with ours, and they contain but few foreign works'.[2] In her famous book, *The City of the Sultan and*

[1] Sir James Porter and Sir George Larpent Larpent, *Turkey; Its History and Progress: From the Journals and Correspondence of Sir James Porter, Fifteen Years Ambassador at Constantinople; Continued to the Present Time with a Memoir of Sir James Porter by His Grandson Sir George Larpent, Bart.*, 2 vols., vol. II (London: Hurst and Blackett, 1854), 140. In fact, the sections about Ottoman cultural life, probably written by his grandson, seem to be direct translations from Abdolonyme Ubicini's account. See A. Ubicini, *Lettres sur la Turquie, ou, Tableau statistique, religieux, politique, administratif, militaire, commercial, etc. de l'Empire ottoman, depuis le khatti-cherif de Gulkhané (1839)* (Paris: Librarie Militaire de J. Dumaine, 1853), 198–199.

[2] James Ellsworth de Kay, *Sketches of Turkey in 1831 and 1832 by an American* (New York: J. & J. Harper, 1833), 142. There is now an excellent study on this peculiar aspect of Ottoman intellectual life, that is, purpose-built libraries of the eighteenth century. See Yavuz Sezer, 'The Architecture of Bibliophilia: Eighteenth-Century Ottoman Libraries' (PhD diss., Massachusetts Institute of Technology, 2016).

Domestic Manners of the Turks in 1836, Julia Pardoe also supported these observations by noting:

Perhaps, with the single exception of Great Britain, there exists not in the world a more reading nation than Turkey. I have no doubt that this assertion will startle many individuals in Europe who have been accustomed and indeed led to believe that the natives of the East are as a people plunged in the profoundest ignorance. It is nevertheless a fact that nearly every man throughout the Empire can read and write, and there are, at this moment, upwards of eight thousand children scattered through the different schools of the capital. But the studies of the Osmanlis of both sexes have, with a few exceptions, hitherto been confined to the Koran, and to works of an inconsequent and useless description, the mere playing of an idle hour, incapable of inspiring one novel idea, or of leaving upon the mind impressions calculated to exalt or to enlighten it.[3]

Naturally traveller accounts should be handled with caution. But the implications attached to this recurring sneer are important to understand the nature of change in the Empire. In other words, one needs to ask what were intellectuals reading at a time when the Empire was undergoing profound social and economic changes? Was it possible to establish some sort of correlation between the reading material easily available for consumption and ideas in the air? Was it possible to detect a concept of the public infiltrating into contemporary literature as it was percolating into the Ottoman public sphere? And was there, as widely suggested for Europe, a certain secularisation or 'extension' of the available corpus as the years went by, or did the literature manage to remain, as it were, 'untouched by the storm-clouds of the political sky'?[4]

These questions remain unanswered in the field. The complications are of different sorts. The first challenge is a universal one for anybody interested in the circulation of ideas: as Roger Chartier points out, it is difficult to know the reading habits of an 'anonymous multitude who neglected to confess what they read'.[5] As far as the nineteenth-century

[3] Miss Pardoe, *The City of the Sultan and Domestic Manners of the Turks in 1836*, 2 vols., vol. I (London: Henry Colburn, 1837), 205–206.

[4] Karl Marx, *Capital: A Critical Analysis of Capitalist Production*, ed. Friedrich Engels, trans. Samuel Moore (London: Half-Guinea International Library, 1897), 352.

[5] Roger Chartier, *Cultural History: Between Practices and Representations*, trans. Lydia G. Cochrane (Ithaca, NY: Cornell University Press, 1988), 151.

Ottoman Empire is concerned, there are only a few cases where a diligent reader cared to note his or her library in detail and of course it is impossible to know how sincere they were in their 'confessions'.[6]

When the period between 1820s and 1860s is surveyed, there are also difficulties specific to the Ottoman case. The survival of the manuscript culture well into the nineteenth century and the government monopoly over published material until the 1860s, for instance, render a simple print-based investigation unable to address these inquiries. As a result, this chapter examines the estate records belonging to government officers who died between 1830 and 1840 in Istanbul to have a sense of what these people were reading at the beginning of the nineteenth century. The aim here is not to give definitive answers to above-stated questions, but rather to open up further lines of research and fill in gaps in the understanding of the Tanzimat era. The archival material that is consulted for this study is *kismet-i askeriyye*, the probate section of Istanbul *kadi* court that dealt exclusively with the proceedings of the *askeri*, or ruling class.[7]

Reading Habits of the Ottoman Elite

Although this collection is very important as a source of Ottoman material culture and has barely been used, one needs to search thoroughly to find the signs of a reading culture throughout the dusty volumes.[8] Books rarely appear in the records to begin with and when one finds them, if they are not the Quran, they are either compilations

6 See, for instance, the list of the books that Mehmed Murad (d. 1848) read during his lifetime. Feridüddin Attar, *Kitâb-ı Mâ Hazar Şerh-i Alâ Pend-i Attâr*, ed. Hâfız Mehmed Murad Nakşibendî (İstanbul: Dar'üt-Tıbaat ül-Amire, 1285/1868), 257–262.

7 The entire catalogue spans a period of 333 lunar years – from 1000 to 1333 – and consists of 2,142 volumes. This book uses 230 successive tomes, each around 200 pages and dating from 1245 (1830) to 1255 (1840). These volumes are located between the catalogue numbers 1258 and 1488. As Barkan points out the concept of *askerî* class was quite liberal and included a wide array of members of the society. In this case, it was not infrequent to come across non-Muslims who were *askerî* by profession. See Ömer Barkan, 'Edirne Askerî Kassamı'na Âit Tereke Defterleri (1545–1659)', *Belgeler* III, no. 5–6 (1966): 7–9.

8 The only exception is Şükrü Hanioğlu's book in which he 'examined the inventories of estates left by members of the *askerî* class who died between 1750 and 1800'. M. Şükrü Hanioğlu, *A Brief History of the Late Ottoman Empire* (Princeton, NJ: Princeton University Press, 2010), 27.

of poetry, religious classics, or dictionaries of Arabic and Persian languages. One of the most striking characteristics of the collection is the rarity of the printed material that it displays for the first quarter of the nineteenth century. This is maybe striking though not surprising. Compared to Western Europe the Ottoman engagement with the printing press was a relatively late phenomenon (1727). This 'lateness' in fact has turned into a point of embarrassment and criticism for generations of historians and more often than not offered as an obvious explanation for the cultural isolation of the Empire from the West.[9]

Yet maybe more meaningfully, the success and durability of the printing press came even later. The Ottomans were certainly aware of the technology from the very beginning since there were printing presses in Constantinople as early as the fifteenth century.[10] But it was only after the emergence of a print culture – a rise of 'print capitalism' to use Benedict Anderson's terminology – fostered by successful newspapers in the 1860s, that publishing turned into a viable business venture.[11] The first Ottoman printing press went out of business after producing only sixteen books and scribes dominated the literary scene for at least another century.[12] For these reasons, one rarely comes across published material in this timeframe, between 1820 and 1830, and when one does, it is easy to differentiate since they are conveniently marked as *basma* (printed).[13]

From the research undertaken, it is almost possible to argue that a great majority of Ottoman *askeri* class did not read anything but *Delâilü'l-Hayrat* (or *Dala'il al-Khayrat*, henceforth *Delâil*) – an Islamic

[9] This question of lateness is perhaps not very meaningful. As Kemal Beydilli asks, 'To a station where no passenger waits, what difference does it make whether bus comes early or late?' Kemal Beydilli, 'Müteferrika ve Osmanlı Matbaası: 18. Yüzyılda İstanbul'da Kitâbiyat', *Toplumsal Târîh*, no. 128 (2004): 51.

[10] The Jewish community, for instance, printed their first book in 1496. An Armenian printing house was also active in Istanbul in the 1560s. See Alpay Kabacalı, *Türk Kitap Târîhi: Baslangıçtan Tanzimat'a Kadar*, 2 vols., vol. I (İstanbul: Cem Yayınevi, 1989), 20–24.

[11] Benedict Anderson, *Imagined Communities: Reflections on the Origin and Spread of Nationalism* (London: Verso, 2006), 47.

[12] See Orlin Sabev, *İbrahim Müteferrika ya da İlk Osmanlı Matbaa Serüveni (1726–1756)* (İstanbul: Yeditepe Yayınevi, 2006), 231, 87–303.

[13] See, Ş.S.KISASKMAH. 1295, 26a, Ş.S.KISASKMAH. 1314, 78b, 86a, 92a, Ş. S.KISASKMAH. 1326, 4b, Ş.S.KISASKMAH. 1328, 42a, Ş. S.KISASKMAH. 1331, 6a, 1342, 77b, Ş.S.KISASKMAH. 1341, 32a.

Book of Hours compiled in the fifteenth century by Şeyh Cezuli (Imam al-Jazuli) of Morocco.[14] Some like Es-seyid Mehmed Efendi or Ebu Bekir Ağa did not even have their own copies of the Quran but had only *Delâil* to rely on for their salvation.[15] One sees other standard books of piety such as *Muhammediyye* of Yazıcızâde Mehmed (d. 1451) every now and then, but there existed nothing to rival the monopoly of this extremely popular compilation of devotions and litanies, which was also published many times after 1844.[16] Among history books, *Târîh-i Vassaf* was the most popular choice for the Ottoman elite. For a modern reader, this seems an odd predilection. One would expect to see more of the distinguished Ottoman chroniclers such as Kemal Paşa-zâde (d. 1534) or Naîmâ (d. 1716) rather than Vassaf, or Wassaf, (d. 1324), a medieval Persian 'panegyrist' at the Ilkhanate Court who has been infamous for his turgid style among later academics.[17] His book, Charles Rieu argued, 'was unfortunately set up as a model, and has exercised a baneful influence on the later historical compositions in Persia'.[18] Was this predilection for Vassaf just a stylistic interest on the part of Ottomans then? This could be a plausible enough explanation considering that Persian remained the language of refinement for the Ottoman elite even during the modernisation period: a 'bellwether of cultural orientation', as Benjamin Fortna puts it.[19] Nâmık Kemal once mentioned that in the eighteenth century, admittance to the Imperial Chancery Office (*Dîvân Kalemi*) depended upon an examination from Vassaf's *History*.[20] But perhaps the Ottoman *askeri* class also found something familiar in this account, as the Serbs or Greeks increasingly protested the '*pax ottomanica*'. Vassaf, as a state officer, was writing for the crumbling Ilkhanate

[14] Roger Chartier also mentions how *the Book of Hours* was more popular than Bibles among the country people. See Chartier, *Cultural History*, 157–158.

[15] Ş.S.KISASKMAH. 1268, 19a, Ş.S.KISASKMAH. 1284, 92a.

[16] Fehmi Edhem Karatay, *İstanbul Üniversitesi Kütüphânesi Arapça Basmalar Alfabe Kataloğu* (İstanbul: İstanbul Üniversitesi Yayınları, 1953), 441.

[17] His official title was 'His Majesty's Panegyrist'. See Charles Rieu, *Catalogue of the Persian Manuscripts in the British Museum* (London: British Museum, 1879), 162. Browne described the book 'as important as it is unreadable'. Edward Granville Browne, *A History of Persian Literature Under Tartar Dominion* (Cambridge: Cambridge University Press, 1920), 68.

[18] Rieu, *Catalogue of the Persian Manuscripts in the British Museum*, 162.

[19] Benjamin C. Fortna, 'Education and Autobiography at the End of the Ottoman Empire', *Die Welt des Islams* 41, no. 1 (2001): 28.

[20] Nâmık Kemal, 'Hâriciye Nezâreti', *Hürriyet*, 26 April 1869, 5.

Court (1256–1335) during the final years of their state, and Joan-Pau Rubiés commented how his work mirrored, along with that of Rashid al-Din, the 'cosmopolitan views of the Persian Ilkhanids'.[21]

In the collection, one can associate, by and large, certain books with certain professions. *Kadis*, for instance, had fatwa collections or physicians read medical books. But it is not surprising to see judges with extensive medical book collections and *vice versa*.[22] The records, in this respect, defy easy generalisations.[23] The Sheikh (*postnişîn*) of Mustafa Efendi Lodge in Eyüp, Şeyh Hasan Ahmed Efendi for instance, if his book collection is any indication, appears to have been more interested in politics and history than religious devotion. Among his collection of sixty manuscripts, he had books like *Târîh-i Vassaf* or *Kâbûsnâme* (*Qabus-nama*), an eleventh-century Persian Mirror for Princes, but no Quran or *Delâil*.[24] One also does not know what to make of a madrasa professor who had only four books – one of them being the Quran – in his entire collection,[25] or a school teacher (Mekteb Hâcesi Hâfız Ahmed Efendi), clearly a memoriser of the Quran as his title *Hâfız* suggests, but who did not have any books at all.[26]

There is also another and somewhat richer side to the monotonous picture that the archive generally portrays. The collection of a former Şeyhülislam, Es-seyid Mehmed Arif Efendi (d. 1826), a member of the famous *ulemâ* dynasty, Feyzullahzâdes, is astonishing with more than 500 manuscripts – a collection containing the works of most distinguished calligraphers such as Hâfız Osman (d. 1698).[27] Perhaps not as broad, but certainly more interesting from the perspective of intellectual history, through these volumes one also finds the booklist of Keçecizâde Mehmet İzzet Molla (d. 1829) who was in the words of

[21] Joan-Pau Rubiés, *Travel and Ethnology in the Renaissance: South India Through European Eyes, 1250–1625* (Cambridge: Cambridge University Press, 2002), 69. Also see Russell G. Kempiners Jr., 'Vaşşâf's Tajziyât al-Amşâr wa Tazjiyat al-A'şâr as a Source for the History of the Chaghadayid Khanate', *Journal of Asian History* 22, no. 2 (1988): 160–187.

[22] See, for instance, the library of Esseyid Mehmed Arif Efendi, former *kadi* of Üsküdar. Among his eighty-nine books, the majority is on medicine. Ş. S.KISASKMAH. 1293, 72ab.

[23] It is also puzzling to see, for instance, a former *kadi* of Sofia, Mehmed Efendi, who had neither Quran nor *Delâil* in his collection of thirty-one books. Ş. S.KISASKMAH. 1258, 14ab.

[24] Ş.S.KISASKMAH. 1347, 49a.

[25] Müderisin-i kirâmdan Es-seyid Mustafa Efendi, Ş.S.KISASKMAH. 1265, 51b.

[26] Ş.S.KISASKMAH. 1327, 38b.

[27] Ş.S.KISASKMAH. 1258, 17a–20b.

E. J. W. Gibbs, 'one of the most eminent and celebrated men of Sultan Mahmúd's reign'.[28]

The father of a famous Grand Vizier (Fuâd Pasha) and son of a distinguished Kadıasker (Sâlih Efendi), İzzet Molla himself was not only a renowned *kadi* but also a significant poet whose *Mihnet-i Keşan* (*the Affliction of Keşan*), is considered the birth of realism in the Ottoman literature.[29] It should be noted that the overlap between the emergence of a 'public' discourse and the appearance of this realism exemplified by a 'verse in a simpler and more natural manner than had hitherto been accounted literary' is probably not a coincidence.[30] As Robert Wuthnow underlines, 'if cultural products do not articulate closely enough with their social settings, they are likely to be regarded by the potential audiences ... as irrelevant, unrealistic, artificial, and overly abstract, or worse, their producers will be unlikely to receive the support necessary to carry on their work'.[31] Consequently not only the high literature of the elite but also the folk literature of the era adapted itself to changes in the political climate.[32]

This assumption holds true not only for poetry but also for the political prose of the time. İzzet Molla himself actually propounded a Quranic verse, a section from the third chapter, *Al-Imran*, to encourage popular discussions before the government took any political decision.[33] In his words, and from a *lâyıha* (report) written to Mahmud II in 1827:

[28] Ş.S.KISASKMAH. 1258, 35a. E. J. W. Gibb, *A History of Ottoman Poetry*, ed. Edward G. Brown, 6 vols., vol. IV (London: Luzac, 1905), 311. According to İbnülemin, when Molla decided to commit suicide before his rise to fame, he was only stopped by a certain Bucharestian noble residing in Istanbul, who, in fact, asked for his help to decipher the difficult parts in Vassaf's history. See İbnülemin Mahmud Kemal İnal, *Son Asır Türk Şâirleri*, 3 vols., vol. II (İstanbul: Orhaniye Matbaası, 1930), 724.

[29] Ahmet Hamdi Tanpınar, *XIX. Asır Türk Edebiyâtı Târîhi*, ed. Abdullah Uçman (İstanbul: Yapı Kredi Yayınları, 2006), 88–89. Also see Keçecizâde İzzet Molla, *Manzumet-ül Müsemmâ be-Mihnetkeşan*. (İstanbul: Ceride-i Havadis Matbaası, 1269/1853). The title of the book can also mean 'those who suffer' if it is read as *Mihnet-keşan*.

[30] Gibb, *A History of Ottoman Poetry*, 279–280.

[31] Robert Wuthnow, *Communities of Discourse: Ideology and Social Structure in the Reformation, the Enlightenment, and European Socialism* (Cambridge, MA: Harvard University Press, 1989), 3.

[32] See Tanpınar, *XIX. Asır Türk Edebiyâtı Târîhi*, 105.

[33] In the eighteenth century, other Ottoman writers also referred this verse with similar arguments but not with the same insistence. See Subhi Subhi Mehmed Efendi, *Subhi Târîhi: Sâmî ve Şakir Târîhleri ile Birlikte 1730–1744 (İnceleme ve Karşılaştırma Metin)*, ed. Mesut Aydıner (İstanbul: Kitabevi, 2007), 394.

Figure 3.1 A 1853 depiction of Keçecizade Mehmet İzzet Molla, one of the pioneers of Ottoman realism.
Keçecizade İzzet Molla, *Manzumet-ül Müsemmâ be-Mihnetkeşan* (İstanbul: Ceride-i Havadis Matbaası, 1269/1853).

As a consequence of holy command of *take counsel with them in all matters of public concern; then, when thou hast decided upon a course of action, place thy trust in God*,[34] in the state of Muhammad, all the matters of importance were turned over to the authorities of the council to which people were appointed not for their rank but because of their exceptional intelligence. In other saying only those who were the savants of the state and mentioned verily as *them* in the phrase *take counsel with them*, were chosen. The holy *sunna* also concurs with it and requires that the authorities of the council should be worthy of the assembly. But in the last hundred years or so, the authorities of the council remained only in appearance and none of the imperatives of the consultancy (*şerait-i meşveret*) were abided. In truth, the consultative assembly is the foundation of the whole world order and if the consultancy is spoiled, in keeping with the dictum of *building something corrupt in a corrupt manner is corruption;*[35] the world order is also spoiled. According to the hearsay of the people, the assembly of the council now consists only for sycophancy before the grandees of the Sublime State and its members would easily turn the world upside down by saying that this is the word of our master.[36]

This verse, *take counsel with them*, it should be noted, was later used extensively by the Young Ottomans for their constitutional claims, and for a time it was at the centre of ardent debates as the 'authorities of the council' could not agree upon who was meant by 'them' in the holy command. Other than this specific section, Molla's language also often leaned towards what he dubbed 'public benefit' (*menâfi'-i âmme*), which was, to him, a significant category of reckoning.[37]

[34] Arabic in the original. Al-Imran-159, *The Message of the Qur'an*, trans. Muhammad Asad (Beirut: Dar al-Andalus, 1980), 92. Or 'consult with them upon the conduct of affairs. And when you are resolved, then put your trust in Allah' as William Pickthall translated it. *The Meaning of the Glorious Qur'an: Text and Explanatory Translation*, trans. Marmaduke William Pickthall (Beltsville, MD: Amana, 1996), 63. It should be noted that there are currently eleven different English translations of the Quran and Muhammad Asad's version (formerly Leopold Weiss) is the only one using the word 'public' in this verse. His former life as a part of Viennese intellectual circles had probably a bearing upon this particular interpretation, as there is nothing to justify the word 'public' in the original.

[35] Arabic in the original.

[36] Keçecizâde Mehmet İzzet Molla,'*Islâh-i Nizâm-ı Devlete Dair Risâle* (İstanbul: Üniversitesi Türkçe El Yazmaları No: 9670), 8a.

[37] See, for instance, İzzet Molla,'*Islâh-i Nizâm-ı Devlete Dair Risâle*, 22b. Also, see his pacifist draft written against the idea of a war with Russia. Its full text was given in Lûtfi Ahmed Lutfi Efendi, *Târîh-i Lutfi*, 8 vols., vol. I (İstanbul: Matbaa-i Amire, 1290 [1873/1874]), 391–401.

One can see this sensitivity throughout his writings, perhaps best in the end of his report where he wrote, 'I cannot vouch with utmost confidence if the points that I have humbly written down are the truth and only truth. They need to be discussed with persons of understanding one by one as the instruction given by a single man's mind cannot gain the public's approval (*makbûl-i âmme olamaz*)'.[38]

Yet when this remarkable man died in exile in 1829 – banished because of his 'conflicting ideas with the royal opinion and the consensus of public decisions/*efkâr-ı şâhâne ve karar-ârâ-i umûmîyeye muhâlif*',[39] – in his collection of thirty-two books he had all the classical examples of 'advice literature' such as *Ahlâk-i-Alâî* by Kınalızâde (d. 1572) or *Zahiret-ül-Mülûk* by Sururi Çelebi (d. 1562), but little illuminated his inclination for the nascent Ottoman public. Even though in his report, he recommended translations from European languages (*kütüb-i efrenciyye*),[40] there was not a single Western book in his library.

Of course, one thing to keep in mind is the possibility that maybe these old texts gained a new meaning simply because their readers were changing.[41] As Michel de Certeau points out 'whether it is a question of newspapers or Proust, the text has a meaning only through its readers; it changes along with them'.[42] In a given society, the implication of any text depends very much upon the conditions through which they are received, as it is argued for Vassaf's history. But this fact does not necessarily exclude the probability of new texts circulating. The collection of İsmail Ferruh Efendi for instance, the putative founder of the first Masonic lodge of Istanbul, was quite remarkable in this regard for its eclectic content.[43]

38 İzzet Molla,'*Islâh-i Nizâm-ı Devlete Dair Risâle*, 36b.
39 Lutfi Efendi, *Târîh-i Lutfi I*, 293.
40 İzzet Molla,'*Islâh-i Nizâm-ı Devlete Dair Risâle*, 37b.
41 See D. F. McKenzie, *Bibliography and the Sociology of Texts: The Panizzi Lectures, 1985* (London: British Library, 1986), 20.
42 Michel de Certeau, *The Practice of Everyday Life*, trans. Steven Rendall (Berkeley: University of California Press, 1984), 170.
43 Ş.S.KISASKMAH. 1461, 52a–54a.

The Library of İsmail Ferruh Efendi

In fact, İsmail Ferruh Efendi's only publication, a translation from a famous *sufi* scholar, Hüseyin Vâiz Kâşifî (d. 1504/5), exhibits probably the earliest example of what one might call a distinct concern for 'commoners/*avâm*'.[44] In his preface, Ferruh Efendi openly stated that he had translated this book not for the elite but for the commoners 'after realizing how difficult it was for them (*emr-i asîr*) to comprehend religious texts'.[45] 'Since', Ferruh Efendi wrote, 'the real purpose (*asıl maksad*) is to help their understanding, writing in an elevated style (*elfâz-ı münşiyâne*) was deliberately avoided and the book was composed in a coarse Turkish (*kabaca lisân-ı türki üzerine tâbir olunub*)'.[46] This attitude set the mood for the remainder of the century and the literary language became gradually easier and easier for the benefit of the expanding public.[47] But in case of Ferruh Efendi, was there a connection between his reading material and this new concern?

When one goes through the list of the books that he owned, it is easy to see that Ferruh Efendi, too, had his fair share of classical canon such as *Makamat-ül Hariri*, widely held book of anecdotes written by Mediaeval Arabic scholar Hariri of Basra (d. 1122) or the *Dîvân* of Ebu Tayyib, also known as al-Mutanabbi (d. 965), one of the most

44 Among his books, it was recorded as '*Tefsir-i Mevahib Müsveddesi*' and '*Mevakib fi tercüme-i tefsir-il mevahib*'.

45 Hüseyin Vaiz el-Kaşifi, *Tefsir-i Mevakib: Tercüme-i Tefsir-i Mevâhib*, trans. İsmail Ferruh Efendi (İstanbul: Matbaa-i Amire, 1246/1830), 2.

46 Ibid., 3. Cf. Eric Auerbach, *Literary Language and Its Public in Late Latin Antiquity and in the Middle Ages*, trans. Ralph Manheim (Princeton, NJ: Princeton University Press, 1993), 50–51. Ferruh's choice of Kashifi was by no means coincidental. As Kristin Zahra Sands points out, Kashifi's exegesis was famous for its simple and accessible style and was very popular throughout the Islamic world. See Kristin Zahra Sands, 'On the Popularity of Husayn Va'iz-i Kashifi's Mavāhib-i 'âliyya: A Persian Commentary on the Qur'an', *Iranian Studies* 36, no. 4 (2003): 469.

47 See, for instance, Mustafa Sâmî's travelogue which was dedicated to the 'commoners of his nation/*avâm-i milletime*'. Mustafa Sâmi Efendi, *Avrupa Risâlesi* (İstanbul: Takvim-i Vekayi Matbaası, 1257/1840), 3. The word '*avâm* عوام shares the same root with *âmme* (public). James W. Redhouse, *An English and Turkish Dictionary in Two Parts: English and Turkish and Turkish and English* (London: B. Quaritch, 1856), 833.

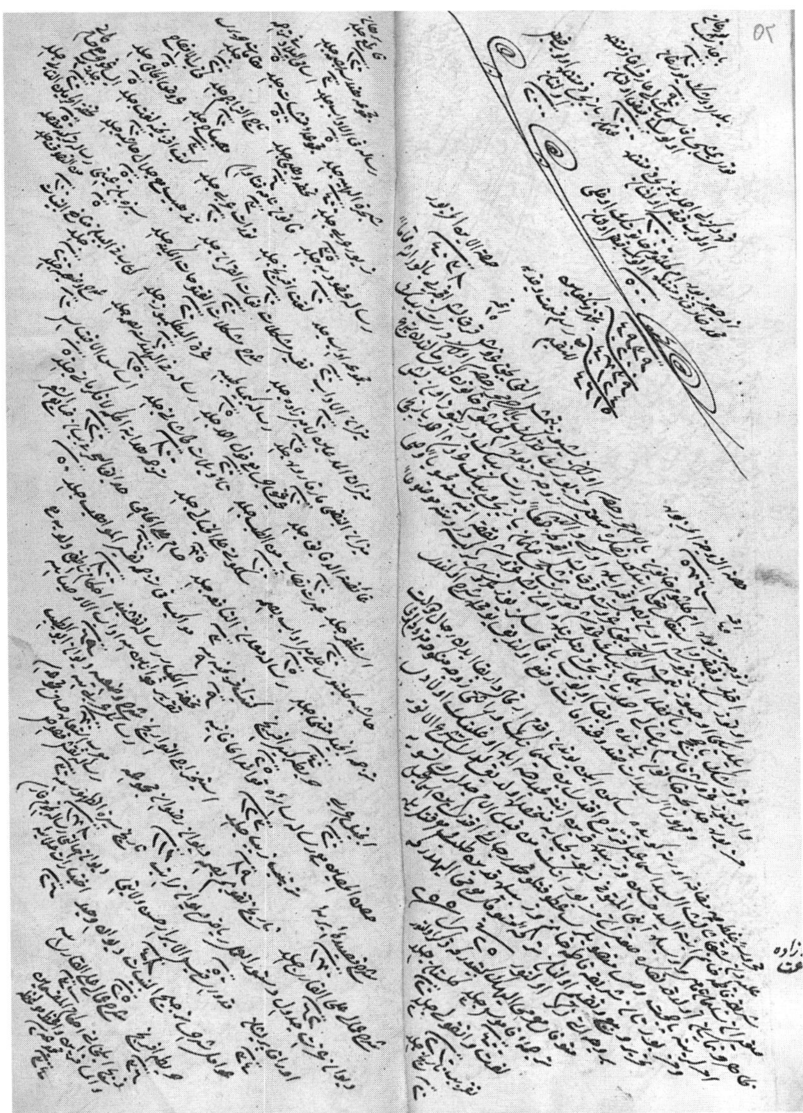

Figure 3.2 The inventory of books left by İsmail Ferruh Efendi.
Ş.S.KISASKMAH. 1461, 52a-54a.

prominent examples of early Arabic poets.[48] The lack of a Quran and *Delâil* as well as the absence of works by certain well-known conservative benchmarks such as İbni Teymiye (d. 1328) or İmam Birgivi (d. 1573) might suggest his latitudinarian tendencies.[49] Another member of his circle, Recâîzâde Ahmed Cevdet (d. 1831) did not have a Quran or *Delâil* either in his collection of twenty-eight books.[50] Was this more than just a coincidence? It is difficult to say. Building an argument based on absence can be problematic, particularly when perishables are in question. But one can say that *Delâil* did not have the 'rustic' connotations that *The Book of Hours* had in Europe.[51] Sophisticated intellectuals of the time, such as Halim Giray (d. 1823),[52] a descendant of the Crimean Khans and historian or Şânîzâde Mehmed Ataullah Efendi (d. 1826),[53] the palace chronicler (*vakânüvis*) and physicist, had its valuable copies in their private collections. It was one of the books that Abdülaziz requested to read during the troubled days leading to his deposition in 1876.[54] Even though complaints about corrupt probate officers were not infrequent,[55] these clerks (known as *kassam*) were generally meticulous and precise in record keeping, registering everything from 'some soap' to 'some

48 For Hariri and his reception, see Jaakko Hämeen-Anttila, *Maqama: A History of a Genre* (Göttingen: Harrassowitz, 2002), 148–77, especially 73–77. For Mutanabbi, see Margaret Larkin, *Al-Mutanabbi: Voice of the 'Abbasid Poetic Ideal* (London: Oneworld, 2008), passim.

49 A close friend of İsmail Ferruh Efendi and a member of his circle, Kethüdâzâde Arif Efendi often criticised Birgivi for being too strict in religious matters. See Emin Efendi, *Menâkıb-ı Kethüdâzâde el-Hac Mehmed Ârif Efendi* (İstanbul: s. n., 1305/1887), 285.

50 Ş.S.KISASKMAH. 1310, 27a.

51 Roger Chartier, for instance, remarks how *the Book of Hours* was exclusively read by country people. See, Chartier, *Cultural History*, 157–158.

52 Ş.S.KISASKMAH. 1274, 26a.

53 Ş.S.KISASKMAH. 1193, 94b.

54 İsmail Hakkı Uzunçarşılı, 'Sultan Abdülaziz Vak'asına Dair Vak'anüvis Lütfi Efendi'nin Bir Risâlesi', *Belleten* VII, no. 28 (1943): 358. Abdülmecid's 'pious and prodigal' daughter, Refia Sultan (d. 1880) also commissioned a lavish copy from a famous calligrapher for her modest book collection. See Ali Akyıldız, *Mümin ve Müsrif Bir Padişâh Kızı: Refia Sultan* (İstanbul: Tarih Vakfı Yurt Yayınları, 1998), 14. In her estate, the only other book mentioned by name was, strangely enough, Ferruh Efendi's translation. Ibid., 15.

55 Bilgin Aydın, İlhami Yurdakul, İsmail Kurt, *Şeyhülislamlık (Bab-ı Meşihat) Arşivi Defter Kataloğu* (Istanbul: Türkiye Diyânet Vakfı İslâm Araştırmaları Merkezi, 2006), 224.

sugar'.[56] In any case, such venal *kassams* were mostly interested in orphans' estates and would not have dared to be mixed in any wrong-doing when the families in question were well-connected. Hence this should not be a simple omission. Perhaps the remaining members of the families may have swept certain books aside for money or sentimental values attached.[57] This is now impossible to know. But something is certain: in the library of İsmail Ferruh Efendi there were signs of another world or rather signs of an interest in another world. Among his hundred-odd books, he had two *Frenk* (European) dictionaries, two different maps printed in Europe, two copies of the Bible – one is in Arabic, the other probably in Turkish – and nine other undifferentiated European works, along with various treaties on astronomy, chemistry, and mineralogy.[58]

Naturally İsmail Ferruh Efendi was not the first one to read foreign literature in the history of the Empire – that is to say other than in *elsine-i selâse*, or the three constituent languages of the official idiom: Arabic, Persian, and Turkish. The estate records are sprinkled with random Western lexicons and manuals.[59] Some prominent members of the non-Muslim elite, such as Barutçubaşı Bogosyan, coming from the famous and influential Armenian family, Dadians, had rather wide-ranging collections for their time.[60] Without going any further, the

[56] See Ş.S.KISASKMAH. 1286, 83a, Ş.S.KISASKMAH. 1626–91a. Some information on *kassams* can be found in İsmail Hakkı Uzunçarşılı, *Osmanlı Devletinin İlmiye Teşkilatı* (Ankara: Türk Tarih Kurumu, 1965), 121–125.

[57] The Court of Probate was invited when there was a problem with the execution of an inheritance. According to an *Adâletnâme* (*Book of Justice*), if the inheritors were adult and present (*hâzır ve kibar*), probate officers (*kassam*) were not supposed to be involved in the process unless they were called for. See Barkan, 'Edirne Askerî Kassamı', 3, fn. 4.

[58] In the late seventeenth century, a Polish convert named Ali Ufkî Efendi (originally Wojciech Bobowski) translated the Bible into Ottoman, which remained as the sole translation until the mid-nineteenth century. See Cem Behar, *Ali Ufkî ve Mezmurlar* (İstanbul: Pan Yayıncılık, 1990), 28–32.

[59] See, for instance, Ş.S.KISASKMAH. 1268, 29b, Ş.S.KISASKMAH. 1299, 48b–50a.

[60] He had 10 Turkish books (150 kuruş), 35 Armenian books (400 kuruş), and 24 Western books (160 kuruş). This renders, according to the calculations of the Ottoman probate officer, each Turkish book 15 kuruş, Armenian book 11.5 kuruş, and Western book 6.5 kuruş. See Ş.S.KISASKMAH. 1355, 60ab. About the family see, Anahïde Ter Minassian, 'Une famille d'amiras arméniens: Les Dadian', in *Histoire économique et sociale de l'Empire ottoman et de la Turquie (1326–1960): Actes du sixième congrès international tenu à Aix-en-Provence du 1er au 4 juillett 1992*, ed. Daniel Panzac (Paris: Peeters, 1997), 505–519.

library of Ferruh's close friend, Şânîzâde Mehmed Atâ'ullah,[61] contained thousands of books in Western languages: a staggering example of cultural interaction between the Empire and Europe.[62] Here it should be mentioned that the idea of a public was one of the most important subtexts, a *zeitgeist*, for the books that Şânîzâde composed. In his writings, he often expounded the relationship between government and public from what he called philosophical perspective (*felasife kavliyle*).[63] One reads parables implying the importance of public approval in all governmentality (*umûr-ı cumhûr*) in his *Târîh-i Şânîzâde*.[64] Was this because of the time he lived in or because of the books that he read? Again, it is not easy to say, and this is not a mutually exclusive relationship. In any case, he was a man who could write about public consensus (*ittifâk-i âmme)*, democracy (*kanûn-i demokrâti*), or parliamentary regime (*parlemento*) as tantalising examples from Europe on the same page.[65] Perhaps Şânîzâde himself did not use the very expression of 'public opinion' as such, but his modern readers casually employed the phrase as shorthand to express the meaning behind his convoluted terminology.[66] In other words, he often meant it. Yet this idiosyncratic man, who also singlehandedly laid the foundations of modern medicine in the Empire and read Latin,

[61] When Şânîzâde died, his mother, Şakire Hanım, declared that her son owed some money, 600 kuruş, to İsmail Ferruh Efendi. Ş.S.KISASKMAH. 1193, 96b. But İsmail Ferruh's name appears only once and *en passant* in his history. Şânîzâde Mehmed 'Atâ'ullah Efendi, *Târîh-i Şânîzâde*, 4 vols., vol. I (İstanbul: Ceride-i Havadis, 1291 [1874/1875]), 242.

[62] Ş.S.KISASKMAH. 1193, 94b–96b. Unfortunately, the probate officer did not give a precise number of books, but from the value he attached, an educated guess is possible. For İsmail Ferruh Efendi's nine Western books, he assigned nine kuruş. For Şânîzâde's books, he remarked, 'some western books' and assigned 2,000 kuruş once and another time 150 kuruş. According to this calculation, Şânîzâde probably had thousands of Western books, whether in Latin, French, or Italian.

[63] See, for instance, Şânîzâde Mehmed 'Atâ'ullah Efendi, *Târîh-i Şânîzâde*, 394–395.

[64] See ibid., 353. Also see where he compares *menfaat-i mahsûsa* (personal benefit) to *menfeat-i âmme* (public benefit), ibid., 28. One can see the importance of *menfaat-i âmme* in ibid., 134, or in Şânîzâde Mehmed 'Atâ'ullah Efendi, *Târîh-i Şânîzâde*, 4 vols., vol. III (İstanbul: Ceride-i Havadis, 1291 [1874/1875]), 134.

[65] Ibid., 134, or in Şânîzâde Mehmed 'Atâ'ullah Efendi, *Târîh-i Şânîzâde*, 4 vols., vol. IV (İstanbul: Ceride-i Havadis, 1291 [1874/1875]), 64, 71.

[66] See, for instance, Mert Sunar, 'Cauldron of Dissent: A Study of the Janissary Corps, 1807–1826' (PhD diss., State University of New York at Binghamton, 2006), 166.

French, and Italian, should be treated as a fascinating and suggestive exception.[67]

It must be also noted that long before the nineteenth century, Western literature was not an unknown to some members of the Ottoman elite. Before the end of the sixteenth century, when the Ottomans felt safer, the cultural interactions seem to have been more frequent with more porous borders between the Empire and Europe. Mehmed II (r. 1451–1481), 'Conqueror' of Constantinople, for instance, is reported to have had an important collection of Latin and Greek manuscripts.[68] Even around the early seventeenth century, an eccentric figure like Kâtip Çelebi (d. 1657) could write his book, *the Greek, Roman and Christian History for the Confused*, from Western sources.[69] This list can be stretched further if one insists.[70] But the case of İsmail Ferruh Efendi, coming after years of cultural isolation and political struggle, is different from these examples. Following Michel Foucault's argument, this book envisages modernity as an 'attitude' rather than a period of history, as 'a mode of relating to contemporary reality; a voluntary choice made by certain people'.[71] İsmail Ferruh

[67] See, Abdulhak Adnan [Adıvar], *La science chez les Turcs ottomans* (Paris : Maisonneuve, 1939), 159–160. Edhem Eldem shows that the introduction of Şânîzâde's history is almost identical with Voltaire's article on History, published in the famous Encylopédie in 1765. For details, see Edhem Eldem, 'Hayretü'l-Azime fi İntihalati'l-Gâribe: Voltaire ve Şânîzâde Mehmed Ataullah Efendi', *Toplumsal Târîh*, no. 237 (2013): 18–28.

[68] See Julian Raby, 'A Sultan of Paradox: Mehmed the Conqueror as a Patron of the Arts', *Oxford Art Journal* 5, no. 1 (1982): 4. In this case, one needs to add that Greek was not really a foreign language (nor really was Latin) as he considered himself an heir to the Byzantine throne, *Kayzer-i Rum*. See İlber Ortaylı, *Üç Kıtada Osmanlılar* (İstanbul: Timaş Yayınları, 2007), 18.

[69] *İrşadü'l-Hayara İla Târîhi'l-Yunan ve'r-Rum ve'n-Nâsâra*. The title can be also translated as 'for bewildered, or 'for dummies'. See Bekir Kütükoğlu, *Vekâyi'nüvis Makaleler* (İstanbul, 1994), 32–33. In another work, he mentions 'In the European history, which I translated from the Latin into Turkish'. See Haji Khalifah [Kâtip Çelebi], *The History of the Maritime Wars of the Turks*, trans. James Mitchell (London: Printed for the Oriental Translation Fund by A. J. Valpy, 1831), 14. Also see Orhan Şaik Gökyay, *Kâtip Çelebi* (Ankara: Kültür ve Turizm Bakanlığı, 1986), 30, 51.

[70] Hezarfen Hüseyin Efendi also used Greek and Latin materials for his studies – probably through his friends', Marsigli and Antonia Galland, assistance. See Bernard Lewis, *Islam in History: Ideas, People, and Events in the Middle East* (Chicago: Open Court Publishing, 2001), 220.

[71] Michel Foucault, 'What Is Enlightenment?', in *The Foucault Reader*, ed. Paul Rabinow (New York: Pantheon Books, 1984), 39.

Efendi's attitude signifies a change in the stance of his class, a break with the tradition. He was not an exceptional scholar like Şânîzâde or Kâtip Çelebi. He was not a ruler like Mehmed II interested in Byzantine legitimacy. What makes İsmail Ferruh Efendi interesting is that he is one of the first examples of what became known as a Tanzimat man. In other words, he was a precursor of what was soon going to be the norm.[72]

Tanzimat Man

The presence of foreign literature in İsmail Ferruh Efendi's library does not have the same implications as 'the European Book' that Homi Bhabha describes as the 'signifier of authority' in the Indian context.[73] For Bhabha, 'it is precisely to intervene in such a battle for the *status* of the truth that it becomes crucial to examine the *presence* of the English book. For it is this *surface* that stabilizes the agonistic colonial space; it is its *appearance* that regulates the ambivalence between origin and *displacement*, discipline and desire, mimesis and repetition'.[74] It suggests, he emphasises, the 'triumph of the writ of colonialist power'.[75] It should be noted that Ottoman relations with imperial powers of the nineteenth century are too intricate to explain with colonialism taken as a frame of reference. The Empire remained an independent power until the very end as a result of its eclectic and defensive modernity.

Nevertheless, by having recourse to European epistemology, İsmail Ferruh Efendi digressed from two interlaced canons: Ottoman and Islamic. Until the second half of the nineteenth century, the Ottoman Empire shared a common world of knowledge with the rest of the

[72] After his death, his wives Zübeyde and Fatma Hanıms fell into serious financial difficulties. One certain Recâî Efendi, a senior officer from the Imperial Council (*Dîvân-ı hümâyun hâcegânı*), tried to lay his hands on İsmail Ferruh Efendi's estate – probably seeing his disgrace as an opportunity – while his wives desperately struggled to retrieve it. BOA, HAT 1321/51602-A, 4 Rebiülevvel 1255 (18 May 1839), BOA, HAT 1321/51602, 29 Zilhicce 1255 (4 March 1840). The story ended happily for the wives and Recâî Bey was sent to prison. During this crisis, his library was acquired by the state for the collection of freshly founded state schools, although certain items were missing from the new list compared to the original. There are only eight volumes of foreign works with one dictionary and one does not see any newspaper, and so on. See BBO, A. {DVNS.BUY.iLM.d. No. 03, 8 Safer 1255 (23 April 1839).

[73] Homi K. Bhabha, *The Location of Culture* (London: Routledge, 1994), 110.

[74] Ibid. [75] Ibid., 107.

Muslim world. Even though from time to time different cultures emphasised dissimilar features in this framework, Islamic societies lived under uniform cognitive foundations.[76] Nelly Hanna, for instance, has already pointed out the importance of *Delâil* in the Egyptian context, which was, according to her, 'copied again and again, perhaps more than any other book in the eighteenth century'.[77] Michael Laffan, in his book on Indonesian Islam, has similarly remarked how 'Banten archives included numerous copies of the *Dala'il al-khayrat*'.[78] In the same vein, *Târîh-i Vassaf* was first published in India in 1853 'with a vocabulary of difficult words'.[79] In this interconnected system, the 'intensive' reader had access to a limited corpus of books, which were 'read and re-read, memorised and recited, deeply understood and possessed and transmitted from one generation to another'.[80]As pointed out by Brinkley Messick, 'recitation and memorization were at the foundation of Muslim pedagogy, in both literal and general methodological senses'.[81] Religious texts were read

[76] See, for instance, Francis Robinson, 'Ottomans-Safavids-Mughals: Shared Knowledge and Connective Systems', *Journal of Islamic Studies* 8, no. 2 (1997): 151–152. According to Robinson, 'the channels along which these ideas spread were in large part, of course, those of the connections of the great supra-regional Sufi orders – for instance, the Khalwatiyya in the eastern Mediterranean lands, but most important of all the Naqshbandiyya which in the third and fourth phases of its development spread not just from India into the Ottoman empire but throughout the whole of the Asian world'. Ibid.

[77] Nelly Hanna, *In Praise of Books: A Cultural History of Cairo's Middle Class, Sixteenth to the Eighteenth Century* (Syracuse, NY: Syracuse University Press, 2003), 94–95.

[78] Michael Laffan, *The Makings of Indonesian Islam: Orientalism and the Narration of a Sufi Past* (Princeton, NJ: Princeton University Press, 2011), 32. Even though now it is almost unknown in Turkey, *Delâil* is still held in veneration in North Africa and used even as an amulet by the Arabs and Berbers. See Pessah Shinar, *Modern Islam in the Maghrib* (Jerusalem: The Max Schloessinger Memorial Series & The Hebrew University of Jerusalem, 2004), 132.

[79] See Sir H. M. Elliot, *The History of India as Told by Its Own Historians: The Muhammadan Period*, ed. Professor John Dowson, 9 vols., vol. III (London, Trübner: 1871), 26.

[80] Guglielmo Cavallo and Roger Chartier, 'Introduction', in *A History of Reading in the West*, ed. Guglielmo Cavallo and Roger Chartier (Amherst: University of Massachusetts Press, 2003), 24–25. Here the intensive versus extensive reading paradigm of European historiography is applied into the Ottoman context.

[81] Brinkley Messick, *The Calligraphic State Textual Domination and History in a Muslim Society* (Berkeley: University of California Press, 1992), 21.

in a style characterised by 'sacrality and authority'.[82] If one keeps this framework in mind, it becomes less surprising to see, for instance, a Şeyh El-Hac Mustafa Efendi with two books, one of them being *Delâil* and the other its commentary.[83] Or an Ömer Aga, who had, when he died, three books in his entire library: a fifteenth-century legal classic, *Câmiu'l Fusuleyn*, and two different copies of the Quran.[84]

Until the second half of the eighteenth century, this 'Islamic' knowledge system worked adequately for the Empire. But even the word 'adequately' here should be used warily. Despite revisionist scholarship's deconstructionist attempts to refute the decline paradigm, one cannot categorically rule out the earlier signs of intellectual depression holding sway in the Ottoman lands (it is perhaps possible to perceive this stagnation as indicative of the 'great divergence').[85] The diminishing number of scholarly works produced in Ottoman academic establishments from the late sixteenth century onwards, for instance, is hard to overlook.[86] If the quantitative evidence regarding the cultural production in the Madrasa of Sahn-i Semân,[87] one of the most prestigious learning institutions of the Empire founded in the fifteenth century, is any gauge, the contrast between two subsequent centuries demonstrates an overwhelming decline.[88] It should be accentuated that it was only around this time that the Ottoman *ilmiye* (the body of higher

[82] Cavallo and Chartier, 'Introduction', 25. [83] Ş.S.KISASKMAH. 1268, 57a.

[84] Ş.S.KISASKMAH. 1286, 82b.

[85] The classical scholarship tends to see the demolition of an observatory in 1580 by the janissaries as the watershed year, or rather the 'the triumph of fanaticism' in the intellectual history of the Ottoman Empire. See, for instance, Halil İnalcık, *The Ottoman Empire: The Classical Age 1300–1600*, trans. Norman Itzkowitz and Colin Imber (London: Weidenfeld and Nicolson, 1973), 179.

[86] If the list of the most popular books read in the Ottoman madrasas is examined, of eighty-five books, four were written in the seventeenth century, one in the eighteenth century, and one another in the nineteenth century. All the others belonged to the 'golden age' of the Empire and of the Islamic civilization. Mefail Hızlı, 'Osmanlı Medreselerinde Okutulan Dersler ve Eserler', *Uludağ Üniversitesi İlahiyat Fakültesi Dergisi* 17, no. 1 (2008): 43–46.

[87] On this madrasa, see Uzunçarşılı, *Osmanlı Devletinin İlmiye Teşkilatı*, 24–37; İnalcık, *The Ottoman Empire: the Classical Age 1300–1600*, 167; Cornell H. Fleischer, *Bureaucrat and Intellectual in the Ottoman Empire: The Historian Mustafa Âli (1541–1600)* (Princeton, NJ: Princeton University Press, 1986), 26.

[88] According to Fahri Unan, between 1470 (when it was established) and 1603, 290 scholars of this high-status madrasa penned 520 treatises. In the seventeenth century, however, while the numbers of books written dropped to a mere 118, the number of scholars increased to 648. See Fahri Unan, 'Osmanlı

religious functionaries) was institutionalised under a few aristocratic families – a phenomenon depicted by Madeline Zilfi as 'unionising'.[89] But rather than heralding a creative stability, this ramification had an adverse effect and slackened Ottoman intellectual life in irrecoverable manner.

The intention here is not to deny the opulent cultural life of the Empire after the 'golden age'. The seventeenth century witnessed renowned specimens of Ottoman prose drawn up by the likes of Veysi and Nergisi.[90] It was also around this time that poets, influenced by *sebk-i Hindi* (Indian style), penned the finest pieces of metaphysical poetry.[91] The same century also saw the formation of a distinct Ottoman music canon, delineated from the Iranian tradition – a distinction which was perfected throughout the eighteenth and early nineteenth centuries.[92] Similar transformations can be observed in the field of architecture as well.[93] Nevertheless, these developments should be understood against the background of a contracting Ottoman cultural world. Even though the present scholarship tends to argue the fictitiousness of an 'iron curtain' separating the Ottoman world from the West,[94] it should be conceded that after the sixteenth century the

Medreselerinde İlmi Verimi ve İlim Anlayışını Etkileyen Amiller', *Türkiye Günlügü*, no. 58 (1999): 97.

89 Madeline C. Zilfi, 'Elite Circulation in the Ottoman Empire: Great Mollas of the Eighteenth Century', *Journal of the Economic and Social History of the Orient* 26, no. 3 (1983): 318.

90 Fahri İz, 'Ottoman and Turkish', in *Essays on Islamic civilization: Presented to Niyazi Berkes*, ed. Donald P. Little (Leiden: Brill, 1976), 118. Edward Browne, however, thinks that they should be interpreted in the framework of Persian literature because of the heavy Persian influence on their vocabulary. See Edward Granville Browne, *Literary History of Persia*, 4 vols., vol. IV (London: T. Fisher Unwin, 1924), 17.

91 See *Ottoman Lyric Poetry: An Anthology*, ed. Walter G. Andrews, Najaat Black, and Mehmet Kalpaklı (Seattle: University of Washington Press, 2006), 147–148; Günay Kut, 'Turkish Literature', *Culture and Learning in Islam* (2003): 268.

92 Walter Feldman, *Music of the Ottoman Court: Makam, Composition and the Early Ottoman Instrumental Repertoire* (Berlin: Verlag für Wissenschaft und Bildung, 1996), 496. Tanpınar, *XIX. Asır Türk Edebiyâtı Târîhi*, 68.

93 Shirine Hamadeh, 'Ottoman Expressions of Early Modernity and the 'Inevitable' Question of Westernization', *Journal of the Society of Architectural Historians* 63, no. 1 (2004): 33.

94 Donald Quataert, *The Ottoman Empire, 1700–1922* (Cambridge: Cambridge University Press, 2000), 75. In the second edition of this book, Quataert removed all the references to the absence of an 'iron curtain' and presented a

exchange of ideas between these cultures became extremely limited (trade, conversion), governed by atypical personalities (Hezârfen Hüseyin Efendi, Kâtip Çelebi), and to some degree incidental (wars and diplomatic exchanges).

But the second half of the nineteenth century brought a gradual end to this introverted picture. Even though the decline of the *kadi* court during the Tanzimat era makes extensive comparisons impossible, even a simple examination of three volumes from the end of our period (1878) demonstrates striking differences that took place in half a century.[95] Three changes are easily discernible: First, the derogatory language used for the non-Muslim elite was replaced with a proper legal parlance fitting to equal citizens.[96] The printed books, replacing the domination of manuscripts, emerged as the main reading medium

more neutral view of the cultural exchange with the outside world. Donald Quataert *The Ottoman Empire, 1700–1922*, 2nd edn. (Cambridge: Cambridge University Press, 2005), 75–77. Also see Suraiya Faroqhi, *The Ottoman Empire and the World Around It* (London: I. B. Tauris, 2004), 2. In her next book, like Quataert, Faroqhi also seems less sure about the imaginariness of the curtain. See Suraiya Faroqhi, *Subjects of the Sultan: Culture and Daily Life in the Ottoman Empire* (London: I. B. Tauris, 2005), 280. But the 'iron curtain' is still a very popular metaphor in the secondary literature. See Rifa'at 'Ali Abou Abou-El-Haj, *Formation of the Modern State: the Ottoman Empire, Sixteenth to Eighteenth Centuries* (New York: Syracuse University Press, 2005), 68. Gábor Ágoston, *Guns for the Sultan: Military Power and the Weapons Industry in the Ottoman Empire* (Cambridge: Cambridge University Press, 2005), 43. Gábor Ágoston, 'The Ottoman Empire and the Technological Dialogue Between Europe and Asia: The Case of Military Technology and Know-How in the Gunpowder Age', in *Science between Europe and Asia: Historical Studies on the Transmission, Adoption and Adaptation of Knowledge*, ed. Feza Günergün and Dhruv Raina (New York: Springer, 2011), 38.

95 For the decline of the *ulemâ* during the modernisation era, see Uriel Heyd, 'The Ottoman "Ulema and Westernization in the Time of Selim III and Mahmud II"', in *Studies in Islamic History and Civilization*, ed. Uriel Heyd (Jerusalem: Hebrew Univeristy, 1961), 63–96; Richard L. Chambers, 'The Ottoman Ulema and the Tanzimat', in *Scholars, Saints, and Sufis: Muslim Religious Institutions in the Middle East since 1500*, ed. Nikki R. Keddie (Berkeley: University of California Press, 1972), 33–46; Carter V. Findley, *Bureaucratic Reform in the Ottoman Empire: the Sublime Porte, 1789–1922* (Princeton, NJ: Princeton University Press 1980), 61–63; John Robert Barnes, *An Introduction to Religious Foundations in the Ottoman Empire* (Leiden: Brill, 1987), 118–153.

96 Before the Reform Decree of 1856, the deceased non-Muslims, for instance, were referred as *hâlik* (perished) in the probate records. After this date, we see them mentioned as *fevt* (died) like their Muslim fellow citizens, even though the word *vefât* (related to the Arabic word *wafa'* meaning fulfilment, redemption) was reserved only for Muslims.

for the Ottoman elite.[97] And maybe most importantly for the present purposes the variety of the book titles began to exhibit an unprecedented diversity and scope. Not only governors of important provinces such as Ömer Fevzi Pasha (d. 1878)[98] but also simple deputy *kadis* (*nâib*), or small clerks had their share of foreign literature.[99]

One can say with some degree of confidence that all of these developments had something to do with the profound changes that occurred in the Ottoman Empire during Ferruh Efendi's saeculum. According to Elias Gibb, Mahmud II transformed the 'old half-Asiatic half-Byzantine Turkey which had carried down into the nineteenth century many of the scenes and not a few of the principles of the days of the Seljuqs and the Paleologi'.[100] This was not an exaggeration of a romantic nineteenth-century scholar. Contemporaries, such as Kethüdâzâde Mehmed Efendi, were very cognizant of the overwhelming transformations that changed the face of the Empire forever.[101] The Ottoman world that İsmail Ferruh Efendi lived in saw tremendous changes which can be best defined as, or likened to, the end of a dominant paradigm in the Kuhnian sense – a stage characterised by lack of consensus.[102] Even though Thomas Kuhn developed his concept of 'paradigm shifts' to illustrate the phases of scientific knowledge,[103] there are unmistakable similarities between the development of 'scientific revolutions' and what was happening in the Ottoman Empire at the beginning of the nineteenth century.

In a nutshell, a scientific revolution emerges, in Kuhn's view, when scientists encounter abnormalities that cannot be explained by the

97 See, for instance, Ş.S.KISASKMAH. 1850, 21a.

98 He had hundreds of books in French. Mostly interested in history, among the books of Ömer Fevzi Pasha the complete absence of religious books is striking. Ş.S.KISASKMAH. 1853,13. He was also the grandfather of famous Behiç Erkin (d. 1961), republican statesman. About Ömer Fevzi Pasha's life and appointments, see Behiç Erkin, *Hâtırat 1876–1958* (İstanbul: Türk Tarih Kurumu, 2010), 1–3.

99 See, for instance, the estate of Üsküdar Nâibi Ahmed Hayreddin Efendi Ş. S.KISASKMAH. 1856, 30.

100 Gibb, *A History of Ottoman Poetry*, 311.

101 See, for instance, Emin Efendi, *Menâkıb-ı Kethüdâzâde el-Hac Mehmed Ârif Efendi*, 57, 312–313.

102 Thomas S. Kuhn, *The Structure of Scientific Revolutions*, 3rd edn. (Chicago: University of Chicago Press, 1996).

103 Ibid., 165. Thomas S. Kuhn, *The Essential Tension: Selected Studies in Scientific Tradition and Change* (Chicago: University of Chicago Press, 1977), 294.

generally established system of knowledge.[104] In this interpretation, the paradigm, which hitherto created all scientific explanations, is not merely a broad frame of principles but, rather, the 'disciplinary matrix' within which everything exists and all the institutions arise.[105] Against this background, certain abnormalities can be flouted as permissible miscalculations (such as defeats and territorial losses).[106] But when enough anomalies have ensued within the current paradigm – in the Ottoman example the Russian victory following the wars of 1768–1774 was probably the final blow; the scientific discipline is thrust into a state of crisis.

To weather the storm, as it were, new ideas, perhaps ones previously cast-off, are reassessed.[107] The reports presented to Selim III for comprehensive changes, which introduced the New Order (*Nizâm-i Cedîd*), can be, for instance, taken as an example of this intermediate stage.[108] Nonetheless eventually a new paradigm becomes inevitable because of the increasing sense of failure. This new paradigm gains its own adherents, and an intellectual 'battle' takes place between the cohorts of the new and the hold-outs of the old, such as the one that took place between Reşid Pasha and Dâmâd Said Pasha in 1840.[109] It is surprising to see how much a contemporary, Cevdet Pasha, described this confrontation in terms of old and the new (*efkâr-ı cedîde eshâbı*).[110] According to Kuhn, and as it took place in the Ottoman Empire, this state might continue for some time but ultimately the new paradigm establishes itself securely as a reference point (hence the paradigm shift) and the framework that governs the knowledge system completely changes.[111] From then on, champions of the *Ancien Régime*, if any left, bore the mark of the old and archaic.

104 Kuhn, *The Structure of Scientific Revolutions*, 52–56.

105 Ibid., 46–48. See also Giorgio Agamben, *The Signature of All Things on Method*, trans. Luca D'Isanto and Kevin Attell (New York: Zone Books, 2009), 11.

106 Kuhn, *The Structure of Scientific Revolutions*, 65, 68.

107 Ibid., 72.

108 *III. Selim'e Sunulan Islâhat Lâyıhaları*, ed. Ergin Çağman (İstanbul: Kitabevi, 2010).

109 See Kuhn, *The Structure of Scientific Revolutions*, 18–19.

110 Cevdet Paşa, *Tezâkir 1–12*, ed. Cavid Baysun, 4 vols., vol. I (Ankara: Türk Tarih Kurumu, 1991), 11.

111 Michel Foucault calls this 'discursive formation'. See Michel Foucault, *Archaeology of Knowledge*, trans. Alan Sheridan (London: Routledge, 2007), 130–132. Suggestively, Giorgio Agamben points out a tension between Foucault and Kuhn in their definitions of 'paradigm'. See Agamben, *The Signature of All Things on Method*, 12–13.

This simplified dichotomic model might look too rudimentary to explain the multifaceted and complex historical realities of the post-janissary era at first glance. For one, the 'battle' fought between two parties was not forthright at all times; the fronts were not always neatly drawn, nor did they coincide with the soldiers' expectations. The paradigms of different ages also co-existed for a long time – something that Kuhn finds rare but conceivable.[112] But all together, this scheme might be a better way of understanding the Ottoman modernity outside the restrictive Westernisation discourse.

Naturally no scientific revolution is implied to have arisen in the Ottoman Empire during the nineteenth century. Yet it is suggested that this paradigm shift, caused by a combination of internal and external pressures, reconditioned the way in which the Ottoman society perceived the world. One does not see, for instance, likes of the fantastic stories, emphasising Mahmud's sainthood in the official newspaper after his death. It would have been, in many people's eyes, absurd – or, if one compares the works of two palace chroniclers of subsequent generations, that of Şânîzâde and that of Cevdet Pasha, it is clear that they were written by people living in completely different worlds.[113] This was not only a question of a dated vocabulary. Şânîzâde was one of the most liberal men of the janissary epoch and Cevdet was among the most conservative reformers of the Tanzimat era. But still, the way they understood the Ottoman Empire indicates a clear transformation in their perceptions of the outside world. They operated in a 'different strategic field'.[114] In its social content, the difference was perhaps greater than what the French Revolution generated in the French society. The most significant outcome of this shift was that the agent of change, which had been up until then embodied by the Sultan, gravitated towards the bureaucratic elite.

[112] Kuhn, *The Structure of Scientific Revolutions*, xi.

[113] Cf. Franz Rosenthal, *Knowledge Triumphant: The Concept of Knowledge in Medieval Islam* (Leiden: Brill, 2007), 1.

[114] 'If the Physiocrats' analysis belongs to the same discourses as that of the Utilitarians, this is not because they lived in the same period, not because they confronted one another within the same society, not because their interests interlocked within the same economy, but because their two options sprang from one and the same distribution of the points of choice, one and *the same strategic field*'. Pierre Bourdieu, *The Rules of Art: Genesis and Structure of the Literary Field* (Stanford, CA: Stanford University Press, 1996), 197–198.

4 The Schooling of the Public

Introduction

This chapter adds to the analysis made in the previous chapters by examining the Ottoman Empire's reforms to state education. However, rather than summarising the achievements, or failures, of the Ottoman state in this endeavour, this chapter follows a selective approach and is concerned only with one dimension of this multi-faceted phenomenon: the scheme of the schooling of the public (*terbiye-i âmme*). Developed initially during the reign of Abdülmecid in 1845, this policy, to date, has never been adequately examined by historians. It was, however, the most ambitious and influential imperial formula of late Ottoman history.[1] Over years, *terbiye-i âmme* was gradually adopted by various elements of the society, including women intellectuals who linked its success to the expansion of female education.[2] Islamic modernists, on the other hand, presented it as the only possible way in which one could eliminate superstition from contemporary society.[3] The pashas of the Tanzimat era repeatedly pointed out its importance for the

[1] In his book on the modernisation of Ottoman education, Selçuk Akşin Somel only mentions it *en passant* without any connection with the subsequent events. See Somel, *The Modernization of Public Education*, 37, 58–59. In her book Emine Evered, on the other hand, does not mention it at all. Emine Evered, *Empire and Education Under the Ottomans: Politics, Reform and Resistance from the Tanzimat to the Young Turks* (London: I. B. Tauris, 2012).

[2] See Anonymous, "Kızların Tahsili Hakkında Bir Mütâlaa II', *Hanımlara Mahsûs Gazete*, 30 Teşrinievvel/10 November 1313/1895, 1. It can also appear in similar formats such as the 'schooling of the nation'. See Anonymous, "Kadınlarda Tahsîl ve Terbiye', *Hanımlara Mahsûs Gazete*, 27 Teşrîn-i Sânî/9 December 1313/1897, 2. Anonymous, 'Avrupa'da Terbiye-i Nisvâniyye', *Hanımlara Mahsûs Gazete*, 1 Kanûn-i Sâni/13 January 1313/1898, 2. 'It is clear', an unsigned article declared, 'at this day and age what occupies *public opinion* most is the schooling of the women'. See Anonymous, 'Terbiye-i Nisvân', *Hanımlara Mahsûs Gazete*, 3 Nisan/15 April 1313/1897, 5, emphasis mine.

[3] Muhammed Mekkî b. Azzûz, 'İslâmiyet'in Bahşettiği Hûrriyet-i Âmme', *Sırat-ı Müstakim* II, no. 27 (1327–1909): 2.

establishment of an 'Ottoman nation' in their private reports written for the Sultan (*lâyıha*).[4] It appeared in newspapers, in novels, and in translations.[5] Even after the collapse of the 'well-protected domains', the young republic, despite its explicit rejection of the Empire's many political and cultural premises, inherited this formula as the focal point for its own educational programmes.[6]

This chapter begins with a short account of the introduction of modern education into the Ottoman Empire, followed by a brief discussion of how this affected and changed the perceptions on mass education, or the schooling of the public. Next it examines the construction of the first Ottoman University, *Dârülfünun*, as an example of this changing attitude in governmental circles. This chapter then explores the emergence of new type of *cemiyets*, or societies, that began surfacing around the beginning of the 1860s while the pasha *konaks* were slowly losing their public character and monopoly over the opinion-making process. Here it is argued that these 'epistemic communities', by strengthening the Empire's sense of cultural identity and providing new forms of sociability, contributed to the establishment of new participatory spheres, civic awareness, and citizenship in the burgeoning Ottoman public sphere. Finally, it

[4] See, for instance, *lâyıhas* written by, respectively, Âli Pasha, Said Pasha (two of them), and Cevdet Pasha (last two). BOA, Y. EE. 91 / 29, 3 Şaban 1284 (30 November 1867), BOA, Y. EE. 83 / 70, 25 Ramazan 1297 (31 August 1880), BOA, Y. EE. 82 / 58, 2 Safer 1300 (13 December 1882), BOA, Y. EE. 39 / 5, 6 Rebiülahir 1327 (27 April 1909), BOA, Y. EE. 38 / 124, 6 Rebiülahir 1327 (27 April 1909).

[5] See, for instance, Emin Nihad Bey, *Müsameretnâme: Kapı Kethüdâsı Behçet Efendi İle Makbûle Hanım'ın Sergüzeşti*, 12 vols., vol. II (Istanbul: s.n., 1289/1872–1873), 3–4. Ahmed Rasim, *Fuhş-i Âtîk* (Istanbul: İkdam Matbaası, 1340/1922), 339. The last one, published during the final year of the Empire, had a pessimistic approach about the scheme: 'while the moral principal, which is called the schooling of the public was slowly losing its importance'. Also compare Nâmık Kemal's translation of Montesquieu and the original text: '*Oraca medeniyetin bidayet-i zuhûrunda terbiye-i umûmîyeyi ittihaz eden cumhûr reîsleri*'. Nâmık Kemal, 'Romalıların Esbab-ı İkbal ve Zevâli Hakkında Mülâhazat', *Mir'ât* I, no. 2 (1279/1863): 24. '*Dans la naissance des sociétés ce sont les chefs des républiques qui font l'institution*'. Montesquieu, *Considérations sur les causes de la grandeur des Romains et de leur décadence: aussi Dialogue de Sylla et d'Eucrate* (Paris: Didot, 1802), 3.

[6] The very first article of new Republic's education program was dedicated to '*terbiye-i umûmîye*'. See Nuran Dağlı and Belma Aktürk, Hükümetler ve Programları, 3 vols., vol. I (Ankara: TBMM Basımevi, 1988), 15.

concludes with a discussion of the changing attitude of the Ottoman government towards its public.

The Birth of Modern Education in the Ottoman Empire

The Russian victory following the wars of 1768–1774 was a turning point in the Ottoman scholastic world. The humiliating fiasco that the armada suffered at the hands of the Russian fleet in Çeşme (ancient Kysos) in 1770 discredited Ottoman nautical practices. As a result of this demoralising defeat, the Ottomans established the first modern military academy of *Hendesehâne*, or the Chamber of Mathematics, on 29 April 1775. This academy was placed under the charge of Baron François de Tott,[7] an Hungarian nobleman whose father fled to France during the Rakoczi Revolt (1703–1711), and Gilles Jean Marie Barazer de Kermorvan, a French military engineer and something of an adventurer.[8] These two men were assisted by Campbell Mustafa Ağa,[9]

[7] His memoir, published in French in 1784 and next year in English translation, was extremely, and according to Virginia Aksan 'malignly', influential in the formation of a negative Turkish image in Europe. François Tott, *Mémoires du Baron de Tott sur les Turcs et les Tartares*, 4 vols. (Amsterdam: s.n., 1784). François Tott, *Memoires of the Baron de Tott on the Turks and the Tartars*, 2 vols. (London: J. Jarvis, 1785). Virginia Aksan, 'Breaking the Spell of the Baron de Tott: Reframing the Question of Military Reform in the Ottoman Empire, 1760–1830', *The International History Review* 24, no. 2 (2002): 254.

[8] See Jean Bérenger, 'Les vicissitudes de l'alliance militaire franco-turque (1520–1800)', in *Guerres et paix en Europe centrale aux époques moderne et contemporaine: Mélanges d'histoire des relations internationales offerts à Jean Bérenger*, ed. Daniel Tollet (Paris: Presses de l'université de Paris-Sorbonne, 2003), 321. It seems that a year later he offered his services to the United States during the American War of Independence. Thomas Balch cites Chevalier de Kermovan as one of the oldest French volunteers recommended to the Congress as an engineer. A personal friend of Benjamin Franklin wrote to him 'I seriously think that Chevalier de Kermovan is one of the best men your country can obtain ... he is as ready to expose himself to every danger as if he were commander-in-chief. He seems to me well acquainted with the military art'. Thomas Balch, *The French in America during the War of Independence of the United States, 1777–1783*, trans. Thomas Willing Balch (Philadelphia: Porter & Coates, 1891).

[9] Some information on him can be found in William Eton's survey of the Ottoman Empire: 'In speaking of their artillery I ought not to omit mentioning an Englishman in the service of the porte, his name is Campbell, and he is related to a great Scotch family. When very young, he came to Constantinople (the cause of his quitting Scotland is said to be a duel) and without making himself known to any European, he went to the porte and turned Turk.' William Eton, *A Survey of the Turkish Empire* (London: T. Cadell and W. Davies, 1798), 73–74 fn.

a Scottish convert and Seyyid Hasan Hoca, an Algerian who had demonstrated some usefulness in the Ottoman navy.[10] This diversity in terms of the backgrounds of the staff was not a coincidence, and points to a deliberate Ottoman desire to expand the range of their scholastic knowledge and expertise.[11]

This small academy, converted into the Naval Engineering School in 1789, was followed by a sister college, the Military Engineering School, founded in 1795 under the supervision of Swedish experts.[12] The internal revolutions of the palace (the assassinations of Selim III and Alemdâr Mustafa Pasha) and mounting janissary pressure to eliminate anything with the potential to rival their monopoly had blocked these types of innovations for nearly three decades. However, following the abolition of the corps in 1826, numerous institutions based on Western-style curriculums began to proliferate.[13] The Imperial Medical School (1827), the Imperial Music School (1831), and the School of Military Sciences (1834) were all established in relatively short order, and were celebrated with ostentatious opening ceremonies. These new institutions, especially the Medical School, constituted a significant channel through which cutting-edge new forms of knowledge and expertise were transmitted to the Empire.[14] The Sultan

10 Giambatista Toderini, who visited the Empire around that time, was quite impressed with his talents: 'the first professor is an Algerian, Seyyid Hasan Hodga. Apart from Arabic and Turkish, he knew English, Italian and French. Very habile mariner who knows the best books of Europe and the instruments of navigation'. Abbé Toderini, *De la littérature des Turcs*, trans. Abbé Cournand, 2 vols., vol. I (Paris: Chez Poinçot Libraire, 1789), 162. Later he was executed with the order of Abdülhamid I and his book collection was taken by the recently founded Naval Engineering School. See Fevzi Kurtoğlu, *Deniz Mektepleri Târîhçesi* (İstanbul: Deniz Matbaası, 1941), 1. For the libraries of these institutions, also see Kemal Beydilli, *Türk Bilim ve Matbaacılık Târîhinde Mühendishâne: Mühendishâne Matbaası ve Kütüphânesi* (İstanbul: Eren, 1995).

11 Even though Daniel Panzac writes about the 'disastrous conditions' of the Naval School during the reign of Mahmud II, there was also a certain level of success. In 1829, the Imperial shipyard managed to construct the largest sailing warship of the time, *Mahmudiye*. See, respectively, Daniel Panzac, 'Entre carrière et politique: Les officiers de marine ottomans a la fin de l'empire (1863–1923)', *Turcica*, no. 33 (2001): 63. Lawrence Sondhaus, *Naval Warfare 1815–1914* (London: Routledge, 2001), 17.

12 Mesut Uyar and Edward J. Erickson, *A Military History of the Ottomans: From Osman to Atatürk* (Santa Barbara, CA: Praeger Security International, 2009), 123.

13 Somel, *The Modernization of Public Education*, 20–23.

14 See, for instance, Charles MacFarlane, *Kismet: or, The Doom of Turkey* (London: Thomas Bosworth, 1853), 99. Also see Mahmud II's address to the

also launched a scheme for the creation of student missions that sent 150 pupils, mainly to Paris but also to other parts of Europe such as England, to study diverse sciences.[15] Later on some of these students, Macfarlane pointed out, were 'favourably known even at Cambridge'.[16]

The increasing awareness of new, innovative Western-style education programmes espoused by statesmen helped to fashion a new understanding among the Tanzimat reformers. The Ottoman elite, who were at best uninterested and at worst hostile to the idea of widespread education,[17] began to see formal training as the only way to defend the Empire against further European encroachment. By the 1860s, public education began to be presented as the tonic to every social ailment.[18] It was the avenue through which the reformers believed they could acculturate the lower classes, and inculcate those values deemed appropriate for the new Ottoman society into non-Muslims.[19] Intellectuals saw it as a magical panacea, which would awaken public opinion in an indolent society.[20] According to Ali Pasha (d. 1871), five-time Grand Vizier, pushing forward education

students where he explained how they had to study in French for the time being as it was the language of the science. See Rıza Tahsîn, *Mir'ât-ı Mekteb-i Tıbbiyye* 2 vols., vol. I (Dersaâdet: Kader Matbaası, 1328/1910–1911), 18–22.

15 Mahmud Cevâd İbnü'ş-Şeyh Nâfi, *Maârif-i Umûmîye Nezâreti Târîhçe-i Teşkilat ve İcraatı*, ed. Muhammed Ali bin Kemal (İstanbul: Matbaa-i Âmire, 1338–1919/1920), 4–5.

16 MacFarlane, *Kismet*, 87.

17 See the views of Rifat Pasha in Somel, *The Modernization of Public Education*, 62.

18 See, for instance, Münif Efendi, 'Mukayese-i İlm ü Cehl', *Mecmûa-ı Fünun* I, no. 1 (1279/1862): 21–34. Münif Efendi, 'Ehemmiyet-i Terbiye-i Sıbyan', *Mecmûa-ı Fünun* I, no. 5 (1279/1862): 176–85. Anonymous, 'Dâire-i Maârif-i Umûmîye', *Mecmûa-ı Fünun* I, no. 24 (1280/1864): 495–99. As an earlier example also see Sâmî Efendi, *Avrupa Risâlesi*, 53–54.

19 BOA., Y. EE. 91 / 29, 3 Şaban 1284 (30 November 1867).

20 Hersekli Arif Hikmet Bey (d. 1903), one of the founders of the Society of Poets, once wrote: 'from general experiences, it has been understood that most mischief in human societies spring from idleness and idleness itself is induced by want of education. Consequently, countries, which attained true civilization (*medeniyet-i sahiha*), put their utmost exertions in making education widespread. Naturally with the proliferation of science and education, ignorance and vagrancy decrease, the individuals of the community are put into training and learning, and [as a result a] public opinion awakens'. Hersekli Arif Hikmet, 'Levayihü'l-Hikem'den: Lâyıha', in *Müntahabat-ı Bedayi-yi Edebiye: Mensur Kısmı / Müntehibi*, ed. Bulgurluzâde Rıza (Istanbul: Kader Matbaası, 1327/1910), 155–156.

in the Empire was almost a religious duty. 'If this is not materialised, we cannot stand out and will have to surrender. Whatever we do', he stressed, 'even if we put up a wall encircling us like the Great Wall of China, nations with knowledge will beat us down and deprive us of everything that we have, one by one'.[21]

The Schooling of the Public

As early as 1824, Mahmud II introduced compulsory education to Istanbul. Even though what he had in mind was mostly religious teaching through *sibyan mektebleri* (primary schools), there was a still certain sense of common good visible throughout the *hatt* that he issued.[22] Some years later, Mahmud Cevad explained this move as the government's attempt to create some sort of cultural levelling and standardisation among a diverse population. 'Naturally', he reasoned, 'it is not possible to have a union of opinion *(ittihâd-ı efkâr)* among men who grow and develop from different springs. As a result of the lack of schools in the Ottoman state, men were not brought up to have any unity of ideas. Hence the vessel of the state remained shaken for a long time amidst the waves of controversy'.[23]

The extension of education was also a crucial concern of the Council of Public Works (*Meclis-i Umûr-u Nâfia*) established in 1838 and functioned under the close supervision of Mahmud II.[24] A committee

21 BOA., Y. EE. 91 / 29, 3 Şaban 1284 (30 November 1867).

22 Such as '*ekser-i halk* or *ekser-i nâs* (most of the people)', '*herkes* (everybody)', or '*ale'l-umûm* (publicly)'. For the whole text, see Cevdet Paşa, *Târîh-i Cevdet*, 12 vols., vol. XII (Istanbul: Matbaa-i Osmaniye, 1301/1883–1884), 277–79; Nâfi, *Maârif-i Umûmîye Nezâreti*, 1–3.

23 Ibid., 5. Cf. 'A common opinion cannot be developed before people have an occasion to discuss with one another, before they have been drawn from the isolation of lonely thought into a public world in which individual opinion can be sharpened and tested in discussion with others.' Lewis A. Coser, *Men of Ideas: A Sociologist's View* (New York: Free Press, 1965), 20.

24 This is how Stanford Shaw chose to translate it. See Stanford J. Shaw and Ezel Kural Shaw, *History of the Ottoman Empire and Modern Turkey: Reform, Revolution, and Republic: The Rise of Modern Turkey, 1808–1975*, 2 vols., vol. II (Cambridge: Cambridge University Press, 1977), 37. Niyazi Berkes calls it 'the Board of Useful Affairs'. *Niyazi Berkes, The Development of Secularism in Turkey* (London: Routledge, 1964), 105. It should be noted that Mahmud II followed the Council very closely and every decision was presented to him for approval. See, for instance, BOA, HAT 490/24017, 17 Safer 1245 (2 May 1839).

of its members was appointed to draft suitable resolutions regarding public education, and the result was published in the official newspaper.[25] The report accentuated the importance of learning in daily affairs and alluded to the will of the government to take action in order to repair the negligence of the past. The uneducated, the statement asserted, 'not only would have difficulties in gaining profit and income, but they would also not be able to advance in the trade that they actively pursued. They would have nothing to do with the state under its auspices they come about and they would not know anything about the love of one's country (*hubb-ı vatan*)'.[26]

Yet the first serious attempts towards this goal were realised during the reign of Sultan Abdülmecid, who superseded his royal father in July 1839. At the beginning of 1845, in a *hatt* that was later published in the official newspaper, Abdülmecid registered in a rather dramatic tone his frustration with how his reform programmes had been thwarted. 'My loyal and reliable vizier', he wrote:

> I believe everybody construed that the idea of justice that we have avowed and proliferated through my various imperial decrees and our compassionate orders that we have shadowed closely since the beginning of my regal enthronement are only for the welfare of the country and subjects, and also by the same token to perpetuate our sublime religion as well as our exalted state. Consequently even though it is not deemed necessary to recite and remind them again, it cannot be denied that despite all the various royal attempts and enterprises aimed at the realisation of this auspicious undertaken – *I do not know if this is because nobody has their heart in the work* – up until now from our various royal ambitions only military reforms have enjoyed a certain level of success.[27]

The Sultan, after complaining about how 'his regal sorrow and grief' were abysmal, and how 'his royal peace and ease' were stolen, urged the formation of a committee composed of scholars and ministers to

[25] See Mahmud II's order for the report to be published in the official newspaper, BOA, HAT 494/24232, 14 Zilkade 1254 (29 January 1839).

[26] Anonymous, 'Meclis-i Umûr-i Nafi'anın Lâyıhası', *Takvîm-i Vekâyi*, 21 Zilkade/5 February 1254/1839, 1. The full text was also given in Cevad Nâfi, *Maârif-i Umûmîye Nezâreti*, 6–10.

[27] See BOA, A. AMD. 374, 4 Muharrem 1261 (13 January 1845), 30, emphasis mine. For the same text, see Anonymous, 'Sûret-i Hattı-ı Hümâyun-ı Şevket-Makrûn', *Takvîm-i Vekâyi*, 12 Muharrem (21 January) 1261/1845, 1. For its French translation see Anonymous, 'Hat Imperial', *Journal de Constantinople*, 21 Janvier 1845.

come up with a plan. More importantly, however, he also outlined a new direction for future reforms. The solution he proposed was *terbiyet-i âmme* through the construction and invention of new schools.

Âmme can be simply translated, as it is done through the text, as 'public'. Yet it is difficult to render the word *terbiye(t)* with its various nuances into English. It is an Arabic word that fuses education and punishment into one compound.[28] Ottomans, throughout ages, mostly used the term with negative connotations in order to denote 'chastising' or 'disciplining'. Armed bandits or unruly janissaries were always corrected with *terbiye*.[29] But the term did not simply mean the retribution for the wicked; it was also an attitude that enabled to escape from punishment. While rowdy public behaviour, for instance, was severely penalised, onlookers putting their *terbiye* on remained safe from the sultanic infliction (*fakat terbiyesi ile seyrangâhları seyr ü temâşâya gidenlere ilişilmemesi*).[30] A disgraced vizier, like Saadeddin Paşazâde Nasuh Paşa, could gain favour with the Sultan again through the acceptance of *terbiye*.[31] Around the beginning of the nineteenth century, the expression began to be used more in reference to the schooling and education of soldiers.[32] But still the Serbian rebels or difficult *â'yâns* had to be disciplined through its mechanisms.[33] During the Greek War of Independence (1821–1832), an Ottoman fleet was sent to Samos to subject its inhabitants to *terbiye*.[34] For practicality, this

[28] In the nineteenth century, famous lexicographer James Redhouse translated it as 'the doing something to a thing in order to improve its quality; education; sauce for meats; preparation for stuffs; good and polite manners; punishment'. Redhouse, *An English and Turkish Dictionary in Two Parts*, 580.

[29] For an order sent to the Governor of Damascus for '*mevâli urbânın terbiyesi için*' or to knock sense into the heads of the nomadic desert tribes, see BOA, C.. DH.. 139/6945, 29 Muharrem 1134 (19 November 1721). See also an order sent to Vidin Muhâfızı Yeğen Ali Paşa for the *terbiye* of janissaries who were in preparation for a mutiny, BOA, C..AS.. 1138/50536, 29 Şaban 1193 (11 September 1779).

[30] BOA, C..ZB.. 70/3467, 30 Muharrem 1177 (10 August 1763).

[31] BOA, C..DH.. 96/4794, 29 Zilhicce 1201 (12 October 1787).

[32] See, for instance, BOA, C..AS.. 108/4866, 29 Muharrem 1219 (10 May 1804), BOA, C..AS.. 1220/54764, 1 Receb 1219 (6 October 1804), BOA, C..ML.. 524/ 21407, 12 Şaban 1219 (16 November 1804).

[33] For an order given to Vezir Halil Paşa for the *terbiye* of Serbian rebels, see BOA, C..AS.. 1027/45046, 25 Safer 1222 (4 May 1807). Also see BOA, C..ADL. 75/ 4526, 23 Zilhicce 1208 (22 July 1794) where former *â'yân* of Štip, Nâzıroğlu Kör Ahmed, was banished from his land till he assumed his *terbiye*.

[34] BOA, C..AS.. 2/59, 25 Şaban 1236 (28 May 1821).

book employs the term in order to refer to 'schooling', but its other connotations should also be kept in mind since *terbiye* conveys the deliberate attitude of the Ottoman state towards its 'public'.

Pursuant to the Sultan's encouragement, the Supreme Council (*Meclis-i Vâlâ*) instructed to set up an Ad Hoc Committee (*Meclis-i Muvakkat*) to look into the schooling of the public.[35] After deliberations lasting over a year, the report prepared by the committee was published in the official newspaper with the 'cover letter' of the Sultan himself.[36] In this letter, Abdülmecid expressed his appreciation for the dedication that everyone exhibited towards the rule of law (*usûl-i adliye*), and declared his faith that the Empire would survive these temporary difficulties. He reminded readers that his major concern was to adorn the 'subject and the people of *our Sublime State* with justice and prosperity'. Such diplomatic language, more becoming to a politician than a sultan, is interesting to note here. The Sublime State, which had been the personal estate of the reigning sultan up until then and had always been used as in first person possessive form (*Devlet-i Âliyem*), was slowly turning into a common property.

In terms of providing the requisite educational and intellectual skills to the general population for the betterment of society, the report proposed a three-stage plan of action: a reform of primary schools, the improvement of middle-school curriculum and the establishment of a university. These proposals were presented to the Sultan and approved forthwith as, the report emphasised 'this beneficial schooling of the public scheme (*terbiyet-i umûmîye*) has the force of being virtually the foundation of the state. Those who are not aware of learning and science cannot possibly know the love of motherland (*muhabbet-i vataniye*) nor would they know the meaning of divine or daily justice. They would stay, [the statement pointed out] in the state of animal existence'.[37]

35 BOA, İ..MSM. 25/653, 11 Safer 1261 (19 February 1845). The committee began working at the beginning of March. See BOA, İ..DH.. 99/4972, 24 Safer 1261 (4 March 1845).

36 Anonymous, 'Sûret-i Münife-i Hatt-ı Hümâyun', *Takvîm-i Vekâyi*, 27 Receb/21 June 1262/1846, 1. Ali Fuat Bey argued that especially important *hatts* were 'edited' by the Sublime Porte before they were put in the newspapers. Fuat, 'Ricâli tanzimattan Rifat Paşa', 3.

37 Anonymous, 'Sûret-i Münife-i Hatt-ı Hümâyun', 2.

A Public University

At the beginning of June, shortly after the publication of the report, the government began to look for a suitable location for the construction of the university.[38] The Italian-Swiss architect Giuseppe Fossati (d. 1891), who was assisting his older brother Gaspare (d. 1883) for the construction of the Russian Embassy in Istanbul, was named chief architect for the project.[39] The site that was eventually chosen was quite symbolic and signified the transformation the Empire was undergoing: 'Abdul Medjid had decreed that a stately university should be erected near to the mosque of Santa Sophia in an open square on site of one of the barracks of the destroyed Janissaries.'[40]

According to MacFarlane, who foresaw the failure of the enterprise from the very beginning in February 1848, the university was originally supposed to be 'provided with most eminent professors and endowed with funds the maintenance of a vast number of students ... The stone was laid, [he added], with great pomp and ceremony and with a flourishing of trumpets by the Pera journalists'.[41] Yet like many other Tanzimat projects what had started as a promising idea quickly turned into a quagmire. The edifice of the structure cost vastly more time and money than the government had originally anticipated.[42] The Qajars, for instance, though taking their cue from the Ottoman example, completed their '*Dar-ul Funun*' at the end of 1851.[43] That same year, the Ottomans were still struggling to train teachers, which they reckoned, was the 'source and the soul of the schooling of the public'.[44] The timing of the project also proved to be less than perfect. The financial resources for one had to be vigilantly

[38] BOA, İ..MSM. 25/656, 18 Cemaziyelahir 1262 (13 June 1846).

[39] BOA, İ..MSM 25/686, 12 Safer 1264 (19 January 1848). About the Fossati Brothers, see Zeynep Çelik, *The Remaking of Istanbul: Portrait of an Ottoman City in the Nineteenth Century* (Berkeley: University of California Press, 1986), 133–140.

[40] MacFarlane, *Turkey and Its Destiny II*, 292. [41] Ibid.

[42] The Sublime Porte probably thought that the architect was trying to embezzle money, which might have been the case. For an order suspending the payments that were not estimated in the original project, see BOA, A.}MKT.MVL. 64/8, 24 Ramazan 1269 (1 July 1853).

[43] Maryam Dorreh Ekhtiar, 'The Dar al-Funun: Educational Reform and Cultural Development in Qajar Iran' (PhD diss., New York University, 1994), 116.

[44] '*Dârülmuallimin ise terbiyet-i umûmîyenin menbaı ve ruhu mesabesinde olduğundan*'. BOA. İMVL. 195/6008, 9 Safer 1267 (14 December 1850).

marshalled as Abdülmecid had already embarked upon the construction of a lavish, European-style palace, Dolmabahçe, in 1843.[45] The outbreak of the Crimean War also diverted the attention of the reformers for a few years. During this conflict, the unfinished building first served as a hospital for wounded French soldiers,[46] and was later converted into an asylum for Muslim refugees from Dagestan.[47]

Near the end of the 1850s, the relationship between the palace and the architect worsened. Abdülmecid, dreadfully concerned with the expenses of palace women, must have been disheartened by the unending project.[48] By the beginning of the 1860s, Fossati mounted an increasing number of complaints over his unpaid salary. In 1861 the palace finally terminated his contract.[49] Only a few months later, Sultan Abdülmecid died at the age of thirty-eight. Had it not been for the colossal, albeit unfinished, building constantly reminding the failure of the enterprise, it is easy to imagine the idea of a university being completely written off for the time being. As Osman Ergin pointed out, ownership of a building was vital for the endurance of official bodies in the Ottoman Empire.[50] This is why military schools always attained a certain level of success, and civil schools did not. Hence its imposing physical presence, which had been originally the cause of the problems, saved the project from possible termination.

[45] It could be finished only in 1856. See Pars Tuğlacı, *The Role of the Balian Family in Ottoman Architecture* (Istanbul: Yeni Çığır Kitâbevi, 1990), 113–116. The British Palace was also being constructed around the same time and interestingly Stratford Canning, the ambassador, had problems with his architect too: 'the costs of the new embassy continued to mount, and in 1851 the grounds were still a building site. Canning had had enough of the architect'. Geoff Berridge, *British Diplomacy in Turkey, 1583 to the Present: A Study in the Evolution of the Resident Embassy* (Leiden: Brill, 2009), 18. It is probable that the logistics that Istanbul could provide around that time was not enough for the increasing construction demand.

[46] BOA, İ..HR.. 118/5781, 7 Cemaziyelahir 1271 (25 February 1855), BOA, A.} AMD. 60/28, 1271 (1854/1855).

[47] BOA, İ..MVL. 439/19469/M, 29 Rebiülahir 1277 (14 November 1860).

[48] Cevdet Paşa, *Tezâkir 13–20*, 4.

[49] For his complaints about the unpaid salaries, see BOA, HR.MKT. 328/41, 17 Şaban 1276 (10 March 1860), BOA, HR.MKT. 335/52, 29 Şevval 1276 (20 May 1860), BOA, HR.MKT. 337/25, 15 Zilkade 1276 (4 June 1860), BOA, HR.MKT. 348/61, 24 Safer 1277 (11 September 1860), BOA, HR.MKT. 357/15, 8 Cemaziyelevvel 1277 (22 November 1860). For the termination of the contract, see BOA, İ..MVL. 447/19893, 23 Ramazan 1277 (4 April 1861).

[50] Ergin, *Türk Maârif Târîhi*, 302.

Figure 4.1 A view of the Ottoman *Darülfünun* positioned between Hagia Sophia and Blue Mosque: Unfortunately (or perhaps as some said fortunately) the building burnt down completely in 1933.
Abdullah Frères, [*Light house at Ahırkapı*]. With the permission of Istanbul University, Rare Book Collection, 90813.

In 1862 the state returned to the question of 'schooling of the public', which, according to an article in the official newspaper, constituted the 'very fulcrum of the civilized countries (*ümrân-ı memleketin esâs-ı kavisi*)'.[51] Sâmî Pasha, who was appointed as the Minister of Education to prepare necessary rules and regulations consistent with this policy, set to work with great enthusiasm.[52] Under Sultan

[51] Anonymous, '[Ümrân-ı Memleketin Esâs-ı Kavisi]', *Takvîm-i Vekâyi*, 26 Zilhicce/24 June 1278/1862, 3.

[52] '*Şeref-sunuh-u sudûr buyrulan irâde-i seniyye-i cenâb-i mülükanenin iktizâ-i âlisi üzerine terbiye-i umûmîye için derecât-ı mütenevvieden olarak memâlik-i mahrûsa-i hazret-i şâhânede her bir sınıfın tedrîs ve tâlimleri için bulunacak kâffe-i mekâtibin nizâmat ve usûlüne nezâret etmek üzere Maârif-i Umûmîye Nâzırı nâsb ve tayin bulunmuş olan Meclis-i Âli-i Tanzimat azâ-ı fihâmından Devletlü Sâmî Paşa hazretlerinin…*' BOA, İ.MMS 28/1204 1280/1863. This was the beginning of what one might call a ministerial dynasty. His son,

Abdülaziz, who was anxious to show the progressive face of his reign, the Ottoman university finally began its public career – though somewhat precipitately.[53]

While Ottoman historians have tended to translate '*Dârülfünun*' as 'university' (literally, 'House of Sciences' in Arabic), it functioned initially more in the manner of early modern Europe's humanitarian seminaries. It was not a degree-granting body but, rather, a government organisation that was put together in haste to deliver public lectures (*ders-i âmm*) on various branches of literature and science. Even though Niyazi Berkes argued that the idea was probably inspired by the *conferences publiques* initiated in France by Jean Victor Duruy,[54] the phenomenon was a continuation, or rather an extension, of an old practice.[55] Ottoman chroniclers, including Mecdi Mehmed Efendi (d. 1591) and Selaniki (d. 1600), began to refer to this term, *ders-i âmm*, in the sixteenth century to indicate open lectures, taking place either in mosques or in one of the adjacent structures – such as libraries or madrasas, for the Muslim population.[56] As Lisa Golombek

Abdüllâtîf Suphi Paşa, also became the Minister of Education, so did his grandson, Hamdullah Suphi Tanrıöver who actually served as the first Minister of Education of the Turkish Republic.

53 'When Abdülaziz Khan succeeded to the throne, he said to Rıza Pasha, "I cannot, like the brother did, have fun with girls and boys in the palace. Put me to work (*beni işe alıştırın*)".' Cevdet Paşa, *Tezâkir 13–20*, 151.

54 'The French educational reformer and Minister of Education who played the role of the first foreign educational advisor to the Turkish Government.' *Berkes, The Development of Secularism in Turkey*, 179. Mehmed Ali Ayni asserted that the idea of giving free public lectures came from the Grand Vizier, Keçecizâde Fuâd Pasha. Mehmet Ali Ayni, *Dârülfünun Târîhi*, ed. Aykut Kazancıgil (Istanbul: Kitâbevi, 2007), 13. These are not of course mutually exclusive. But the role of the French reformer should not be exaggerated as he left Istanbul rather hastily because his suggestions were not followed. See M. Challemel-Lacour, 'Les hommes d'état de la Turquie – Aali-Pacha et Fuâd-Pacha', *Revue des Deux Mondes* 73, no. Février (1868): 887.

55 *Tasvîr-i Efkâr*, one of the first Ottoman newspapers, did not miss this connection and took the tradition all the way back to Ibn-i Sina (Avicenna) who, they claimed, taught sciences to public (*umûma fünun tedrîs ederdi*). 'And now', the article continued, 'in Europe ministers who are competent give public lectures … as it is their duty of gratitude to make public beneficiary from the fruits of knowledge that they have gained thanks to the life of civilization (*hayât-ı medeniye*)'. Anonymous, 'Havâdis-i Dâhiliye: Pay-i Taht', *Tasvîr-i Efkâr*, 9 Şaban/30 January 1279/1863, 1.

56 Taşköprülüzâde Ahmed bin Mustafa, *Tercüme-i Şakayık-ı Nu'maniye*, trans. Mecdi Mehmed Efendi (Istanbul: Dar'üt-Tabaat ül-Amire, 1269/1852), 57. Selaniki Mustafa Efendi, *Târîh-i Selaniki*, 2 vols., vol. II (Istanbul: İstanbul

points out, in the Islamic world 'one of the major functions of the large mosque was teaching; [and] eminent scholars in various branches of the religious sciences held 'chairs' in the great mosques'.[57]

In the following centuries and following this tradition, the Ottoman state commissioned *ders-i âmms* more and more, and chiefly during the period of three sacred months of the Islamic calendar, in order to convey useful religious information (*va'z ve nâsihat*).[58] Mahmud II, who was as mentioned in the first chapter rather public-minded, even tried to manipulate the institution in an effort to attract popular support and build legitimacy for his controversial reform programmes.[59] With the foundation of the university, however, the term was used for the first time in a new way, devoid of religious connotations.[60]

It is rather interesting to follow the contemporary discussions taking place in the burgeoning Ottoman press. *Mecmuâ-i Fünun* for instance, around this same time established as the first scientific journal, announced the forthcoming inaugural lecture with great excitement.[61] Mehmet Derviş Pasha, a London-educated statesman,[62] was going to deliver the first talk on physics under the supervision of Edhem Pasha, one of the four pupils sent to Paris in 1830 as a part of the first Ottoman student mission.[63] The article highlighted the importance of

Üniversitesi Edebiyât Fakültesi Yayınları, 1989), 748. The reference to this institution increased dramatically in the following century See, for instance, Şeyhi Mehmed Efendi, *Eş-Şekaiku'n-Nu'maniyye ve Zeyilleri: Vekâyiü'l-fudala*, ed. Abdülkadir Özcan (Istanbul: Çağrı Yayınları, 1989), 106, 46, 291, 482, 509, 27, 77.

57 Lisa Golombek and Donald Wilber, *The Timurid Architecture of Iran and Turan*, 2 vols., vol. I (Princeton, NJ: Princeton University Press, 1992), 45.

58 BOA, A.}DVN. 56.3, 29 Zilhicce 1265 (15 November 1849).

59 Esra Yakut, *Şeyhülislâmlık: Yenileşme Döneminde Devlet ve Din* (Istanbul: Kitâbevi, 2005), 157. İsmail Hakkı Uzunçarşılı, 'Asâkir-i Mansure'ye Fes Giydirilmesi Hakkında Sadr-ı Âzam Takrîri ve II. Mahmud'un Hatt-ı Humayunu (2 resmle birlikte)', *Belleten* XVIII, no. 70 (1954): 229.

60 This was probably again an example of what Marx called the conjuring up the 'spirits of the past' to 'borrow from them names, battle cries and costumes in order to present the new scene of world history in this time-honoured disguise'. See Marx, *The Eighteenth Brumaire of Louis Bonaparte*, 10.

61 And with specific references to the schooling of the public, see Münif Efendi, 'Dârülfünun'da Ders-i Âmm Küşâdı', *Mecmûa-ı Fünun* I, no. 5 (1279/1862): 260.

62 BOA, İ..MVL. 481/21829, 17 Şaban 1279 (7 February 1863).

63 Compare with Muhammad Ali who sent his first students to Italy in 1809 and Abbas Mirza to England in 1811. Bernard Lewis, *The Muslim Discovery of Europe* (New York: Norton, 2001), 133. Vanessa Martin, 'An Evaluation of

physics for the 'extension of opinion', and promised, as much as possible, a jargon-free language (*ta'birat-i vâziha*).[64]

When the day arrived, three hundred people were present at the hall.[65] Derviş Pasha began his address with a eulogy to the Sultan for the importance he placed on the 'schooling of the public'. His lecture focused on the characteristics of 'air, electrical power and other similar things'.[66] By using 'special equipment', he carried out several experiments in front of the audience. It should be noted that in the Western world, especially before the second half of the nineteenth century, the distinction between entertainment and education was more of a notion than a reality.[67] As a result, amusing 'itinerant lecturers' dominated public talks throughout the eighteenth and early parts of the nineteenth centuries.[68] The Ottoman example should also be understood within this framework. Even though Derviş Pasha was a serious scholar and was single-handedly responsible for the introduction of modern physics and chemistry into the Ottoman lands through his publications,[69] his conferences were decidedly watered-down. Osman Ergin, for instance, called the content of his talks 'rather rudimentary and superficial'.[70] The Pasha was aware that science and technology were not immediately relevant to spectators in Istanbul, and that it was therefore

Reform and Development of the State in the Early Qājār Period', *Die Welt des Islams* 36, no. 1 (1996): 21.

64 Münif Efendi, 'Dârülfünun'da Ders-i Âmm Küşâdı', 259.

65 Münif Efendi, 'Dârülfünun'da Ders-i Âmm Vuku'-u Küşâdı', *Mecmûa-ı Fünun* I, no. 7 (1279/1862): 301.

66 Ibid.

67 Ian Inkster, 'The Public Lecture as an Instrument of Science Education for Adults — the Case of Great Britain, c. 1750 – 1850', *Paedagogica Historica* 20, no. 1 (1980): 83.

68 J. L. Heilbron, *Elements of Early Modern Physics* (Berkeley: University of California Press, 1982), 154.

69 See Feza Günergun, 'Derviş Mehmed Emin Pacha (1817–1879), serviteur de la science et de l'Etat ottoman', in *Médecins et ingénieurs ottomans à l'âge des nationalismes*, ed. Méropi Anastassiadou-Dumont (Paris: Maisonneuve et Larose & Institut Français d'Etudes Anatoliennes, 2003), 171–83. Hyde Clark also mentions him in the following manner: 'Dervish Pasha, Director-General of Mines, a man educated in the schools of England and France, is commonly the President of the Council of Public Instruction, and sometimes the under secretary. He takes an active and zealous interest. He was one of the promoters of the scheme of a university and gave public lectures on natural philosophy.' Hyde Clarke, 'On Public Instruction in Turkey', *Journal of the Statistical Society of London* 30, no. 4 (1867): 513.

70 Ergin, *Türk Maârif Târîhi*, 554.

crucial for his lectures to be entertaining in order to attract a sizable audience. He transmitted, for instance, an electric shock through the body of a volunteer who ended up emitting a blue glow – iterating what Jean Antoine Nollet, member of the *Académie Royale des Sciences*, had done with royal guards more than a century earlier to amuse Louis XV in Versailles.[71]

This approach turned out to be very successful. For the second and third lectures approximately five hundred people attended – a number that was far beyond the capacity of the hall (*ve dershânenin bundan ziyâde tahammülü olmadığından*).[72] Attendance at these lectures turned into something like an index of civility for Istanbul gentlemen. Grand Vizier Keçecizâde Fuâd Pasha, or Minister of Foreign Affairs, Âli Pasha, with other members of high bureaucracy, all appeared as auditors to set a high example for the public (*âmmeye mûcib-i şevk ve gayret olmak üzere*).[73] Before too long, with the permission of the Sultan a course on general history and natural sciences began to be offered. Each class was attended by hundreds of audience members.[74] Eventually, Ahmed Vefik Efendi's lectures on the prehistoric ages and Sâlih Efendi's on natural sciences were serialised in the newspapers for wider consumption.[75] Derviş Pasha's books, and those of his students,

[71] Münif Efendi, 'Dârülfünun'da Ders-i Âmm Vuku'-u Küşâdı', 302. About Nollet's experiment, see J. L. Heilbron, *Electricity in the 17th and 18th Century: A Study of Early Modern Physics* (Berkeley: University of California Press, 1979), 318. Some information about the content of the lectures can be also found in Anonymous, 'Fünun', *Takvîm-i Vekâyi*, 22 Zilkade/11 May 1279/1863, 3.

[72] Münif Efendi, 'Dârülfünun'da Ders-i Âmm Vuku'-u Küşâdı', 302. Hyde Clarke again mentioned that 'a university was planned by the great Sultan Mahmood, and an extensive building erected, but not fitted. He proposed that this monument of the new regime should be placed on the site of the barracks of the extinguished janissaries . . . Of late years men of eminence, as Ahmed Vefik Effendi and Dervish Pasha, have given courses on the natural and moral sciences, history, &c., to *crowded audiences*'. Clarke, 'On Public Instruction in Turkey', 519, emphasis mine.

[73] Münif Efendi, 'Dârülfünun Dersleri', *Mecmûa-ı Fünun* I, no. 8 (1279/1869): 332.

[74] Ibid., 331.

[75] See Anonymous, 'Tefrika [Hikmet-i Târîh]', *Tasvîr-i Efkâr*, 8 Ramazan/27 February 1279/1863, 4. Anonymous, 'Tefrika [Târîh-i Tabi'i]', *Tasvîr-i Efkâr*, 6 Şevval/27 March 1279/1863, 4. These and subsequent pages in the Hakkı Tarık Us collection of Istanbul University were cut out, probably for binding purposes.

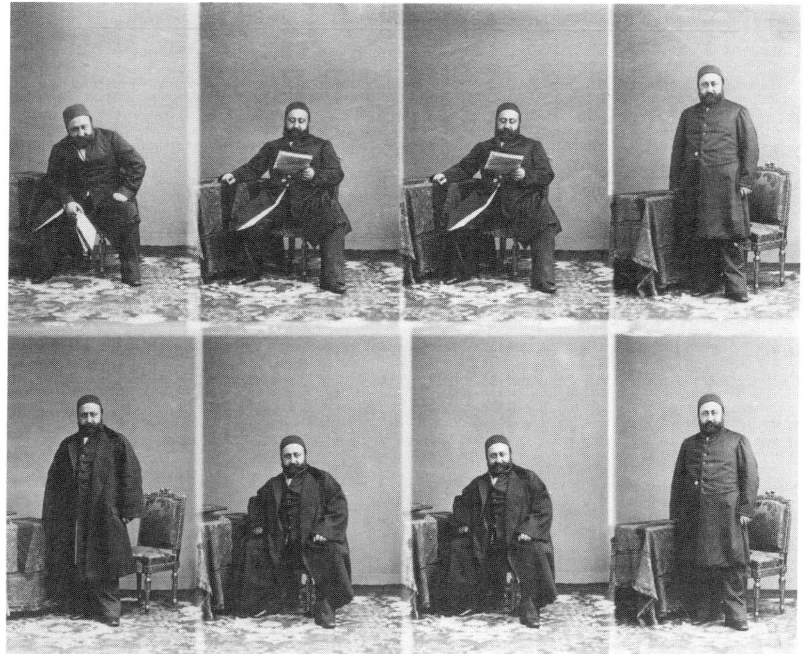

Figure 4.2 Ahmed Vefik Pasha, one of the lecturers of *Darülfünun* and the first translator of Molière to Ottoman Turkish.

Bahattin Öztuncay, *Hâtıra-i Uhuvvet (Portre Fotoğrafların Cazibesi: 1846–1950)* (İstanbul: Aygaz, 2005), 65.

started to be sold with specific references to his lectures.[76] Such interest was encouraging for Münif Efendi, a great supporter of the organisation. These educators, he vowed, 'will succeed in disseminating the light of science and learning among the public'.[77]

Although the *Dârülfünun* did not play any prominent role in the formation of an intellectual class until very late in the nineteenth century, and offered only sporadic education, these courses engendered a perennial interest in science and helped it, to a certain extent, enter into the public imagination – a phenomenon perhaps akin to the Royal

[76] Anonymous, 'İ'lânât [Usûl-i Kimya]', *Tasvîr-i Efkâr*, 2 Şaban/23 January 1279/1863, 3; Anonymous, 'İ'lânât [Hikmet-i Tabiyye ile ilgili bir kitâbın satışı]', *Tasvîr-i Efkâr*, 14 Şaban/4 February 1279/1863, 3.

[77] Münif Efendi, 'Dârülfünun Dersleri', 332.

Institution Christmas Lectures given by Michael Faraday in the 1850s.[78] References to new inventions in written works thrived noticeably after this point, and Ottoman readers began to learn about the latest scientific discoveries in newspapers and journals.[79] The 'scientific novels' of Ahmed Mithat Efendi, Ottoman encyclopaedist, in particular, fuelled the popularisation of modern knowledge among the urban classes.[80] This had one significant long-term effect. By offering new forms of cultural and intellectual authority, scientific knowledge helped promote a unified public opinion over the fragmented and multicultural urban population of the Empire.[81] The emergence of positivist intellectuals, such as Beşir Fuâd or Abdullah Cevdet, in subsequent years cannot be fully comprehended without this background.[82]

The lectures are also significant in that they indicate the formation of an idea of a public surfacing clearly in the contemporary imagination.

[78] See John Meurig Thomas, *Michael Faraday and the Royal Institution: The Genius of Man and Place* (New York: Taylor & Francis, 1991), 192. For the relationship between experimental physic and Enlightenment, see Michael R. Lynn, *Popular Science and Public Opinion in Eighteenth-Century France* (Manchester: Manchester University Press, 2006), 9–10.

[79] Though somewhat later, the title page of *Manzara*, literary journal, is quite telling: Mehmed Ramiz, 'Mebâhis-i Fennîyye ve Edebiyye, Hıfzıssıhha, Seyâhat, Terâcim-i Ahvâl ve Roman Gibi Mütenevviadan Bahseder', *Manzara* I, no. 1 (1303/1887): 1. Among the Ottoman periodicals of Hakkı Tarık Us Collection, 151 titles have the name *fennî* (scientific) in their colophon. See Abdurrahman M. Hacıismailoğlu Selahattin Öztürk, and Muhammed Hızarcı, *Hakkı Tarık Us Kütüphânesi Kataloğu: Süreli Yayınlar* (İstanbul: İstanbul Büyükşehir Belediyesi Kültür ve Turizm Dâire Başkanlığı Kültür Müdürlüğü, 2006), passim.

[80] See, for instance, Ahmed Mithat Efendi, *Fennî Bir Roman yahud Amerika Doktorları* (Istanbul: s.n., 1305/1887–1888). As it says on the first page, this novel was first serialised in *Tercüman-ı Hakikat*. Also see M. Orhan Okay, *Batı Medeniyeti Karşısında Ahmed Midhat Efendi* (Ankara: Atatürk Üniversitesi Edebiyât Fakültesi, 1975), 61–63. Even Zeki Velidi Togan, a native of Bashkortostan cites Midhat's oeuvres as his introduction to liberal ideas like those of John William Draper (d. 1882), English-American scientist and philosopher. Zeki Velidi Togan, *Hâtıralar* (Ankara: Türkiye Diyanet Vakfı Yayınları, 2015), 63.

[81] John Bradley, for instance, writes 'Perhaps more important, the diffusion of applied science, combining utility with entertainment, created a public'. John Bradley, *Voluntary Associations in Tsarist Russia: Science, Patriotism, and Civil Society* (Cambridge, MA: Harvard University Press, 2009), 29.

[82] M. Orhan Okay, *İlk Türk Pozitivist ve Natüralisti Beşir Fuâd* (Istanbul: Dergâh Yayınları, 1969); Şükrü Hanioğlu, *Doktor Abdullah Cevdet ve Dönemi* (Istanbul: Üçdal Neşriyat, 1981).

The newspaper advertisements announcing the date of the inaugural lecture, which actually took place during the sacred month of Receb, repeatedly emphasised that *Dârülfünun* was set up to 'teach and educate the public and is open to whomever desiring to listen'.[83] This was a radical break from the traditional Ottoman practice of religious segregation and became only possible with the proclamation of the 1856 Reform Decree guaranteeing equality before the law for all the Ottoman citizens. As Robert Wuthnow has emphasised, social conditions and cultural innovations very often went hand in hand.[84] This is perhaps a simple, nonetheless important point to keep in mind, and will be explored in further detail in the following chapters. Here, however, it can be briefly mentioned that the traditional structure of the Ottoman society was going through a period of profound transformation during this decade.[85] Not only were the vertical lines separating different religious groups waning under political and commercial pressure, but the horizontal lines dividing high culture (*has*) and folk culture (*avâm*) were also starting to fall apart.[86] As such, Münif Efendi was rather startled by the idea of common people (*avâm-ı nâs*) freely attending these lectures for their own amusement (*âdetâ bir oyun gibi temâşâsıyla eğlenmek üzere*).[87] However, by this time, the idea of an

83 '*Saye-i Maârif-Vaye-i Hazret-i Padişâhide umûma tedrîs ve tâlim olunmak ve her kim isterse gelib istima etmek üzere*'. Anonymous, 'Vuku'ât-ı Resmiye', *Takvîm-i Vekâyi*, 7 Receb/29 December 1279/1862, 1. The same advertisement also appeared in *Tasvîr-i Efkâr* ten days later. But this time, it excluded a crucial part (under shadow of his imperial majesty, benefactor of education). This was probably not a simple omission. See Anonymous, 'Madde-i Resmiye [I]', *Tasvîr-i Efkâr*, 18 Receb/9 January 1279/1863, 1, box brackets in the original.

84 Wuthnow, *Communities of Discourse*, 5.

85 Cf. 'The official disestablishment of the four traditional statuses of Tokugawa society-warrior, peasant, artisan, merchant-and legal equalization of the populace as imperial subjects did more than lay the infrastructure of national identity. It created a "public world" not necessarily coterminous with imperial subjecthood as *officially defined*.' Andrew E. Barshay, *State and Intellectual in Imperial Japan: Public Man in Crisis* (Berkeley: University of California Press, 1988), 6.

86 Or rather a new category called *âmme* was slowly emerging and this was causing increasing pressure on the traditional vision of the society. A book written a few years later divided the population into three distinct classes consisting of, respectively, high (*havas*), low (*esafil-i nâs*), and *âmme*, corresponding to middle class. The author explained how one needed to deal with each individual case. Osman Hayri Mürşit Efendi, *Terbiyetü'l-Ezhân* (Istanbul: Matbaa-ı Âmire, 1289/1872), 42–43.

87 Münif Efendi, 'Dârülfünun'da Ders-i Âmm Vuku'-u Küşâdı', 303.

expansive public sphere had begun to be integrated into the normative political culture of the Empire. Münif Efendi also expressed in a weighty manner the impossibility of curtailing their participation. 'Since these lectures are public (*işbu ders-i âmm olduğu cihhetle*)', he wrote, 'distinguishing or separating these two classes is surrounded with great difficulty (*müteassir*) and beset with valid obstacles (*müteazzir*).'[88]

Contemporary articles also constantly accentuated what one might call the representative role of the audience on behalf of the general public. This is interesting for two reasons. First, it, along with contemporary literature, helped to engender what Benedict Anderson has called 'simultaneity' by letting people imagine themselves as members of distinct homogeneous *âmme* or *umûm* existing in measurable time and within a spatially delineated geography.[89] This was a process that began with the official gazette and was carried on by a new type of literature that was exemplified in novels and plays. Second, they presented those attending science lectures as representative of the new public. *Takvîm-i Vekâyi* and *Tasvîr-i Efkâr*, for instance, frequently remarked that the lectures were open *for* (*umûma tedrîs olunmak üzere*),[90] or rather *reserved* for the public (*umûma mahsûs olarak tedrîs olunmak husûsuna*).[91] In the same vein, when the attendants were portrayed, they were portrayed as *public* without any discrimination from the wider whole (*Dârülfünun'da umûma verilen*).[92] Sensitivity to this type of portrayal can also be seen in the writings of Münif Efendi. For him, the lectures were delivered in front of the public (*âmme huzurunda*) with people from every class attending (*her sınıf ahâlîden*).[93] And naturally whenever these spectators showed their appreciation, it was in fact the appreciation of the whole Ottoman

88 It should be underlined that by two classes Münif Efendi did not mean *has* and *avâm* but rather those who were truly interested in science and those who went there for entertainment. Ibid.
89 Anderson, *Imagined Communities*, 23–25.
90 Anonymous, 'Vuku'ât-ı Resmiye', 1; Anonymous, 'Havâdis-i Dâhiliye (Pay-i Taht)', *Tasvîr-i Efkâr*, 4 Receb/26 December 1279/1862, 1.
91 Anonymous, '[Bundan Akdem İlan Olunduğu Üzere]', *Takvîm-i Vekâyi*, 26 Şevval/4 April 1280/1864, 2.
92 Anonymous, 'Havâdis-i Dâhiliye: Pay-i Taht', 1.
93 Münif Efendi, 'Dârülfünun'da Ders-i Âmm Vuku'-u Küşâdı', 301. In the same vein, his suggestions and recommendations for the audience by no means was to criticise the institution but just 'to cause public benefit (*umûm hakkında hayırlı olmak*)'. Ibid., 304.

public that they were epitomising (*âmme tarafından fevkel me'mûl zuhûra gelen hüsnü kabul*).[94]

Amidst these developments, we can see the first examples of the internalisation of the state's modernist agenda by private people (again in the widest sense of the term) in the public sphere. Halil Bey (later pasha), one of the Ottoman plenipotentiaries present at the Congress of Paris in 1856 following the Crimean War and later the Ottoman ambassador in St. Petersburg, lodged a petition, along with a few of his colleagues, including Münif Efendi, asking permission to establish an Ottoman scientific society, *Cemiyet-i İlmiye-i Osmaniye*, to express their gratitude 'for the opportunities of good education provided either here or in Europe by the imperial benevolences'. The aim of the Society, according to the petition, was to 'strive and endeavour, as much as possible, to circulate and make public the essential science and education in the well protected domains of His Imperial Majesty'. The members were going to 'compile and translate all kind of books about science and education, with the exception of ones touching on religion and politics, and organise public lectures on specific days'. This was, they emphasised, 'in complete accord with the well-known imperial scheme of the *schooling of the public*'.[95]

It is perhaps possible to detect some Russian influence at work here. By the second half of the nineteenth century, Russia was full of comparable civic associations that 'were sanctioned and patronized by the state, and [in many of them] government officials were prominent charter members'.[96] Before Halil Bey, Derviş Pasha, the very first lecturer of *Dârülfünun*, happened to be the previous Ottoman ambassador in St. Petersburg and was undoubtedly aware of the public lectures organised there in early 1861, following the closure of the city's university by Alexander II as a result of political turbulence.[97]

94 Ibid., 302. Or '*âmme tarafından hüsn-i telakki*' in Münif Efendi, 'Dârülfünun Dersleri', 330.

95 BOA, İ. DH. 472/31671, 8 Şevval 1277 (19 April 1861). Halil or Khalil Bey was an important art collector and sensational gambler who, while in Paris, amassed the portraits of great European masters. See Francis Haskell, 'A Turk and His Pictures in Nineteenth-Century Paris', *Oxford Art Journal* 5, no. 1, Patronage (1982): 42.

96 Bradley, *Voluntary Associations in Tsarist Russia*, 8.

97 John McNair, 'The "Reading Library" and the Reading Public: The Decline and Fall of "Biblioteka dlia chteniia"', *The Slavonic and East European Review*, 70, no. 2 (1992): 214.

Although Egypt has often been seen as the model by which the Ottoman Empire distilled Western modernity into its system, Russia was probably not less influential.[98] These two empires experienced similar paths towards modernity, though the Russian case was arguably swifter and less problematic.[99] Peter the Great (r. 1682–1725) shook off his version of the janissaries, the '*streltsy*', more than a century earlier than Mahmud II did for instance.[100] The Russian state also completed its 'bureaucratic revolution' by the mid-eighteenth century (and the sequence between eliminating an ancient military elite and establishing an efficient bureaucracy here is probably no coincidence).[101] Because of the idea of a shared Christian world, the tsars always felt more at home in a Western setting than their Ottoman counterparts, ultimate outsiders.[102] This idea of association helped them to internalise Western values more easily, and at an earlier date.[103] While on the face of it the Ottomans were bitterly deploring

[98] See, for instance, Robert Mantran, 'Prelude Aux Tanzimat: Presse et Enseignement, Deux Domaines de Reforme de Mahmud II', in *Tanzimat'ın 150. Yıldönümü Uluslararası Sempozyumu, Ank., 31 Ekim-3 Kasım 1989* (Ankara: Türk Târîh Kurumu, 1994), 51.

[99] Particularly after the seventeenth-century upheavals, which were called the *Celâlis* by the Ottomans and the *Smuta* by the Russians. Cf. Chester S. L. Dunning, *Russia's First Civil War: The Time of Troubles and the Founding of the Romanov Dynasty* (Philadelphia: Pennsylvania State University Press, 2001), 13–45; Mustafa Akdağ, *Büyük Celâli Karışıklıklarının Başlaması* (Erzurum: Atatürk Üniversitesi Fen-Edebiyât Fakültesi, 1963), 1–2.

[100] David B. Ralston, *Importing the European Army: The Introduction of European Military Techniques and Institutions in the Extra-European World*, 1600–1914 (Chicago: University of Chicago Press, 1996), 17–24. Also see Gábor Ágoston, 'Military Transformation in the Ottoman Empire and Russia, 1500–1800', *Kritika: Explorations in Russian and Eurasian History* 12, no. 2 (2011): 295–296.

[101] James Cracraft, *The Petrine Revolution in Russian Culture* (Cambridge, MA: Harvard University Press, 2009), 144.

[102] See his 'Grand Embassy' to Europe, Evgenii V. Anisimov, T*he Reforms of Peter the Great: Progress Through Coercion in Russia*, trans. John T. Alexander (New York: Sharpe, 1993), 17–19. About the otherness of the Ottomans, Talal Asad, 'Muslims and European Identity: Can Europe Represent Islam?', in *The Idea of Europe: From Antiquity to the European Union*, ed. Anthony Pagden (Cambridge: Woodrow Wilson Center Press and Cambridge University Press, 2002), 212–213; Deringil, *The Well-Protected Domains*, 4.

[103] See the beginning of Tsar Peter's *General'nyi reglament*: 'Whereas H[is]. Ts [arist]. M[ajesty]. our most merciful lord, on the example of other Christian [= European] realms, has been pleased to conceive the most merciful intention, for the sake of the orderly administration of his state affairs.' Cracraft, *The Petrine Revolution in Russian Culture*, 166. Also see Robert Collis, *The Petrine*

their northern neighbour, constantly referred as the 'Muscovite infidel'.[104] But they were also very much aware of the similarities and followed Russia all too closely through reports written by ambassadorial agencies and later through Russian newspapers.[105]

It should be also mentioned that Halil Bey's organisation was not the first properly constituted learned society to have left a record in the Ottoman Empire. There had been several institutions and associations, mostly dominated by foreigners and non-Muslims, functioning in the capital around the time of the Crimean War. *La Societe Impériale de Médecine*, for instance, was founded in 1856 under the imperial

Instauration: Religion, Esotericism and Science at the Court of Peter the Great, 1689–1725 (Leiden: Brill, 2011), 360.

104 'It was known that the Sultan [Mahmud II] had accepted the offer of Russian assistance ... Were it the English, they might bid them welcome; but to invite the Muscovite infidel, their bitter and hereditary foe, was inadmissible; they would rather leave the event to Providence.' Miss Pardoe, *The Beauties of the Bosphorus* (London: G. Virtue, 1838), 156, emphasis mine. This popular appellation (*Moskof Gavuru*) found its way even into government documents. See BOA, C..AS.. 959/41715, 23 Zilhicce 1182 (30 April 1769).

105 Mehmed Ağa of Niş, for instance, wrote a detailed account of his embassy (*sefaretnâme*) that took place between 1722 and 1723 at the court of Peter I. Faik Reşit Unat, *Osmanlı Sefirleri ve Sefaretnâmeleri*, ed. Bekir Sıtkı Baykal (Ankara: Türk Târîh Kurumu, 1968), 62–65. A few years later, in 1731, İbrahim Müteferrika penned an advisory book (*nâsihatnâme*) to present Mahmud I. Müteferrika's language towards Peter I was surprisingly praising, describing him as a wise ruler (*âkil ve dana*) who created a strong empire out of some hunters and gatherers. İbrahim Müteferrika, *Usûl ül-hikem fi nizâm il-ümen* (Istanbul: Dar ül-Taba'at ül-'Amire, 1144/1732), 47a. Just before the Tanzimat era, Kethüdâzâde mentioned Catherine II in a similar vein. See Emin Efendi, *Menâkıb-ı Kethüdâzâde el-Hac Mehmed Ârif Efendi*, 84. This interest never faded away and Istanbul watched very closely what was going on in Russia through its newspapers and reports. See BOA, HAT, 307/18139, 29 Zilhicce 1231 (20 November 1820), BOA, HAT 1163/46027/B 29 Zilhicce 1241 (4 August 1826), BOA, İ..HR.. 151/7966, 3 Cemaziyelevvel 1274 (20 December 1857), BOA, İ..HR.. 168/9027, 26 Şevval 1275 (29 May 1859), BOA, İ..HR.. 176/9647 9 Zilkade 1276 (29 May 1860), (the first three were newspaper reports and the last ones were written by Ottoman ambassadorial agents residing in the city, which included a report of Derviş Pasha of *Dârülfünun*). If the similarities concerning the local reforms made in the Ottoman Empire after 1839 (*Muhassıl Meclisleri*) and in Russia after 1864 (*Zemstvo*) are any indication, the Russians were also looking at their southern neighbour to see how it dealt with similar problems. Cf. Catherine Evtuhov, *Portrait of a Russian Province: Economy, Society, and Civilization in Nineteenth-Century Nizhnii Novgorod* (Pittsburgh, PA: University of Pittsburgh Press, 2011), 12–22; İlber Ortaylı, *Tanzimattan Sonra Mahalli İdâreler, 1840–1878* (Ankara: Sevinç Matbaası, 1974), 15–18.

patronage with the explicit aim of 'accomplishing the scheme of public health'.[106] With its gazette dedicated to this new concern (*santé publique*),[107] the Society organised open lectures and competitions in Istanbul up until the late nineteenth century.[108] Although clearly of no immediate popular consequence, considering the epidemics ravaging the city, its articles such as '*Hygiène Publique*' contributed to the increasing significance of 'protection of public health/*hıfz-ı sıhhât-i âmme*' in the administrative circles.[109]

Among these early endeavours, the most important one was a government initiative, put together a decade earlier at the Sultan's behest, for the scheme of *terbiye-i âmme*. In February 1851, a report prepared by the Commission of Public Education had underlined the requirement 'of forming a society, as soon as possible, from the talented and accomplished to produce the most indispensable and required books for the public (*âmmeye ehemm ü elzem olan*)'.[110] As a result, in July of the same year, an Ottoman Society of Sciences (*Encümen-i Dâniş*) was founded 'along the lines of the Parisian assembly called Academy' and like the *Académie française* itself, it had forty seats and set about with the idea of compelling a comprehensive dictionary of the Ottoman language.[111]

In the official correspondences, *Encümen* was repeatedly presented as the catalyst to transform the nascent idea of *the schooling of the public* into a reality.[112] The project was motivated by an almost

106 '*Sıhhat-i umûmîye maddesinin ikmâline say ve ikdam için*'. BOA, İ..HR.. 139/7208, 7 Cemaziyelevvel 1273 (3 January 1857).

107 '*Elle tiendra ses lecteurs au courant de toutes les nouvelles intérressant la santé publique*'. Anonymous, 'Constantinople, 13 Février 1857', *Gazette Médicale d'Orient* 1, no. 1 (1857): 1.

108 See, for instance, Anonymous, 'Variété', *Gazette Médicale d'Orient* 1, no. 1 (1857): 16.

109 Dr. Verrollot, 'Hygiène Publique: Rapport sur une motion relative à l'hygiène publique, lu dans la séance du 10 Avril 1857', *Gazette Médicale d'Orient* 1, no. 3 (1857): 33–37. There was also the British Literary Institution of Constantinople, a popular reading circle. Even though now completely faded from historical memory, with hundreds of members, including some Ottoman officials, its committee organised public lectures for the educated strata of the city at the beginning of the 1860s. See, for instance, Anonymous, '[The Committee of British Literary Institution]', *Levant Herald*, 21 November 1860, 956.

110 Cevdet Paşa, *Tezâkir 40*, 48.

111 Ibid., 46–47.

112 '*Terbiyet-i âmme maslahat-ı mühimmesinin kuvveden fiile sürat-i ihracını*'. BOA, İ..MVL. 208/6740, 13 Cemaziyelahir 1267 (15 April 1851).

fanatical faith on part of the Ottoman statesmen in education as a modernising force.[113] Similar to many other government initiatives of the Tanzimat era, the opening of *Encümen* began with inspiring speeches and grand ceremonies. Reşid and Hayreddin Pashas delivered their inaugural addresses in the presence of the Sultan along with other dignitaries, and emphasis was given to the status of science and education in the modern society.[114] The members were presented to Sultan Abdülmecid and decorated with the usual Ottoman paraphernalia – signifying the importance ascribed to this project by the Sultan himself.[115] The manifesto, drawn up by Cevdet Pasha and published in the official newspaper, stressed the importance of language simplification and translation from other languages for the public good.[116] The text was again awash with casual references to the significance of the 'schooling of the public' in the eye of the sultanate.[117] In fact, according to Cevdet Pasha, this auspicious enterprise was a direct result of this imperial campaign, which could only be successful, he emphasised, 'by spreading multifarious sciences in public'.[118]

Albeit ceremonial, among the members of the *Encümen-i Dâniş*, there were a number of highly prominent and distinguished men.[119] The Grand Vizier Reşid Pasha, Şeyhülislam Arif Hikmet Efendi, Rüşdü Pasha, Âli Pasha, and scholars such as James Redhouse, Xavier de Bianchi, or Joseph von Hammer-Purgstall all numbered among the founding members of the Society. Yet despite the initial confidence that 'many required books will be produced and public benefit (*fevâid-i âmme*) will be catered in a very short period of time',[120] and

113 'In the Exalted State as well, such books, which are respected and worthy of a study for everybody, are also going to be translated from Arabic, Persian and foreign languages into an easy Turkish, as much as possible, in a form which will be appreciated by common people (*avâm-pesend*) so that benefits and advantages will be made public.' Ibid.

114 Cevdet Paşa, *Tezâkir 40*, 56–57.

115 BOA, A.}MKT.NZD., 8 Ramazan 1267 (7 July 1851).

116 Cevdet Paşa, *Tezâkir 40*, 50–52; Anonymous, '[Müstağni-i Beyân Olduğu Üzere]', *Takvîm-i Vekâyi*, Gurre-i Şaban/1 June 1267/1851, 2–4.

117 Two references were made to *terbiye-i âmme* and one was to *terbiye-i umûmîye*.

118 Cevdet Paşa, *Tezâkir 40*, 51.

119 For the roster, see Anonymous, '[Müstağni-i Beyân Olduğu Üzere]', 4. Also BOA, İ..DH.. 237/14310, 15 Ramazan 1267 (14 July 1851).

120 BOA, İ..MVL. 208/6740, 13 Cemaziyelahir 1267 (15 April 1851).

after many meetings filled with heated debate and hours of technical study, the outcome failed to live up to expectations. Even though Mahmud Cevad called the *Encümen* 'the first institution of high science in the Ottoman state',[121] few tangible results can be attributed to this enterprise – the chief among them being Cevdet Pasha's '*Târîh-i Cevdet*'.[122] A few books were published and even fewer translations were attempted.[123] Before long, the whole project sank into oblivion, disappearing from the government yearbooks without even being officially abolished.[124]

Consequently, Halil Bey's proposal for a scientific society was welcomed by the government as this projected to remove some of the responsibility from the shoulders of the state. Since the beginning of the 1860s, it was not surprising to see newspaper articles assailing the 'tardiness with which the schooling of the public was moving'.[125] Halil Bey's petition also contained a latent criticism of the state's education policies, expressed carefully in the form of lamenting.[126] The government eventually allocated a building for the Society in one of the central areas of the city, seeing as how its members were going to 'concern themselves with useful means such as publishing and translating educative books and pamphlets as well as giving public lectures on specific days'.[127] This was, the permit underlined, 'completely in line with the government's proposed extension of the *schooling of the public*'.[128]

121 Cevad Nâfi, *Maârif-i Umûmîye Nezâreti*, 57.

122 This was, Cevdet Pasha claimed, a turning point in the Ottoman literature for a simpler language: 'Târîh-i Cevdet was written in a coarse Turkish without circumlocution (*bir tarz-ı tersîl üzere kaba Türkçe ile yazıldı*)'. Cevdet Paşa, *Tezâkir 40*, 72.

123 For the list of the books, see Taceddin Kayaoğlu, *Türkiye'de Tercüme Müesseseleri* (Istanbul: Kitâbevi, 1998), 77–90.

124 Belin, 'De l'instruction publique et du mouvement intellectuel en Orient', *Le Contemporain Revue d'économie Chrétienne* XI, August (1866): 220.

125 Anonymous, 'Maârife Dair Bend-i Mahsûsdur', *Tercüman-ı Ahvâl*, 2 Zilkade/3 May 1277/1861, 2. Also see '*usûl-i terbiyenin sakemeti*' or 'the failure of *terbiye* method' in 'Kemal, 'Me'mûrlara Dair', 3.

126 'Since means of education (*vesa'it-i tahsiliyye*) have not yet attained their desirable state'.

127 Anonymous, 'Emir-Nâme-i Sâmî Sûreti', *Mecmûa-ı Fünun* I, no. 5 (1279/1862): 174.

128 BOA, İ..DH.. 472/31671, 13 Zilkade 1277 (23 May 1863).

An Ottoman Scientific Society

At first glance, *Cemiyet-i İlmiye-i Osmaniye* was akin to other contemporary initiatives towards public education that were created in different parts of the world; the Society for the Diffusion of Useful Knowledge in Great Britain and the Lyceum Movement in the United States to name only a few.[129] As Joseph Bradley has emphasised, 'during the course of the nineteenth century, more and more societies of science and natural history in Europe and the United States regarded their mission to be the popularization of knowledge'.[130] Accordingly, the Society began by publishing a thick, pocket-sized journal, named *Mecmuâ-i Fünun* (the Collection of Sciences), whose purpose was to make scientific knowledge popularly accessible. It was published monthly in 'an easy language', and contained scholarly articles on economics, history, and a diverse range of sciences.[131] Though initially avowing to remain out of political and religious controversies (*diyânet ve zaman-ı hâl politikası*) in the preamble of its charter,[132] the writers in due course embraced ostensibly harmless political debates revolving around the American Civil War or the French intervention in Mexico as writing on these subjects Münif Efendi reckoned, were almost like 'recitation and discussion of history'.[133]

Overall, *Mecmuâ* was an eclectic intellectual project that aimed to create a unified and informed Ottoman public within the framework of the imperial scheme of *terbiye-i âmme*. Münif Efendi likened his

[129] The Society for the Diffusion of Useful Knowledge, founded in 1826, can be also seen as a mixture of government and private initiatives as it was established at the instigation of Lord Brougham (d. 1868), a British statesman who later became Lord Chancellor. See Aileen Fyfe, *Science and Salvation: Evangelical Popular Science Publishing in Victorian Britain* (Chicago: University of Chicago Press, 2004), 43.

[130] Bradley, *Voluntary Associations in Tsarist Russia*, 128.

[131] '*Herkesin anlayabileceği surette sehl-ül ibare olmak üzere... fünun ve sanaiye müteallik mâlumat-ı nafiyeye müştemil olacaktır*'. Münif Efendi, 'Mukaddime', *Mecmûa-ı Fünun* I, no. 1 (1279/1862): 19.

[132] Cf. 'The associations of northern and central Germany relied on the Prussian government for more than an annual donation: they existed only insofar as they could prove to the officials that they had no political agendas and were organizations for "purely scholarly purposes".' Susan A. Crane, *Collecting and Historical Consciousness in Early Nineteenth-Century Germany* (Ithaca, NY: Cornell University Press, 2000), 91.

[133] Münif Efendi, 'Mecmûa-i Fünun'un Mazhar Olduğu Hüsn-ü Kabulden Dolayı Âmmeye Teşekkür', *Mecmûa-ı Fünun* I, no. 4 (1279/1862): 135.

journal and Şinâsi's newspaper (*Tasvîr-i Efkâr* or *the Portraitist of Public Opinion*)[134] to twin brothers (*birâder-i tev'em*), working together while helping and supporting each other for the same purpose, 'the schooling of the public'.[135] It was strongly emphasised that the Society, including its journal, was not organised around religious or racial lines and welcomed any constructive criticism from learned circles. As a result, its contributors included prominent members of the non-Muslim elite such as Ohannes Vahanyan (d. 1891),[136] Alexander Karatheodori Pasha (d. 1906),[137] and Sakızlı Ohannes Efendi (d. 1912).[138]

Its content, albeit at an elite level, indicates a clear shift in the political culture of the Empire. What is meant here is not so much new information, like a Trojan horse, infiltrating into the Empire through printed pages. This is, to a certain extent, true and important in its own right. But more meaningfully, inspired by Western political discussions and internal dynamics of the Empire, these writers were steadily moving away from the classical Ottoman political ideals, orbiting around the state and religion (*din ü devlet*) or justice (*adl*), and beginning to incline towards an expanding public as the ultimate point of reference.

There are many examples of this new sensitivity. One early debate, in particular, embodies the rupture from traditional political philosophy quite lucidly. '[L]et's assume', wrote Münif Efendi in the very first issue of the journal, that 'the poverty and deprivation that we observe in refined countries is a negative result of civilization. Since the [ultimate] aim is the happiness of the public (*maksad umûmun saâdet-i hâli olduğundan*), if one per cent or two per cent is subjected to extreme poverty, what harm is there in it'![139] This seemingly innocuous statement was, at the time, quite daring. Even though because of the deeply

134 This is at least how Belin, a contemporary, translated it, '*la Peinture de l'opinion publique*'. See Belin, 'De l'instruction publique et du mouvement intellectuel en Orient', 232.

135 Münif Efendi, 'Zuhûr-i Tasvîr-i Efkâr', *Mecmûa-ı Fünun* I, no. 1 (1279/1862): 46.

136 Vahan Efendi, 'Fevâid-i Şirket', *Mecmûa-ı Fünun* I, no. 8 (1279/1863): 343–353.

137 Aleksandr [Alexander Karatheodori], 'Usûl-i Te'mîniye', *Mecmûa-ı Fünun* I, no. 16 (1280/1863): 191–195.

138 Sakızlı Ohannes Efendi, 'İlm-i Servet-i Milel', *Mecmûa-ı Fünun* I, no. 2 (1279/1862): 86–92.

139 Münif Efendi, 'Mukayese-i İlm ü Cehl', 127.

embedded notion of justice (*adl*), subjects came to be seen as something entrusted by God to the Sultan,[140] the idea of their happiness was simply irrelevant in the Ottoman political thought. The etymological root of the word that the Ottomans used for common people is very telling here: *reâya* (or *ra'iyya*), which denoted tax-paying subjects for centuries, in Arabic originally referred to the herding of cattle or sheep.[141] Hence, while as a 'good shepherd', the Sultan was responsible for the well-being of his flock,[142] his ultimate *raison d'être*, however, was to preserve the stability of the state and the sanctity of religion.

In the second issue of the journal, then–Minister of Foreign Affairs, Âli Pasha responded to this contention in a 'Letter of Compliment' written to congratulate the beginning of *Mecmuâ-i Fünun*. The tone of his message was quite laudatory; complimenting it on its sense of patriotic and national duty (*azim-i vezâif-i hubb-u vatan ve millet*).[143] However, as one of the most conservative statesmen of the era, Âli Pasha also perceived the role of the individual in the society rather differently. 'In fact', his letter read, '[what we call] public benefit is just an aggregation of personal benefits. As such, saying that the common people should never pay attention to their individual advantage but serve only the public interest is not only against human nature but also against the necessities of civilization ... This must be the most important consideration to take into account in the *schooling of the public*.'[144]

These discussions, or rather insinuations, did not always need to be so blatant in order to capture the shifting social landscape of the Empire. As Natascha Vittinghoff emphasises in comparable examples from China, the line between 'objective information' and

[140] Halil İnalcık, 'Osmanlı Padişâhı', *Siyasal Bilgiler Fakültesi Dergisi* XII, no. 4 (1958): 74–75.

[141] *Reâya* began to be used, after the eighteenth century, to denote mostly non-Muslim population. See Erol Özbilgen, *Bütün Yönleriyle Osmanlı Adab-ı Osmaniyye* (İstanbul: İz Yayınları, 2003), 416.

[142] See Dennis P. Hupchick, *The Bulgarians in the Seventeenth Century: Slavic Orthodox Society and Culture Under Ottoman Rule* (Jefferson, NC: McFarland, 1993), 19.

[143] Ali Paşa, 'İltifatnâme-i Mezkûrun Sûretidir', *Mecmûa-ı Fünun* I, no. 2 (1279/1862): 52.

[144] Ibid., 53.

'public-opinion making' was not so easy to distinguish in early newspapers.[145] Although the members of the Society, as mentioned earlier, were compelled – perhaps not directly but consequentially – to abstain from political discussions, even the seemingly most innocuous articles, could be 'publicly' relevant. Halil Pasha's article on the ancient kings of Egypt is a good example of this. For Halil Pasha, the rulers of ancient Egypt, for instance, 'understood before everyone else that the outcome of ruling a country should only be maintaining the safety and security of the public (*âmmenin husûl-u emn ve asâyişi hâlleri kaziyyesinden ibaret olduğu*)'.[146] According to his reading, or version, of Egyptian history, sovereigns, like regular subjects, had to abide by the rules and regulations of the country (*kavânîn-i mevzuiyeye tevfik etmekte mecbur idiler*) and every aspect of daily life in ancient Egypt was organised according to strict regulations including the provisions of the kings.[147]

According to Halil Pasha, ancient Egypt was practically ruled by a judicial council, which was composed of the ruler and his thirty *meb'ûs*, (a word later used for the members of the parliament which literarily means deputy), chosen from the thirty cities constituting the kingdom. The Pasha, who was born in Cairo as a member of the Turkish-speaking elite, also argued in a very striking passage that after the Egyptian rulers died, their bodies would be carried into a square (*meydan*) where the public formed a pseudo tribune (*âdetâ bir mahkeme*) in order to decide upon the fate of the corpse. If they believed that the former king, (probably because of the negative religious stigma attached to it, he never used the word *fir'avn* or pharaoh in the article), served his country well, he would be mummified and put into a magnificent tomb. If the people felt unenthusiastic about their former sovereign owing to his tyranny (*zulm*), negligence (*teseyyüb*), or lust (*şehevât*), he would be left a prey to the mountain birds, and the beasts that roamed through the land.[148]

145 Natascha Vittinghoff, 'Readers, Publishers and Officials in the Contest for a Public Voice and the Rise of a Modern Press in Late Qing China (1860–1880)', *T'oung Pao* 87, no. 4/5 (2001): 428.

146 Halil Bey, 'Kudemâ'-i Mülûk-i Misriyye Târîhi', *Mecmûa-ı Fünun* I, no. 1 (1279/1862): 36.

147 Ibid., 37.

148 Ibid. Similar arguments can be also found in the extracts published in the journal from the translation of 'Les aventures de Télémaque', the first Western book to be fully translated into Ottoman. See Yusuf Kâmil Paşa, 'Mevâd-i Hikemiye-i Telemak', *Mecmûa-ı Fünun* I, no. 12 (1279/1863): 488–495.

Before long, the Society also began to organise its own lectures series on a range of subjects which were open to anyone who wished to attend.[149] Giving free public lectures was actually one of the requirements for membership of the *Cemiyet*.[150] As a result, several times a week, classes in foreign languages including English and French or in minority languages such as Greek, and lectures in political economy and law were delivered by the leading intellectuals of the era.[151] We do not know much about the content of the lectures with one exception: a talk given by Münif Efendi on alphabet simplification was also published as a separate article, and it, perhaps unsurprisingly, underlined the importance of the *schooling of the public*.[152] Moreover, aside from this specific example, it does appear that there was a connection between essays that appeared in the journal and the courses given by the Society. If we are to believe Münif Efendi, the lectures were quite successful. French classes, especially, attracted immense participation and needed to be divided into four levels.[153] Years later, Ebuzziyâ Tevfik, who personally participated in some of these courses as a teenager, wrote romantically at some length about the care and attention displayed by Münif Efendi towards the audience.[154]

Retrospectively, it is easy to overstate (or understate) the importance of the Society – and all with good reason. As early as 1910, Ebuzziyâ

[149] Münif Efendi, 'Sûret-i Hal-i Cemiyet', *Mecmûa-ı Fünun* İkinci Sene, no. 24 (1280/1864): 480.

[150] '*Umûm için bir ders okutmağa mecbur olacaklardır*'. Anonymous, 'Cemiyet-i İlmiye-i Osmaniye Nizâmnâmesidir', *Mecmûa-ı Fünun* I, no. 1 (1279/1862): 3.

[151] Münif Efendi, 'Sûret-i Hal-i Cemiyet', 480. İsmail Eren, 'Cemiyet-i İlmiye-i Osmaniye'nin Fa'âliyet ve Te'sirleri', *Belgelerle Türk Târîhi Dergisi*, no. 45 (1971): 10. A basic knowledge of Greek and Armenian for the Ottoman elite was actually quite useful. They could follow the Turkish newspaper published in Greek or Armenian alphabets. These papers were probably under less pressure and could be critical of the government.

[152] Münif Efendi talked at length about the importance of the alphabet simplification along with his concerns over possible public reactions to such measure (*kabul-i âmme istihsali mevâd-i müşkileden olub*). Münif Efendi, 'Cemiyet-i İlmiye-i Osmaniye'de 1278 Senesi Zilkadesinin On Üçü Târîhinde Münif Efendinin Husûs-u Mezkûra Dair Telaffuz Eylediği Makaledir', *Mecmûa-ı Fünun* İkinci Sene, no. 14 (1280/1863): 76. According to Ebuzziyâ Tevfik, the lectures were given in a manner of conference (*bir nevi konferans suretinde*). For the details, see Ebuzziyâ, 'Münif Paşa', *Yeni Tasvîr-i Efkâr*, 1 Safer/12 February 1328/1910, 2.

[153] '*Bunların her birinde haylice müdavim-i şakirdan bulunmaktadır*'. Münif Efendi, 'Sûret-i Hal-i Cemiyet', 481.

[154] Ebuzziyâ, 'Münif Paşa', 2.

Tevfik claimed that 'young Ottomans (*erbâb-ı şebâb*), who relished studying it, kept the journal always with them like a holy book and engraved its content into their mind as if memorising it'.[155] Ahmed Hamdi Tanpınar, in a similar vein, compared the members of the Society to French 'Encyclopaedists'.[156] Similar views are still being replicated in modern historiography. According to Ali Budak, for instance, the members of the Ottoman Scientific Society 'realised how book, newspaper and journal had magical powers; they saw very well what could be done with them and demonstrated it to everybody. They made an important contribution in the formation and distribution of new ideas'.[157] Ekrem Işın, on the other hand, held the view that *Mecmuâ-i Fünun* was an 'important vehicle to propagate opposition views in public opinion' and 'laid the foundations of positivist thought in the Ottoman Empire'.[158] Yet as William St Clair, while writing of Shelley's 'the Revolt of Islam' (1818), remarks, 'quantification, however, destroys a good story'.[159]

In an article entitled 'Thanks to the Public Because of *Mecmuâ-i Funün*'s Handsome Acceptance', Münif Efendi stated that the number of their subscribers, drawn mostly from government departments and agencies, reached a mere three hundred.[160] It is possible to speculate about a somewhat wider circulation with unsubscribed readers added to this figure. Ebuzziyâ mentions, in glowing terms, how there were approximately six hundred readers outside of Istanbul (*taşra*).[161] We know that some of the issues, such as the first one, had to be reprinted due to popular demand and that the administration issued a warning against pirated editions from the very beginning (though this can be a mere adaptation of the Western practice).[162] Moreover, even years after, it is possible to find the name of *Mecmuâ-i Fünun* appearing in the probate court records of the Ottoman elite, which at least attests a

155 Ibid. 156 Tanpınar, *XIX. Asır Türk Edebiyâtı Târîhi*, 172.

157 Ali Budak, *Mecmûa-i Fünun: Osmanlının İlk Bilim Dergisi* (Istanbul: Bilge Kültür Sanat, 2011), X.

158 Ekrem Işın, 'Osmanlı Bilim Târîhi: Münif Paşa ve Mecmûa-i Fünun', *Târîh ve Toplum* I, no. 11 (1984): 63.

159 William St Clair, *The Reading Nation in the Romantic Period* (Cambridge: Cambridge University Press, 2004), 189.

160 Münif Efendi, 'Mecmûa-i Fünun'un Mazhar Olduğu', 137.

161 Ebuzziyâ, 'Münif Paşa', 2.

162 Dündar Akünal, '[Server Tanilli'nin *Târîh ve Toplum*'un]', *Toplumsal Târîh* I, no. 11 (1984): 63.

certain importance given by Ottoman readers to this journal.[163] Even still, however, when compared to Mikhail Katkov's *the Russian Messenger* (*Russkii Vestnik*) and Smirdin's *the Reader's Library* (*Biblioteka Dlya Chteniya*), both 'thick' literary journals founded in Russia around the same time in a country with parallel literacy rates, the sales figures of the *Mecmuâ* were rather meagre.[164]

Although low literacy rates in the Ottoman Empire offer one ready explanation for the limited circulation of this journal, the Russian example suggests this was not the sole reason. Moreover, Istanbul was a city of officials and by the 1860s reading and writing was a prerequisite to obtain civil service positions.[165] Another and probably more immediate reason for the limited success of the *Mecmuâ* was its high sale price. According to Ebuzziyâ, 'the fact that each issue was 5 kuruş deprived many irregular readers from its readership. As such saving 5 kuruş throughout the month to buy the upcoming issue at the start of each month was a reason for affliction for me. Sparing 5 kuruş from my needs was an exertion. Nonetheless, I was struggling to buy.'[166] One can clearly see how traumatic it was for Ebuzziyâ to pay 5 kuruş (approximately equivalent to 18 pounds sterling in

163 See, for instance, the probate court record taken in 1877 for the list of books owned by İsmail Sabri Pasha, Ş.S.KISASKMAH. 1850, 17a.

164 In I862, The Russian Messenger had a circulation of 7,000. See Andreas Renner, 'Defining a Russian Nation: Mikhail Katkov and the 'Invention' of National Politics', *The Slavonic and East European Review* 81, no. 4 (2003): 666. *Biblioteka* again enjoyed a wide circulation, something between 5,000 and 7,000 around the 1840s, see John McNair, 'The 'Reading Library' and the Reading Public', 213. Although they were, one must note, exceptionally successful compared to the circulation figures of other Russian journals and newspapers, see Anne Lounsbery, '"Russia! What Do You Want of Me?": The Russian Reading Public in Dead Souls', *Slavic Review* 60, no. 2 (2001): 369. One can add to this picture *The Penny Magazine* of the Society for the Diffusion of Useful Knowledge that reached a circulation of two hundred thousand around 1832. See Harold Perkin, *The Origins of Modern English Society: 1780–1880* (London: Routledge & Kegan Paul, 1969), 307.

165 The graduates of new schools were slowly replacing the illiterate officers, see BOA, A.}MKT.MVL. 118/94, 17 Muharrem 1277 (5 August 1860). One can easily find documents attesting this change. See, for instance, an unsuccessful application of a certain Sâlih Bey, an immigrant from Crimea, who could not be employed at the customs since he was illiterate. BOA, A.}MKT.NZD. 385/88, 15 Cemazeyilahir 1278 (18 December 1861), or another one in which a Hacı Ahmed Ağa was refused a job as he was, again, unable to read and write, see BOA, A.}MKT.UM.. 432/54, 3 Rebiülahir 1277 (19 October 1860).

166 Ebuzziyâ, 'Münif Paşa', 2.

2016).[167] Considering that he was coming from a well-off family, it is unsurprising that the journal was forced to close down in 1867 after forty-seven issues as a result of general apathy and the withdrawal of government support.[168]

But even if we cannot assign a wide popular influence to the Society or its journal, it is easier to insist on a consequential influence. Only a few months after its establishment, a new society, the *Cemiyet-i Kitâbet* (Society of Composition) was inaugurated by what İsmail Eren describes as 'second or third rate intellectuals'.[169] This new society also published its own journal, *the Mecmuâ-i İber-i İntibah* or *the Collection of Lessons of Vigilance*.[170] The government again allocated a building for this new association in one of the central areas of the city as the members were going to 'concern themselves with matters pertaining to useful sciences'.[171]

As Elizabeth Kendall rightly points out 'very little is now known about these early endeavours in Istanbul'.[172] It is not easy to explain the reason for such a widespread indifference of the Ottoman historians towards early newspapers and journals if it is not because of 'the archive fever'.[173] As if to make her own point stronger, even Kendall

[167] 1 English Pound (*İngiliz Lirası*) in 1862 was worth 250,75 *Kuruş* (250 *Kuruş* and 30 *Para*). Anonymous, 'İ'lânât: İstanbul'da Akçenin Raici', *Tasvîr-i Efkâr*, 5 Muharrem/3 July 1279/1862, 3. Hence the journal was sold approximately for 0.02 Pound. This was equivalent of, using the index of income value, £18.1, in 2016. Its output worth, on the other hand, is £47.50. See Lawrence H. Officer and Samuel H. Williamson, 'Purchasing Power of British Pounds from 1245 to Present', in *MeasuringWorth* (2016).

[168] There is an attached paper to *Meclis-i Vâlâ* (High Council) document that illustrates the change of heart in the government circles: 'even though previously it was written to the Exalted Ministry for this money to be paid, as the situation is going to be handled differently from now on, this money should not be given anymore'. BOA, İ..MVL. 873/80, 16 Şevval 1282 (4 March 1866).

[169] Eren, 'Cemiyet-i İlmiye-i Osmaniye'nin Fa'âliyet ve Te'sirleri', 12.

[170] Throughout the official correspondence, one can clearly see how *Mecmuâ-i Fünun* turned into a point of reference for the Ottoman public servants in such a short time. They either likened the new journal to *Mecmuâ-i Fünun* (*Mecmuâ-i Fünun missullu*) or they considered it to be in line with it (*Mecmuâ-i Fünun'a tevfikan*), see BOA, İ..MVL. 482/21861, 10 Ramazan 1279 (1 March 1863).

[171] BOA, İ..MVL. 864/47, 2 Rebiülahir 1281 (September 4, 1864).

[172] Elizabeth Kendall, 'Between Politics and Literature: Journals in Alexandria and Istanbul at the End of the Nineteenth Century', in *Modernity & Culture: From the Mediterranean to the Indian Ocean*, ed. Leila Tarazi Fawaz and C. A. Bayly (New York: Columbia University Press, 2002), 338.

[173] In the Ottoman historiography, the repositories of the state have an epistemological supremacy over printed material, which is considered somewhat tangential. This can be thought as an example of what Spivak called

confuses what little we know about the *Mecmuâ-i İber* and its successor, *Mecmuâ-i İbretnümâ*, in her next sentence.[174] Unfortunately, this lack of knowledge holds true not only for scholars from other adjacent fields visiting the Ottoman historiography but also for the most erudite historians of the period.[175]

Part of this historiographical neglect can be attributed to the fact that this new journal was not particularly interesting or original. It is easy to see why İsmail Eren would call the contributors 'second or third rate'. Compared with *Mecmuâ-i Fünun*, the content of *İber-i İntibah* does look elementary and somewhat lopsided. However, the very same discussions and sensitivities that we observe in *Mecmuâ-i Fünun* are still easily discernible throughout its pages – albeit expressed in a somewhat dated vocabulary. Like *Mecmuâ-i Fünun, İber-i İntibah* also begins with a reference to 'every class of the Exalted Sultanate' and contains exemplary stories about the importance of the protection of human rights (*muhâfaza-i hukuk-i ibâd*).[176] Strangely enough, the parable that our writer, Ali Haydar Bey, chose to make his points, albeit much shorter, is again taken from the 'history of ancient Egypt'. This is most likely because Egypt came to be seen as a conflict-free foundation for Ottoman modernity.[177] One can sense an intuitive

'the archival fetish'. See Gayatri Chakravorty Spivak, 'The Rani of Sirmur: An Essay in Reading the Archives', *History and Theory* 24, no. 3 (1985): 248–250. Also Jacques Derrida, *Archive Fever: A Freudian Impression* (Chicago: University of Chicago Press, 1998).

174 '*Mecmuâ-i İber-i İntibah*, Turkey's first specialised literary journal, was published by a group of enthusiastic literary-minded young men and ran only eight issues in 1862–1864; *Mecmuâ-i İbretnümâ* was published by the *Cemiyet-i Kitâbet* and ran to only 16 issues in 1865–66'. Kendall, 'Between Politics and Literature', 338. Actually *Cemiyet-i Kitâbet* published both of the journals and after the eighth issue, the journal changed its name to *Mecmuâ-i İbretnümâ*. See Anonymous, 'İ'lânât', *Tasvîr-i Efkâr*, 27 Cemazeyilahir/12 November 1282/1865, 4.

175 See, for instance, 'a general indication of the restlessness of the Turkish men of letters in the early 1860's', Şerif Mardin writes, 'may be seen in that the organ of the Society of Writers (*Cemiyet-i Kitâbet*), the *İbar-ı İntibah* was suspended almost immediately after the first number appeared'. Mardin, *The Genesis of Young Ottoman Thought*, 245–46.

176 Ali Haydar, 'Mecmûa-i İber-i İntibah – Mukaddime', *Mecmûa-i İber-i İntibah* I, no. 1 (1279/1862): 2.

177 Anonymous, 'Nesâih-i Hükema', *Mecmûa-ı İber-i İntibah* I, no. 1 (1279/1862): 5. This sudden interest in times of pharaohs might also have something to do with al-Tahtawi's influence on the Ottoman literary. Al-Tahtawi, as Gershoni and Jankowski point out, 'was perhaps the first modern Egyptian writer to view

desire to fashion ancient Egypt into an 'Eastern version' of Classical Greece here. Coincidentally, one of the first books that the Ottomans ever published was actually on the history of the ancient Egyptians.[178] While nominally Egypt was still part of the Empire's dominions and by using the fertile lands of the Nile delta as the bedrock for their idea of modernity, these writers were able to construct a more inclusive and equitable conception of citizenship for the Empire's multi-ethnic population than the later, Islamic 'golden age' myth.

Apart from the usual sorts of clichéd scientific articles such as *Fevâid-i Fünun* (Benefits of Sciences),[179] the *Mecmuâ-i İber* also contained curious engravings, which was something of a novelty to the Ottoman public. This gave them a chance to see random but exotic scenes such as the 'Sponge Divers of Tripoli'.[180] But today the importance of the journal lies in a single sentence written as a part of its charter.[181] In the second issue, Ali Haydar Bey announced that they

the entire civilized history of Egypt as a continuum and to formulate an embryonic theory of an Egyptian national character that extended from the ancient Egyptians to his contemporaries'. Israel Gershoni and James P. Jankowski, *Egypt, Islam, and the Arabs: The Search for Egyptian Nationhood, 1900–1930: The Search for Egyptian Nationhood, 1900–1930* (New York: Oxford University Press, 1986), 11. Also see Donald Malcolm Reid, *Whose Pharaohs?: Archeology, Museums, and Egyptian National Identity from Napoleon to World War I* (Berkeley: University of California Press, 2002), 50–58. A few years later, the Ottoman writers such as Nâmık Kemal or Ahmed Mithat tried to postulate a similar type of relationship with the early Ottoman past. See Ahmet A. Ersoy, 'On the Sources of the 'Ottoman Renaissance:" Architectural Revival and Its Discourse During the Abdülaziz Era (1861–1876)" (PhD diss., Harvard University, 2000), 335–344.

178 Süheyli Efendi, *Târîh-i Misr-ı Cedîd, Târîh-i Misr-ı Kadim*, ed. İbrahim Müteferrika (Istanbul: Dar ül-Taba'at ül-'Amire, 1142/1730). Later on, other than a few articles, the Ottoman writers published quite a few books on the history of ancient Egypt as well. One translation from Arabic, dealing with the history of pyramids, is particularly interesting. See Mahmud Paşa Falâki, *Mısır Ehramları: Kangı Maksada Mebni Vücuda Getirilmiş ve Ne Vakit Bina Edilmiştir?*, trans. M. Muhiddin (Istanbul: Karabet Matbaası, 1311/1893).

179 Lûtfi, 'Fevâid-i Fünun', *Mecmûa-ı İber-i İntibah* I, no. 2 (1279/1863): 51–52.

180 Arif, 'Urban Târîhi', *Mecmûa-ı İber-i İntibah* İkinci Sene, no. 7 (1280/1864): 175.

181 These charters themselves are actually important since they were written, in what Margaret C. Jacob calls 'the new language of constitutionalism', and the 'implication here is that laws and societies-not just the lodge-are human institutions and they can be altered by the will of the majority'. Margaret C. Jacob, *Living the Enlightenment: Freemasonry and Politics in Eighteenth-Century Europe:* (New York: Oxford University Press-USA, 1991), 47.

would accept political articles on condition that they were not composed 'with the deliberate intention of spoiling the public opinion'.[182] What we witness here is the first use of this abstract concept in what one might liberally call the mass media. Although *Mecmuâ-i Fünun* had wrestled with this idea, its writers somehow could never bring themselves to utter the phrase. While historians of the Empire have tended to bestow this honour onto Şinâsi for an article which appeared a year later, the term public opinion was 'released' for the first time by Ali Haydar Bey, an otherwise unknown man in a journal that is now almost as obscure as its owner.[183]

This chapter does not intend to provide a detailed inventory of Ottoman societies or their publications, even though such a work is sorely needed. This was a period when these organisations were in their infancy, and by 1870s they had expanded and multiplied into a number of very active societies throughout Istanbul, including an anti-tobacco league.[184] Some of these, such as *Darüşafaka*, were quite long-lived and carried on their customs and traditions into the republican era.[185] Others, such as the *Cemiyet-i Edebiye*, simply vanished, leaving little traces behind aside from their names. All of them, however, had one thing in common: by offering and encouraging new forms of sociability, they all contributed to the formation of an Ottoman public.

On the face of it, the government welcomed this civic spirit. The *İttifâk-i Âmme* (public alliance) that Mahmud II (r. 1808–1839) so

182 Ali Haydar Bey, 'Mecmûanın Nizâmı', 29. Though initially this journal avowed to remain out of politics as well, see BOA, İ..MVL. 482/21861, 10 Ramazan 1279 (1 March 1863).

183 There is some biographical information on Ali Haydar Bey in Niyazi Akı's history of nineteenth-century Ottoman theater as Ali Haydar wrote the first examples of Ottoman tragedy. See Niyazi Akı, *XIX. Yüzyıl Türk Tiyatrosu Târîhi* (Ankara: Ankara Üniversitesi Basımevi, 1963), 54–59. Although the same confusion prevails here since Akı claims that Ali Haydar Bey published these journals for the education of children. Ibid., 54, fn. 1. Also see Metin And, *Tanzimat ve İstibdat Döneminde Türk Tiyatrosu: 1839–1908* (İstanbul: Türkiye İş Bankası Kültür Yayınları, 1972), 341–342.

184 Mehmet Ö. Alkan, 'Osmanlı'da Cemiyetler Çağı', *Târîh ve Toplum* 40, no. 238 (2003): 6.

185 The school founded by *Cemiyet-i Tedrîsiye-i İslamiye* in the 1860s was probably the most successful of these early organisations. It was initially established by intellectuals such as Nâmık Kemal to teach the Muslim population how to read and write. According to Şerif Mardin, its '*Lycée*' is still a centre of conservatism. Mardin, *The Genesis of Young Ottoman Thought*, 219.

desperately longed for against the formidable janissaries was slowly coming to fruition.[186] A report, which was read during Abdülaziz's visit to *Meclis-i Vâlâ* in June 1865, applauded these *cemiyets* initiated by 'the good-doers and the scholars' of the country while stressing that they could only have been materialised because of the constant royal support for the *schooling of the public*.[187] The Empire's tutelary bureaucracy knew that it was the duty of a modern, i.e. Western, government to sponsor such unions and associations. As a result, not only local *cemiyets* in Istanbul, or other cities of the Empire, but also a society of zoology and botanic sciences in Paris,[188] a trade association in Manchester,[189] or a Mozart society in Brussels benefited from imperial munificence.[190]

Signs of restlessness in government circles however were also beginning to manifest themselves. The Ottoman state invoked the help of private initiative in *the schooling of the public*, but they preferred it to be on their own terms and without political complexities involved. The proliferation of contemporary knowledge about the outside world and the involvement of these societies in this process, however, opened the government up to certain risks. For example, despite strict surveillance and censorship, it was becoming extremely difficult to filter out the 'malicious information', coming from abroad that could 'corrupt' and 'degenerate' people's minds.[191] Even though Ottoman officers seemed certain that 'no one in their right mind would take heed of this kind of sedition', they also did their best to ensure that such temptations were not available. Even the personal books of *Dârülfünun*'s architect, Fossati, were kept at the customs office for inspection, and were handed back to him only after they were deemed to be 'not harmful'.[192] Nevertheless, in spite of all these protective measures, 'detrimental books', which were 'capable of perverting the minds (*izlâl-i ezhâna mûcib olacak*)', could sometimes end up in the middle of Istanbul, in a shop in Mahmutpaşa and then baffled custodians would

186 See Chapter 1, esp 42–64.

187 Cevad Nâfi, *Maârif-i Umûmîye Nezâreti*, 90.

188 BOA, İ..HR.. 171/9297, 12 Rebiülevvel 1276 (9 October 1856).

189 BOA, İ..HR.. 229/13414, 28 Receb 1284 (25 November 1867).

190 Especially the last document shows this desire of being one of them quite clearly: 'since this society has been supported in various degrees by the great rulers of Europe (*Avrupa hükumdaran-ı fehamı*)'. BOA, İ..HR.. 263/15745, 13 Rebiülevvel 1291 (30 April 1874).

191 BOA, HR.MKT. 360/76, 11 Cemaziyelahir 1277 (25 December 1860).

192 BOA, HR.MKT. 264/5, 1 Rebiülahir 1275 (8 November 1858).

run enquiries in order to determine how they had slipped through the customs.[193]

In other words, once the Pandora's box was opened, there was no containing it. In its inaugural issue, *Mir'ât*, the first Ottoman journal to be published with pictures (February 1863), warned statesmen against the possible side effects of the schooling of the public. 'As it is known to experts of propriety and knowledge', Refik (d. 1865), the editor-in-chief posited:

Civilisation, which means the attainment of perpetual affluence and contentment for a human society can only be achieved through the good *schooling of the public* (*hüsn-i terbiyet-i umûmîye*). But people who reside in this circle are also capable of, because of the nature of the civilization, evil deeds (*ef'al-i sey'ie*) on account of their experience and knowledge made in an exercise of some degree of freedom.[194]

The emergence of the Young Ottomans, who were also called '*cemiyet*', gave the ruling elite an unpleasant shock. Only a few years later, in 1867, the Society of Literature implicitly threated the government with armed resistance if no action were forthcoming to organise a national assembly.[195] Needless to say, its newspaper *Mecmuâ-i Maârif*

[193] BOA, HR.MKT. 292/16, 13 Zilkade 1275 (14 June 1859).

[194] '*Ehl-i edeb ve arifana mâlum olduğu vechile cemiyet-i beşeriyenin refah ve saâdet-i hal-i daimiye mazhar olması demek olan medeniyet esâsı hüsn-i terbiyet-i umûmîyedir. Çünkü tabiat-i medeniyet iktizasınca bu dâirede bulunan halk az çok nâil olacağı serbestliği tecarib ve mâlumat-ı muktesebesiyle ef'âl-i sey'iede dahi istimale muktedir olacağına ve bundan tevakki ve mücanebet edebilmesi mutlaka tehzib ahlakına menut olub, bunun husûlude terbiyet-i umûmîyeye mutavâkif bulunduğuna binaen hüsn-i terbiye esâs-i medeniyet oldugu âşikârdir*'. [Mustafa Refik], 'Esâs-ı Medeniyet', *Mir'ât* I, no. 1 (1279/1863): 2. About Refik, see İbnülemin Mahmud Kemal İnal, *Son Asır Türk Şâirleri*, 3 vols., vol. III (İstanbul: Orhaniye Matbaası, 1930), 1387–94.

[195] 'If I had one hundred thousand breech-loading rifles with people who would defend the rights of the Exalted State and if there were *people who were capable of conducting fluent and agreeable discourse*, only then I would have said with impunity "now this is the National Assembly of the Ottomans". But in this situation that we are in there is no doubt that conceiving such an idea is just dreaming'. Hayreddin, 'Mesâil-i Osmaniye', *Mecmûa-ı Maârif*, 27 Receb/ 13 November 1285/1868, 1, emphasis mine. *Cemiyet-i Edebiye* or the Society of Literature emerged again with promised open lectures with public benefit regarded as a fundamental policy in its charter. İsmet Efendi, 'Mukaddime: Cemiyet Nizâmnâmesidir', *Mecmûa-ı Maârif* I, no. 1 (1283/1866): 2–3, see especially the articles III–IV and V. Even though now it is even more obscure

or the '*Journal of Education*' was suspended for five years the very next day. But the word was already on the street. An article written in the form of an open letter to Mithat Pasha in 1872 shows this increasing tension between the government and the emerging public quite clearly:

The government, taking nothing into account and not listening to the words, which have been uttered, has this preconceived idea that "we do not have a public opinion." Even if they accept the existence of a public opinion, it does not amount to much: they think that if people become free (*serbest*), they will start bouncing off the walls. Because it is believed that people should be scared of the government. In their view, it should strike terror into their hearts. We want education. We want to mend our ways. We want to be civilized. The government takes away the education from us because it fears that, thanks to its influence, once the eyes of the people are opened, they will not be easily subdued.[196]

This feeling of mutual suspicion characterised the 1870s and lasted until the deposition of Sultan Abdülaziz. The following chapters examine in greater detail how the relationship between state and society shift from collaboration to confrontation. In short, however, the Ottoman public that the Tanzimat pashas animated with their schools, vitalised with their societies, and educated with their newspapers began to hold the government in contempt for political reasons. As Ahmed Hamdi Tanpınar, an early critic of the Ottoman literature and probably one of the most sophisticated authorities of the era, so elegantly put it: 'the reversing of the roles in such a manner had one explicit meaning: 'the regulating motion, which came about from above and outside by the fiat of the state was interiorized and turned into a revolution.'[197]

than *İber-i İntibah*, as far as the early journals are concerned, *Mecmuâ-i Maârif* was a success and ultimately turned into an almost-daily newspaper.

196 Ahmed Midhat Efendi, 'Midhat Paşa Hazretlerine Hitab', *Devir*, 17 Ağustos/29 August 1288/1872, 3.

197 Tanpınar, *XIX. Asır Türk Edebiyâtı Târîhi*, 150.

5 *The Emergence of a Reading Public after c. 1860*

Introduction

Before writing about a reading public which comprises not only intellectuals but also great masses of people, it might be useful to begin this chapter with a few concluding remarks on government endeavours to modernise and spread education. The introduction of the Regulation of Public Instruction (*Maârif-i Umûmîye Nizâmnâmesi*) in 1869,[1] another touchstone of Ottoman educational history, was a part of this effort.[2] It reflected the state's on-going centralisation efforts in the domain of education. The law structured the entire Ottoman school system in a very meticulous manner (consolidated under five headings and 198 articles) and adopted a standard curriculum for every state student, Muslim and non-Muslim alike. According to regulations, four-year schools were to be opened in every village and district with the attendance of boys between the ages of seven and eleven years and girls between six and ten years compulsory. Following this, the government embarked upon a nationwide literacy campaign and opened schools throughout the country.[3]

[1] It divided the whole school system between private and state schools and gave free hand to private schools in internal matters. For the full text, see BOA, Y..EE.. 112/6 24 Cemaziyelahir 1286 (1 October 1869). For the published text, see *Düstûr*, Tertîb-i Evvel ed., 4 vols., vol. II (İstanbul: Matbaa-i Amire, 1289–1872/1873), 184–219; Cevad Nâfi, *Maârif-i Umûmîye Nezâreti*, 469–510.

[2] See Ekmeleddin İhsanoğlu, *Science, Technology, and Learning in the Ottoman Empire: Western Influence, Local Institutions, and the Transfer of Knowledge* (Aldershot, UK: Ashgate/Variorum, 2004), 302.

[3] See, for instance, these two reports; the first one is a feasibility report prepared by the Council of the State (*Şûrâ-ı Devlet*) on schools to be opened to make teaching and education public. The second is on the 'latest literacy campaign' and the teachers who were to be employed in recently opened schools. BOA, İ..MMS. 37/1541, 7 Rebiülevvel 1286 (17 June 1869), BOA, MF.MKT. 3/92, 6 Cemaziyelahir 1289 (11 August 1872).

How these joint efforts by the state and the learned societies on the 'schooling of the public' translated into real life is another, more complicated question. The usual diligence of Ottoman civil servants in keeping numerical data was not traditionally associated with literacy whose rates remained largely speculative before the republican era. In François Georgeon's estimation merely 10 to 15 per cent of the whole population could read and write at the beginning of the twentieth century.[4] While Carter Findley gives a slightly lower figure (5 to 10 per cent),[5] Cem Behar puts the adult literacy rate at around 25 per cent at the end of the nineteenth century.[6] These numbers are low compared to other modernising empires, let alone any European power.[7] Japan, for instance, enjoyed a literacy rate of about 40 per cent for males and 15 per cent for females as early as 1870s.[8] China had a similar ratio attained for males, though a much lower female literacy rate.[9] Russia was roughly comparable to the Ottoman Empire for most of the period (with 6 per cent literacy rate around the 1850s) and achieved a phenomenal escalation around the end of the century.[10]

A statistic from 1894–1895, prepared by Mehmed Behiç Bey, on the other hand, portrays a rather different picture. According to his figures, 77.95 per cent of Istanbul population over ten years of age could read and write, and adult literacy across the Empire was almost 66 per cent.[11]

[4] François Georgeon, 'Lire et écrire à la fin de l'Empire ottoman: Quelques remarques introductives', *Revue du monde musulman et de la Méditerranée*, no. 75–76 (1995): 173.

[5] Carter Vaughn Findley, *Ottoman Civil Officialdom: A Social History* (Princeton, NJ: Princeton University Press, 1989), 139.

[6] Behar, *A Neighborhood in Ottoman Istanbul*, 206, fn. 62.

[7] See David Vincent, *The Rise of Mass Literacy: Reading and Writing in Modern Europe* (Cambridge, UK: Polity, 2000), 1–26.

[8] Peter Kornicki, *The Book in Japan: A Cultural History from the Beginnings to the Nineteenth Century* (Honolulu: University of Hawai'i Press, 2001), 275.

[9] Evelyn Sakakida Rawski, *Education and Popular Literacy in Ch'ing China* (Ann Arbor: University of Michigan Press, 1979), 140.

[10] E. Anthony Swift, *Popular Theater and Society in Tsarist Russia* (Berkeley: University of California Press, 2002), 42–43.

[11] The statistics published in Karpat, *Ottoman Population 1890–1914*, 221. The numbers are given in 'illiteracy forms' and they are converted into the literacy figures for the sake of simplicity. Also see Mehmed Behiç Bey, *Yevmiye Kâtibi Mehmet Behiç Tarafından Tanzim Olunan İstatistik Defteri* (İstanbul Üniversitesi Türkçe El Yazmaları No: 9075).

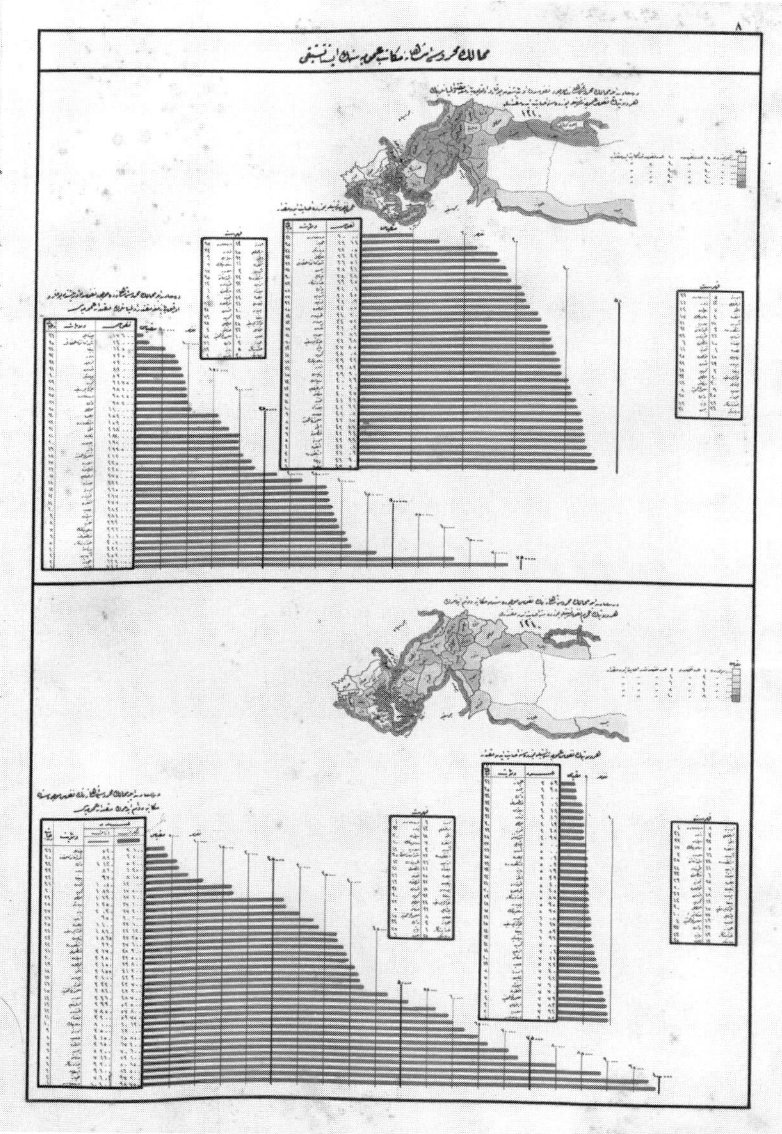

Figure 5.1 A statistic from 1894–1895, prepared by Mehmed Behiç Bey, suggested that 77.95 per cent of Istanbul population over ten years of age could read and write, and adult literacy across the Empire was almost 66 per cent.
Mehmed Behiç Bey, *Yevmiye Kâtibi Mehmet Behiç Tarafından Tanzim Olunan İstatistik Defteri* (İstanbul Üniversitesi Türkçe El Yazmaları No: 9075), 8

The data looks puzzling.[12] But one needs to remember that Istanbul was a true cosmopolitan city: '*la vraie tour de Babel*' as Théophile Gautier named it,[13] with a population of almost one million (873,575) in 1885.[14] Of this number, 55.94 per cent was non-Muslim and of the Muslim population, a considerable portion (almost 50 per cent of the males) consisted of civil servants (22,894) and students of religious and public schools (73,199).[15] While Kemal Karpat, who previously used this data, stated that there was no information regarding the procedure employed in its collection, it clearly must be from the first modern Ottoman census conducted between 1881 and 1893. Mehmed Behiç Bey was an employee of the Public Registry Office (*Nüfûs-ı Umûmîye İdâresi*), which ran the survey.[16] He stood out there for his 'statistical talents' and was eventually transferred to the Office of Statistics.[17] He became its director just after the Young Turk Revolution in 1908 and at one point even attempted to publish a popular scientific journal named *Mecmuâ-i İstatistik* (*Journal of Statistics*).[18] In other words, these figures might look questionable, but they are not negligible. Even though Carter Findley finds these illiteracy rates 'implausibly low',[19] it is difficult to ignore the increasing cultural complexity, which was stimulated rather than stifled by the political problems, throughout the second half of the nineteenth century.

[12] According to the figures Kemal Karpat gives, 89,000 illiterate made up 22.05 per cent of the Istanbul population which would give the total number as 403,628 people. If you add to this number the children younger than ten during the census, one effectively has the population of the inner city, see Kemal Karpat, 'Ottoman Population Records and the Census of 1881/82–1893', *International Journal of Middle East Studies* 9, no. 2 (1978): 273.

[13] Théophile Gautier, *Constantinople*, Nouvelle Èdition ed. (Paris: Michel Lévy Frères, 1865), 79.

[14] See Stanford J. Shaw, 'The Population of Istanbul in the Nineteenth Century', *International Journal of Middle East Studies* 10, no. 2 (1979): 266.

[15] Ibid., 271. These numbers do not include non-Muslim state employees (1,128) and students (80,020). In other words, even if the merchants and traders were completely illiterate, half of the male population of the city had to know how to read and write because of their professions.

[16] See his personal record, BOA, DH.SAİD.MEM 18/14, 29 Zilhicce 1275 (30 July 1859). From his obituary, we understand that after the proclamation of the Republic, he took the surname Erberk. See Anonymous, '[Ölüm İlanı]', *Cumhûriyet*, 27 May 1938, 4.

[17] BOA, İ..TNF. 7/1315/L-03, 9 Şevval 1315 (3 March 1898).

[18] BOA, BEO. 3387/254015, 2 Şaban 1326 (30 August 1908), BOA, DH.MKT. 2816/54, 27 Rebiülahir 1327 (18 May 1909).

[19] Findley, *Ottoman Civil Officialdom*, 139, fn. 28.

This brings us to the theme of this chapter, which can be broadly summarised as the emergence of a cultural public sphere in the Ottoman Empire. The chapter begins with a discussion of *Cerîde-i Havâdis* (1840) as the first example of private newspapers in the Ottoman Empire. Its comparison with the dailies of the 1860s provides us a chance to see a number of important changes taking place in this period. Here the chapter briefly underlines the importance of printing houses as political spaces and examines the commodification of discourse through the birth of the professional author. Next, by focusing on Nâmık Kemal as the prime example, it is argued that a new relationship between public and intellectuals was established during this period. Close attention to Kemal's articles reveals the growing importance of the term 'public opinion' in daily political language. Through his writings and other contemporary examples, the chapter also explores the significance of unofficial spaces, such as steamboats, in providing discursive communication, including discussions of transparently political questions. It is argued that these places had an underestimated effect in solidifying imperial and eventually national identities. Throughout the chapter the division between journalism and literature is also deliberately disregarded as this is anachronistic (appeared only in the late nineteenth century) and makes little sense when much of the prose written by Tanzimat novelists was first serialised in newspapers and published only later in book forms.[20]

The Birth of Private Newspapers

The first non-official newspaper in Turkish, *Cerîde-i Havâdis* (*Register of News*) was founded in 1840 by an Englishman named William Churchill (Vilyam Çörcil). In a strange way, this was a direct result of the increasing European presence in the capital. While hunting birds in the vicinity of Istanbul in 1837, Churchill accidentally shot a Turkish boy and was imprisoned. It is not clear what transpired in prison, but the impression was that the Ottoman authorities maltreated him during his time in the custody.[21] The threats of John Ponsonby, British ambassador to Constantinople, to bring down the Ottoman Empire if

[20] For this discussion, see Matthew Rubery, *The Novelty of Newspapers: Victorian Fiction after the Invention of the News* (Oxford: Oxford University Press, 2009), 11.

[21] See BOA, HAT, 1231/ 47986/E, 29 Zilhicce 1252 (6 April 1837).

Âkif Paşa, then Secretary for Foreign Affairs, did not immediately liberate Churchill caused a minor diplomatic crisis between the Porte and the British embassy.[22] Even though the Russian ambassador claimed that this was just a 'British scheme' to disturb the good relations of the Ottoman Empire with his country, Âkif Pasha, who had surprisingly good rapport with St. Petersburg,[23] was eventually sacked and Churchill was released from the prison after three days.[24]

Though subsequent Ottoman histories depicted Churchill as a freelance journalist,[25] as Orhan Koloğlu points out this assertion seems rather dubious.[26] Especially after the abolition of the janissaries, there came more and more 'European adventurers who roam through Turkey, ready at five minutes' notice to undertake the drill of a

[22] For the details from the Ottoman perspective or rather from the perspective of Âkif Pasha, see Akif Pacha, *Un diplomate ottoman en 1836: Affaire Churchill, Trad. annotée de 'l'Éclaircissement" (Tebsireh) d'Akif Pacha, Ministre des Affaires Etrangeres de Turquie*, trans. Arthur Alric (Paris: Ernest Leroux, 1892), esp. 12–14. For the Turkish edition, see Âkif Paşa, *Tabsıra-i Âkif Paşa* (Istanbul: Ebuzziyâ Matbaası, 1300/1882–1883), esp. 10–12. Also see BOA, HAT 1231/ 47986/B, 29 Zilhicce 1252 (6 April 1837).

[23] See, for instance, 'We learn, by a letter of the 28th Sept., from Constantinople, that the English fleet, along with the Turkish, was then in the Dardanelles, and that it was fully expected that the English would pass into the Black Sea. The. ex-minister of the interior, Âkif Pacha, had been sharply remonstrated with for having received the Russian ambassador at his residence. There was a warm contest in the Turkish ministry between the influence of Russia and that of England. The part acted by France in the struggle was not positively known'. *Army and Navy Chronicle*, ed. Benjamin Homans, 13 vols., vol. VI (Washington, DC: Benjamin Homans, 1839), 335. Also see Christine M. Philliou, *Biography of An Empire*, 140. Âkif Pasha argued in a similar vein: '*L'affaire ne meritait pas de prendre de pareilles proportions… En se conduisant comme on l'avait fait des le debut, on voulait uniquement grosser I'incident, afin de provoquer ma destitution et mon remplacement*'. Âkif Pacha, *Un diplomate ottoman en 1836*, 14, 39.

[24] BOA, HAT 1231/ 47986/I, 29 Zilhicce 1252 (6 April 1837). Even Prince Metternich interfered and, according to the Ottoman sources, criticised the behaviour of Ponsonby. See BOA, HAT, 962/41198/E, 29 Zilhicce 1251 (16 April 1836), or BOA, HAT, 1205/47278/B, 29 Zilhicce 1254 (15 March 1839). Probably it was indeed an excuse to get rid of Âkif Pasha.

[25] Enver Behnan Şapolyo, for instance, after attributing to him high family connections, claimed that he was the Istanbul correspondent of *Morning Herald*. Enver Behnan Şapolyo, *Türk Gazetecilik Târîhi ve Her Yönüyle Basın* (Ankara: Güven Matbaası, 1969), 109.

[26] See Orhan Koloğlu, *Miyop Çörçil Olayı: Cerîde-i Havâdis 'in Öyküsü* (Ankara: Yorum Yayıncılık, 1986), 21–24. Although he does not use Ottoman archival sources, Koloğlu's account of the event is very detailed.

battalion, the service of an hospital, or the construction of a battery, turns Turk for a year or two, and then leaves the country'.[27] He might well have been one of those wanderer 'fellow-Europeans' that Benedict Anderson mentions as a global phenomenon.[28] But knowledge about his previous life is very limited. In any case, as later events demonstrated, he was at least interested in journalism since, either because of the connections that he established during the incident or because of a promise made to him during the reparations, he obtained permission for the first non-official newspaper in Turkish in 1840.[29]

Churchill must have seen potential in Istanbul. Especially the integration of the Ottoman Empire into the world economy made the rapid exchange of information essential for a new class of people living in the Empire and there were already a few foreign weeklies running in major trade centres such as Smyrna.[30] The petition that he presented for the necessary paperwork shows that he had done his homework. He highlighted, for instance, the potential of newspapers to 'enslave and enthral hearths of the public (*kulûb-i âmme*) and opinions of the people (*efkâr-ı kâffe*)'.[31] He also emphasised the functional benefit of transparency in governmental decision making, one of the main points of *Takvîm-i Vekâyi*'s inaugural issue. Public opinion as a term in Ottoman Turkish did not yet exist in the 1840s, but this statement (hearths of the *public* and *opinions* of the people) is close enough. Churchill specified that his newspaper was going to be in an easy enough language 'for everybody to benefit, virtually a coarse Turkish

[27] Andrew Archibald Paton, *The Modern Syrians; or Native Society in Damascus, Aleppo, and the Mountains of the Druses, from Notes Made in Those Parts during the Years 1841–2–3* (London: Longman, Brown, Green, and Longmans, 1844), 261. Also see Charles MacFarlane, *Constantinople in 1828 II*, 337.

[28] See Anderson, *Imagined Communities*, 58.

[29] The whole scandal was actually solved only with the Sultan taking the initiative. Churchill was freed, awarded an indemnity, and presented with a diamond-studded imperial decoration. Âkif Pacha, *Un diplomate ottoman en 1836*, VII.

[30] In 1828, Charles MacFarlane even criticised these papers' political engagements and remarked: 'if Smyrna must have a paper, let it be what it ought, – a register of the arrival and departure of ships, and a chronicle of the rates of exchange, and of the prices of figs, opium, and cotton bales'. Charles MacFarlane, *Constantinople in 1828: A Residence of Sixteen Months in the Turkish Capital and Provinces: With an Account of the Present State of the Naval and Military Power and of the Resources of the Ottoman Empire*, 2 vols., vol. I (London: Saunders and Otley, 1829), 263.

[31] Kaynar, *Mustafa Reşit Paşa ve Tanzimat*, 313.

and without strange Arabic and Persian words', another important concern for the Tanzimat elite.[32] The Consultative Assembly (*Meclis-i Meşveret*), as a response, pointed out that the money that Churchill requested for the initial expenses was 'not that much', 'public benefit (*menâfi'-i umûmîye*) of such a undertaking could not be denied', and a second newspaper in Istanbul could be in fact useful, as they accentuated twice, 'to reform the people's mind (*ıslah-ı ezhân-ı nâs*)'.[33]

The circumstances surrounding the birth of *Cerîde-i Havâdis* are strangely akin to those of *Shenbao*, the first non-official newspaper in China. *Shenbao* was also founded after a court case, although not of a very similar character, by a British businessman living in Shanghai in the 1870s.[34] The newspaper intended, as Barbara Mittler reports, to 'edify and instruct its reader' through 'easy-to-understand language' and promised, as its foremost goal, to 'renew all the people'.[35] But the similarity basically ends there. *Shenbao* was an enduring success and *Cerîde-i Havâdis* was not (it was actually a long-lasting failure).[36] In many ways, Churchill's paper was a bad copy of *Takvîm-i Vekâyi*, the official gazette. It contained no striking innovations; there was nothing different in its arrangement and one needed to be an articulate reader to make sense of the news replete with circumlocution.[37] With the exception of occasional breaks during major crisis, such as the

[32] Ibid., 314. [33] Ibid., 316.

[34] Vittinghoff, 'Readers, Publishers and Officials in the Contest for a Public Voice', 397–398.

[35] Barbara Mittler, *A Newspaper for China?: Power, Identity, and Change in Shanghai's News Media, 1872 – 1912* (Cambridge, MA: Harvard University Press, 2004), 13–14.

[36] According to Ami Ayalon, 'the public's disinterest in such papers did not result solely from the fact that they represented the voice of the authorities. When an Englishman, William Churchill, tried to publish the first nonofficial paper in Istanbul in 1840, he quickly found himself giving it away in the streets free of charge, for nobody would buy it. Failing to elicit sufficient public interest in this novelty, he was forced to shut it down after a while'. Ami Ayalon, *The Press in the Arab Middle East: A History* (Oxford: Oxford University Press, 1995), 147. Ayalon here is probably wrong in not perceiving *Cerîde* as a 'voice of the authority'. It should be also noted that the newspaper continued with ups and down for almost thirty years and was not 'shut down after a while' as he argues.

[37] Selim Nüzhet points out that '*Cerîde-i Havâdis*'s outline, writing style and content are almost identical with *Takvîm-i Vekâyi* at the beginning'. It should be noted that according to Nüzhet, the paper gradually embraced an easier Turkish. Selim Nüzhet, *Türk Gazeteciliği 1831–1931* (İstanbul: Devlet Matbaası, 1931), 36–37.

Crimean War, *Cerîde* always depended on a government subsidy for its survival and it never reached a popular acclaim.[38] It was for this reason that later republican historians chose to criticise the paper stating that 'it was in Turkish but it was not Turkish (*Türkçe idi, fakat Türk değildi*)'.[39] While *Shenbao* became truly a Chinese newspaper, for many Ottomans *Cerîde* was just a foreign interloper with dubious connections.[40]

But this does not mean that it was inconsequential. First of all, according to Cevdet Pasha, its print shop provided the very ground, ideologically and organisationally, upon which tangible political activities took off and gained momentum in the Empire.[41] For Cevdet Pasha, people who met at that '*de facto* academy' because of their aversion to Âli Pasha created the true political opposition in Istanbul. This might be dismissed as an exaggeration. However, like *konaks* and other venues of sociability, printing houses were also critical hubs of cultural exchange. Especially after the decline of *konak* sociability in the late 1850s,[42] the role that these places played, as the centres of intellectual activity, became more pronounced. For the Young Ottomans, the print shop of *Le Courrier d'Orient* (1860–1870), for instance, was almost a sanctuary because of the legal protections it enjoyed as a foreign investment.[43] It was through its editor, Jean Pietri (or Giampietri), that Mustafa Fâzıl, the sponsor of the Young

38 Churchill was practically on a government payroll. This payment, however, depended upon his 'performance' and was occasionally suspended because of the 'fallacious articles' appearing in his paper. See for instance, a warning to Churchill, BOA, İ..DH.. 45/2230, 12 Şaban 1257 (29 September 1841). Two years later, he was cut out because of his 'poor performance', but reinstalled to the payroll again a year later. See respectively, BOA, İ..HR.. 22/1035, 3 Receb 1259 (30 July 1843), BOA, İ..HR.. 26/1239, 19 Receb 1260 (4 August 1844).

39 Server İskit, *Türkiye'de Matbuat İdâreleri ve Politikaları* (İstanbul: Başvekâlet Basın ve Yayın Umûm Müdürlüğü Yayınları, 1943), 4.

40 A. D. Jeltyakov, *Türkiyenin Sosyo-Politik ve Kültürel hayâtında Basın (1729–1908)* (Ankara: Basın Yayın Genel Müdürlüğü, 1979), 53. Tevfik, *Yeni Osmanlılar Târîhi I*, 457.

41 In his words, 'its print shop turned into a gathering place for the intellectuals of the time and it became a home for young men who later became known as Young Turks'. Cevdet Paşa, *Tezâkir 13–20*, 35.

42 See Chapter 2, esp. 106–09.

43 Because of the long history of capitulations, the Empire was a safe haven for foreign investments. See V. Necla Geyikdağı, *Foreign Investment in the Ottoman Empire: International Trade and Relations 1854–1914* (London: I. B. Tauris, 2011), 53–73.

Ottomans, made contact with Nâmık Kemal and Ziyâ Pasha.[44] On many occasions, the members of the society ensconced themselves in its office.[45] The print shop of *Tasvîr-i Efkâr*, also known as *Dârün-Nedve* or House of Consultancy by contemporaries, was also a regular meeting point for dissidents like Nâmık Kemal or Ayetullah Efendi.[46] Kemal's 'satellites' went through their intellectual education there 'in constant exchange of ideas'.[47] Especially because of their religiously mixed environment (Strauss reports that as late as 1914, most printing presses in Istanbul were still managed by non-Muslims),[48] these spaces offered a distinctive conviviality in which people of different creeds and beliefs could socialise.[49] Perhaps it should be mentioned that some of the most important opposition newspapers in later years, such as *Muhbir/Informer* (1866–1868), *İbret/Exemplary* (1870–1773), *Diyojen/Diogenes* (1870–1873), or *Sabah/Morning* (1876–1922) were all owned by non-Muslim Ottoman citizens and they sometimes worked in close collaboration with names like Suâvi or Nâmık Kemal against political compulsion.[50]

But more importantly *Cerîde* served an example for the subsequent papers to emulate, albeit somewhat belatedly. With the emergence of *Cerîde*, the newspaper turned for the first time into something non-governmental, something belonging to the civil sphere of the society.[51]

44 Roderic H. Davison, *Reform in the Ottoman Empire, 1856–1876* (Princeton, NJ: Princeton University Press, 1963), 202, fn. 108. Though Davison does not cite any reference for this information, his source must be Ebuzziyâ's account; see Tevfik, *Yeni Osmanlılar Târîhi I*, 62.

45 Ebuzziyâ, *Yeni Osmanlılar Târîhi I*, 70, 85–87.

46 Sâmî Paşazâde Hasan Bey, 'Ayetullah Bey ve Yeni Osmanlılar', 3. '*Darün-Nedve*' was something of a town hall in Mecca in the time of Muhammad. Ahmed Cevdet, *Kısas-ı Enbiya ve Tevârih-i Hülefa*, ed. Mahir İz, 3 vols., vol. I (Ankara: Milli Eğitim Bakanlığı Kültür Yayınları, 1972), 212.

47 Tevfik, *Yeni Osmanlılar Târîhi I*, 56–57.

48 Strauss, 'Kütüp ve Resail-i Mevkute', 228.

49 Jeltyakov, *Türkiyenin Sosyo-Politik ve Kültürel hayâtında Basın (1729–1908)*, 54.

50 This is also true for important publishing houses such as *Vatan Kütübhânesi* or *Asır Kütübhânesi*, both owned by Armenian-Ottomans. Ottoman intellectuals were also regularly reading Turkish newspapers written in Armenian alphabet. Unfortunately, our knowledge about those papers is very limited. See, for instance, Ahmet İhsan, *Matbuat Hâtıralarım, 1888–1923: Meşrûtiyet İlânina Kadar*, 2 vols., vol. I (İstanbul: Ahmet İhsan Matbaası, 1931), 43–44.

51 International and domestic political problems intensified public debate. See, for instance, a spy report from 1840 discussing the Egyptian affair: 'They have not

As Ahmed Emin highlighted in 1914, 'the Crimean War and the general eagerness to get war news gave a new turn to the position of the press, extending the circle of readers and making the ground ready for self-supporting and independent newspapers'.[52] Indeed the decades following the war saw a dizzying proliferation in the number of papers appearing in the Empire. Quantitatively speaking, from the foundation of *Takvîm-i Vekâyi* in 1831 to 1860, an Ottoman had only four journals or newspapers to peruse with his or her morning coffee. By 1876, this number was 130.[53] The lion's share fell to Istanbul. In 1876, the imperial capital boasted seventy-two newspapers apprising citizens of the latest news.[54] These provided the information necessary for 'any kind of informed political debate; the essential prerequisite for the formation of opinion'.[55] Especially the detailed publication of the Ottoman budgets, the *compte-rendus*, fuelled ardent discussions in the press.[56] Robert Walsh, living in the Empire in the 1830s noticed this as 'the most extraordinary communication ... that would please

had the peace published in the *Takvîm* [newspaper]. They must be embarrassed.' Kırlı, 'The Struggle Over Space', 219.

52 Ahmed Emin [Yalman], *The Development of Modern Turkey as Measured by Its Press* (New York: Colombia University, 1914), 33. According to Stefanie Markovits, 'the world fashioned by the mass media during the Crimean War, though doubtless the product of commercialization, functioned as a public sphere in reality as well as in appearance'. Stefanie Markovits, 'Rushing into Print: "Participatory Journalism" during the Crimean War', *Victorian Studies* 50, no. 4 (2008): 561. Similar views were also presented for the Russian Empire. See Renner, 'Defining a Russian Nation', 659–660.

53 Orhan Koloğlu, *Osmanlı'dan Günümüze Türkiye'de Basın* (İstanbul: İletişim Yayınları, 1992), 37.

54 Roderic H. Davison, 'The Question of Ali Paşa's Political Testament', *International Journal of Middle East Studies* 11, no. 2 (1980): 220.

55 Hannah Barker, *Newspapers, Politics, and Public Opinion in Late Eighteenth-Century England* (Oxford: Oxford University Press, 1998), 4.

56 After 1863, they also began to be published separately, see *Devlet-i Âliye'nin Yetmiş Dokuz Senesi Muvâzene Defteridir* (İstanbul: Matbaa-i Amire, 1280/1863–1864). Sublime Porte Ministère des Finances, *Budget des recettes et des dépenses de l'exercice 1863–1864 et Compte-Rendu de l'emploi des ressources extraordinaires crées pour le retrait du Papier-monnaie et le remboursement de la dette flottante* (Constantinople: Imprimerie du Journal de Constantinople, 1863). For the details, see Abdüllatif Şener, *Osmanlı Mâliyesinin Şeffaflaşması: Yayımlanan İlk Bütçeler* (İstanbul: Kapı Yayınları, 2008). Interesting detail of this transparency was given by an hitherto unnoticed article, see Saint-Marc Girardin, 'Les voyageurs en Orient: De la Moralité des finances turques', *Revue des Deux Mondes* 31, no. Janvier/Février (1861): 473–476.

Mr. Hume'.[57] Consequently, men like Nâmık Kemal after scrutinising the figures published by the official newspaper could give a thorough account of the Ottoman financial situation and compare it with other countries in detail.[58] This helped, as in France, to crystallise public opinion.[59]

The Commodification of Literature

There was one crucial difference between early didactic journals such as *Mecmuâ-i Fünun* (*Journal of Sciences*) and popular newspapers of a slightly later period such as *İbret*. The former ones were written by enlightened civil servants with an explicit aim of 'schooling' their public.[60] The latter, in contrast, were written by professional journalists (such as Ebuzziyâ and Ahmed Mithat Efendi) who while potentially concerned with education for understandable reasons, were also interested in their own finances. Obscure articles on electricity, stratosphere or geology, couched in a patronizing style, were gradually

57 'This is a thing', he continued, 'before unheard of in Turkish policy, where public money was a mystery, and everything concerning it kept secret, both in its collection and expenditure'. Rev. R. Walsh, *A Residence at Constantinople during a Period Including the Commencement, Progress, and Termination of the Greek and Turkish Revolutions*, 2 vols., vol. II (London: Frederick Westley and A. H. Davis, 1836), 282–283. 'Mr. Hume' that Walsh referred to is not David Hume (d. 1776), philosopher, economist, and historian, but rather Joseph Hume (d. 1855), doctor and radical MP, his contemporary. 'Beginning in 1819, and continuing throughout the 1820s, Hume operated as the "watchdog of the British treasury". He carefully dissected every budget matter brought before the Commons'. Ronald K. Huch and Paul R. Ziegler, *Joseph Hume: the People's M.P* (Ephrata, PA: American Philosophical Society, 1985), 19.

58 Nâmık Kemal, 'Muvâzene-i Mâliye', *Hürriyet*, 30 August 1869, 1–4. To another article, he began by saying 'I wonder if you had a chance to examine the budget of this year'. Nâmık Kemal, 'Matbaa-i Amire', *Hadîka*, 15 Şevval/16 December 1289/1872, 1.

59 See Gail Bossenga, 'The Financial Origins of the French Revolution', in *From Deficit to Deluge: The Origins of the French Revolution*, ed. Thomas E. Kaiser and Dale K. Van Kley (Palo Alto, CA: Stanford University Press, 2011), 56; Baker, *Inventing the French Revolution*, 191–192. Writing in 1950, Hans Speier also remarked how 'we know more about the history of literacy, the press, the law of sedition, and censorship than about the relationship between the struggle for budget control and the history of public opinion'. See Hans Speier, 'Historical Development of Public Opinion', 380.

60 In the first issue of his newspaper, *Asır*, Mehmed Tevfik Bey wrote in 1870 'we hope it will be understood that we have not undertaken this responsibility to indulge in pedantry'. [Mehmed Tevfik] *Asır*, 4.

replaced by learned articles and translations from foreign dailies.[61] This also coincided with the period in which *ulemâ* began to lose its grip on discursive monopoly. Its two strongholds, law and education, were facing daily challenges from the outside world and newspapers were instrumental in providing the most advanced developments in these fields to every nook and cranny of the society.

In most cases what animated individuals to run enterprises like a newspaper was the potential of a profitable market. With the expansion of the Ottoman public through the 1860s and 1870s (quantitatively and qualitatively), newspapers became a part of daily life and were perceived as lucrative business opportunities.[62] Though numbers are scanty and sometimes speculative,[63] according to various sources, some issues of *Tasvîr-i Efkâr* sold twenty-four thousand copies in the early 1860s and the newspaper eventually built up a circulation unprecedented in the Empire.[64] Similar figures were also given for *İbret* whose first issue supposedly sold twenty-five thousand copies.[65] Even if these numbers are dismissed as retrospective overstatements, one can rely more on contemporary testimonies, such as that of Ali Efendi who stated that during the Franco-Prussian War of 1870, his paper, *Basîret* (*Watchfulness*), was selling around ten thousand copies per day.[66]

61 See, for instance, some examples of early articles, Kadri Bey, 'Alaim-i Semaviye', *Mecmûa-i Fünun* I, no. 1 (1279/1862): 37–44; Edhem Paşa, 'Medhal-i İlm-i Jeoloji', *Mecmûa-ı Fünun* I, no. 2 (1279/1862): 68–75; Safvet Paşa, 'Suyun Mahiyet ve Enva-i ve Havass-i Hekimiye ve Kimyeviyesi', *Mecmûa-ı Fünun* I, no. 10 (1279/1983): 419–424.

62 Kuntay mentions admiringly the enormous money that Nâmık Kemal made as a journalist (three hundred gold lira per month). See Kuntay, *Nâmık Kemal Devrinin İnsanları I*, V.

63 Palmira Brummett mentions how, even at the beginning of the twentieth century, 'most gazettes did not include circulation statistics as an integral part of the published subscriber information'. Palmira Brummett, *Image and Imperialism in the Ottoman Revolutionary Press: 1908–1911* (New York: State University of New York Press, 2000), 43.

64 Jeltyakov, *Türkiyenin Sosyo-Politik ve Kültürel hayâtında Basın*, 55.

65 Koloğlu, *Osmanlı'dan Günümüze Türkiye'de Basın*, 39.

66 [Basîretçi] Ali, *İstanbul'da Yarım Asırlık Vakayi-i Mühimme* (İstanbul: Matbaa-i Hüseyin Enver, 1325/1909), 6. With his publication, he openly supported Prussia and after the war, he was invited to Berlin by Bismarck, met him and showered with gifts including a latest technology printing press. Ibid., 14–24. This at least shows the influence that Bismarck ascribed to the Ottoman press. A contemporary humour magazine, *Çaylak/Novice*, while complaining 'lamentable situation' of Ottoman newspapers compared to Europe in 1877, mockingly gave *Basîret* as an example selling only 5,675 copies per day and read

Ebuzziyâ Tevfik, another contemporary and a partner in *İbret*, also noted how, after its nineteenth issue, the newspaper raised its daily publication twelve thousand in 1872.[67]

If these statistics are genuine, compared to contemporary sale figures of Russian or Japanese newspapers, the Ottoman figures are quite substantial.[68] In fact even compared with Germany where 'a circulation of 10,000 was large for any newspaper in the years 1850–1900 ...[or] a circulation of 2,000–5,000 was significant',[69] the Ottoman press proved to be vibrant and resilient. It should be also remembered that the newspapers in the West were products of a mature print culture. Their Ottoman counterparts were not. The journalism in the Empire lagged behind in what Paul Starr has described as the 'information price revolution' which resulted from the sharp decline in the cost of publishing.[70] Before this took place in the mid-nineteenth century, even in England 'no paper had a daily circulation of more than five thousand readers', and they 'all maintained average circulations under seven thousand even at the height of the Napoleonic wars'.[71] With a slight increase in its sale figures, and only around the

exclusively by *paçacı esnafı* (merchants of an Ottoman delicacy made of calves' feet). Cited in Hamdi Öziş, *Osmanlı Mizah Basınında Batılılaşma ve Siyaset: 1870–1877* (İstanbul: Libra, 2010), 105.

67 Tevfik, *Yeni Osmanlılar Târîhi I*, 417.

68 Writing of two 'important' newspapers of the 1860s Japan, Fabian Schäfer remarked that 'the former once reached a circulation of more than 1,500 copies'. Fabian Schäfer, *Public Opinion – Propaganda – Ideology: Theories on the Press and Its Social Function in Interwar Japan, 1918–1937* (Leiden: Brill, 2012), 9. Russian figures are comparable to the Ottoman ones. '*Moskovskie Vedomosti* continued to grow, reaching its apogee in 1867 with a circulation of 13,750. For a decade *Moskovskie Vedomosti* remained the biggest of all the political newspapers in Russia (with a circulation between 12,000 and 13,000).' Renner, 'Defining a Russian Nation', 673.

69 Abigail Green, 'Intervening in the Public Sphere: German Governments and the Press, 1815–1870', *The Historical Journal* 44, no. 1 (2001): 173. Germany, after unification, and the Ottoman Empire had similar populations, around 40 million. Cf. Karpat, *Ottoman Population 1890–1914*, 25; Hajo Holborn, *A History of Modern Germany: 1840–1945*, 3 vols., vol. III (Princeton, NJ: Princeton University Press, 1982), 367.

70 Paul Starr, *The Creation of the Media: Political Origins of Modern Communications* (New York: Basic Books, 2004), 124. Also see Ahmed Rasim's account about how Ottoman printing houses were not able to keep up with the demand, especially during important political events. Rasim, *Matbuat Hâtıralarından*, 2.

71 Rubery, *The Novelty of Newspapers*, 6.

1830s, *The Times* began to lead the market with a daily sale of around ten thousand copies.[72] But after the removal of the Stamp Duty in June 1855 and with accompanying technological developments in printing, the numbers increased incomparably.[73] In a similar vein, following the abolition of the Stamp Tax in 1900 in the Ottoman Empire, some papers like *İkdam* were able to sell fifty thousand or more copies on special occasions.[74]

Moreover a paper's influence was not solely circumscribed by its circulation figures, especially in a culture where 'public reading' (*kır-âât-ı umûmîye*) was a frequent practice.[75] Examining the Tanzimat period, Ahmed Emin Yalman deduced that 'a single copy could reach a great many more people through the medium of the coffee house and through the evening gatherings of neighbors in the different houses of the neighborhood'.[76] In 1883, Nâmık Kemal, after remarking how intellectual curiosity increased a hundred times in women and men in last fifteen years, noted that one copy of newspaper could reach at least fifteen thousand people through coffeehouses and other public venues: 'the shop owners and servants read newspapers in Istanbul now', he approvingly wrote and added: 'at any rate they listen'.[77]

Indeed, as early as the 1830s, Robert Walsh noticed the popularity of the 'news-rooms' where 'a stool is placed in the centre, on which the man who can read sits, and others form a circle round him and listen ... There was no mirth or laughter excited, but all seemed to listen with profound attention, interrupted only sometimes by a grave

72 See, Andrew King and John Plunkett, *Victorian Print Media: A Reader* (Oxford: Oxford University Press, 2005), 339–340.

73 See, for instance, the influence of steam-driven press on production, Hannah Barker and Simon Burrows, 'Introduction', in *Press, Politics and the Public Sphere in Europeand North America, 1760–1820*, ed. Hannah Barker and Simon Burrows (Cambridge: Cambridge University Press, 2002), 6.

74 Ahmed Emin, *The Development of Modern Turkey*, 78, 132. Benjamin Fortna makes a similar argument through children literature. See Benjamin C. Fortna, *Learning to Read in the Late Ottoman Empire and the Early Turkish Republic* (London: Palgrave, 2011), 154–174.

75 See Necip Asım [Yazıksız], *Kitâb* (İstanbul: Matbaa-i Safa ve Enver, 1311/1894), 140. According to Necip Asım even janissaries had heroic and epic books composed for communal reading in their companies. It should be noted that 'communal reading' of newspapers was a very frequent practice in Europe as well. See Rubery, *The Novelty of Newspapers*, 6–7.

76 Ahmed Emin, *The Development of Modern Turkey*, 47.

77 Nâmık Kemal, *Mukaddime-i Celal* (İstanbul: Matbaa-i Ebuzziyâ, 1305/1888), 4.

Figure 5.2 The private secretary of Midhat Pasha, reading him daily newspapers.

Osman Nuri, *Abdülhamid-i Sani Devr-i Saltanatı Hayat-ı Hususiye ve Siyasiyesi*, 3 vols., vol. I (İstanbul: İbrahim Hilmi Kitabhanesi, 1327/1909–10), 58.

ejaculation of "*Inshallah*", or "*Allah Keerim*".'[78] Especially in literary coffeehouses, which were becoming more and more fashionable throughout the city,[79] members of the Ottoman public, 'from gentry and gentlemanly class', converged, to the much dismay of the government, to deliberate over the affairs of the state.[80] Some societies, such as *Cemiyet-i İlmiye*, also established reading clubs where members could consult a broad range of foreign and local newspapers (and books) for a nominal membership fee.[81] Even schools provided aspiring pupils an opportunity to examine the content of a newspaper

78 Walsh, *A Residence at Constantinople* 283. Using government spy reports, Cengiz Kırlı also revealed how newspapers were read in coffeehouses in the 1840s. See Kırlı, 'The Struggle Over Space', 118, 219.

79 See, for instance, an article praising the opening of a literary coffeehouse in Üsküdar, Anonymous, 'Mütâlaa', *Basîret*, 27 Şevval/30 January 1286/1870, 3. Also see, Anonymous, 'Bir Zât Tarafından Gönderilen Varakadan Hulasa Edilmiştir: Kırâathânede', *Diyojen*, 28 Kanûn-ı Sâni/9 February 1286/1871, 3–4; Anonymous, 'Al Sana Bir Merak Daha', *Diyojen*, 11 Kanûn-i Sâni/23 January 1287/1872, 1–2. Other than the famous literary coffeehouse of Sarafim which was mentioned in Chapter 2, there were quite a few of these establishments all around the city. Some of them, such *Sultan Ahmed Kırâathânesi* (also called public coffeehouse, or *Sultan Ahmed Kırâathâne-i Umûmîsi*), *Tophâne Kırâathânesi, Şehzâdebaşı Mehmed Efendi Kırâathânesi, Köprübaşı Kırâathânesi* and *Okçularbaşı Kırâathânesi* were also selling books and we could ascertain their existence only through Books and advertisements. See Anonymous, 'Ecel-i Kaza', *Diyojen*, 25 Ağustos/6 September 1288/1872, 4; Anonymous, 'Tercüme-i Hikâye-i Heft Peyker', *Diyojen*, 6 Eylül/18 September 1288/1872, 4; Anonymous, '[Gelibolu Mutâsârrıfı Kemal Beyefendi]', *Diyojen*, 12 Eylül/24 September 1288/1872, 4; Anonymous, 'İlan', *Diyojen*, 22 Eylül/4 October 1288/1872, 4; Anonymous, '[Mühendishâne- i Berri-i Hümâyun Hâcelerinden]', *Diyojen*, 3 Teşrin-i Evvel/15 October 1288/1872, 4; Anonymous, '[1067 Senesinde Kâtip Çelebi Merhum]', *Basîret*, 1 Zilkade/2 February 1286/1870, 4. From its cover, we also learn that *Mecmuâ-i Maârif* (*Journal of Education*) was sold 'only' in Sarafim's coffeehouse, this indicates the interesting but unstudied relationship between these places and the reading public. Cf. Markman Ellis, 'Coffee-House Libraries in Mid-Eighteenth-Century London', *The Library: The Transactions of the Bibliographical Society* 10, no. 1 (2009): 3–40.

80 '*Efendi ve ağa takımından*'. BOA, Y..EE.. 42/217, 13 Cemaziyelahir 1295 (14 June 1878).

81 According to the article of Münif Efendi, readers had a chance to read, other than Ottoman dailies, ten French, five English, four Armenians, three Greek newspapers at the Society reading room. Münif Efendi, 'Cemiyet Merkezinde Kırâathâne Küşâdı', *Mecmûa-ı Fünun* II, no. 22 (1280/1864): 423–427. The book collection included names like Adam Smith, Shakespeare, Francis Bacon, Montesquieu, and Lamartine. See Anonymous, 'Ba'zı Zevat Tarafından Cemiyete Verilen Hedaye', *Mecmûa-ı Fünun* II, no. 22 (1280/1864): 432–434.

without necessarily buying it.[82] This naturally created a ripple effect and gazette patrons carried substantive political and economical weight.

The commercialisation or commodification of newspapers also had a contiguous relationship with the liberation of men of letters from the domination of imperial and noble patrons. Before the nineteenth century, the Ottoman court was the locus of an 'economy of gift', in which 'artistic products, at the highest level, are directly supported and purchased by the state'.[83] Besides its imperial craftsmen called *Ehl-i Hiref*, the state sponsored many poets and artists through an extensive and systematic network of gifts and allowances.[84] Along with the imperial palace in Istanbul, princely courts of Anatolia and later *â'yân* households in different cities of the Empire attracted aspiring artists looking for remuneration.[85] This was similar to what took place in Western Europe throughout the early modern period. In both cases, the system 'kept men of letters as it kept servants, but literary production based on patronage was more a matter of a kind of conspicuous consumption than of serious reading by an interested public. The later, [Habermas argues] arose only in the first decades of the eighteenth century, after the publisher replaced as the author's commissioner and organized the commercial distribution of literary works'.[86]

In Europe, Alvin Kernan connects the rise of professional authorship to the 1710 copyright act, the Statute of Anne, arguing that this act ratified a proprietorial relationship between the author and his literary creation.[87] But this did not occur until a certain level of sophistication

[82] Ahmed Rasim, for instance, mentioned how he engaged in political arguments, which sometimes ended in physical confrontations, with his classmates over newspaper articles that they barely understood. Rasim, *Matbuat Hâtıralarından*, 46–47.

[83] Walter G. Andrews, 'Singing the Alienated 'I': Guattari, Deleuze and Lyrical Decodings of the Subject in Ottoman Poetry', *The Yale Journal of Criticism* VI, no. 2 (1993): 214.

[84] See, for instance, Halil İnalcık, *Şâir ve Patron* (Ankara: Doğubatı, 2003); Fahri Unan, 'Osmanlı Resmi Düşüncesinin 'İlmiye Tariki'' İçindeki Etkileri: Patronaj İlişkisi', *Türk Yurdu* 45, no. 391 (1991); Nusret Çam, 'Türk Sanatında Sultanların İşveren Olarak Estetik Rolleri', *Vakıflar Dergisi*, no. XXVII (1999): 5–14.

[85] Haluk İpekten, *Dîvân Edebiyâtında Edebi Muhitler* (İstanbul: Milli Eğitim Bakanlığı Yayınları, 1996), 210.

[86] Habermas, *The Structural Transformation of the Public Sphere*, 38.

[87] Alvin Kernan, *Samuel Johnson & the Impact of Print* (Princeton, NJ: Princeton University Press, 1989), 35–36.

and dissemination of printed materials was reached in the eighteenth century.[88] A similar saturation point can be located in the history of the Ottoman Empire after the 1850s. The century following the establishment of a printing press in Istanbul in 1727 saw only 180 books intermittently printed. However between 1830 and 1876, the number of the published books rose to more than three thousand.[89] Other than newspapers, some political pamphlets such as Ziyâ Pasha's *Zafernâme* (*the Book of Victory*) were said to be printed in hundreds of thousands in the Istanbul of the 1870s.[90] Such an increase naturally required some sort of protection of the author's rights.[91] Although some thoughts on the issue had been presented by the Ottoman Academy of Sciences in the past, the first Ottoman copyright act was issued in 1872.[92]

After this date, complaints about pirated editions, mostly coming from authors, grew.[93] This also had to do with the rising impact of capitalist ideology, which, as Roland Barthes comments, 'has attached the greatest importance to the "person" of the author'.[94] Consequently, newspapers blamed each other bitterly for unauthorised reprints.[95]

[88] Terry Belanger, 'Publishers and Writers in Eighteenth-Century England', in *Books and Their Readers in Eighteenth-Century England*, ed. Isabel Rivers (London: St. Martin's, 1982), 5–26.

[89] See Jale Baysal, *Müteferrika'dan Birinci Meşrûtiyete Kadar Osmanlı Türklerinin Bastıkları Kitaplar* (İstanbul: Edebiyât Fakültesi Basımevi, 1968), 14–15. A Hungarian convert called İbrahim Müteferrika founded the first Ottoman printing press in 1727. About his printing press, see Sabev, *İbrahim Müteferrika*, passim.

[90] Tevfik, *Yeni Osmanlılar Târîhi I*, 204–205.

[91] This does not include, one must note, *Zafernâme*, which was published under a *nom de guerre* as a satirical attack.

[92] For the details, see Fatmagül Demirel, 'Osmanlı Devleti'nde Telif Hakları Sorunu', *Bilgi ve Bellek* III, no. 5 (2006): 93–103.

[93] See, for instance, a complaint by a certain Necib Efendi against the owner of *La Turquie* printing press for the unauthorized publishing of his *elifba* (alphabet) book. BOA, MF.MKT 2/135, 12 Cemaziyelevvel 1289 (18 July 1872).

[94] Roland Barthes, *Image-Music-Text*, trans. Stephen Heath (London: HarperCollins, 1977), 143.

[95] *Diyojen*, for instance, protested against *Phare du Bosphore* in referring 'property' rights in an article entitled 'Don't journalists have honour?' which read: 'When we publish something from a newspaper, don't we have a tradition of putting its name somewhere on top or on the bottom of the page? *Phare du Bosphore* does not follow this custom and we understand that it publishes someone else's property as if it belongs to his father ... What a fool!' Anonymous, 'Gazetecilerin Namusu Yok Mu', *Diyojen*, 12 Teşrin-i Sâni/ 24 November 1286/1870, 3.

Especially for popular writers like Nâmık Kemal, this turned into a serious point of contention.[96] But the birth of the modern author in the Ottoman Empire perhaps can be traced back to a single incident. When the first issue of *Tasvîr-i Efkâr* was presented to Abdülaziz in 1862, the Sultan sent five hundred gold coins to Şinâsi, the editor-in-chief and the lead author of the newspaper. He, in return, refused the imperial donation, stating that he did not need that kind of money.[97]

Whether the story is true or not, it is difficult to say and not really important. The fact that some time later Şinâsi lost his post in the civil service due to his publishing activities at least indicates the tension between him and the government.[98] But more importantly Şinâsi's rejection was believable for many Ottomans. His attitude here, whether invented or not, presents a striking contrast with the writers of earlier generations and can be likened to Samuel Johnson's famous refusal of Lord Chesterfield's gesture of patronage in 1754.[99] In the nineteenth century, the Empire witnessed the emergence of a critical and politically engaged intellectual class, which relied on the emerging public as the ultimate benefactor.[100] For this reason, Ebuzziyâ Tevfik criticised Nâmık Kemal because of his liaisons with the Crown Prince, Murad. According to his account, he repeatedly refused Kemal's attempts to present him to the Prince.[101] After Kemal's return from Europe in 1870, he 'gave him friendly advice, [and] implored him to break off this connection with Murad'. 'Let them', he wrote, 'slug it out, squabble and quarrel for their aspirations. What business would

[96] See Kuntay, *Nâmık Kemal Devrinin İnsanları ve Olayları Arasında II*, 42. Also see BOA, MF.MKT 148/46, 29 Muharrem 1310 (23 August 1892).

[97] Tevfik, *Yeni Osmanlılar Târîhi I*, 237–238.

[98] 'As he has always been writing on governmental matters in a hostile manner (*mu'terizane*).' BOA., İ. DH. 510/34687, 17 Muharrem 1280 (4 July 1863).

[99] According to Kernan, this letter 'still stands as the Magna Carta of the modern author'. Kernan, *Samuel Johnson & the Impact of Print*, 105. For newspapers, this liberation was somewhat later, even in Europe. According to Mathew Rubery the 1830s was a 'crucial step in the transition from party control to editorial independence'. See Rubery, *The Novelty of Newspapers*, 5.

[100] Nâmık Kemal asserted that it was Şinâsi who managed to build the Ottoman press and printing on a 'public opinion'. He is 'the real inventor of', he wrote, 'independent printing and unsalaried [from the palace] journalism'. See Nâmık Kemal, 'Matbuat-i Osmaniye', *Hadîka*, 18 Ramazan/19 November 1289/1872, 1.

[101] Tevfik, *Yeni Osmanlılar Târîhi I*, 437. Ebuzziyâ's criticism might also stem from his exile, which was caused by this relationship between Kemal and the Prince. See Mardin, *The Genesis of Young Ottoman Thought*, 67.

we have among them as people who work for the country, nation and God?'[102] Before long, at the end of the century, for a writer sustaining any relationship with the palace turned into something to be condemned, mocked, and even attacked.[103]

This mutual relationship between newspapers and their public however was not easy to establish – nor was it easy to maintain. Especially after the 1860s, when the relative liberty of the Tanzimat era slowly vanished, the government tried to silence the opposition through coercion and censorship. During the first Grand Vizierate of Mahmud Nedim Pasha in 1871–1872, for instance, there was an unprecedented pressure on newspapers.[104] But even at the peak of his power, he could not control the press.[105] When Basîretçi Ali was advised by palace men to write laudatory remarks for the government, he, according to his account, rejected it by saying 'Sir, I am aware of the Grand Vizier's power. But yet, alas! Here we have public opinion much more stronger than him'.[106] Ironically enough, Ali was arrested for 'agitating public opinion' some time later.[107]

[102] Tevfik, *Yeni Osmanlılar Târîhi*, 532. Compare with what Andrew Barshay writes for Fukuzawa of the 1870s. Barshay, *State and Intellectual in Imperial Japan*, 6.

[103] See, for instance, the reaction of the *Edebiyât-ı Cedîdeciler* (supporters of the new literature) to Ali Ekrem and Ahmed Reşid for their clerkship in the palace. Halit Fahri Ozansoy, *Edebiyâtçılar Çevremde* (Ankara: Sümerbank Kültür Yayınları, 1970), 264–265.

[104] Alpay Kabacalı, *Başlangıçtan Günümüze Türkiye'de Basın Sansürü* (İstanbul: Gazeteciler Cemiyeti Yayınları, 1990), 44–47; Mehmet Zeki Pakalın, *Mahmud Nedim Paşa* (İstanbul: Ahmet Sait Matbaası, 1940), 84–89. For the censorship during the reign of Abdülhamid, see Fatmagül Demirel, *II. Abdülhamid Döneminde Sansür* (İstanbul: Bağlam Yayıncılık, 2007). This eventually led to, in the words of Arifi Pasha, Mahmud Nedim's attraction of the 'public hatred (*nefret-i âmme*)' and subsequent downfall. İnal, *Son Asır Türk Şâirleri II*, 1180. For details, see Chapter 6, esp. 222–32.

[105] It should be mentioned that he did this in the name of the Sultan. According to Butrus Abu Manneh, 'about a decade before he became grand vizier, Mahmud Nedim had written a treatise in which he criticized the Tanzimat and advocated an alternative system of government rooted in an idealized concept of early Ottoman history; in it he saw the Sultan as an all-powerful ruler who attended in person to the daily affairs of the state. During his tenure as grand vizier, Nedim tried to apply the principles that he had advocated'. See Butrus Abu-Manneh, 'The Sultan and the Bureaucracy: The Anti-Tanzimat Concepts of Grand Vizier Mahmud Nedim Paşa', *International Journal of Middle East Studies*, 22, no. 3 (1990): 257.

[106] Ali, *İstanbul'da Yarım Asırlık Vakayi-i Mühimme*, 29.

[107] Ibid., 34.

But newspapers' language of claiming rights transcended political coercion and they managed to become a key component of the expanding public. In going through inaugural issues of the early Ottoman newspapers, one can detect a sense of deliberate purpose strikingly building over time. At one end is the preamble to *Cerîde-i Havâdis*, which appeared on the last day of July 1840, awash with references to the importance of education.[108] Twenty years later, in contrast, in the inaugural issue of the 'first' private Ottoman newspaper, the attitude differs: 'since so many legal duties are incumbent on public', Şinâsi wrote haughtily, 'they consider it one of their vested rights to give their opinion, by writing and saying, as to the benefit of their state'.[109] In the first issue of *Tasvîr-i Efkâr* in 1862, again from the pen of Şinâsi, the government was delegated to the position of a mere political representative of the public (*müvekkil*).[110] In 1869, Basîretçi Ali likened the newspaper to a national assembly where the opinion of the people could be formed.[111] Especially after the 1870s, direct references to public opinion in inaugural issues began to emerge.[112] *Diyojen*, a humorous magazine published by a Greek-Ottoman, Teodor Kasap, after lauding the role of the press in 'guiding public opinion', even protested against the rhetoric of 'paternal advice and admonition (*pederâne pend ve nâsihat*)' used by previous newspapers in their first issues.[113]

108 Anonymous, 'Mukaddime', *Cerîde-i Havâdis*, Gurre-i Cemazeyilahir/31 July 1256/1840, 1.

109 İbrahim Şinâsi, 'Mukaddime', *Tercüman-ı Ahvâl*, 6 Rebiülahir/22 October 1277/1860, 1.

110 İbrahim Şinâsi, 'Mukaddime', *Tasvîr-i Efkâr*, 15 Haziran/27 June 1278/1862, 1.

111 'The exchange of opinion in such a big nation cannot be made, as members of parliaments do, in person but only through newspapers. A nation who aspires civilization should first work to promote and endorse newspapers, which are among the principal causes of civilization, so that their desire can be achieved. As students of history know very well publishing is the main reason which saved Europe from misery and brought it to this advanced point. If there is no liberty (*serbestiyet*) of publishing in a country, civilization cannot be achieved. This is as exact as a mathematical science. It is the first duty of individuals of the nation to espouse and encourage publishing. Our endeavour can stand only with public's predilection (*bizim gayretimiz umûmun rağbetiyle kaimdir*)'. See Basîretçi Ali, 'Mukaddime', *Basîret*, 20 Şevval/23 January 1286/1870, 1–2.

112 See, for instance, the first issue of *İbret*; Nâmık Kemal, 'İstikbal', *İbret*, 7 Rebiülahir/14 June 1289/1872, 1.

113 Teodor Kasap, 'Mukaddime', *Diyojen*, 12 Teşrin-i Sâni/24 November 1286/1870, 1.

These newspapers, like the other methods of literary life, sought to respond to specific needs of their changing society. They had a contiguous relationship with the socio-economic changes that the Empire was going through. By expanding the sphere for the public discussion, they led individuals to raise objections to the established setting in which political decisions were made and subsequently helped to weaken the complex balance of socio-political relations that had formed the traditional Ottoman society. They turned into a vehicle for communicating and shaping the opinions of the incipient public. This decisive role that newspapers played, however, is probably best understood in the context of a single man, Nâmık Kemal.

Birth of a Public Intellectual

Nâmık Kemal was born in 1840, in Tekirdağ (ancient Bysanthe, part of Eastern Thrace). He came from a prominent family, which likely had ties with the Ottoman dynasty through a female branch.[114] He went through a classical Ottoman education, learning Persian and Arabic at an early age and saw different parts of the Empire because of his grandfather's, Abdüllâtîf Pasha (d. 1859), appointments. This unequivocally influenced his early political and intellectual formation. He was, for instance, in Kars during the Crimean War and in Sofia just after the famous Siege of Silistra in 1854 (hence his celebrated tragedy, *Fatherland or Silistra*). Later when he went back to Istanbul as a young man, he was employed in the Translation Bureau in 1857 and learned French there.[115]

114 For the details of his early life and family, see Süleyman Nazif, *Nâmık Kemal* (İstanbul: İkdam Matbaası, 1340/1922), 4–7; Ebuzziyâ Tevfik, *Merhum Nâmık Kemal* (Istanbul: s.n., 1327/1909), 4; Ali Ekrem Bolayır, *Nâmık Kemal*, Büyük Adamlar Serisi Nr: 2 (Devlet Matbaası, 1930), 2–9; Sadettin Nüzhet Ergun, *Nâmık Kemal: Hayâtı ve Şiirleri* (İstanbul: Yeni Şark Kitaphânesi, 1933), 5–25; Rıza Nour, *Revue de Turcologie: Nâmık Kemal* (Alexandria: Imp. Hamouda, 1936), 484–487; Nihal Atsız, 'Nâmık Kemal', *Çınaraltı*, no. 22 (1942): 8–9; Kuntay, *Nâmık Kemal Devrinin İnsanları I*, IX. For an analysis of his political views, see Mardin, *The Genesis of Young Ottoman Thought*, 283–336.

115 In one of his articles in *Hürriyet*, however, he was very critical of the bureau. See Kemal, 'Hâriciye Nezâreti', 5–6. His French teacher, Mehmed Mansur Efendi, later known as *Kemal Hocası* (Kemal's master), was a converted Macedonian Christian who learnt French and English from James Redhouse. See Johann Strauss, 'The Greek Connection in Nineteenth-Century Ottoman

After this date, the details of his life in large part overlap with the trajectory that this book has followed. He was the youngest member of the Society of Poets gathered around Leskofçalı Gâlib in 1861.[116] A year later, he began to work for Şinâsi at *Tasvîr-i Efkâr*.[117] This was, one might call, his apprenticeship. Though today he is mostly remembered as a poet (his everyday sobriquet is *vatan şâiri*, or the poet of the fatherland), his contemporary importance actually came from his newspaper articles.[118] Kemal's talent for striking phrases and succinct verdicts on the political issues of the day soon made him the *enfant terrible* of Ottoman journalism.[119] This association with the press led to his radicalisation, and, he later became one of the founders of the Young Ottoman movement (1865). This caused his first serious estrangement from the ruling elite, forcing him to flee the country in 1867. While in Europe he made connections with Eastern European liberals such as Władysław Plater or Simon Deutsch, probably to negotiate an alliance against the Russian Empire. When he returned three years later, beyond being a firm constitutionalist, he was also a freemason and an ardent dramatist.[120]

In the midst of political turmoil, Kemal looked for a fundament upon which to build his ideal political system. His traditional upbringing and exposure to novel political ideas created a multifaceted and

Intellectual History', in *Greece and the Balkans: Identities, Perceptions and Cultural Encounters Since the Enlightenment*, ed. Dimitris Tziovas (Farnham, UK: Ashgate Publishing, 2003), 55; Mardin, *The Genesis of Young Ottoman Thought*, 211; Tevfik, *Yeni Osmanlılar Târîhi I*, 112.

116 See Chapter 2.

117 Nâmık Kemal, *Nâmık Kemal'in Talim-i Edebiyât Üzerine Bir Risâlesi*, ed. Necmettin Halil Onan (Ankara: Milli Eğitim Bakanlığı, 1950), 37.

118 As in Europe after the Romantic period, in the nineteenth century there was a change in public taste in the Ottoman Empire and reading of poetry became less common as people moved towards less demanding types of reading such as novels. Cf. Clair, *The Reading Nation in the Romantic Period*, 175.

119 See, for instance, Şerif Mardin's comments: 'Nâmık Kemal, on the other hand, went further in the use of the vernacular than his predecessors such as Şinâsi and Münif Paşa and thereby reached an even wider audience than these precursors of the simplification of the Turkish language. Besides the simplicity of his Turkish, the power of his style was remarkable.' Mardin, *The Genesis of Young Ottoman Thought*, 283.

120 Kaya Bilgegil, *Ziyâ Paşa Üzerinde Bir Araştırma* (Ankara: Atatürk Üniversitesi Basımevi, 1970), 115. Also see Michael L. Miller, 'From Liberal Nationalism to Cosmopolitan Patriotism: Simon Deutsch and 1848ers in Exile', *European Review of History: Revue europeenne d'histoire* 17, no. 3 (2010): 379–393.

complex political system. He struggled to justify his constitutionalist position through an idealised version of Islamic and Ottoman history.[121] It is possible to divide his articles roughly in two. The ones written abroad (either in Paris or in London for *Hürriyet*) were naturally of a sharper nature. There he did not mention 'public opinion' often (only twice) and was more interested in convincing the people that sovereignty belonged to them.[122] He had other key words and concerns. For instance, he argued that while the Islamic community was not legally allowed to elect a *kadi* (because appointing judges was a sultanic prerogative), if they wished to do so, they had every right to nominate a new caliph – hence a new sultan.[123] For him what was missing was the '*supervision* of the community (*nezâret-i ümmet yok*)'.[124] Even the control of the budget should have been under the '*supervision* of the public (*umûmun nezâreti*)'.[125] As members of the public bound to be affected from any decision, they had every right to '*supervise* the government activities (*ef'al-i hükümete nezâret*)'.[126] Now that education 'drew aside the curtain of ignorance inhibiting people from perceiving the truth',[127] it was impossible for the public to acknowledge the government 'without direct *supervision* (*bizzât idâreye nezâret*)'.[128]

In these articles, Kemal rarely blamed the Sultan and followed the age-old tradition of accusing viziers. According to him, Abdülaziz had all the good intentions, but between him and the truth barriers,

[121] 'In the past', he wrote, 'even though our government ostensibly was in the shape of an absolutist rule, in reality it was a constitutional government which enjoyed the utmost degree of freedom. Scholars ruled, sultan and ministers executed, and the armed people oversaw the execution'. Nâmık Kemal, 'Hasta Adem', *Hürriyet*, 7 December 1868, 1.

[122] Nâmık Kemal, 'İhtilafi ümmeti rahmetün', *Hürriyet*, 6 July 1868, 4; Kemal, 'Veşavirhum fi'l-Emr', 2. But the term was used in translations from foreign newspapers. See, for instance, an article translated from *L'Internationale*, in the form of a letter written from Istanbul. Anonymous, 'Fransızca Londra'da Basılmakta Olan İnternasyonal Nam Gazetenin 20 Teşrin-i Evvel Târîhiyle İstanbul'dan Alıp Neşr Eylediği Mektûbun Hülasasıdır', *Hürriyet*, 2 November 1868, 7.

[123] Kemal, 'Veşavirhum fi'l-Emr', 1.

[124] Ibid., 2.

[125] Nâmık Kemal, 'Sekizinci Numaradaki Mâliye Bendine Zeyl', *Hürriyet*, 31 August 1868, 3.

[126] Nâmık Kemal, 'Usûl-i Meşverete Dair Geçen Nümerolarda Münderic Mektûbların Üçüncüsü', *Hürriyet*, 29 September 1868, 7.

[127] Nâmık Kemal, 'Fransa İhtilâli', *Hürriyet*, 21 June 1869, 6.

[128] Kemal, 'Veşavirhum fi'l-Emr', 3.

'reminding the Great Wall of China', had been implemented by tyrannical ministers.[129] He argued that they forbade giving petitions to the Sultan. This is actually an interesting point.[130] The Near Eastern states and governments had a special view of justice which was based upon the people's right of presenting their complaints directly to the ruler.[131] As a part of his omnipotent and omnipresent image, the Sultan was supposed to be accessible and receive petitions from supplicants who, in return, expected an 'immediate justice'.[132] But the trouble was, with the improving communication technologies and growing political awareness in the late nineteenth century, while the Sultan was indeed omnipresent, his 'omnipotence' was severely damaged. With the administrative ramifications, one of the concerns of the Ottoman bureaucracy also became the implementation of *trias politica*, the separation of powers, as a way to ensure bureaucratic efficiency.[133]

[129] Kemal, '[İngiltere Hâriciye Vekili Lord Stanley]', 1–2.

[130] The relationship between public opinion and innovative uses of petitions in the Western historiography is also worth noting here. See, for instance, James E. Bradley, *Religion, Revolution and English Radicalism: Non-conformity in Eighteenth-Century Politics and Society* (Cambridge: Cambridge University Press, 1990), 326–330; David Zaret, *Origins of Democratic Culture: Printing, Petitions, and the Public Sphere in Early-Modern England* (Princeton, NJ: Princeton University Press, 2000), 217–265; Cowans, *To Speak for the People: Public Opinion and the Problem of Legitimacy in the French Revolution*, 71. David Zaret especially draws attention to the importance of published petitions for the construction of an early public opinion in the seventeenth century. Though petitions were not published as such in the Ottoman Empire, reader contributions written in the form of a complaint must have been influential to create informed opinions. See, for instance, a petition-letter written by a certain Yusuf about the conditions of the roads. Yusuf, 'Varaka', *Basîret*, 2 Zilkade/3 February 1286/1870, 2.

[131] Halil İnalcık, 'Şikayet Hakkı: Arz-ı Hâl ve Arz-ı Mahzar'lar', *Osmanlı Araştırmaları*, no. VII-VIII (1988): 33.

[132] Ebru Boyar and Kate Fleet, *A Social History of the Ottoman Empire* (Cambridge: Cambridge University Press, 2010), 37.

[133] See, for instance, 'As legal courts (*Mehâkim-i Hukukiye)* are not allowed to accept petitions, it has been asked whether the civil service or the courts were responsible for handling the paperwork regarding judicial conduct. Because it has been confirmed, through various royal decrees and the Constitution, that judicial power is separated from legislation, members of the civil service do not have any influence whatsoever in the functioning of judiciary system.' Anonymous, 'Adliye Nezâretinden 11 Nisan Sene 95 Târîhiyle Vilâyet ile Müstakilen İdâre Olunanan Mutâsârrıflıklara Yazılan Telgrafnâme Sûretidir', *Cerîde-i Mehâkim*, 12 Receb/2 July 1296/1879. Similar views can be also found in Anonymous, 'Adliye ve Mezahib Nezâretinin ve Devair-i Merbutasının Vezaifi Nizâmnâmesidir', *Cerîde-i Mehâkim*, 19 Receb/9 July 1296/1876, 10.

This fixated civil servants on the formal right to receive petitions. This privilege, first bestowed upon legal courts (*Mehâkim-i Hukukiye*), was extended to commercial courts (*Mehâkim-i Ticâriye*) only after long deliberation.[134] Even though it remained important as a symbolic gesture,[135] the bureaucracy was not ecstatic about this archaic tradition for understandable reasons.[136] But Kemal considered their apprehension as coveting a sultanic prerogative. 'What kind of time are we living in?' he asked and answered: 'it is such a time that the Sublime Porte legislates, the Sublime Porte rules and the Sublime Porte executes. To the execution of laws, the Sublime Porte attends. When we say *Padishah*, the Sublime Porte is understood. When we say law, again it is the same. Assembly, court, it all is the same . . . The Sultan, [he wrote] has only has power to tyrannise over his immediate family'.[137]

These complaints had something to do with the mounting power of the bureaucracy that has been mentioned in the previous chapters.[138]

[134] *Journal of Courts* (*Cerîde-i Mehâkime*) is laden with rules and protocols regarding the right to receive petitions. See for instance, Anonymous, 'Adliye Nezâretinden 11 Nisan Sene 95 Târîhiyle Vilâyet ile Müstakilen İdâre Olunanan Mutâsârrıflıklara Yazılan Telgrafnâme Sûretidir', 3–4; Anonymous, 'Adliye Nezâretinden 21 Nisan Sene 95 Târîhinde Vilâyete Yazılan Telgraf', *Cerîde-i Mehâkim*, 12 Receb/2 July 1296/1879, 6–7; Anonymous, 'İlan: [Deavi-i Vakinin Sürrati ve Serbest-i Ceryanı Emrinde]', *Cerîde-i Mehâkim*, 14 Şevval/1 October 1296/1879, 101; Anonymous, 'Fi 20 Şevval Sene 96 ve fi 24 Eylül Sene 95 Târîhleriyle Adliye Nezâretinden Bil-Cümle Vilâyet ile Adliye Müffettişliklerine ve Müdde-i Umûmîliklere Yazılan Tahrîrât Sûretidir', *Cerîde-i Mehâkim*, 28 Şevval/15 October 1296/1876, 115; Anonymous, 'Adliye Nezâretinden 14 Mayıs Sene 95 Târîhiyle Umûm Vilâyete ve Ressen İdâre Olunan Mutâsârrıflıklara ve Merkez Vilâyet Ticâret Mahkemeleri Riyasetlerine Yazılan Telgrafıdır', *Cerîde-i Mehâkim*, 12 Receb/2 July 1296/1879.

[135] See, for instance, the incident where a private soldier (*nefer*) managed to give a petition to the Sultan. Though, this was deemed against the regulations (he should have gone through his superiors, it was duly noted), his petition was accepted and necessary orders were given to attend to the matter. BOA, Y.. PRK.BŞK. 14/43, 27 Safer 1306 (2 November 1888).

[136] Even in the late sixteenth century officials 'tried, where possible, to block such petitions, not always successfully and sometimes with disastrous results. The janissary *ağa* was removed from his post by Mehmed III at the beginning of his reign, after he had seen the janissaries preventing the people of Ruse and Silistria from approaching him after Friday prayer'. Boyar and Fleet, *A Social History*, 39.

[137] Kemal, 'Hasta Adem', 2.

[138] The helplessness that Abdülmecid felt against the independent conduct of Reşid Pasha in governmental affairs, for instance, is clearly seen from contemporary testimonies. Once he unburdened himself in a private conversation with the French ambassador, Edouard Antoine de Thouvenel (d. 1866), stating 'Reshid

But it was also a roundabout, and hence more acceptable, way of criticising the system. Even the revolutionary assembly of 1920 did not denounce the Sultan directly and put the blame on 'evil ministers who kept him ignorant of his subjects' concerns'.[139] Not to alienate his public, Kemal also adhered to this old rhetoric of 'evil viziers, being masters of guile',[140] and distinguished himself from more radical opponents such as Mehmed Emin Bey (d. 1874) who by pronouncing Abdülaziz, to put it mildly, mentally incapable, declared the whole sultanate illegitimate and pled a swift revolution from his paper with a panoply of insults and vitriolic attacks.[141] For Kemal, maybe not its particular individuals, but the family of Osman remained inviolable, and this extended his popularity among many young Ottomans.[142]

Pasha, in a most clear manner, as the source of all of his troubles and scourges'. Louis Thouvenel, *Trois années de la question d'Orient, 1856–1859: D'après les papiers inédits de M. Thouvenel* (Paris: C. Lévy, 1897), 194. If we are to believe existing rumours, he was even seen crying, while praying to God for salvation from the 'hands of such a man'. Abdurrahman Şeref, *Târîh Musâhabeleri* (İstanbul: Matbaa-i Amire, 1339/1923–1924), 106. But soon after his prayers were heard, when Reşid Pasha died in 1858, the Sultan realised that the trouble was not the player but the game. There was no salvation from the hands of new pashas touching him on the raw. On one occasion, he found himself inviting Mehmed Ali Pasha, once Grand Vizier, to a duel and asked, '*are you counting on your office*?' Cevdet Paşa, *Tezâkir 13–20*, 54–55, emphasis mine.

139 Andrew Mango, *From the Sultan to Ataturk: Turkey: The Peace Conferences of 1919–23 and Their Aftermath* (London: Haus Publishing, 2010), 89.

140 Anonymous, *The Arabian Nights: Tales of 1,001 Nights*, ed. Robert Irwin, trans. Malcolm C. Lyons and Ursula Lyons, 3 vols., vol. III (London: Penguin, 2010), 490.

141 His *İnkilab* (*Revolution*), published in Geneva in the 1870s, was the severest critic of the Ottoman government. See Bilgegil, *Yakın Çag Türk Kültür ve Edebiyâti Üzerinde Araştırmalar*, 143. In a letter written to his father, Nâmık Kemal mentioned it admiringly, saying, 'I am sending you the third issue of *İnkilab*. This is not like *Muhbir* and *Hürriyet*. It uses a very harsh language and distributed regularly to every nook and cranny of the country.' See Kuntay, *Nâmık Kemal Devrinin İnsanları I*, 418. Burak Onaran, *Détrôner le sultan*, esp. 370–386. Also see Bilgegil, *Yakın Çag Türk Kültür ve Edebiyâti Üzerinde Araştırmalar I*, 354–407. Some information about Mehmed Bey can be also found in İnal, *Son Asır Türk Şâirleri II*, 942–949; Bernard Lewis, *The Emergence of Modern Turkey*, 155–156; Kuntay, *Nâmık Kemal Devrinin İnsanları I*, 414–418.

142 Kemal once wrote: 'We always want the Family of Osman, we always want constitutional government.' Nâmık Kemal, 'Usûl-i Meşveret Hakkında Dördüncü Nüshamızdaki Ben Üzerine İrad olunan Ba'zı İtirazlara Cevâben Bir Zâta Yazılmış Mektûb', *Hürriyet*, 14 September 1868, 6.

The articles written in the Ottoman Empire had a different tone. He chose to chide pashas who were safely dead. Fuâd Pasha (d. 1869), for instance, was belittled for leaving important government work aside just to expurgate Şinâsi's article on stray dogs.[143] Though Kemal did not mention it, this is the famous article in which Şinâsi used the term public opinion for the first time in 1864.[144] The Pasha, who was well versed in Western political literature, might have actually seen the possible implications of Şinâsi's terminology. But leaving aside his old feud with Âli and Fuâd Pashas, here Kemal's animosity was directed against a new class of men whom he mockingly called *nâzik* (kind), *nâzenin* (delicate), or *çelebi* (gentleman).[145] These new men, whose Francophile mannerisms became an object of scorn and disdain for various elements of the society,[146] emerged under the influence of the Western culture in the second half of nineteenth century and mostly in Istanbul.[147] Many important works of Tanzimat literature, such as *Felatun Bey ve Râkım Efendi* (1875), *Bahtiyarlık* (1875), *Şık* (1888), or *Araba Sevdası* (1898) ridiculed this type of protagonist, who was not dissimilar to earlier notions of *petit-maitre* in France or dandy in Britain.[148]

143 Nâmık Kemal, 'Türkçe Matbuat', *İbret*, 16 Zilkade/15 January 1289/1873, 1.

144 Şinâsi, 'Bend-i Mahsûs: İstanbul Sokakları Tenvîr ve Tathîri Hakkındadır', 1–2.

145 See, for example, his articles, Nâmık Kemal, 'Cevap', *İbret*, 27 Rebiülahir/4 July 1289/1872, 2; Nâmık Kemal, 'Hadd-i Tedib', *İbret*, 27 Rebiülahir/4 July 1289/1872, 3–4; Nâmık Kemal, 'Hadd-i Sâni', *İbret*, 30 Rebiülahir/7 July 1289/1872, 4.

146 See Mustafa Nihat Özön, *Türkçede Roman* (İstanbul: İletişim Yayınları, 1985), 196; Ercüment Kuran, *Türkiye'nin Batılılaşması ve Milli Meseleler* (Ankara: Diyânet Vakfı Yayınları, 1994), 35; Edhem Eldem, 'Batılılaşma, Modernleşme ve Kozmopolitizm: 19. Yüzyıl Sonu ve 20. Yüzyıl Başında İstanbul', in *Osman Hamdi Bey ve Dönemi*, ed. Zeynep Rona (Istanbul: Târîh Vakfı Yurt Yayınları, 1993), 12–26. Also see Berna Moran's very interesting analysis, differentiating between the naïve francophone of the Tanzimat era and the francophone traitor of the 1920s. Berna Moran, *Türk Romanına Eleştirel Bir Bakış: Ahmet Mithat'tan Ahmet Hamdi Tanpınar'a*, 3 vols., vol. I (İstanbul: İletişim Yayınları, 1995), 196–202.

147 They perhaps exemplified what Amanda Anderson calls 'aesthetic practice of detachment'. See Amanda Anderson, *The Powers of Distance: Cosmopolitanism and the Cultivation of Detachment* (Princeton, NJ: Princeton University Press, 2001), 29.

148 Jean-Pierre Saidah, 'Le dandysme: continuité et rupture', in *L'honnête homme et le dandy*, ed. Alain Montandon (Tübingen: Narr, 1993), 127–130.

In fact, these protagonists usefully epitomise the changes that have been discussed so far. Both Felatun Bey (of *Felatun Bey ve Râkım Efendi*) and Bihruz Bey (of *Araba Sevdası*) were avid collectors of French books, although not great readers. In many ways Bihruz Bey was a caricature of a Tanzimat man. He was employed in one of the new bureaus through his father's connections, but he was not interested in official work (in particular, his Ottoman Turkish was not very good).[149] When he had free time from his French classes,[150] he was obsessed with being seen in public places, particularly in one '*jardin publique*'.[151] 'Wherever Bihruz Bey went, wherever he was', Mahmud Ekrem wrote, 'his purpose was not to see while being seen. It was just to be seen'.[152]

This statement is rather important.[153] As in many parts of Europe, during the nineteenth century, the Ottoman Empire's commercial growth led urban centres to become venues of sociability, accommodating an increasing number of people.[154] As wealth grew, the members of the public were able to dedicate more of their time to communicating with each other.[155] Even simple innovations, like public transportation, provided new urban spaces where the 'suffocated' city folk could interact.[156] These types of technologies 'removed

[149] Recâîzâde Mahmud Ekrem, *Araba Sevdası: Musavver Milli Hikâye* (İstanbul: Âlem Matbası, 1314/1896), 48–49.

[150] Ibid., 35–40.

[151] French in Arabic script in the original, ibid., 10.

[152] Ibid., 9.

[153] Probably this had something to do with Timothy Mitchell's now famous adaptation of Heidegger's 'the world as an exhibition' formula. See Timothy Mitchell, *Colonising Egypt* (Berkeley: University of California Press, 1988), 10–13.

[154] Cf. J. H. Plumb, 'The Commercialization of Leisure in Eighteenth-Century England', in *The Birth of a Consumer Society: The Commercialization of Eighteenth-Century England*, ed. Neil McKendrick, John Brewer, and J. H. Plumb (London: Europa Publications, 1982), 275–280. Peter Borsay, *The English Urban Renaissance: Culture and Society in the Provincial Town 1660–1770* (Oxford: Clarendon Press, 1991), 16–18; Richard Sennett, *The Fall of Public Men* (London: Penguin Books, 2002), 17–18.

[155] Melton, *The Rise of the Public in Enlightenment Europe*, 204. The increasing trade relations following the Crimean War and the commercial treaty of 1838 created what Cevdet Pasha dubbed '*servet-i kazibe*/false fortune' in the Empire. See Cevdet Paşa, *Tezâkir 1–12*, 20.

[156] In the words of Vakanüvis Lûtfî Efendi, 'after a serious amount of money poured into the country, Istanbul became suffocating for some people'. Cited in Şirket-i Hayriye, *Boğaziçi: Şirket-i Hayriye: Târîhçe, Sâl-nâme* (İstanbul: Ahmet İhsan ve Şürekası, 1914), 2.

many of the constraints on coordination and control that in the past had limited organisational expansion and the physical separation of subunits, and they provided the means of centralising and integrating activities on an unprecedented scale'.[157]

Specifically the introduction of regular steamboat service in 1854 – 'to create public benefit' – dramatically changed the physiognomy of the city.[158] Not only did the city grow longitudinally (towards the Bosporus), but steamboats also provided a critical urban space for the city's residents.[159] For centuries, boatmen, whom Karolyna Suchodolska referred to as the 'reflectors of public opinion', had conducted the journey between the European and the Asian sides of Istanbul.[160] But the boats they used were flimsy little vehicles, which offered little or no chance of interaction among passengers.[161] Before the establishment of *Şirket-i Hayriye* (the Company of Goodwill), the boats of various groups in the Empire, such as the patriarchates, ministries, or princedoms – like Wallachia – were all different and strictly regulated by the shape and number of their oars.[162] This had to do with the

157 D. Eleanor Westney, *Imitation and Innovation: The Transfer of Western Organizational Patterns to Meiji Japan* (Cambridge, MA: Harvard University Press, 1987), 10.

158 Anonymous, '[Müstezil-i Saye-i Râfetvaye]', *Takvîm-i Vekâyi*, 2 Muharrem/ 7 November 1267/1850, 2.

159 According to Ahmed Lûtfî Efendi, before the foundation of *Şirket-i Hayriye* most of the villages around the Bosporus were 'unknown territories/*bilad-ı meçhule*' for Istanbul people. Rarely you would find a person, he wrote, who visited the Kavaks (Rumeli Kavağı-Anadolu Kavağı). The *Şirket* brought, according to him, 'life' to those parts of the city. Cited in Şirket-i Hayriye, *Târîhçe, Sâl-nâme*, 1. Fatma Âliye Hanım also mentions the growth of urban sprawl in her biography of her father. Fatma Âliye Hanım, *Ahmed Cevdet Paşa ve Zamanı* (İstanbul: Kanaat Matbaası, 1913), 81.

160 Wanda, *Souvenirs anecdotiques sur la Turquie*, 10.

161 See, for instance, this passage from Slade: 'Sit down cry the caikgis [boatmen] authoritatively, seeing they have to do with a greenhorn. You obey, and place yourself on what appears to be a seat, but so far from gaining steadiness, the bark reels to an inch of the tide each way. 'Sit down! Down in the bottom of the boat!" again shout the caikgis, who, half frightened, endeavour to counteract your awkwardness by balancing their supple bodies; 'sit quiet, unless you wish the boat to be over you instead of under!' Adolphus Slade, *Records of Travels in Turkey, Greece, etc. and of a Cruise in the Black Sea, with the Capitan Pasha, in the Years 1829, 1830, and 1831*, 2 vols., vol. I (London: Saunders and Otley, 1833), 113. Similar views were also expressed in Richard Burgess, *Greece and the Levant, or, Diary of a Summer's Excursion in 1834*, 2 vols., vol. I (London: Longman, 1835), 145.

162 Şirket-i Hayriye, *Târîhçe, Sâl-nâme*, 2.

'representative publicness' briefly discussed in Chapter 1. The villages farther along the strait had their own 'bazaar boats' too.[163] Against the background of this complex picture, the steamers of *Şirket-i Hayriye* can be thought as embodiments of the expanding public.

In the novel, the steamboat was one of the places where Bihruz Bey was frequently depicted. He bought his newspaper (*Le Courrier d'-Orient*) on-deck, read it and was 'seen' by his peers.[164] The steamboats of the city became one of the standard topoi of Tanzimat literature from the very beginning. *Müsâmeretnâme* of Emin Nihad (1872), the first modern Ottoman novella, for instance, begins with a description of Rifat Bey, the hero, waiting and watching fellow passengers with an inquisitive eye. The whole story is actually based on Rifat Bey's friendship with a foreigner (*ecnebî*) aboard a *Hayriye* steamer.[165] This was not far-fetched. The physical shape of a boat and the nature of its journey were immensely more suitable to social interactions than that of an underground system or streetcars. Above all, its seating arrangements were more conducive to speaking than other means of public transportation.[166] An Ottoman steamboat in fact can be likened to a colossal coffeehouse with its *kahvecis* (literally coffeehouse-keepers) working its deck, regularly serving drinks and providing backgammon for their customers.[167]

163 Sâmîha Ayverdi, *Boğaziçi'nde Târîh* (İstanbul: Kubbealtı Neşriyâtı, 2008), 54–55. Also see Musâhipzâde Celâl, *Eski İstanbul Yaşayışı* (İstanbul: Türkiye Yayınevi, 1946), 181.

164 Ekrem, *Araba Sevdası*, 83.

165 Little did he know that through this seemingly harmless friendship, he was going to be offered the 'body' of his friend's daughter in exchange for his conversion to Christianity. According to the author, the novella was based on a 'true story'. Emin Nihad Bey, *Müsâmeretnâme: Binbaşı Rıfat Bey'in Sergüzeşti*, 12 vols., vol. I (İstanbul: Midhat Efendi Matbaası, 1288/1872), 54. Ahmed Mithat's heroes in *Vah* all met during a streamer journey. His *Müşâhedat* also begins with the hero, in this case Ahmed Mithat himself, overhearing a conversation on a *Şirket-i Hayriye* steamer.

166 A very interesting article appeared in *Gazette Médicale d'Orient* on the ill effects of timetable irregularities of the *Şirket* on the mental health of the people. Though the idea looks rather far-fetched, according to the author, the company was indirectly responsible for quite a few casualties, at least for shortened lives, because of their irresponsible attitude. See Sinapian, 'Le Chirket-i-Hairié: Influence de ce service sur la santé des passagers', *Gazette Médicale d'Orient* VII, no. 1 (1863): 1–8.

167 See, for instance, two complaints about *kahvecis*: Anonymous, '[Mâlum ya Fevâid Kumpanyası]', *Dijojen*, 12 Ağustos/24 August 1287/1871, 2; Anonymous, '[İşte Bu Alâ]', *Diyojen*, 4 Eylül/16 September 1287/1871.

٤٩ مصور رومانه

[بهروز بك واپورده غزته اوقویور ایدی]

صغیر] كلمه‌لرینی نصلسه طانیه‌مدیغندن
عباره‌نك معناسنی اكلایه‌مدی . اكلامغه
چاره دوشونوركن باشا بدر مرحوم طرفندن
مخدوم بك ایچون الدیرلمش وفقط مخدوم
بكك تحصیلی بالاخره بتون بتون الافرانغه‌یه
دوكلمسیله یالدیزلی مالدیزلی .. جیجیلی بیجیلی ..
یك حجم .. یكنسق كتب متنوعهٔ افرنجیه ایله
كسب انتظام و زینت ایدن میشه اغاجندن
معمول .. اویمالی اوروپا كاری كتبخانه‌سی ایچنده
یاقشمدیغندن طولایی بر طاقمی شونك بونك
طرفندن اشیریلان .. دیكر بر طاقمی ایسه حرم
دائره‌سنك الت قاتنده دولاب التلری .. یوك
قیلیری كبی یرلره پریشان بر صورتده آتیلوب
براغیلان تركجه عربی فارسی كتابلرك ارەسنه
قارشمش اولان [لغات عثمانیه] نامنده‌كی تركجه
دیقسیونر خاطرینه كلدی . حال بوكه
[لغات عثمانیه] نك [ردحاوز] اسمنده
برانكلیز طرفندن تألیف اولنمش اولدیغنی
ایكی ای اول بر كون قلمده قولاق مسافری
اولدیغی بر بحث ادبی ایچنده ایشیدیر ایشتمز
بوكتابی كوزلجه تجلید ایتدیره‌رك ینه
كتابخانه‌سنه قبول ایتمه‌یی تصمیم ایتمشیدی .

Figure 5.3 Bihruz Bey, the hero of *Araba Sevdası*, frequently read his newspaper (*le Courrier d'Orient*) on the deck of a steamboat.

Recaizade Mahmud Ekrem, *Araba Sevdası: Musavver Milli Hikaye* (İstanbul: Alem Matbası, 1314/1896), 49.

In other words, ordinary individuals of different creeds and beliefs were put in a 'sailing coffeehouse' for a few hours and left to talk. The company announced that in the second half of 1871 they transported almost a million people (876,321) across the city.[168] Its ferries could carry up to one thousand passengers at a time.[169] Contemporary complaints and testimonies reveal that women and men sometimes travelled in mixed company, previously isolated from each other in the public sphere by tenets of religion and custom.[170] Lucy Garnett noted, for instance, how one would meet Turkish women 'on the steamers plying between Galata and the many suburbs on the Bosporus'.[171] As a result the steamers also became, in the literature of the time (and probably in reality as well), a place where one could meet, see, and wait for their beloved. It was there, for instance, where Bihruz Bey ran into his adored Periveş Hanım after believing for a long time that she was dead.[172] In Nâmık Kemal's *İntibah* (1876), Ali Bey also waited for his Mahpeyker at the deck hoping that she would emerge from the next steamer.[173]

168 Anonymous, 'Bu Hesaba Ne Buyurursunuz?', *Diyojen*, 5 Nisan/17 April 1288/ 1872, 2. According to the official statistics in 1895, this number was almost 10 million. In 1906, the number of passengers was over 12 million. See Chirket-I-Hairié, *Annuaire de la Société conetenant un historique de l'enterprise et une monographie du Bosphore, élaboré par la Direction* (Constantinople: Ahmed Ihsan & Cie, 1914), 12, 16. Unfortunately, there has not been scholarly interest on this important part of the late Ottoman history. Such negligence is, for example, demonstrated by Kemal Karpat, a prolific historian, who repeatedly declared that *Şirket-i Hayriye* was 'a French controlled navigation society'. Karpat, *Ottoman Population 1890–1914*, 97; Karpat, *Studies on Ottoman Social and Political History*, 270. In fact Şirket was one of the few successful Ottoman enterprises. See Zafer Toprak, *Türkiye'de Mili İktisat: (1908–1918)* (Ankara: Yurt Yayınevi, 1982), 40. Also see Chirket-I-Hairié, *Annuaire de la Société*, 1.

169 See, for instance, the capacity of its famous boats such as 'Souhoulet' and 'Sahilbend', Chirket-I-Hairié, *Annuaire de la Société*, 20.

170 Anonymous, 'Üsküdar Vapularlarından Şikayet', *Diyojen*, 12 Haziran/24 June 1287/1871, 3. This probably was not regular. See, for instance, a complaint letter written by a woman. Though she saw *Şirket-i Hayriye* as 'a sign of the civilization', she was offended because they refused allocating a starboard cabin to her, with two other women, on the ground that it was reserved for men. Anonymous, 'Bir Hanım İmzasıyla Aldığımız Varakadır', *Diyojen*, 14 Kanûn-i Evvel/26 December 1288/1872, 3–4.

171 Lucy M. J. Garnett, *Turkish Life in Town and Country* (New York: G. P. Putnam's Sons, 1904), 87.

172 Ekrem, *Araba Sevdası*, 119.

173 Nâmık Kemal, *İntibah: Ali Bey'in Sergüzeştine Havidir* (Istanbul: s.n., 1291/ 1876), 105–106.

Clearly there were unwritten rules regulating the conduct of conversation aboard. Peter Stallybrass and Allon White emphasise the 'cultural conditions' of a space controlling 'what may and may not be said, who may speak, how people may communicate and what importance must be given to what is said'.[174] It is easy to imagine that in its ideal form, the conversation between strangers was civic but not governmental. They would for instance complain about the conduct of a certain newspaper.[175] The dialogue could occasionally acquire political overtones, as happened, for instance, when an elderly statesman, Musa Kâzım Pasha (d. 1890), a truculent man apparently, 'overheard' the discussion of young Francophiles admiring Europe.[176] A careless passenger could be also caught disparaging a philanthropic act of an Egyptian prince.[177] But more politically minded passengers were aware of the vigilance of spies and preferred to abstain from dangerous dialogues before a multitude.[178] They were right. The agents of the state often monitored the conversations taking place aboard.[179] Nevertheless this did not stop other less cautious types or those who were less bound by the statutes of the Ottoman state. A middle-aged European lady, for instance, thought that it was a perfectly safe place to invite passengers to Christianity and distribute pamphlets in Greek and Ottoman.[180] On-board Armenian dissidents also tried to organise a big public demonstration

174 Peter Stallybrass and Allon White, *The Politics and Poetics of Transgression* (London: Methuen, 1986), 80.

175 See Anonymous, 'Dünyada Herze-Vekili Yalnız Diyojen Midir?', *Diyojen*, 25 Mart/6 April 1287/1871, 3.

176 See İnal, *Son Asır Türk Şâirleri II*, 807–08. From İnal's account it seems that the Pasha was in the habit of eavesdropping in ferries and then getting into awkward arguments with complete strangers. For a more 'philosophical' argument also see, ibid., 804. It should be noted that each episode ended with the Pasha's calling his interlocutors 'jackass' (*eşek*).

177 From a letter by Nâmık Kemal to his father: 'His Highness Mustafa Fâzıl Pasha is getting his sons circumcised. Along with them, fifteen hundred poor boys are also getting circumcised. Now that is humanitarianism. Yesterday on one of the Bosporus boats, I heard one idiot saying, "this is a necessity of fortune." I know so many men ...' Kuntay, *Nâmık Kemal Devrinin İnsanları I*, 327.

178 İnal, *Son Asır Türk Şâirleri II*, 1038.

179 See, for instance, a report presented by Mahmud Celaleddin Pasha in İbnülemin Mahmud Kemal İnal, *Son Sadrâzamlar*, 4 vols., vol. I (İstanbul: Milli Eğitim Basımevi, 1964), 387.

180 BOA, Y..PRK.ASK. 18/13, 12 Receb 1300 (19 May 1883).

to protest against what later became known as the Hamidian massacres of 1894–1896.[181]

Because of its ephemeral nature, there are only small fragments of what was probably spoken on board (*verba volant*). The conversation among acquaintances tended to be more political. The existence of cabins also made private, less conspicuous conversations possible. Mîzâncı Murad described in detail how he and a family friend talked about the Grand Vizier in the protection of a cabin aboard.[182] Maybe for this reason, *Şirket* steamboats also became a favoured meeting place for certain secret societies.[183]

It is highly unlikely that the Ottoman steamboats (*vapurs*) turned into Habermas's eighteenth-century London coffeehouses where regulars putatively engaged in high-minded discourse. But maybe they can be imagined as a part of the urban fabric that enabled the formulation of public opinion.[184] They brought people from various strata of society together in a new context and became more influential than any coffeehouse or social club that existed during that era.[185] Haughty pashas and modest city dwellers inevitably mingled in an ambiance of relative equality. It was also during this era; the public began to acquire an increasingly similar appearance because of the mass production of clothes and lost the visible signs of difference – a global phenomenon described by C. A. Bayly as the uniformity of 'bodily practices'.[186] Not everybody liked this democratisation, of course. As 'waiting with the

181 BOA, İ..HUS. 44/1313/C-63, 28 Cemaziyelahir 1313 (December 16, 1895). The date of the massacres is sometimes given as 1894–1896 and sometimes as 1894–1897, even on the same page. See, for instance, Aram Arkun, 'Into the Modern Age: 1800–1913', in *The Armenians: Past and Present in the Making of National Identity*, ed. Edmund Herzig and Marina Kurkchiyan (Oxford: RoutledgeCurzon, 2005), 81.

182 [Mîzâncı Murad], 'İfâde-i Mahsûsa - İzâhat-ı Lâzıme', *Mîzân*, 30 Receb/20 January 1312/1895, 2356–2357.

183 One of the secret societies discussed in Chapter 2 made a habit of meeting in *vapurs*, probably for security reasons. See BOA, Y..EE.. 23/13, 26 Safer 1296 (19 February 1879).

184 Cf. Christina Parolin, *Radical Spaces Venues of Popular Politics in London, 1790 – c. 1845* (Canberra: Australian National University, 2010), 158.

185 Lisa Wedeen, for instance, underlines the importance of 'ordinary activities undertaken by men and women in pursuit of their daily lives' to inculcate national values when the state institutions are ineffective. Lisa Wedeen, *Peripheral Visions*, 3.

186 C. A. Bayly, *The Birth of the Modern World, 1780–1914* (Cornwall: Blackwell Publishing, 2004), 1. Also see Sennett, *The Fall of Public Men*, 20.

public on the deck, vexed or offended Ahmed Vefik Pasha' (d. 1891), famous statesman and one of the public lecturers in Chapter 3, he supposedly lingered until the last minute in his library while his household followed the movement of the boat from a window to let him know the exact moment of its arrival.[187] But *Şirket* provided a critical public sphere for a new generation when there were few available. Perhaps for these reasons, Ahmed Rasim counted it among the most important initiatives, along with the Ottoman Academy of Sciences, which connected the country with progress after the Crimean War.[188]

In fact it was over a boat conversation that Nâmık Kemal made his strongest protest against the Francophile circles. In a letter published in his paper (*İbret*), one young admirer after writing rather excessively on the logic of argument and importance of soldiering in the Ottoman society 'with various proofs and evidences', implored him to help convince his friends. He was unsophisticated, the reader accepted without hesitation.[189] For this reason he asked Kemal's opinion as someone 'whose ideas, like everybody he venerated, and whatever he says it would be accepted as truth without any proof or evidence'.[190] His letter was about a discussion that the reader had with his friends on a boat to the Asian side of the city. They saw two soldiers behaving rather improperly aboard and one of his friends complained about their obnoxious treatments of non-Muslims. 'The other', he wrote:

> taking it to the philosophical direction (*felsefiyet cihhetine saparak*), and maybe even further, categorized soldiers as a bunch of savages who are under orders (*me'mur*) to obliterate civilized society and added that for this reason he did not like them at all. I, on the other hand, tried my hardest to

187 İbnülemin Mahmud Kemal İnal, *Son Sadrâzamlar*, 4 vols., vol. II (İstanbul: Dergah Yayınlar, 1982), 731. He was in fact the first translator of Molière and prepared a dictionary of the Ottoman language with etymological roots. If the books that he owned were any indication, he was a well-rounded intellectual. Among his thousands and thousands of books, there were Arabic, Persian, Chagatai, Turkish, French, English, Latin, German, Italian, Greek, Spanish, Russian, Polish, Rumanian, and Hungarian books. For the list of his books prepared for auction after this death, see *Catalogue de la bibliothèque de feu Ahmed Véfyk pacha* (Constantinople: Baghdadlian, 1893).

188 Rasim, *İstibdaddan Hakimiyet-i Milliyeye*, 286.

189 Anonymous, 'Nev-Residegan-ı Maârifetten Bir Zâtın Varakasıdır', *İbret*, 27 Rebiülahir/4 July 1289/1872, 2.

190 Here the owner of the letter writes in third person.

Figure 5.4 Namık Kemal when he was the editor-in-chief of *İbret*, c. 1872–1873.
With the permission of Istanbul University, Rare Book Collection, 90625.

persuade them with *various proofs and evidences*, but I could not succeed. The reason for me to present this object before you is to plea if there is anything wrong in what I am saying, owing to my immaturity and inexperience, to be corrected; but if my opinions are valid, then to implore you to write a special editorial to explain what soldiering is and from what their *terbiye* is made of to save our young minds from such feeble ideas.[191]

This letter, if genuine, is interesting for several reasons. First of all, it is an example of the 'philosophical' conversations taking place in public transport and demonstrates the value of these places for opinion-making. The language that the fledgling reader used is also noteworthy here. His constant reference to proofs and evidences (*delâil ve senedât*) and his explanations of the logic of argument can be taken as an allusion to his *münâzara* skills. Not surprisingly, he does not use the word, which, as mentioned in Chapter 2, had become slightly obsolete by then.[192] Secondly, it indicates Kemal's position as a public arbiter. Richard Posner cites this kind of 'authority' as one of the conditions of being a public intellectual.[193] In this letter, the reader relinquishes his authority to Kemal and entreats him to make a decision for or against his ideas (although he seems sure of Kemal's approval). And the third is the strange antimilitary stance of the interlocutors in question. In traditional Ottoman political thought, which glorifies *jihad* as an Islamic ideal, there are only a few examples where an author could write about the 'advantages of peace'.[194] When we ponder the conversation, their sympathy towards non-Muslims over Muslim soldiers can be interpreted as a sign of internalisation of certain Tanzimat values such as Ottoman citizenry above religious identity. But such a strong antimilitarist tone is puzzling. It is possible to connect it with some European philosophies such as Utilitarianism of Bentham or deontological Pacifism of Kant. But even for these thinkers there was an acceptable version of warfare as decoded by

[191] Anonymous, 'Nev-Residegan-ı Maârifetten', 2.

[192] In his answer, Kemal employed the word *münâzaa* (as in 'those who had a *münâzaa* with you'), which is a less systematic and more argumentative type of argument. For details, see Chapter 2, 96–109.

[193] Richard A. Posner, *Public Intellectuals: A Study of Decline* (Cambridge, MA: Harvard University Press, 2001), 46.

[194] See, for instance, the late sixteenth-century account of Akhisari (d. 1616) on '*Des Avantages de la Paix et de l'Inviolabilité des Traités*', in Garcin de Tassy, 'Principes de sagesse touchant l'art de gouverner par Rizwan-ben-abd'oul-mannan Ac-hissari', *Journal Asiatique* I, no. IV (1824): 289. After the eighteenth century, however, with the evident decline of power, the idea of peace became more prevalent among Ottoman intellectuals. Aksan, *An Ottoman Statesman in War and Peace*, 199.

Walter Benjamin's formulas for 'legitimate' or 'sanctioned violence'.[195] This man, if not a misrepresentation, might be, in fact, the first Ottoman conscientious objector to be documented.

Kemal's answer was less exciting. As an enthusiast of early Ottomans conquests against their medieval enemies (*fütûhât*), he saw soldiers as the successors of Ottoman martyrs and ghazis. Even though he acknowledged the destructions caused by the military profession, he was also aghast at the mere suggestion of any antipathy towards Muslim soldiers. 'Those who say such things', he wrote, 'are among the kind gentlemen whose existence we do not wish to see in the fatherland'. 'Pray', he added, 'let's not act so unfeelingly towards our soldiers to deny them a warm place aboard. In the moment of danger, neither *Şirket* nor those flamboyant gentlemen can protect our lives and comfort'.[196]

But what makes Kemal a pivotal figure in this study was not so much his arbitration in these kinds of disagreements, but rather his turning the nascent idea of public opinion into a powerful rhetorical and discursive tool through his writing. It was by his hand that the notion found its voice and became an important power on the Ottoman political platform. Through his books and articles, he presented governmental issues to what he termed the 'tribunal of public opinion/ *efkâr-ı umûmîyenin nazargâh-ı muhâkemesi*'.[197] In this world, even the laws were subjugated to the protection of this mighty force.[198] It

195 See, for example, this passage from an early compilation of Bentham: 'Thus, judging that there were circumstances which would justify declarations of war, he appealed to the *tribunal of public opinion* regarding the method of conducting hostilities towards the desired end.' Jeremy Bentham, *Benthamiana: or Select Extracts from the Works of Jeremy Bentham. With an Outline of His Opinions on the Principal Subjects Discussed in His Works*, ed. John Hill Burton (Philadelphia: Lea & Blanchard, 1844), 423, emphasis mine. For Kant's idea of 'just war', see Andrew Fiala, *The Just War Myth: The Moral Illusions of War* (Plymouth, UK: Rowman & Littlefield, 2008), 47. Also see Benjamin's essay, Critique of Violence in Walter Benjamin, *Reflections: Essays, Aphorisms, Autobiographical Writings*, ed. Peter Demetz (New York: Harcourt Brace Jovanovich, 1978), 279.

196 Kemal, 'Cevap', 2. For an analysis of 'Ottoman Medieval Romanticism', see Ersoy, 'On the Sources', 335–347.

197 Nâmık Kemal, 'Konsoloslar', *İbret*, 15 Şevval/16 December 1289/1872, 1. Or alternatively to the 'appreciative eye of the public opinion/*efkâr-ı umûmîyenin nazar-ı takdirine arz*'. See Nâmık Kemal, '[İbret Gazetesi]', *İbret*, 26 Zilkade/25 January 1289/1873, 1.

198 Nâmık Kemal, 'İbret', *İbret*, 11 Rebiülahir/18 June 1289/1872, 1.

was the 'true guardian to a foundation of civilization', as he put it in 1872.[199] The intellectuals of his country awaited its emergence for a very long time, and when it finally appeared, he argued, it was much stronger and effective than they had ever expected.[200]

He explained the meaning of public opinion to his readers through different examples. If one considers the great Parliament in London, he wrote in 1872, for instance, 'if one only takes a look at that great building where the grandeur and endurance of public opinion found embodiment against the sight of the administration, it can be reasoned that its formidable shape turned into stone only to suggest that it is safe from any calamity and decay'.[201] For Kemal, public opinion was an 'impetuous deluge with no chance of building a barrier against it'.[202] It was an unstoppable juggernaut, as he asserted in another article in 1868,[203] or it was inexorable, as he put it a few years later.[204] 'When the public opinion begins exploding like volcanoes', he questioned in 1872, 'could private benefit or personal inclination possibly stand against such a force?'[205]

This was the political conundrum faced by Ottoman intellectuals and not everybody agreed with Kemal's answers. Was it really public opinion or was it just the opinion of the people who were good at making their opinion public?[206] Ali Suâvi, for instance, writing from

199 Nâmık Kemal, 'Tanzimat', *İbret*, 5 Ramazan/6 November 1289/1872, 2.

200 Nâmık Kemal, 'İfâde-i Meram', *İbret*, 27 Receb/30 September 1289/1872, 1.

201 Nâmık Kemal, 'Terakki', *İbret*, 3 Ramazan/4 November 1289/1872, 1.

202 Nâmık Kemal, 'Meyelân-ı Âlem', *İbret*, 30 Rebiülahir/7 July 1289/1872, 2.

203 He argued, for instance, in an article written for *Hürriyet* in 1868, 'we are living in such a time that nobody can resist public opinion'. Kemal, 'Veşavirhum fi'l-Emr', 2.

204 In September 1872 and this time for *İbret*, he wrote everybody realized the 'unstoppable power (*mukâvemet nâ-kâbil*) of public opinion in our country'. Kemal, 'İfâde-i Meram', 2.

205 Kemal, 'Meyelân-ı Âlem', 2.

206 One day Nâmık Kemal, Ziyâ Paşa, Menapirzâde Nuri, and Kayazâde Reşad, the sacred circle of the Young Ottoman movement, took a *caique* to go to the Asian side of Istanbul. As the boat glided over the Bosporus, the city's famous southwest wind started to shake the vessel. Nâmık Kemal asked his frightened friend, Kayazâde Reşad Bey, if he was afraid of death. 'No', Reşad Bey answered, 'no, I am not afraid of death. But I am afraid that if the boat sinks, public opinion will sink with us'. The anecdote, narrated by Kemal's son, is meaningful as it encapsulates how some of his contemporaries perceived Kemal. Ali Ekrem Bolayır, *Ali Ekrem Bolayır'ın Hâtıraları*, ed. Metin Kayahan Özgül, Türk Büyükleri Dizisi (Ankara: Kültür Bakanlığı, 1991), 406–407.

Paris in 1870, asserted that even the Russian Empire, which he found somewhat primitive, was behind the protective shield of public opinion; alas, not the Ottomans. 'O people of understanding', he wrote, 'if you contemplate carefully on this comparison, you shall understand which side is going to win'.[207] Another contemporary Ottoman newspaper, *Hakayık*, in February 1872, after referring to what it called the 'frailty' of public opinion even in civilized countries, or the absence of modern books and schools in the Ottoman Empire commented rather derisively from its editorial: 'claiming that there is public opinion with us', it read, 'would be like saying that there is life and existence among the residents of the underworld (*ehl-i kubûr*)'.[208]

As a response, Nâmık Kemal penned a long article entitled 'Public Opinion' and criticised *Hakayık*'s negative attitude. The article itself is remarkable for its daring tone, with its discussions of constitutional charters (*sened-i meşrûtiyet*) and justified revolutions (*lüzum-i hakiki*).[209] But it is also noteworthy as it clearly shows Kemal's understanding of the concept. Keith Baker in his study of the French Revolution distinguishes between the two different understandings of public opinion. One assumes its presence as 'a perpetual noise in the system which must in some way be taken account', and the other sees it as a 'specific phenomenon of modern societies, brought into being by long-term changes in literacy, by the growth of capitalism and the commercial expansion of the press'.[210] For Kemal, it was clearly the former. He perceived it as something transcending of human history, a ruling principle. It was thanks to its power that the Romans became the 'king of nations' in the past. 'Were not those heroes, who saved our nation from the cruel and corrupt claws of tyrants such as Feyzullah Efendi and İbrahim Pasha', he asked, 'clear examples of public opinion? Were they reading French and German books of political science in the barracks of Janissaries? In brief there is no time and nation in human history which could be thought destitute of public opinion'.[211]

207 Ali Suâvi, 'Rusya'da Dahi Efkâr-ı Umûmîyye Var Bizde Yok' *Ulum [Muvakkaten]*, 10 Şaban/16 November 1286/1869, 141.
208 Anonymous, 'Terbiye-i Siyâsiye', *Hakayık*, 4 Şaban/7 October 1289/1872, 1.
209 Nâmık Kemal, 'Efkâr-ı Umûmîye', *İbret*, 26 Şaban/28 October 1289/1872, 1–3.
210 Baker, *Inventing the French Revolution*, 168.
211 Kemal, 'Efkâr-ı Umûmîye', 2.

Kemal's association of public opinion with two major rebellions from Ottoman history that caused the deposition of two sultans (Mustafa II in 1703 and Ahmed III in 1730) is quite remarkable, especially during the reign of a sultan who was supposed to be an avid reader of history.[212] But he went even further. This was just a beginning (*fâtiha-i zuhûr*) he wrote:

> The public opinion that we see waking up from its silence is the precious offspring of every member of this fatherland and the saviour of our nation. For its nourishment, it is absolutely necessary for everybody to show more attention and care than they do for their own children. And to realize the goal, it is imperative to know that if political ethics is corrupt in a society, public opinion needs to stay in a demonstrative state (*dâimâ bir nümâyiş hâlinde*) to keep the government in the circle of justice.

'It does not rebel', he finally warned, 'unless it is harassed to the last extremity as it happened in Russia'.[213] The message was clear. The public was going to rebel when harassed to that level.[214]

This article is also interesting in that it elucidates why he used this term, public opinion, incomparably more in his articles written in the Empire. He projected it as a political contriving, which was meant to limit the power of an absolute ruler by making him believe that there was something stronger than him, something that he could not possibly control. When Kemal could write his demands for a constitutional government without anxiety, he did not need the protection of this abstract notion. He could threaten the government with a violent revolution.[215] Public opinion was not written or explained for the

212 See, Kuntay, *Nâmık Kemal Devrinin İnsanları I*, 518–519.

213 Kemal, 'Efkâr-ı Umûmîye', 2.

214 His prophecy was precise. Only a few years later, on 30 May 1876, the army overthrew Sultan Abdülaziz after popular demonstrations in the city. This was presented as a victory of public opinion by the newspapers and intellectuals. Mahmud Nedim Pasha, Grand Vizier, pressured the people to the last extreme, many intellectuals agreed. But this 'public revolution' shall be discussed in the next chapter. Perhaps it is also wrong to call this a fulfilment of a prophecy since the word denotes a distance; a non-involvement as Kemal did the best he could to bring down Abdülaziz's reign.

215 He wrote for *Hürriyet* in London in the form of a letter: 'You know what I am afraid of. While those who oppose certain things work respectfully to make things smoother, hunger and starvation can get the better of the mob. If they arm once, God forbid, *Istanbul will turn into a slaughterhouse and perhaps this excuse will be the end of the state*.' Nâmık Kemal, 'Usûl-i Meşverete Dair Geçen Nümerolarda Münderic Mektûbların Beşincisi', *Hürriyet*, 19 October

interest of the public (at least not exclusively), but for the Sultan's benefit. He hoped that the Sultan would read his articles and understand the meaning between the lines. For some time, there was a general feeling that he actually did read and understand. When Abdülaziz established the Council of the State (*Şûrâ-i Devlet*) in 1868, Kemal described this as a victory for Young Ottomans and the recognition of public freedom (*hürriyet-i âmme*).[216] But when the Sultan's understanding was slower than societal expectations (with which his were quite interlaced), he invoked public opinion as the *ulemâ* had invoked janissaries in the past.[217] Yet there were hesitations in the scope of public opinion's authority. Janissaries, who were for one very visible, proved themselves fierce through many revolutions and upheavals, whereas public opinion was untested and ill defined. So his evocations were also mixed with wishful thinking. He may have been sure of its presence, but like many others, he was not sure of its power.

There is a reason why Nâmık Kemal is called a 'public intellectual' and not his contemporaries.[218] Şinâsi was maybe the first intellectual of the Tanzimat era, but he was too much an eccentric to become a

1868, 8, emphasis mine. From his private letters, however, we know that he was not actually very hopeful about any reaction coming from Istanbul people. See a letter written to his father, Kuntay, *Nâmık Kemal Devrinin İnsanları I*, 418–419.

216 Indeed Abdülaziz, in his royal speech, mentioned 'the protection of people's law of liberty in every circumstance' as the main duty of every government. For the whole text, see Anonymous, 'Havâdis-i Dâhiliye: Pay-i Taht', *Tasvîr-i Efkâr*, 18 Muharrem/11 May 1285/1868, 1–2. For Kemal's comment, see Kemal, 'İhtilafi ümmeti rahmetün', 4. Levant Herald described this as the 'creation of the new institution with all the importance of great constitutional epoch in the history of the Empire', and wrote: 'in its general organisation, the Turkish Council of the State, as we anticipated, *is modelled after the Russian 'Council of the Empire'*. This comment is rather interesting as it shows how the Russian influence that we have mentioned in Chapter 3 was visible to contemporaries. See Anonymous, 'Constantinople, Wednes: May 13', *Levant Herald*, 13 May 1868, 100, emphasis mine.

217 In a letter to Ali Suâvi, he wrote 'I swear to God, the Ruler does not read the newspaper [*Hürriyet*]. Even if he read it, he would not understand. Even if he understood, he would not be upset. Even if he was upset, he cannot do anything about it!' Kuntay, *Nâmık Kemal Devrinin İnsanları I*, 500.

218 About public intellectuals and their political involvements see, Posner, *Public Intellectuals*, 19–20.

public figure.[219] Kemal's fluent wielding of the editorial 'we' was sustained by the popular perception that he did actually speak for the people.[220] In his books and articles, he deliberately chose early Islamic and Ottoman parables to appeal the Muslim population's conscience.[221] Thanks to his influence, a new vocabulary, which was devised to address political questions, found its way into daily language.[222] Perhaps he was not a member of that elegant club which Michel Foucault deferentially called 'founders of discursivity'.[223] He did not come up with an extensive political agenda. He was a practical man interested in political improvement. For his purposes, he used

[219] As Kuntay emphasised 'Kemal's political side did not begin rapidly. Kemal the Rebellious was not around. Because his master Şinâsi was not a revolutionary thunder but rather a revolutionary gentleman. He was going to destroy the old through calculation and mathematics.' Kuntay, *Nâmık Kemal Devrinin İnsanları I*, 56–57.

[220] See, for instance, his acknowledgement in the name of the whole Ottoman public (*umûm-i Osmanlılar tarafından beyân-ı teşekkür*) Nâmık Kemal, 'Bir Muvafakkiyet', *İbret*, 16 Muharrem/16 March 1290/1873.

[221] In a letter to his father, the Court Astronomer Mustafa Asım Efendi, he asked for Persian classics such as *Ravzâtü's Safâ* or *Ravzâtü'l-Ahbab* 'to show examples from the Islamic past in the upcoming writings (*yazılacak şeylerde*)'. Kuntay, *Nâmık Kemal Devrinin İnsanları I*, 308, 488–489. Sebastian Conrad, on the other hand, focuses on Kemal as the Voltaire of the Ottoman Empire, citing Ebuzziyâ. Conrad argues, 'Young Ottomans such as Namik Kemal (1840–1888) legitimized their cause by citing the works of Locke, Rousseau, and Montesquieu, which were beginning to be translated.' Even though Kemal referred to Rousseau and Montesquieu quite a few times as people of great understanding, it still is very difficult to think of them as sources of legitimacy in the Ottoman context. See Sebastian Conrad, 'Enlightenment in Global History: A Historiographical Critique', *American Historical Review* 117, no. 4 (2012): 1018.

[222] Mithat Cemal Kuntay wrote: 'how much he cried for Kars, how happy he became after Sebastopol. But there was no sign of these joys and tears in his [early] poetry book. Because these excitements did not have any correspondence in the language; this child was going to find the word *Vatan* (fatherland), but much later'. Kuntay, *Nâmık Kemal Devrinin İnsanları I*, 3. Though he did not invite them, the expressions such as *vatan, hürriyet* (liberty) and *meşrûtiyet* (constitutional government) became popular as a result of his writings. For the evolution of the term *vatan*, see Bernard Lewis, 'Watan', *Journal of Contemporary History* 26, no. 3/4 (1991): 530.

[223] Foucault, 'What Is an Author?', 113–114. According to Foucault, people belonging to this club such as Marx and Freud 'are unique in that they are not just the authors of their own works. They have produced something else: the possibilities and the rules for the formation of other texts . . . [they] have established an endless possibility of discourse'. Ibid., 114.

newspapers, which constituted, he argued, the 'language of the public',[224] or the ultimate school that transformed the country into 'an assembly of friends'.[225] 'Even if the government organised free lectures on politics for years', he once wrote, 'they would not have served public opinion as much as newspapers have done'.[226] Indeed, it was mostly because of the impact of the press and Kemal that political participation became possible in the Ottoman context. By giving a more definitive sense of time and space to their readers, they both helped the formation of an imperial citizenry.[227] Although eventually they failed to keep it up, they once created an Ottoman public.

After the opening night of his famous play, *Fatherland or Silistra* in 1873, amidst the cries of 'Long Live Kemal' and 'Long Live the Nation', something of a riot ensued in the city.[228] As a result, the government exiled him; the semi-official *La Turquie* made no secret that this was indeed due to his '*popularité*'.[229] The *Levant Herald*, after expressing its regret at Kemal's 'rustication', blamed his over-zealous style. 'In its present infant stage of existence', the paper reasoned, '*public opinion* in this country requires to be strengthened by sound and wholesome instruction, not to be stimulated to

224 '*Lisân-i umûm makamında olan gazeteler*'. Kemal, 'Usûl-i Meşverete Dair Geçen Nümerolarda Münderic Mektûbların Üçüncüsü', 7.

225 See Nâmık Kemal, 'Gazeteciliğe Dair', *İbret*, 21 Zilkade/20 January 1289/1873, 1. With this expression, *meclis-i ülfet*, he implicitly compared the extensive public with earlier pasha *konaks*.

226 Kemal, 'Türkçe Matbuat', 2.

227 As Benedict Anderson argues, the press brought individuals together through simultaneous acts of reading, which enabled them to imagine themselves as a national body. Anderson, *Imagined Communities*, 24–25.

228 Şeref, *Târîh Musâhabeleri*, 182. Also see Talat S. Halman, *Rapture and Revolution: Essays on Turkish Literature* (Syracuse, NY: Syracuse University Press, 2007), 105. This piece, according to Kemal Karpat, played 'an important part in the ideological indoctrination of Ottoman and Turkish officers in the nineteenth and twentieth centuries'. See Karpat, *Studies on Ottoman Social and Political History*, 237.

229 '*D'une pièce de Kémal bey dans laquelle se trouvaient de allusions très-offensantes pour le gouvernement impérial. Si l'autorité s'est montrée assez tolérante pour les scènes tumultueuses qui ont eu lieu lors de la première représentation de cette pièce, elle ne pouvait naturellement souffrir que ces représentations devinssent le prétexte de menées coupables, et permissent à une personnalité ambitieuse d'asseoir sa popularité sur les sentiments malveillants qu'elle exploitait*'. Anonymous, '[D'une pièce de Kémal bey]', *La Turquie*, 12 April 1873, 1.

precocious action by theories which intoxicate and enfeeble the immature judgment'.[230]

The decision to exile him, however, turned out to be a poor one for the authorities. It only served to entrench Kemal's legendary fame. Even twenty years after his death, which incidentally caught him during another 'rustication' in 1888, government spies still reported of stores secretly selling his photographs,[231] or dissidents singing his poetry.[232] His writings remained banned because of the 'excitement it might cause in people'.[233] Another report referred to the possible negative effects of his publications on the 'schooling of the public'.[234] Even old style compilations were reported by the spies of Abdülhamid II because of their inclusion of his historical prose. The aim of this kind of publication, the informer patriotically articulated was to 'poison public opinion (*efkâr-i umûmîyeyi tesmim*)'.[235] Yet despite his untimely death, according to Ahmet Hamdi, Kemal had two great achievements: 'When he died there were two things in the country which had not existed during the years he was born and educated: public opinion and literature. On the first one, his share was colossal but the second one came entirely out of his benevolence. He taught his society to engage in their own matters'.[236] Maybe for this reason, Süleyman Nazif (d. 1927), one of the most esteemed names of the

230 Anonymous, '[The Rustification of Kemal Bey]', *Levant Herald*, 16 April 1873, 124, emphasis mine. The article continued in an interesting vein: 'The geographical limits of Turkey are so disproportioned to the ethnical importance of the dominant race that '*La Patrie*' as a watchword in the mouth of a Turk, is nonsense'.

231 BOA, Y..EE..KP.. 16/1598 23, Cemaziyelevvel 1320 (28 August 1902).

232 BOA,Y..EE.. 15/114, 6 Rebiülahir 1327 (27 April 1909).

233 BOA, MF.MKT. 628/7, 16 Safer 1320 (25 May 1902).

234 BOA., Y.PRK. MF 4/60, cited in Demirel, *II. Abdülhamid Döneminde Sansür*, 100.

235 BOA, Y..EE.. 15/43, 16 Rebiülahir 1327 (7 May 1909). Ostensibly, the informer reasoned, maybe Kemal's stories were about the first four caliphs but there were references to today which were too clear to miss: 'It reads, he wrote 'the obedience to the Caliph hinges on his obedience to people. In fact, the real reason is to propagate the idea that Islam was subject to republic.' The book in question was *Hadîkat-ül Üdebâ* (*the Garden of Writers*). See Osman Emin, *Hadîkat-ül Üdebâ* (İstanbul: Matbaa-ı Aramyan, 1299/1883). According to the list that Fatmagül Demirel published this book appears to be among the volumes garnered and burnt by the censorship agents in 1902. Demirel, *II. Abdülhamid Döneminde Sansür*, 184.

236 Tanpınar, *XIX. Asır Türk Edebiyâtı Târîhi*, 331.

Turkish literature, wrote with deference: 'do not look for Kemal's oeuvres only in books, newspapers or journal collections. From Recâî-zâde Ekrem to Faruk Nafiz, we are all, according to our talent and aptitude, great and small production of the great writer. It was God who created us and it was Kemal who brought us up'.[237]

[237] Nazif, *Nâmık Kemal*, 27. According to Jale Parla, Nâmık Kemal became a 'father figure for Tanzimat writers, and those who followed him imitated this role in their fatherhood'. See Jale Parla, *Babalar ve Oğullar: Tanzimat Romanının Epistemolojik Temelleri* (İstanbul: İletişim Yayınları, 1993), 54–55.

6 'The Turkish Revolution'

The following is what one might call the denouement of this book, which seeks to situate the immediate circumstances surrounding the overthrow of Sultan Abdülaziz in May 1876. This momentous event, it is argued, represented the apogee of public opinion as a political force in the Ottoman Empire. It was only then that the notion truly became the 'impetuous deluge' that Kemal mentioned in his many articles. Despite many schisms and divisions among the Ottoman elite, from the liberal Midhat Pasha to the conservative Cevdet, contemporaries of the event all believed that it was the 'wrath of public opinion' which wrought the fall of their old master so decisively.[1]

This charting is interesting not only for obvious reasons. It also has a historiographical significance: in the prevailing view of Ottoman political culture, this explanation is ignored almost in its entirety.[2] If today a contemporary of Abdülaziz studied the scholarship regarding the events of May 1876, he or she would be struck by the complete absence of the 'public' in scholarly discussions. The deposition of the Sultan is overwhelmingly portrayed as a *coup d'état*, which was secretly carried out and executed by high-ranking military and bureaucratic elite.[3] The events of May, which this chapter addresses, were described, if mentioned at all, as agitations deliberately provoked by

[1] Midhat Paşa, *Midhat Paşa: Hayât-ı Siyâsiyesi, Hidâmatı, Menfâ Hayâtı: Tabsıra-i İbret*, ed. Ali Haydar Midhat, 2 vols., vol. I (İstanbul: Hilal Matbaası, 1325/1908), 161; Cevdet Paşa, *Tezâkir 40*, 152; Mahmud Celâleddin Paşa, *Mir'ât-ı Hakikat*, 3 vols., vol. I (İstanbul: Matbaa-i Osmaniye, 1326/1908), 87; Mehmed Memduh, *Mir'ât-ı Şuûnât* (İzmir: Ahenk Matbaası, 1328/1910–11), 55.

[2] Roderic Davison should be mentioned as one prominent exception. See Davison, *Reform in the Ottoman Empire*, 312–313.

[3] See, for instance, Erik J. Zürcher, *Turkey: A Modern History* (London: I. B. Tauris, 2004), 73; Caroline Finkel, *Osman's Dream: The Story of the Ottoman Empire 1300–1923* (New York: Basic Books, 2005), 481; Hanioğlu, *A Brief History of the Late Ottoman Empire*, 111.

pro-reform statesmen without any proof, except the later allegations of Sultan Abdülhamid himself.[4]

This line of explanation is naturally very convenient for a historiography whose principal source is the state archives. As Tim Harris rightly notes, 'once the crowd is placed outside the political nation, it is easy to become sceptical about the degree of political awareness that we can justifiably attribute to the members of the crowd'.[5] Instead, however, this chapter takes a different approach and suggests that rather than translating the manifestations of 1876 as riots or crowd behaviour with little or no reference to the political consciousness behind it, it might be more pertinent to see them as examples of public participation in politics through debate and demonstration.[6]

Thus, the chapter has two objectives, which can be expressed in a single proposition. Through a reading of domestic and foreign primary sources, it aims to establish firmly the contemporary impression of public opinion as the driving force behind Ottoman politics.[7] By doing so, it shall also prove, it is hoped, the present hegemony of the official discourse in Ottoman historiography. Perhaps this point can be explained further: in slighting the agency of public opinion, Ottoman historians almost unanimously depict the overthrow of Abdülaziz as an example of bureaucratic and military hypertrophy. This is, however, nothing but a modern, and perhaps more sophisticated, reiteration of the 'official history',[8] conveniently promoted by the palace to remove a dangerous precedent before Sultan Abdülhamid.[9] If one can

[4] See, for instance, Mardin, *The Genesis of Young Ottoman Thought*, 70, 77.

[5] Tim Harris, *London Crowds in the Reign of Charles II: Propaganda and Politics from the Restoration Until the Exclusion Crisis* (Cambridge: Cambridge University Press, 1990), 15–16.

[6] See, for instance, Richard Cust's study of early modern political consciousness using discussion of newsletters and oral news. See Richard Cust, 'News and Politics in Early Seventeenth-Century England', *Past and Present* 112, no. 1 (1986): 60–90.

[7] In other words, 'it should matter now', as Adam Fox has remarked while discussing newsmongering in Elizabethan England, 'because it clearly mattered so much to contemporaries'. Adam Fox, 'Rumour, News and Popular Political Opinion in Elizabethan and Early Stuart England', *The Historical Journal* 40, no. 3 (1997): 598.

[8] Ahmed Hamdi aptly called this the 'argument of the palace/*sarayın tezi*'. Tanpınar, *XIX. Asır Türk Edebiyâtı Târîhi*, 407. Also see Nükhet Esen, *Modern Türk Edebiyâtı Üzerine Okumalar* (İstanbul: İletişim Yayıncılık, 2006), 13.

[9] The first reference to the 'public' provocation of the statesmen was given by Mahmud Celâleddin Pasha, a close confidant and loyal statesman of

peel away the layers of historical gossip and prejudices, a close reading of contemporary sources leaves us with a rather different picture, a picture of strands of political discourse and purposive action. Even Ahmet Midhat Efendi, who was actually 'commissioned by Abdülhamid to write a history book to strengthen [the Sultan's] position',[10] after pointing out personal animosities instigating the pashas against Abdülaziz, could not help admitting reluctantly the grim reality:

> In our humble opinion if the *public opinion* had not been favourable in this case, three or four personalities from the government, let alone succeeding in such a tremendous affair like replacing a sultan, could not have dared to venture it. For in a matter like this, which can shake the world, the force that *public opinion* can manifest is naturally greater than the force of three or four individuals. The thing called *public opinion* cannot be compared with private opinion, which is bound to be affected by personal malice and hatred. In any case, the overwhelming importance of such an affair would have doubtlessly led the most courageous man to dismay and hopelessness.[11]

Naturally what has been argued so far does not mean that the pashas were not involved in the act of deposition in any way. Their role as the communicators, or the messengers, of the event cannot be disputed. But it is suggested that rather than orchestrating it, they simply followed the political climate. Later trials clearly demonstrated that they had little or no influence over the public agenda, and when they experienced political persecution, they simply had to accept their fate, as Midhat Pasha's life sadly illustrates, without a protest or resistance coming from the people.[12] In other words, they were not the movers and shakers of the Ottoman public, as it is usually claimed, but rather its meek followers.[13]

Abdülhamid. According to him, Midhat and Hüseyin Avni Pashas planned a 'public uprising/*gulüv-i âmm*' to remove Mahmud Nedim from the Grand Vizierate. See Mahmud Celâleddin Paşa, *Mir'ât-ı Hakikat I*, 91.

10 Mustafa Nihat Özön, *Son Asır Türk Edebiyâtı Târîhi* (İstanbul: Maârif Matbaası, 1941), 310.

11 Ahmet Midhat, *Üss-i İnkilab*, 2 vols., vol. I (İstanbul: Takvîmhâne-i Âmire Matbaası, 1294/1877–78), 216. It should be also noted that Ahmed Midhat was trying to legitimise Abdülhamid's rule. This reference to public opinion can be also taken as Midhat's effort to show the expiration of Sultan Abdülaziz's reign, hence the legitimacy of his master's rule.

12 For the details, see İsmail Hakkı Uzunçarşılı, *Midhat Paşa ve Tâif Mahkûmları* (Ankara: Türk Târîh Kurumu Basımevi, 1950), passim.

13 After Hüseyin Avni Pasha pointed out that 'public opinion' was most favourable to the deposition of Abdülaziz, Mithat Pasha said to him menacingly 'you should remember that if you leave this alliance of purpose (*maksad-ı ittifâk*), this

In order to probe the role of Ottoman public opinion in the events of May 1876, the chapter first examines the outburst of political exuberance towards Sultan Abdülaziz and his Grand Vizier, Mahmud Nedim Pasha, prior to the affair in question. Thus, at one level, it demonstrates how the 'reading public' engaged in political interaction and rendered the government accountable to its citizens. Next, it goes through the actual deposition of the Sultan. Close attention to the discourses surrounding Sultan Aziz's fall reveals public opinion as the most important political force in Ottoman politics. After briefly summarising the short, and ill-fated, reign of Murad V, the chapter analyses the background of Abdülhamid's policies and shows how much of his later 'peculiarities' were in fact related to his public-mindedness.

The Fall of a Sultan

In his famous book, *The Interpretation of the Dreams*, Sigmund Freud makes an interesting political analogy to describe a patient's diagnosis. 'Let us imagine a society', the great psychoanalyst has written, 'in which a struggle is in process between a ruler who is jealous of his power and an alert *public opinion*. The people are in revolt against an unpopular official and demand his dismissal. But the autocrat, to show that he need take no heed of the popular wish, chooses that moment for bestowing a high distinction upon the official, though there is no other reason for doing so'.[14] This imaginary scenario portrays quite accurately the unfortunate circumstances preceding the deposition of Sultan Abdülaziz at the end of May 1876.

Rumours had been circulating about the mental health of the Sultan for some time. The situation was actually somewhat similar to pre-Revolution France. Exile *libellistes* were doing their best to discredit Abdülaziz in the public eye. Mehmed Emin Bey (d. 1874), in his newspaper published in Geneva, accused him of decorating his winning goats (Abdülaziz was fond of blood sports) and his lackeys with sacred Ottoman orders.[15] 'Because the downfall of this government is

nation will tear you up in Beyazid Square'. Mahmud Celâleddin Paşa, *Mir'ât-ı Hakikat I*, 105. If one can believe Mahmud Celâleddin Paşa, this comment worried the former Grand Vizier immensely.

14 Sigmund Freud, *The Interpretation of Dreams*, trans. James Strachey (New York: Basic Books, 2010), 169, emphasis mine.

15 About Mehmed Emin Bey, see İnal, *Son Asır Türk Şâirleri II*, 942–951.

imminent', he wrote, 'God first maddened the Sultan. His reign is rotten and turned into carrion. A revolution', he added decisively, 'is absolutely necessary/*bir inkılâba kat'i suretle lüzum vardır*'.[16]

'The charge brought against him by *public opinion* was that of gross extravagance'.[17] The Sultan was very careless with his expenditure, or at least people thought so.[18] The increasing fiscal crisis and severe droughts that wracked Ottoman society created widespread unrest and poverty among the lower classes. 'Various circumstances – some of them of remote, some of recent date – have contributed to give the *prolétariat* of the city enormous proportions'.[19] While struggling with social problems, the Sultan's decision to make unpopular Mahmud Nedim Pasha Grand Vizier in August 1875, for a second time, only added insult to injury. He was by far the most hated statesman of the late Ottoman history. Corruption rumours constantly swirled around his name.[20] Nothing was too low for him, Ahmed Saib Efendi declared with disgust.[21] The head chamberlain of Abdülaziz variously described

16 Cited in Bilgegil, *Yakın Çag Türk Kültür ve Edebiyâti Üzerinde Araştırmalar I*, 143, emphasis mine. Ismail Kemal Bey, a principal figure in the Albanian Independence, gives a similar account of the Sultan. Ismail Kemal Bey, *The Memoirs of Ismail Kemal Bey*, ed. Sommerwille Story (London: Constable, 1920), 93. Also see Ahmed Saib, *Vak'a-i Sultan Abd'ül-Aziz* (Kahire: Hediye Matbaası, 1326/1908–1909), 103. Cf. Simon Burrows, *Blackmail, Scandal and Revolution: London's French Libellistes, 1758–1792* (Manchester: Manchester University Press, 2006), 25.

17 Edwin Pears, *Forty Years in Constantinople: the Recollections of Sir Edwin Pears, 1873–1915* (London: Herbert Jenkins, 1916), 53, emphasis mine.

18 Midhat Cemal Kuntay claimed that, the personal budget of his predecessor, Abdülmecid, was seven times more than that of Abdülaziz in francs (15,400,000 FF versus 2,400,000 FF). See Kuntay, *Nâmık Kemal Devrinin İnsanları I*, 125, fn. 12. This does not, however, seem true. According to the published statistics, there is a clear decline in royal budgets as time went by. In 1277 (1861/62) for instance, when Abdülaziz became the Sultan, the royal budget consisted almost 10 per cent (9.3) of the total expenses, with 129,864 kurus allocated. In 1291 (1875/76), however, it was less than 5 per cent (4.6) with a total of 133,776 kurus. See Tevfik Güran, *Osmanlı Mali İstatistikleri: Bütçeler 1841–1918*, 7 vols., vol. VII, Târîhi İstatistikler Dizi (Ankara: Devlet İstatistik Enstitüsü, 2003), 14. But it was also alleged that published budgets lost all of their importance during this era and were prepared only to please the Sultan. See Mehmed Galib Bey, *Sâdullah Paşa yâhûd Mezardan Nidâ* (İstanbul: Matbaa-i Ebüzziyâ, 1327/1909), 82–83.

19 Anonymous, 'The Riot at Constantinople (From Our Special Correspondent)', *The Times*, 18 May 1876, 10.

20 See Şeref, *Târîh Musâhabeleri*, 190.

21 See Saib, *Vak'a-i Sultan Abd'ül-Aziz*, 94–95.

him as 'infidel/*kâfir*', 'mad/*deli*', 'treacherous infidel/*hâin kâfir*', or 'mad infidel/*deli kâfir*'.[22] Even the successive deaths of three former grand viziers, such as Mustafa Naili Pasha (d. 1871), were interpreted as a premonition, as 'their unwillingness to live in a world where Mahmud Nedim Pasha was the Grand Vizier'.[23]

But the pashas left behind many people who had to live in such a world. The first signs of a serious crisis became apparent near the beginning of March 1876. A letter addressed to 'Lord Derby' in French, and signed by '*les patriotes Musulmans*', asked for the support of the international community to depose Abdülaziz. 'After having read the above', the author explained, 'your Highness will probably find it peculiar that while the law allows us to save the country from a sovereign who is mad or evil (*fou ou pervers*), we do not depose Sultan Abdul-Aziz, who is evil and mad at the same time'.[24] As Britain's Secretary of State for Foreign Affairs, Edward Stanley (d. 1893) was used to receiving letters of complaint from Ottoman dissidents. Only a year previously, for instance, Ali Suâvi had also sent a dispatch and criticised the Ottoman government for not organising a General Assembly to create 'public consensus'.[25] But this latest epistle was the harshest in its tone.

Following the news through the domestic press after this point is difficult. From the very beginning, Mahmud Nedim's government encountered intense criticism from newspapers. Especially Nâmık Kemal's articles in *İbret* were 'moving public opinion [against him] to the last degree'.[26] As a result, the Grand Vizier began to use preemptive

[22] See Hâfız Mehmed, *Hakayik ül-Beyân fi Hakk-ı Cennetmekân Sultan Abdül'aziz Hân* (İstanbul: s.n., 1324/1908), 28–33.

[23] See Ahmed Lûtfî Efendi, *Vak'a-Nüvis Ahmed Lûtfî Efendi Târîhi*, ed. Münir Aktepe, 15 vols., vol. XII (Ankara: Türk Târîh Kurumu Basımevi, 1990), 32. In short, as Midhat Pasha argued, 'he was a man who had become the object of public's hatred and animosity/*âmmenin gayz ve adavetine müşted olmuş*'. Midhat Paşa, *Tabsıra-i İbret*, 162.

[24] Anonymous, 'TÜRKEI. – Adresse muselmännischer Patrioten an Lord Derby', in *Das Staatsarchiv: Sammlung der officiellen Actenstück zur Geschichte der Gegenwart*, ed. H. V. Kremer-Auenrode and Ph. Hirsch (Leipzig: Duncker & Humblot, 1877), 217. The letter was originally published in a French newspaper of Istanbul after the deposition of Sultan Aziz. See Roderic H. Davison, 'Turkish Attitudes Concerning Christian-Muslim Equality in the Nineteenth Century', *The American Historical Review* 59, no. 4 (1954): 863, fn. 51.

[25] Ali Suâvi published the translation of his letter as a pamphlet. Suâvi, *Sua[v]i'nin fi 28 Desambr 1875 (Evahir zi'lkada 1292) Târîhiyle İngiltere Hâriciye Nâzırı Lord Derbi'ye Yazmış Olduğu Mektûbun Türkçe Tercümesi*, 2.

[26] Süleyman Nazif, *İki Dost* (İstanbul: Kanaat Kütüphânesi, 1343/1925), 34.

censorship to stop the 'agitations of public opinion'.[27] This was a novelty for the Empire and further increased Mahmud Nedim's unpopularity. But he had reached an impasse. Some journalists, like Basîretçi Ali Efendi, after being reprimanded for 'agitating public opinion' by the Grand Vizier himself, were arrested on his order.[28] But Western newspapers monitored the political events closely, and for that matter more freely.[29] *The New York Times*, on 20 March, informed its readers of 'threatening revolutionary placards' appearing in the city, but dismissed rumours about the Sultan's health: 'he is in good health, leads a quiet, orderly life, takes great interest in public affairs'.[30]

The first half of May witnessed unprecedented political synergy among various groups in the Empire. This was 'unprecedented' because social unrest, while certainly not new to Istanbul people, had focused in the past on protecting the existing order. The incidents of 1703 or 1730, for instance, were more like violent rebellions, which resulted in superficial alterations such as removing a ruling sultan. Even though there were personalities like Çalık Ahmed who supposedly suggested the formation of '*a majority rule or a community government*' in 1703, these incidents were eluded by the Ottoman establishment without leaving a permanent mark and the *status quo ante* was established after a short period of time.[31] In contrast, the events of May 1876 signalled a desire, in a newly politicised language,

[27] Ali Mehmed Ata Bey, 'Memâlik-i Osmaniyede Sansürün Târîhi', *İkdam*, 5 Kanûnuevvel/5 December 1334/1918, 2. In other words, in the past while journalists were punished for articles that appeared in their newspapers, Mahmud Nedim Pasha ordered them to submit their articles to the censor before publication.

[28] '*Efkâr-ı umûmîyeyi galeyâna düşüreceksin*', see Ali, *İstanbul'da Yarım Asırlık Vakayi-i Mühimme*, 34.

[29] When Basîretçi Ali tried to defend himself by saying some of his articles were only translations, the Grand Vizier became furious and said: 'they are foreign newspaper, they can write [whatever they want]. Why did you? I will show it to you!'. Ibid.

[30] Anonymous, 'Internal Commotion in Turkey. Popular Feeling Against Mahmoud Dâmâd – Softas Arrested – Revolutionary Placards', *The New York Times*, 20 March 1876, 5.

[31] Naîmâ Mustafa Efendi, *Târîh-i Naîmâ (Ravzâtü'l-Hüseyn fi Hulâsati Ahbari'l-Hafîkayn)*, ed. Mustafa İpşirli, IV cilt, cilt IV (Ankara: Türk Târîh Kurumu, 2007), 1877. Also see Cemal Kafadar, 'Janissaries and Other Riffraff of Ottoman Istanbul: Rebels without a Cause', in *Identity and Identity Formation in the Ottoman World: A Volume of Essays in Honor of Norman Itzkowitz*, ed.

for political change and so for political improvement. They expanded a new horizon and aimed to establish a new system, which made those in political authority responsible to an expanding public. In short, they became a reference point for later political developments.

The Ottoman public wanted change and was ready to act to get it. In the words of Memduh Pasha, 'the compass of public opinion had deviated from its optimist point'.[32] On 15 May, *the Times* reported, 'the Softas [madrasa students] heading the populace', and 'parading the streets crying 'Down with the Grand Vizier!"[33] According to contemporary testimonies, Mahmud Nedim Pasha was chased by an angry crowd through the streets of the Sublime Porte and only barely saved his life by fleeing barefoot.[34] 'He was deposed by the people', Ahmet Midhat Efendi argued admiringly (*sadrâzamın halk tarafından tard edilmesiyle*).[35] This was something of a turning point: afterwards 'the whole city', as George Washburn put it, 'realized that it was at the mercy of revolutionists'.[36]

Western papers praised the news of the Grand Vizier's dismissal. 'A great revolution is thus accomplished', *the Times* remarked: 'This is the first instance since the time of the Janissaries that the Sultan has yielded to popular pressure'.[37] *Le Temps*, in the same vein, lauded the episode: 'Ever since the janissaries disappeared, Muslims have given a similar

Baki Tezcan and Karl. K. Barbir (Madison: the University of Wisconsin Press, 2007), 133.

32 Memduh, *Mir'ât-ı Şuûnât*, 55.

33 Anonymous, 'Turkey (By Telegraph.) (From Our Special Correspondent at Constantinople)', *The Times*, 15 May 1876, 7.

34 Cevdet Paşa, *Tezâkir 40*, 153. Basîretçi Ali also reports that they were calling him a traitor of the state and the nation (*hâin-i devlet ve millet*) to his face when he was coming to the Sublime Porte. Ali, *İstanbul'da Yarım Asırlık Vakayi-i Mühimme*, 43–44. According to Hâfız Mehmed Efendi, the head chamberlain of the Sultan, the Grand Vizier kneeled down before him and begged, saying 'Pray, son! Help me. They will tear me down into pieces/*aman evladım beni parçalarlar, bana sâhib ol*'. Mehmed, *Hakayik ül-Beyân*, 33. In Mahmud Nedim's defence, the practice was not unheard of. One Grand Vizier, Hezarpare Ahmed Paşa, was cut into pieces by janissaries in 1648 (hence his sobriquet *hezar-pare*/thousand-piece in Persian). His pieces were later sold to people as remedy for rheumatism. See, Hâfız Hüseyin Ayvansarayî, *Vefeyât-ı Selâtîn ve Meşâhir-i Ricâl* (İstanbul: Edebiyât Fakültesi Matbaası, 1978), 21.

35 Midhat, *Üss-i İnkilab*, 214.

36 George Washburn, *Fifty Years in Constantinople and Recollections of Robert College* (Boston: Houghton Mifflin Company, 1909), 104.

37 Anonymous, 'Turkey (By Telegraph.) (From Our Special Correspondent at Constantinople)', *The Times*, 16 May 1876, 5.

proof of energy or, as we say it here, boldness for the first time ... Long live the Constitution! Since yesterday, this word comes to conversations every moment'.[38] The mobilisation of *softas* especially attracted their attention. They were called 'priestly janissaries',[39] an association of which *softas* were also conscious and probably enjoyed.[40] Even Mahmud Nedim Pasha recognised this similarity and likened their demonstration to the 'awakening of the abolished house of tyranny/*mülga zorba ocağını uyandırmak*'.[41] Ottoman madrasa students, like their German peers in theological seminaries in 1848, became the motor of the revolution.[42] They were resolute in their decision and were going to depose the Sultan, if necessary by force.[43]

Abdülaziz, by contrast, was slowly losing sight of reality.[44] While his mother was distributing food and money in poor neighbourhoods of the city to buy their support,[45] Abdülaziz merely wandered from one

[38] Anonymous, 'Lettres de Turquie', *Le Temps*, 18 May 1876, 1.

[39] Anonymous, 'The New Turkish Government', *The Times*, 23 May 1876, 8.

[40] Ahmed Lûtfî, for instance, reported how madrasa students, imitating janissaries' refusal of their ration, stopped going to their classes to show their discontent. See, Uzunçarşılı, 'Sultan Abdülaziz Vak'asına Dair Vak'anüvis Lütfi Efendi'nin Bir Risâlesi', 354.

[41] Mahmud Nedim Paşa, *Üss-i İnkılaba Ait Müdafa'anâme*, Ali Emiri Koleksiyonu Târîh El Yazmaları, No. 1032, 89a.

[42] Jonathan Sperber remarked that 'theological seminaries [were] common birthplaces of nationalist movements'. See Jonathan Sperber, *The European Revolutions, 1848–1851* (Cambridge: Cambridge University Press, 2005), 91.

[43] 'A Softa who had just bought a revolver in a shop where I happened to be seeing a Christian who was higgling with the gunsmith about a similar weapon, addressed him, saying, What on earth do you Feringees [foreigners] buy pistols for? Mussulmans buy them because they are afraid of the Christians, but you Christians have no reason to fear us. *It is not with you but with our Government that we have to settle accounts, and if we rid ourselves of the Sultan, it will be as well for you as for us*. So boldly outspoken has everybody in Turkey become.' See Anonymous, 'The Crisis in Turkey (From Our Special Correspondent.)', *The Times*, 20 May 1876, 8, emphasis mine. Cf. Memduh, *Mir'ât-ı Şuûnât*, 66.

[44] When his close advisors warned him about the rumours circulating among the people, he supposedly replied, 'when you say people (*nâs*), if you mean our lot, they do not count (*anların hükmü yok*)'. This comment became, according to Cevdet Pasha, widely known and negatively affected the 'minds of the public/*ezhân-ı âmme*'. See, Ahmed Cevdet Paşa, *Ma'rûzât*, ed. Yusuf Halaçoğlu (İstanbul: Çağrı Yayınları, 1980), 227.

[45] Later, Abdülaziz's mother, Pertevniyal Valide Sultan, wrote a rather sorrowful, and insightful account of the event for Abdülhamid. See, BOA, Y..EE.. 18/114, 27 Rebiülevvel 1301 (26 January 1884).

Figure 6.1 A contemporary picture showing the demonstrations of madrasa students published in *Le Monde illustré*, June 3, 1876. It was reproduced later in Osman Nuri's account as *talebe-i ulumun nümayişi*.
Osman Nuri, *Abdülhamid-i Sani Devr-i Saltanatı Hayat-ı Hususiye ve Siyasiyesi*, 3 vols., vol. I (İstanbul: İbrahim Hilmi Kitabhanesi, 1327/1909–10), 208.

palace to another.[46] 'Neither the number nor the vastness of his Imperial mansions seems to have room enough for him and for the anxious cares which beset him', *the Times* reported.[47] He again asked Mahmud Nedim Pasha to be Grand Vizier. This was circumvented only by the Pasha's excessive demands.[48] According to rumours, the

[46] '*La sultane mère (validé) fait au peuple de ces cadeaux qui entretiennent, l'amitié. Par son ordre, on a distribué des bœufs dans tous les quartiers musulmans. On les a abattus, en signe de reconnaissance envers le ciel pour avoir épargné à Stamboul l'effusion du sang. La chair de ces victimes expiatoires a été distribuée aux pauvres. On prend les noms des enfants en âge d'aller à l'école. On leur donnera des vêtements et de l'argent*'. Anonymous, 'Lettres de Turquie [II]', *Le Temps*, 23 May 1876, 2.

[47] Anonymous, 'The Crisis in Turkey (From Our Special Correspondent)', *The Times*, 26 May 1876, 8.

[48] Mahmud Celâleddin Paşa, *Mir'ât-ı Hakikat I*, 96. Sultan Aziz told Rüşdi Pasha, new Grand Vizier, that he was appointed because 'people want him'. This dangerous compliment met with the evasive responses of the clever Pasha. But

Sultan considered '*une abdication volontaire*'.[49] On 25 May, Sir Henry Elliot, British ambassador in Istanbul dispatched an urgent note to the Foreign Office in which he wrote:

> The word 'Constitution' was in every mouth; that the Softas, representing the intelligent *public opinion* of the capital, knowing themselves to be supported by the nation – Christian as well as Mahometan – would not, I believed, relax their efforts till they obtained it, and that, should the Sultan refuse to grant it, an attempt to depose him appeared almost inevitable; that texts from the Koran were circulated proving to the faithful that the form of government sanctioned by it was properly democratic, and that the absolute authority now wielded by the Sultan was a usurpation of the rights of the people, and not sanctioned by the Holy Law, and both texts and precedents were appealed to, to show that obedience was not due to a Sovereign who neglected the interests of the State.[50]

Many people living in the city felt that a revolution was imminent (*İstanbul'da ihtilâl hâdis olacak imiş*).[51] On 26 May, *The Times* gave Abdülaziz at most twenty days to resign. After that, they were sure that 'Mourad Effendi [*sic* will be] is brought to Eyoub Mosque to gird on Osman's sword'.[52] 'Demanding the replacement of the dignitary was a only pretext, a preamble', *Le Temps* argued on May 29, 'what they want is the country to recover, and that they are determined to go far in their demands and their requirements. This is, in a word, a highly characterized revolutionary movement (*un mouvement révolutionnaire très caractérisé*)'.[53]

Stating the Obvious

The next day, on 30 May, Hüseyin Avni Pasha communicated to Abdülaziz that 'he was deposed by the nation'.[54] The Sultan was immediately removed from the Dolmabahçe Palace, and the heir

the Sultan would not hear it. He repeated again: 'I have nominated you because people want it'. Ibid.

49 Anonymous, 'Lettres de Turquie [III]', *Le Temps*, 27 May 1876, 2.

50 Henry G. Elliot, *Some Revolutions and Other Diplomatic Experiences* (London: John Murray, 1922), 231–232, emphasis mine.

51 Cevdet Paşa, *Tezâkir 40*, 152.

52 Anonymous, 'The Crisis in Turkey (From Our Special Correspondent)', 8.

53 Anonymous, 'Lettres de Turquie [IV]', *Le Temps*, 29 May 1876, 1.

54 Ali, *İstanbul'da Yarım Asırlık Vakayi-i Mühimme*, 51–52.

presumptive succeeded to the throne as Murad V. On 31 May, Ottoman newspapers anonymously presented this news as the victory of 'public opinion' to their readers. *Efkâr/Opinion*, for instance, declared it as 'the day of penitence for the ignoramuses of the age who have denied the spiritual influence of public opinion in the Ottoman Empire (*efkâr-ı umûmîyenin te'sirat-ı mânevisini inkâr eden cehâletperverân-ı asrın yevm-i nedâmeti*)'. 'Now', the writer continued vindictively, 'you see the wrath of public opinion (*efkâr-ı umûmîyenin şiddet-i galeyânı*), which deposed Abdülaziz Khan from his imperial throne of king of kings and installed the son of Abdülmecid, Sultan Murad to the glorious throne of Ottoman'.[55]

Vakit, went a step further than *Efkâr*, and claimed that not only did public opinion depose the Sultan Abdülaziz from his throne and save the country but in fact it was public opinion which had founded the Ottoman state in the first place:

Public opinion, that is the title of our article, is a part of the essential laws established by the sharia, pure and celestial justice. Our whole society is in fact built on this principle. It was public opinion, which founded the Ottoman State (*Devlet-i Âliye-i Osmaniye te'sîs eden efkâr-ı umûmîyedir*). It was *public opinion*, which led all the great triumphs of the Ottoman nation. The regulations, which were in force in the early days of the Sublime State, were all based on *public opinion*. It was *public opinion*, which had legitimized the laws of the Exalted Sultanate. Here the *public opinion* has struck again and eliminated the crisis disconcerting the Ottoman nation for some time. One cannot doubt that *public opinion* exists in Turkey as it exists in other refined countries if one just looks at the unmistakable fate suffered by first Mahmud Nedim Pasha and then later his guardian and protector, Sultan Abdülaziz. *Public opinion in Turkey by elevating His Highness Murad V, adorned with virtue and intelligence, to the throne*, has renewed the hope of the people and assured our future. *Public opinion* has showed that when it comes to searching and securing our legitimate rights, we are equal with Europe.[56]

This last sentence was a common theme in many contemporary accounts. Many frequently alluded to the idea of showing Europe that the Ottomans also had an influential public opinion. 'Our French and English friends', one commented, '[*sic*] shall doubtlessly applaud the

[55] Anonymous, 'Tebşir-i Mânevi', *Êfkar*, 8 Cemaziyelevvel/1 June 1293/1876, 1.
[56] Anonymous, 'Türkistan'da Êfkar-ı Umûmîye', 1.

ایكنجی سنه نومرو ٢٣٤ — (چهارشنبه) — فی ٨ جمادی الاولی ١٢٩٣ سنه

بر سیللكی ١٥٠ آلتی آیلغی ٨٠ اوچ آیلغی ٤٥
پوسته اجرتی سنه‌لكی یمش بش غروشدر
هر نسخه‌سی ٢٠ پاره‌در
فی ١٩ مایس رومی ١٢٩٢

وقت

١٢٩٢

مطبعه و محل اداره‌سی باب عالی جاده‌سنده (٥٤) نومرولی محل مخصوصده‌در
خارجدن كوندریلوبده غزته‌یه درج اولنمیان اوراق صاحبنه اعاده اولنمز
فی ٣١ مایس افرنجی ١٨٧٦

هر نوع حوادثدن بحث ایدر غزته‌در

دونكی علاوه‌مز

یوم مسعود

لطف الهی

تركستانده افكار عمومیه

Figure 6.2 The Cover of *Vakit* a day after the deposition of Sultan Abdülaziz. The article on the left here is entitled 'Public Opinion in Turkey'.
Anonymous, 'Türkistan'da Efkâr-ı Umûmîye', Vakit, May 31, 1876, 1.

level of *public opinion* in the Ottoman Empire and shall be very happy to learn that a constitutional government was established in Istanbul'. Or, as the same writer had mentioned, only a few lines earlier, and this time without irony, the 'Europeans who had denied the existence of public opinion in the Ottoman Empire will be doubtlessly stunned and astonished because of this glorying event, which will ornament the pages of history books'.[57]

The unknown writers were, as mentioned at the beginning of this chapter, wrong in believing that this event would be recorded in the books of history as a glorious victory of public opinion. Yet they rightly foresaw the astonishment, mixed with admiration, which appeared in foreign papers. *Le Temps* described the event as Turkey's *Quatre-Septembre*, the date when Napoleon III fell and the Third Republic was proclaimed in 1870.[58] *The Times* was struck by the whole affair's 'imitation of the procedure of foreign revolutions'.[59] The Empire, it thought, could be in a 'Constitutional path'. *The New York Times*, on the other hand, announced the news from its front-page with headlines pronouncing 'the Turkish Revolution'. The writer was decidedly confused:

> *A popular revolution in Turkey, where the monarchy is nominally absolute, is an anomaly. It may be truly called unique.* Nevertheless, ABDUL AZIZ has been dethroned, and the former heir-apparent, MOHAMMED MURAD reigns in his stead. *An official proclamation from the Grand Vizier announces that all this has been done 'in the presence of the unanimous will of the people', whatever that may be.* The ways of the Osmanli are not less dark than those of the Chinese Celestial.[60]

A Public Madness

Murad V immediately became the object of public affection. His inaugural *Hatt-ı Hümâyun* cited 'the feeling of insecurity apprehending

[57] Anonymous, 'Yaşasun Sultan Murad-ı Hâmis', *Êfkar*, 8 Cemaziyelevvel/1 June 1293/1876, 2.
[58] Anonymous, 'Bulletin du Jour', *Le Temps*, 31 May 1876, 1.
[59] Anonymous, '[Astounding news come to us from Constantinople]', *The Times*, 31 May 1876, 11.
[60] Anonymous, 'The Turkish Revolution', *The New York Times*, 31 May 1876, 1, emphasis mine.

THE ILLUSTRATED LONDON NEWS, JUNE 10, 1876.—560

THE REVOLUTION IN TURKEY.

We had last week to announce the startling news from Constantinople that Abdul Aziz, the Sultan, had been deposed, and that Mourad Effendi, his nephew, the heir-presumptive, had been placed upon the throne. It was suggested, not lightly, but in sad earnest, by our well-known contributor "G. A. S.," commenting in his "Echoes of the Week" upon this revolution in Turkey, that there would be only too much likelihood in the next report informing us of the death of the dethroned Sultan, by some means or other. This conjecture, founded upon an acquaintance with the history of the Turkish monarchy, has already been verified, though not, it is said, in the manner in which such things have been done on former occasions. Abdul Aziz, who had retired under compulsion to the Tcheragan Palace, bled to death there on Sunday morning from wounds in both arms, cutting the arteries inside the elbow and shoulder. It is declared that he inflicted these wounds upon himself with a pair of scissors. He was buried in the Palace on Sunday evening. He was forty-six years of age, and had reigned not quite seventeen years.

The Turkish popular movement which has caused this revolution seems to have originated in the excitement which followed upon the Salonica massacre. For a long time the Softas, or Mussulman students of theology and law, who constitute the "Young Turkey" party, had been agitating for internal reforms and more energetic action concerning the insurrection in the Herzegovina. They objected to the acceptance of the Andrassy Note, as they regarded Montenegro as the cause of much of Turkey's trouble, and they advocated a decisive course of action against that Principality. The consternation into which all classes in Constantinople were thrown by the news of the Salonica outrage gave them at length the opportunity for which they had been waiting. On May 7 a crowd of them, headed by their professors and clergy, gathered in the streets. So menacing was their behaviour that Dervish Pasha ordered the Sultan's guards and the troops in the city to be kept in their respective barracks ready for any emergency. The ironclads which were at that time in the Bosphorus were ordered to draw up in front of the palace and to point their loaded cannon against Beschichtach, Orta Keni, and Arnaout Keni, which were the suburbs from which any attack of the Softas might be expected. Next day, however, Dervish Pasha was turned out of his office as Minister of War—some say in consequence of the Russian Ambassador's intrigues—and was sent away to the Governorship of Diarbekir. The Softas, whose organisation included 20,000 active men in the Turkish capital, were left to agitate against Mahmoud

MOURAD V., THE NEW SULTAN OF TURKEY.

Pasha, then Grand Vizier. Day by day their demands grew louder and more persistent. They asked that Hussein Avni should be recalled from Broussa, in order that he might prosecute an energetic campaign against the Bulgarian and Herzegovinian insurgents. A ship was sent to fetch that able General from his place of retirement. Then they declared that Midhat Pasha should be Grand Vizier, and that politician was actually summoned to the palace. But his demands or conditions were, it appears, so extensive that eventually he was dismissed, and a kind of compromise was offered by the ejection of Mahmoud Pasha, and the appointment of Mahmoud Ruchdi in his place. It is now said that Midhat's chief demands were—firstly, that the Sultan should hand over for the purposes of the State the large sum of money, variously estimated at from three to five millions sterling, which he had hoarded in his palace; and, secondly, that he should give up all idea of diverting the succession to the throne from his nephew (the rightful heir) to his son. To neither of these requests would Abdul Aziz listen—with the results now known. Meanwhile Hussein Avni was appointed Minister of War. Hassan Tehmi Effendi, the Sheik ul Islam, or head of the Moslem lawyers and judges, who had rendered himself obnoxious to the "Young Turkey" party by his intrigues in favour of the Sultan's son, was sent about his business, and Hairoullah Effendi took his portfolio. Abdul Kerim Nadar Pasha was appointed generalissimo of the army, and the Sultan gave out of his own private treasury a sum sufficient to furnish a month's pay to the troops, to whom eight months' stipend was owing. The Sultana Validé or Dowager made large donations of meat and bread to the poor, in the hope of thereby conciliating the mob of discontented people who thronged the streets. But the misguided Monarch at the same moment made a demand upon his Government for £6000, in consideration of his having lent the country two of his private yachts as transports. The personal demeanour of Abdul Aziz showed that he was very uneasy. He changed his residence from palace to palace in a singularly unnecessary manner, testifying to the restlessness of his mind. If reports be credited, he actually dashed his hand through the window of his palace which faced the Bosphorus on noticing the entry of the Russian gun-boat Sokol. The incessant deliberations and demonstrations of the Softas were not calculated to dispel his anxiety. The plot was then under consideration which soon afterwards ripened into his deposition. Midhat Pasha, emboldened by their action, refused to be sent away as Governor of Broussa, and was eventually offered a seat in the new Cabinet without a portfolio, an appointment which he accepted. The outcry for a surrender of some of the money hoarded in the palace increased in strength. To all but the Sultan it was evident that the Softas were gaining daily in strength; that, so far from being a party of disorder, they were emphatically the champions of a more constitutional Government.

On Monday week, affairs being in such a critical state,

Figure 6.3 A contemporary image of Murad V, published in *the Illustrated London News*, on June 10, 1876 in an article entitled 'the Revolution in Turkey'.

public opinion' as the main reason for his enthronement.[61] Thousands of people gathered to watch his first procession through the old city. Antonio Gallenga (d. 1895), an Italian author, described the scene with great animation. The crowd, he wrote, 'saw nothing but perfection in its idol of the moment ... the squalid rabble from Greek, Jew, and Moslem quarters ... the colours of gaudily dressed veiled women clustering like bees at every window'.[62] Levant Herald remarked, 'the cheers of Western Europeans [which] mingled with the *zitos* of the Greeks and the native acclamations of the Mussulmans'.[63] Some commented that Mehmed II, the conqueror of Constantinople, also entered the city on a Tuesday in 1453. This, they thought, was a good augur.[64]

But the following events soon proved them wrong. The incidents surrounding the overthrow of his uncle seemed to sap Murad's mental strength right away, which apparently was lacking because of his heavy alcohol consumption.[65] The *ricâl* (ministers and top officials) immediately noticed that there was something not quite right with him: their suspicions were first aroused when he began to embrace and kiss dignitaries coming to take oaths of allegiance.[66] Regal aloofness was something central in the Ottoman state tradition. The Sultan needed to be awe-inspiring.[67] Murad was not. He was a good crown prince but

61 Anonymous, 'Sûret-i Hatt-ı Hümâyun', *Takvîm-i Vekâyi*, 11 Cemaziyelevvel/4 Haziran 1293/1876, 1. About the writing of this *Hatt*, see Süleyman Paşa, *Hiss-i İnkilab*, 60–61.

62 A. Gallenga, *Two Years of the Eastern Question*, 2 vols., vol. II (London: Samuel Tinsley, 1877), 92.

63 Anonymous, 'Sultan Murad's First Public Visit to Mosque', *Levant Herald*, 5 July 1876, 161.

64 Anonymous, 'Le Sultan Mourad V', *La Turquie*, 31 May 1876, 1.

65 On Murad's alcohol consumption, see Mahmud Celâleddin Paşa, *Mir'ât-ı Hakikat I*, 127. On 4 June, Abdülaziz was found with his wrists slashed – seemingly a suicide but there were unexplained circumstances surrounding it. See Midhat Paşa, *Tabsıra-i İbret*, 170–172; Mahmud Celâleddin Paşa, *Mir'ât-ı Hakikat I*, 116–121. Later on, Abdülhamid II claimed that it was a wilful murder and used it as an excuse to purge the liberals of Ottoman politics such as Midhat Pasha. See for the account in great detail, Uzunçarşılı, *Midhat Paşa ve Tâif Mahkûmları*, passim.

66 Mahmud Celâleddin Paşa, *Mir'ât-ı Hakikat I*, 127.

67 A seventeenth-century writer warned Sultan İbrahim (r. 1640 – 1648) fervently against the dignitaries arriving to kiss his hand: 'Too much esteem is not needed' he wrote to him, and added 'you should sit manfully so that everybody should be frightened'. Koçi Bey, *Koçi Bey Risâlesi*, ed. Ali Kemali Aksüt (İstanbul: Vakit Matbaası, 1939), 111.

Figure 6.4 A rather disturbing image of ex-Sultan Abdülaziz just before he committed 'suicide' on 4 June 1876.
Bahattin Öztuncay, *Hâtıra-i Uhuvvet*, 124.

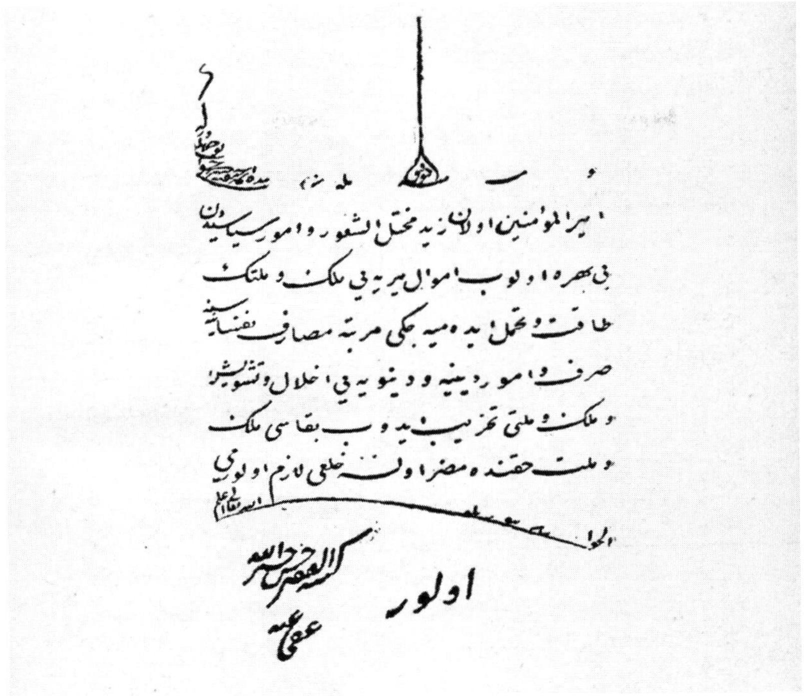

Figure 6.5 The Deposition Fetva of Sultan Abdülaziz.
Reproduced in Mahmud Kemal [İnal], 'Sultan Abdülaziz'e Dair', *Türk Tarihi Encümeni Mecmuası* 15, no. 9 (1925), 188.

not a good sultan. His panic-stricken state became increasingly difficult to conceal. He first threw himself into a garden pool during an evening promenade at the Yıldız Palace.[68] While ministers hoped that this was just due to overexcitement and an isolated incident, he then broke through several windows of the Çırağan Palace to run away after a Friday ceremony (*Cuma selâmlığı*). Servants subdued him with great difficulty, as he climbed over the balustrade of the palace.[69] In short, his nervous breakdowns made obvious that he could not be controlled and was not suitable to command.

[68] Mahmud Celâleddin Paşa, *Mir'ât-ı Hakikat I*, 127; Mithat Paşa, *Tabsıra-i İbret*, 173.
[69] Mahmud Celâleddin Paşa, *Mir'ât-ı Hakikat I*, 167–168.

This was almost tragic-comical because the *fetva*, which led to the deposition of Abdülaziz, was actually given on the mental grounds (*muhtell-üş-şuûr ve umûr-i siyâsiyyeden bi-behre*).[70] Abdülaziz was certainly not the brightest sultan that the Empire had ever seen, far from it. But in spite of all the circulating rumours, he was not hysterical.[71] Naturally all eyes turned to the next heir, Abdülhamid. Yet for the pashas who were in charge, he was someone not *Murad* (literally the desired one), in other words not the liberal charmer, and freemason one should remind,[72] who supposedly fascinated the royal families of Europe as a young prince during the European tour of Abdülaziz in 1867.[73] In the meantime, Osman Nuri reported the uneasiness of 'public opinion' owing to Murad's perceivable absence from state affairs. Threatening placards against the ministers began to appear in the city again.[74] The effect of this rumour-mongering alone shows the importance of public approval in Ottoman politics. If it were a simple question of bureaucratic ambition, the situation would have been ideal for civil servants. A sultan incapable of mingling in state affairs should

[70] For the full text, see Midhat, *Üss-i İnkilab*, 396–397. A contemporary translation runs as follows: 'Question: – If the head of the faithful gives proofs of derangement of mind and ignorance of political affairs – if he employs the public revenues personal expenditure beyond what the State and the nation can support – if he puts confusion into spiritual and temporal affairs – and if his maintenance in power has become injurious to the State and nation – can he be deposed? Answer. – The "Cheriat" [public Mussulman law, according to Koran] says, Yes!' See Anonymous, 'The 'Fetva of Deposition of Sultan Abdul-Aziz', *Levant Herald*, 5 June 1876, 161, brackets in original.

[71] There is an Ottoman translation of Arabic philosophical extracts in manuscript form, which is attributed to Abdülaziz (*Sultan Abdülaziz Han Efendimizin kalem-i hikmet-i şâhâneleriyle*). Even though this is clearly not a proof of his sanity, it is perhaps suggestive. See Abdülaziz, *Ba'z-i Mebâhis-i Hikemiyye ve Mantıkiyye Tercemesi* (Ali Emiri Şeriyye Koleksiyonu, No: 1288), 35.

[72] According to Kératry, Hüseyin Avni Pasha was somewhat annoyed with Murad's egalitarian claims and said to him that these were '*des idées maçoniques*' and needed to be concealed. See E. de Kératry, *Mourad V, Prince Sultan, Prisonnier D'Etat: 1840–1878 (1878) d'apres des témoins de sa vie* (Paris: E. Dentu, 1878), 140. All the high-ranking members of the Young Ottoman movement, including Midhat Pasha were freemasons.

[73] Ahmed Saib, *Târîh-i Sultan Murad-ı Hâmis* (Kahire: Hindiye Matbaası, 1326/ 1908–09), 9. Also see Necib Asım, 'Cennet-Mekan Firdevs-Aşiyan: Sultan Abdülaziz Han Hazretleri'nin Avrupa Seyâhatnâmesidir', *Türk Târîh Encümeni Mecmûası* VIII-XI, no. 9–62 (1335–1337/1919–1921): 90–102.

[74] Osman Nuri, *Abdülhamid-i Sâni Devr-i Saltanatı Hayât-ı Husûsîye ve Siyâsiyesi*, 3 vols., vol. I (İstanbul: İbrahim Hilmi Kitâbhânesi, 1327/ 1909–10), 93.

have been considered providential. But the reality was quite different. The wheels that had deposed Mahmud Nedim and Abdülaziz earlier were in motion again.[75] In panic, Midhat Pasha asked Abdülhamid if he would be willing to act as a regent (*niyâbet-i hükümet*) and received the answer he dreaded. Abdülhamid rejected the proposition flatly. 'It is certain that', he said, 'my brother will not gain his health again'.[76]

The pashas were in a difficult position. There were pressing matters requiring immediate attention, and a healthy sultan was needed if only as a figurehead. They knew that trusting Abdülhamid, with his florid promises of reform and constitution, was difficult.[77] But to distrust him was even more so.[78] Eventually the young prince convinced them of his liberal commitments, and Murad V was deposed at the end of August 1876 as the shortest ruling sultan in Ottoman history.[79] On the spur of the moment, Abdülhamid, the third in line of succession only three months previously and waiting behind a reigning middle-aged uncle and an older brother, who was by far the most popular imperial prince since Selim III (d. 1808), found himself on the throne. But there was one crucial difference. The official declaration, which had referred to the public alliance/*ittifâk-i umûmîye* in Murad's enthronement, this time omitted the critical phrase and confined itself to a dry formula.[80]

Public Judgement?

The following events showed that some revolutionary spirit still existed in the country. A citizen militia, named *Asâkir-i Milliye* (National Soldiers) and modelled after the French *Garde national*, was formed

[75] See Mahmud Celâleddin Paşa, *Mir'ât-ı Hakikat I*, 166.

[76] Nuri, *Abdülhamid-i Sâni*, 94.

[77] See, for instance, Ali Haydar Midhat, *The Life of Midhat Pasha: A Record of His Services, Political Reforms, Banishment, and Judicial Murder* (London: J. Murray, 1903), 97; Mahmud Celâleddin Paşa, *Mir'ât-ı Hakikat I*, 168.

[78] Nâmık Kemal's son, Ali Ekrem Bolayır argued that the Young Ottomans were not, to say the least, fascinated by Abdülhamid's character even when he was a royal prince during the reign of Sultan Abdülaziz. Bolayır, *Ali Ekrem Bolayır'ın Hâtıraları*, 386–389.

[79] Abdülhamid supposedly said to Midhat Pasha: 'I shall not accept a government which is not based on constitution and consultancy/*usûl-i meşrûtiyet ve meşverete mübteni olmayacak bir hükümeti kabul etmem*.' Mahmud Celâleddin Paşa, *Mir'ât-ı Hakikat I*, 168.

[80] See İstanbul Müftülüğü Şeriye Sicilileri Arşivi, İstanbul Mahkemesi, 334, 42ab.

from volunteers coming from 'every class and religion' to defend the forthcoming constitution.[81] Cohorts under the leadership of poet and statesman Ziyâ Pasha marched through the streets of the capital in military formation, singing Nâmık Kemal's adaptation of *La Marseillaise*.[82] The foundation of *Asâkir* was considered a 'moral force, which would attract and appeal to public opinion'.[83] In this politicised atmosphere, intellectuals tried to explain the position of the Sultan in a constitutional monarchy in imaginary dialogues with pamphlets such as *Hükümet-i Meşrûta* (*Constitutional Government*), and various newspaper articles.[84] A national assembly was shown to be inherent to the Islamic and Ottoman state traditions. The constitution was not a novelty; it was suggested through these publications, but rather going back to the proper ways of the past (*usûl-i kadimimiz icâbınca*).[85]

Naturally some of this propaganda was undertaken to intimidate Abdülhamid, who despite all of his promises, did not seem very keen on an Ottoman parliament. At every *meclis* Nâmık Kemal recited, as an allusion to earlier depositions, an old Arabic couplet, meaning 'never two without three!'[86] Yet there seemed to be endless schisms among different fractions, cleverly provoked by the Sultan. Many committees and subcommittees were formed in the following weeks.[87] The trouble was simple: the public was united on Abdülaziz's deposition. But a national assembly, including non-Muslims, was more complicated. Even though some conservative statesmen like Mahmud Celâleddin Pasha considered the constitution a useful 'vehicle to win over and influence public opinion (*efkâr-ı umûmîyenin celb ve*

[81] Süleyman Paşazâde Sâmî, *Süleyman Paşa Muhâkemesi: 1293 Osmanlı - Rus Muharebesi [Rumeli Harb Orduları Umûm Kumandanı Merhum Süleyman Paşa'nın Muhâkemesidir]* (İstanbul: Matbaa-i Ebuzziyâ, 1328/1912), 70–74.

[82] Ibid., 77–78. [83] Mahmud Celâleddin Paşa, *Mir'ât-ı Hakikat I*, 266.

[84] Esad Efendi, *Hükümet-i Meşrûta* (İstanbul: Mihran Matbaası, 1293/1876). The full text is also given in Sâmî, *Süleyman Paşa Muhâkemesi*, 79–89. According to the text, the Sultan's behaviours were, in every respect, limited by the 'public benefit/*menfaat-i âmme*'. If the Sultan did not accept this condition, 'he would be chastened by the barrier of Muslims (*menea-i müslimin onu ıslâh eder*)'. Ibid., 80–81.

[85] ج, 'Meşrûtiyet-i İdâre – Beyân-ı Hakkiyet', *Vakit*, 9 Şevval/28 October 1293/1876, 2.

[86] Mahmud Celâleddin Paşa, *Mir'ât-ı Hakikat I*, 267.

[87] Şeref, *Târîh Musâhabeleri*, 200.

te'mînine bir vâsıta)',[88] the Muslim population at large seemed to hesitate over the issue. As early as 11 June, *Efkâr* reported how '*public opinion* was divided into two on the subject. One is thinking about the public benefit, which will be materialized in case of its construction [parliament]. The other is more concerned with possible harms'.[89] In the meantime, newspapers supporting the constitutionalist cause tried to explain desperately that there was no ground for objection to non-Muslims' inclusion in a national assembly from a religious or legal point of view.[90]

But some members of the *ulemâ* 'by distributing handbills on the street and placarding the walls at night, began to stir up the opinions of common people with fabrications and calumnies (*erâcîf ve türrehât ile avâm-ı nâsın fikirlerini fesada başladıklarından*)'.[91] This emphasis on placarding is interesting and probably shows the prevalence of literacy among the Istanbul population. C. A. Bayly also mentions it as an important, and frequent, means of political debate and social critique in the Indian context.[92] It helped, as he has emphasised, 'to constitute a realm of public knowledge in which political ideas were strenuously debated'.[93] The issues became visible to a wide public. This was a war of 'public opinions' at a clandestine level, and both sides presented their case in their own medium. An anonymous letter supporting the

88 Mahmud Celâleddin Paşa, *Mir'ât-ı Hakikat I*, 220. Similarly, Matthew Giancarlo depicts the parliament as a premier forum 'to manipulate public opinion'. Matthew Giancarlo, *Parliament and Literature in Late Medieval England* (Cambridge: Cambridge University Press, 2007), 66. The same idea was also highlighted in Karin Bowie, *Scottish Public Opinion and the Anglo-Scottish Union, 1699–1707* (Woodbridge, UK: Royal Historical Society, 2007), 32.

89 Anonymous, 'Millet Meclisi Hakkında Bir Mütâlaa', *Êfkar*, 18 Cemaziyelevvel/11 June 1293/1876, 2.

90 ج, 'Meşrûtiyet-i İdâre – Beyân-ı Hakkiyet', 2.

91 Mahmud Celâleddin Paşa, *Mir'ât-ı Hakikat I*, 191. Also see, BOA, İ..DH.. 741/60622, 28 Safer 1294 (14 March 1877). Some members of the *ulemâ* defended that the 'them/هم' in the holy command of '*take counsel with them in all matters of public concern*' did not comprise non-Muslims.

92 C. A. Bayly, *Origins of Nationality in South Asia: Patriotism and Ethical Government in the Making of Modern India* (Oxford: Oxford University Press, 1998), 283; C. A. Bayly, *Empire and Information*, 243, 368. It should be noted that it was also a common practice in the Ottoman Empire. See, for instance, a campaign of placarding by the janissaries against Mahmud II, Câbî Efendi, *Câbî Târîhi I*, 701.

93 Bayly, *Empire and Information*, 368.

constitution appeared in *İttihâd* and strove to assure the masses: 'we are sure that', it went, '*public opinion*, which filled the universe with great admiration as a result of the last revolution will perceive rapidly that the present committee, who became the recipient of nation's every kind of confidence, is of good faith'.[94]

At the end of December 1876, despite Abdülhamid's best attempts, a constitution, heralding a national assembly, was proclaimed. It was accompanied by great pomp, which, Paul Fesch thought, was comparable to that of France on 4 August 1789.[95] In spite of heavy rainfall, thousands of people gathered to listen to the imperial rescript announcing a new era.[96] That night all houses and shops were ornamented and lit up with lamps to celebrate the occasion. Young supporters of liberty (*hürriyet-i efkâr taraftarları gençler*) came together in thousands and brought people before the palace to celebrate the constitution.[97] If one can believe Ali Haydar Bey, son of Midhat Pasha, 'followed by the Softas and students, the representatives of all the corporations, and the populace of the capital, with flags bearing the inscription "Liberty", came to congratulate Midhat, at his own residence, on the new era of liberty'.[98] 'We cannot pride ourselves enough', *Vakit* announced from its front page the next day, 'to live in such an opportune time'.[99]

Compared to his ancestors, however, the Sultan must have felt rather differently about the time in which he lived. The constitution, though not perfect from a legal standpoint,[100] put the life and estate of the Ottoman dynasty under 'public guarantee/*tekâfül-i umûmî*'.[101]

94 Anonymous, 'Varaka', *İttihâd*, 29 Ramazan/18 October 1293/1876, 2.
95 Paul Fesch, *Constantinople aux derniers jours d'Abdul-Hamid* (Paris: Librairie des Sciences Politiques et Sociales, 1907), 234.
96 Şeref, *Târîh Musâhabeleri*, 200.
97 Mahmud Celâleddin Paşa, *Mir'ât-ı Hakikat I*, 224.
98 Midhat, *The Life of Midhat Pasha*, 131.
99 Anonymous, '[Dünkü Gün Umûm Osmanlılar İçin Bir Mebdâ-i Saâdet İdi]', *Vakit*, 8 Zilhicce/25 December 1293/1876, 1.
100 See, for instance, the discussion, revolving around Article 113, which dealt with a state of siege. Davison, *Reform in the Ottoman Empire*, 379.
101 See Article 6 in Anonymous, 'Kanûn-i Esâsi-i Memâlik-i Devlet-i Osmaniye', *Vakit*, 8 Zilhicce/25 December 1293/1876, 2. Roderick Davison argues that there were 'many parallels to be found between the 1876 constitution and the Belgian constitution of 1831'. Davison, *Reform in the Ottoman Empire*, 388. If so, the article in question was not taken from the Belgium example, as there is no similar phrase in the Belgium constitution of 1831. See John Martin Vincent and Ada S. Vincent, 'Constitution of the Kingdom of Belgium', *Annals of the American Academy of Political and Social Science* 7 (1896): 15–40.

This article was probably squeezed in to protect Murad's life against potential palace intrigues. But it also clearly showed how the dynasty had lost its central position as the ultimate guarantor of rights in the public sphere and turned into a state apparatus, whose life and property, in return, needed to be protected by the public authority itself.

The first Ottoman Parliament, assembled for the first time in March 1877, was a true Tower of Babel. It was formed with delegates coming from different parts of the Empire from Bosnia to Hejaz. Among its 115 members, 69 representatives were Muslims and the remaining 46 were non-Muslims.[102] The Sultan expressed, in his inauguration speech, his hope for the country's swift recovery under 'public judgment/*ârâ-i umûmîyye*'.[103] This is an interesting wording on Abdülhamid's part and perhaps needs to be explained: *ârâ-i umûmîyye* is often translated into modern Turkish as 'public opinion/*kamuoyu*'.[104] Yet it is not exactly the same thing. It is a slightly older expression. It almost appears that through his aversion, Abdülhamid avoided using the usual term. For him, it had only negative connotations. Unlike Murad's *hatt*, there was no mention of it in his first *hatt-hümâyun*, for instance.[105] But even this allusion to the power of public was too much of a political concession for the young monarch. When he felt politically stronger, he had this reference to the 'public' removed from reprints of his royal speech.[106] But for the time being, he had to accede. In the words of Ali Haydar Bey, 'he played a deep game'.[107] This aversion of his, however, was lost on the new Prime Minister and deputies. In their vote of thanks, they accentuated 'the feeling of union and confidence rising in *public opinion*, which, [they thought] shall turn the country into a fortified castle (*efkâr-ı umûmîyece husûl bulacak ittihâd ve itimâd ile bir hısn-ı hâsîn olur*). No attempt', they

[102] Ahmet T. Kuru, *Secularism and State Policies Toward Religion: The United States, France, and Turkey* (Cambridge: Cambridge University Press, 2009), 210.

[103] *Meclis-i Meb'ûsan 1293–1877 Zabıt Cerîdesi*, ed. Hakkı Tarık Us, 2 vols., vol. I (İstanbul: Vakit Gazetesi Matbaası, 1939), 11 fn. 11.

[104] See, for instance, Muzaffer Gökman, *Ahmet Rasim: İstanbul'u Yaşayan ve Yaşatan Adam: Hayâtı ve Eserleri*, 2 vols., vol. II (İstanbul: Çelik Gülersoy Vakfı, 1989), 554.

[105] See Anonymous, 'Kısm-ı Resmi', *Takvîm-i Vekâyi*, 23 Şaban/13 September 1293/1876, 1–2.

[106] *Meclis-i Meb'ûsan 1293–1877 Zabıt Cerîdesi*, 11 fn. 11.

[107] Midhat, *The Life of Midhat Pasha*, 98.

emphasised, 'is going to afflict or trouble the piece and unification of our country'.[108]

What happened after is another, and relatively well-documented story: how the 'cunning' Sultan succeeded in playing liberals off against each other and 'prorogued' the parliament for more than thirty years has been the subject of many books and articles.[109] But this begs a final question: how was Abdülhamid able to do this if there was indeed such a politically engaged public in the Ottoman Empire? Does this mean that public opinion suddenly lost its influence and became unable to carry out its leading role in the Ottoman politics? Did people simply stop talking about politics on steamboats?

As previously mentioned, people were extremely divided on the subject of a parliament.[110] Even the most sophisticated statesman of the time, Cevdet Pasha, questioned the necessity of a national assembly since 'a wise sultan/*padişâh-ı âkil*' was in charge.[111] Such a statement is quite interesting, especially as it was made at the beginning of Abdülhamid's reign, before he established his political panopticon. It should also be remembered that Abdülhamid came to the throne after a chain of serious economic and political disasters. Two sultans were deposed in three months, and the economy was in ruins. As early as the 1940s, Ahmed Hamdi Tanpınar noted 'the impossibility of Abdülhamid's absolutism without the preceding economic catastrophe'.[112]

The crisis was partly a result of the long depression, which arose from the panic of 1873 in Europe and North America.[113] But it was also a consequence of the outstanding debt obligations that the Ottoman government contracted during the Tanzimat era.[114] Nature did

108 *Meclis-i Meb'ûsan 1293–1877 Zabıt Cerîdesi*, 14, emphasis mine.

109 There have been a plethora of books and articles written on Abdülhamid since the beginning of his reign. Two books are particularly useful for an introduction. The first one is François Georgeon's biography, giving a detailed account of his life. The other is Selim Deringil's deep analysis of his modernisation policies. See François Georgeon, *Abdülhamid II: Le sultan calife, 1876 – 1909* (Paris: Fayard, 2003); Deringil, *The Well-Protected Domains*.

110 See, for instance, some discussions in Ahmed Saib, *Abdülhamid'in Evâil-i Saltanatı* (Kahire: s.n., 1326/1908–09), 33.

111 Midhat Paşa, *Tabsıra-i İbret*, 188, fn. 1.

112 Tanpınar, *XIX. Asır Türk Edebiyâtı Târîhi*, 152.

113 See Şevket Pamuk, *The Ottoman Empire and European Capitalism*, 12–15.

114 Zafer Toprak, 'The Financial Structure of the Stock Exchange in the Late Ottoman Empire', in *East Meets West – Banking, Commerce and Investment*

not favour the Empire during these troubles either: the crops were failing everywhere, floods ravaged the land, and epidemics broke out in various parts of the Empire.[115] To make matters worse, it was widely known that Russian diplomatic machine was already in motion to provoke an open conflict in the Balkans (hence the Russo-Turkish War of 1877–1878).

Amidst all these problems, Abdülhamid appeared as the sober Caliph who was trying religiously to save his country. This was a political image, one imposed upon him by the Ottoman public as much as by historical reality. The Ottoman sultans had been using the title 'caliph' since the fifteenth century. Yet it was after Selim I's conquest of Egypt in 1517 that they began to be recognised as such by the wider Muslim world.[116] Abdülhamid put new emphasis on the traditional title, which was also supported by the changing demographic profile of the Empire and continued a trend that had already begun during the final years of Abdülaziz.[117] In light of the preceding events, however, Abdülhamid's new insistence was likely intended to influence domestic politics first, and his pan-Islamism was probably an afterthought. Before Abdülaziz was deposed, madrasa students asked him to 'renounce his title of *Khalife*', which rendered him, they believed, 'inviolable'.[118] Abdülhamid must have realised the significance of this political gesture. As a result, he carefully constructed his public image. That he was a sober man was a fact; but his sobriety was heavily accentuated through his

in the Ottoman Empire, ed. Philip L. Cottrell (Farnham, UK: Ashgate, 2008), 152.

115 See Z. Y. Hershlag, *Introduction to the Modern Economic History of the Middle East* (Leiden: Brill, 1964), 63.

116 For the details, see Gilles Veinstein, 'La question du califat ottoman', in *Le choc colonial et l'islam*, ed. Pierre-Jean Luziard (Paris: La Découverte, 2008), 451–468. It should be also noted that the Treaty of Küçük Kaynarca (1774), which concluded the war with the loss of Ottoman suzerainty in Crimea, is considered the beginning of the Ottoman claims to a Universal Caliphate. See Azmi Özcan, *Pan-Islamism*, 30. Also see Colin Imber, *The Ottoman Empire, 1300–1650: The Structure of Power* (New York: Palgrave Macmillan, 2002), 126–127.

117 See Kemal H. Karpat, *The Politicization of Islam: Reconstructing Identity, State, Faith, and Community in the Late Ottoman State* (Oxford: Oxford University Press, 2001), 56–63.

118 Anonymous, 'Deposition of the Sultan (By Telegraph.) (From Our Special Correspondent)', *The Times*, 31 May 1876, 7.

political calculations. For instance, he was not a heavy drinker like his father or brother. Nevertheless, he occasionally enjoyed preprandial cognac or champagne (even punch before his meetings with embassies). Yet he had sense to do this secretly and with various excuses.[119] He immensely appreciated Western drama and opera, enough to build a small theatre at the Yıldız Palace for his amusement. But again, all these were done unobtrusively in the confinements of his private sphere.[120] In public, Abdülhamid was a religious and hardworking sultan who did not have any personal extravagance.

But despite his endearing qualities for the conservative Ottoman public, it proved extremely difficult for Abdülhamid to rule the country without anxiety. This is all the more interesting when one thinks of, for instance, the relative ease with which Napoléon III reigned over France, birthplace of political *salons* and public opinion, for twenty years until his captivity by the Prussian army in 1870.[121] Near the beginning of Abdülhamid's reign, a secret society under the leadership of Ali Suâvi, an estranged dissident and minor *âlim* (sing. of *ulemâ*), organised an unsuccessful raid involving hundreds of people, if not thousand as sometimes reported, to reinstall Murad V on the throne.[122] A day before the event, Ali Suâvi went so far as to hint his plan to the readers of *Basîret* newspaper with specific references to public (*emniyet-i âmme*).[123] But the attempt failed miserably and many died during the attack.[124] Yet it was

[119] Süleyman Kâni İrtem, *Bilinmeyen Abdülhamid*, ed. Osman Kocahanoğlu (İstanbul: Temel Yayınları, 2003), 78.

[120] See ibid., 78–83; Tahsîn Paşa, *Abdülhamit Yıldız Hâtıraları*, 16–17.

[121] Robert Gildea, *Children of the Revolution: The French, 1799–1914* (Cambridge, MA: Harvard University Press, 2008), 231.

[122] See Ali, *İstanbul'da Yarım Asırlık Vakayi-i Mühimme*, 58–60. For Ali Suâvi's life, see Hüseyin Çelik, *Ali Suavî ve Dönemi* (İstanbul: İletişim Yayınları, 1994); Mithat Cemal Kuntay, *Sarıklı İhtilâlci Ali Suâvi* (İstanbul: Ahmet Halit Kitâbevi, 1946).

[123] Mahmud Celâleddin Paşa, *Mir'ât-ı Hakikat*, 3 vols., vol. III (İstanbul: Matbaa-i Osmaniye, 1326/1908), 139.

[124] For the details, see Nuri, *Abdülhamid-i Sâni*, 135–36; Mehmed Gâlib Bey, *Sâdullah Paşa*, 102–103; Mehmed Memduh Paşa, *Esvât-i Sudûr* (İzmir: Vilâyet Matbaası, 1328/1912), 34; Mehmed Memduh Paşa, *Hal'ler, İclaslar* (İstanbul: Matbaa-i Hayriye ve Şürekâsı, 1329/1913), 133.

Figure 6.6 A scene from the unsuccessful raid organised by a secret society under the leadership of Ali Suavi, an estranged dissident and minor *alim*, to reinstall Murad V on the throne. *Le Monde illustré* announced this news as '*une revolution à Constantinople*'.
Le Monde illustré, une revolution à Constantinople, 8 Juin 1878, 372.

enough to set Abdülhamid thinking.[125] He must have guessed that this was just the beginning of many other conspiracies and secret societies that would trouble his reign until he was finally deposed in 1909 after another popular revolution and because of unfavourable 'public opinion'.[126]

125 During the time he was in charge, the Sultan often asked his close advisors for their opinions about the incidents leading up to the deposition of his uncle, as he tried to understand what went wrong and how he could prevent similar problems. A report that Cevdet Pasha presented to him in 1892 went as follows: 'It is evident in history that rulers can assert themselves at will against any individual; only public opinion can restrain them (*onlara karşı yalnız efkâr-ı umûmîye vardır*). In some countries, public opinion is always open and declared, but in others it is latent, and emerges only when provoked to the extreme. In every state, consequently, rules are acutely apprehensive of it.' Cevdet Paşa, *Ma'rûzât*, 227; Ebü'l-Ula Mardin, *Medeni Hukuk Cephesinden Ahmed Cevdet Paşa* (İstanbul: İstanbul Üniversitesi Hukuk Fakültesi, 1946), 10.

126 Anonymous, 'Abdülhamid-i Sâniye Tebliğ-i Karar', 2.

Conclusion

Discussing the invention of certain English words in *the Age of Revolution*, Eric Hobsbawm once argued that 'words are witnesses which often speak louder than documents'.[1] This judgment, given in the European context, is equally valid for the Ottoman Empire, whose intellectuals had to create many new words and expressions in accordance with the times. In fact, a good portion of nineteenth century Ottoman history may be reconstructed from following the trail of new words such as *Dârülfünun* (University), *Hürriyet* (Liberty), or *Meşrûtiyet* (Constitution). These inventions, or sometimes adaptations, gave the Ottoman public a chance to reconstruct the social and political realities around them, and provided new ways of interpreting their Empire and the outside world.

In some cases, we have a complete picture of how a certain word or expression came into being. Cevdet Pasha, for example, described one night, while going through the budget deficits of the year 1267 (1850–1851), how the ministers realized that the economy was in crisis (*crise*), and had to find a new word (ultimately *buhrân*), since there was not an appropriate term in the Ottoman language.[2] In other cases, however, it proves more difficult to reconstruct the circumstances of exact etymological and sociological developments. We know more or less when a certain expression began to be used, but we do not have any means to ascertain where and why. This book has aimed to follow the development of 'public opinion' as a critical expression, belonging to the second category.

[1] Eric Hobsbawm, *The Age of Revolution 1789–1848* (New York: Vintage Books, 2010), 1.

[2] Cevdet Paşa, *Tezâkir 1–12*, 21. The Ottomans, who had lived centuries without *buhran*, literally, found themselves surrounded with the word after that point. The Grand Vizier Said Halim Pasha even wrote a book, which was entitled *Buhranlarımız* or *Our Crises*. Said Halim Paşa, *Buhranlarımız* (İstanbul: Şems Matbaası, 1329/1911). Cf. Bayly, *The Birth of the Modern World*, 88.

The abstract nature of public opinion has made this task difficult. As mentioned at the very beginning, there had always existed similar phrases and expressions used by Ottoman writers, especially when they presaged something ominous and foreboding. But for the first time during the nineteenth century, it was widely accepted that the opinion of the masses could be more valuable than the authority of a few select individuals or even than that of the *ulemâ*, which represented religious knowledge. With its sweeping ramifications, such as the creation of a parliament, the evolution of *efkâr-i umûmîye* was arguably the most important political transformation of the Empire during the nineteenth century.

Such a deep transformation cannot be understood without going back in time, if one is to avoid a *deus ex machina* effect. Naturally, the Ottoman public did not magically come into being. To explain the development of public opinion, this book has first focused on the state-making processes under Selim III and Mahmud II. Broadly, it has argued that the creation of the modern state in the Ottoman Empire redefined both politics and society simultaneously. Especially the removal of centrifugal forces, such as *â'yâns*, and the concentration of power in Istanbul have been presented as key developments in the public formation. By opening a critical space for public authority, particularly with his campaign against janissaries, Mahmud II created the necessary background for public discourse to grow. By propounding a 'public alliance' against the ancient corps of the Empire, he gained new legitimacy for embarking upon such a momentous act. Nevertheless, seeking support through general consensus and not through royal or religious authority had its downsides, as well as advantages. Above all, it meant foregoing a sultanic monopoly on legitimacy and opened the way for the public to take interest in Ottoman politics. It was for this reason that Abdülaziz's deposition was presented as a decision of 'public alliance/*ittifâk-ı umûmîye*'. It had historical precedent.

The next chapter examined the importance of Ottoman *salons* in opinion-making and analysed the symbiotic relationship between the institution of *meclis* and daily politics. With reference to Jürgen Habermas and Reinhart Koselleck, it has been argued that *meclis* provided a critical space for public discourse that, in return, challenged the closed political culture of the Empire. This was not a retrospective reading of the Tanzimat era from a theoretical perspective. Even Sultan Abdülhamid articulated the relationship between public opinion and the Ottoman *salons*, and held these places responsible for the deposition of his uncle. As a result of this, under Abdülhamid the long-standing practice of intelligence gathering turned into a systematic and highly institutionalised means of subjugation. He was certainly successful at dominating the Ottoman politics by creating a reign of surveillance. Yet in the long run, the result of his strict control was paradoxical and paved the way for his overthrow.

The third chapter focused on the connection between the reading material and discursive practices. Through a detailed analysis of probate records, it illustrated that the reading habits of the Ottoman elite changed dramatically over the course of the nineteenth century. This was a result of the paradigm shift that the Empire went through during the Tanzimat era. By examining social and political reasons, which gave rise to this profound transformation, the chapter also furthered the idea that the emergence of notions like public and public opinion were not mere imitations of Western practices but resulted from overwhelming changes that had taken place since the beginning of the nineteenth century.

The next chapter dealt with the introduction of mass education. The Ottomans were very aware of their precarious situation and saw public education as a panacea that would save their country from the ruin hovering over their heads. Theirs was one of the first states to adopt the idea that everyone should receive schooling. This, although surprising at first glance, is perfectly understandable: states which were ethnically and religiously more divided, could benefit more from the putative levelling influence of schooling. While widespread education failed to create the supranational Ottoman identity that the Tanzimat statesmen longed for, the diffusion of scientific knowledge, by offering new formulas of cultural and intellectual authority, helped promote a unified public opinion amongst the fragmented population of the Empire.

Then the book focused on the relationship between the incipient reading public and the Tanzimat press. Ottoman newspapers were both a cause and a consequence of the expansion of public opinion. Ottoman journalists fed their readers with their learned articles and commentaries, teaching them everything from table manners to political philosophy. In return, the expanding public, with its subscriptions and contributions, liberated newspapers from their dependence on royal or noble patronage. This led to the emergence of a critical intellectual class, which found its embodiment in writers like Şinâsi and Nâmık Kemal. These writers enhanced the government's transparency and accountability in the public sphere. For this reason, many contemporaries likened newspapers to a parliament where the voice of the opposition could be heard. It was only natural that the press should assume such an important role in a society where formal channels of citizen participation and political action were very limited. The function of newspapers as the voice of the public became an essential part of Ottoman politics in following years. After demanding the right to petition the Sultan at any time, revolutionaries of May 1876, for instance, also asked that 'only a limited number of newspapers shall be published, and these in Turkish, and the Sultan shall be requested to read each of them in order that he maybe informed of the state of his Empire.'[3] For some, even members of the parliament were not to be trusted with such an important task. Newspapers alone, they thought, could convey the true state of the country to the Sultan.

The last chapter argued against, for want of a better term, historical 'orientalism', which still designates political participation as a Western phenomenon. Just because a state did not follow Habermas's normative transition from civil society to a bourgeois public sphere, it does not mean that it had an inherently 'deviant' structure and insufficient vocabulary for political action. This is, to use Jürgen Osterhammel's phrase, 'to generalize a claim to universality that was invented in the West and whose like is found nowhere else'.[4] Through a detailed narrative of the events leading to the deposition of Sultan Abdülaziz in May 1876, the chapter established the unprecedented level of politicisation attained by Ottoman society at the end of Tanzimat era. By doing so, it uncovered public opinion as the driving force of political change in the late Ottoman history and revealed the modern historiographical biases, which have obscured the contemporary political consciousness and assertiveness of the Ottoman public. Although there is no reason to doubt reports of widespread Ottoman public engagement in politics, which had serious consequences including the deposal of the Sultan, there are genuine grounds to distrust the veracity of later

[3] Anonymous, 'The Rulers of Turkey: Some Facts about the Softas – A Conservative Priesthood – The Governing Power of the Porte', *The New York Times*, 10 June 1876, 5.

[4] Jürgen Osterhammel, *The Transformation of the World: A Global History of the Nineteenth Century*, trans. Patrick Camiller (Princeton, NJ: Princeton University Press, 2014), 515.

testimonies, which ignored the agency of the Ottoman public in the events of 1876. As the final point of the chapter, it was argued that, Abdülhamid's autocratic reign should be understood as a rupture, which became possible only after deep economic and political crises. In other words, it became possible not in spite of but rather because of the tentative, and by no means universal, public support, which eroded in time and resulted in his deposal in 1909.

This book has attempted to give the history of a trajectory, which was decidedly different from the examples experienced in the West: a trajectory that can lead to a more balanced and nuanced understanding of public opinion as a whole. It has sought to trace the origins and nature of the Ottoman public in historical facts, which have hitherto been considered unrelated (such as public borrowings or book inventories). By doing so, it has aimed to reveal the systematic growth of political consciousness, which left its permanent marks on the momentous events of the last years of the Ottoman Empire. It has been shown that the word 'public', with all its implications, was taken quite seriously by Ottomans coming from very different walks of life, be it a sultan or a simple city dweller. As a result, this book has been intended as a beginning, and not the end, of the efforts, which will eventually restore the Ottoman public to its proper place in modern historiography.

Bibliography

Archival Sources

Prime Ministry Archives (BOA – Başbakanlık Osmanlı Arşivi)

A. AMD	(Sadâret Âmedî Kalemi Defterleri)
A.}DVN	(Dîvân/Beylikçi Kalemi Defterleri)
A.DVNS.MHM.d	(Mühimme Defterleri)
A.}DVN.DVE	(Düvel-i Ecnebîye Belgeleri)
A.{DVNS.BUY.iLM.d	(Buyruldu ve İlmuhaber Defterleri)
A.}MKT.MHM	(Sadâret Mektûbi Mühimme Kalemi Evrâkı)
A.}MKT.MVL	(Sadâret Mektûbi Kalemi Meclis-i Vâlâ Evrâkı)
A.}MKT.NZD	(Sadâret Mektûbi Kalemi Nezâret ve Deva'ir Evrâkı
A.}MKT.UM	(Sadâret Mektûbi Kalemi Umûm Vilâyet Evrâkı
A.}MTZ	(Sadâret Eyâlât-ı Mümtâze Kalemi Belgeleri)
C..ADL	(Cevdet Adliye)
C..AS	(Cevdet Askeriye)
C..BH	(Cevdet Bahriye)
C..DH	(Cevdet Dâhiliye)
C..HR	(Cevdet Hâriciye)
C..MF	(Cevdet Maârif)
C..ML	(Cevdet Mâliye)
C..ZB	(Cevdet Zabtiye)
DH.KMS	(Dâhiliye Nezâreti Dâhiliye Kalem-i Mahsûs Evrâkı)
DH.MKT	(Dâhiliye Nezâreti Mektûbi Kalemi)
DH.SAİD.MEM	(Dâhiliye Nezâreti Sicill-i Ahvâl İdâresi Me'mûrin)
HAT	(Hatt-ı Hümâyun Tasnifi)
HR.MKT	(Mektûbî Kalemi Belgeleri)

HR.SYS	(Siyasî Kısmı Belgeleri)
İ.DH	(İrâde Dâhiliye)
İ..DUİT	(İrâde Dosya Usûlü)
İE.HAT.	(İbnülemin Hatt-ı Hümâyun)
İ..HR	(İrâde Hâriciye)
İ..HUS	(İrâde Husûsî)
İ..MMS	(İrâde Meclis-i Mahsûs)
İ..MSM	(İrâde Mesâil-i Mühimme)
İ..MVL	(İrâde Meclis-i Vâlâ)
İ..ŞD	(İrâde Şûrâ-yı Devlet)
İ..TNF	(İrâde Ticâret ve Nâfia)
MF.MKT	(Mektûbi Kalemi)
Y..EE	(Yıldız Esâs Evrâkı)
Y..EE..KP	(Yıldız Sadrâzam Kâmil Paşa Evrâkı)
Y..PRK.ASK	(Yıldız Perâkende Evrâkı Askeri Ma'rûzât)
Y..PRK.AZJ	(Yıldız Perâkende Evrâkı Arzuhâl Jurnal)
Y..PRK.BŞK	(Yıldız Perâkende Evrâkı Başkitâbet Dâiresi Ma'rûzâtı)
Y..PRK.HH	(Yıldız Perâkende Evrâkı Hazine-i Hassa)
Y.PRK. MF	(Yıldız Perâkende Evrâkı Maârif Nezâreti Maruzâtı)
Y..PRK.ZB	(Yıldız Perâkende Evrâkı Zabtiye Nezâreti Ma'rûzâtı)

The Archives of Sharia Court in the Muftiship of Istanbul (İstanbul Müftülüğü Şeriye Sicilleri Arşivi)

Ş.S.KISASKMAH	(Kısmet-i Askeriyye Mahkemesi)
Ş.S.İSTMAH	(İstanbul Mahkemesi)

Manuscripts

Abdülaziz. *Ba'z-i Mebâhis-i Hikemiyye ve Mantıkiyye Tercemesi*: Ali Emiri Şeriyye Koleksiyonu, No: 1288.

Esad Efendi. *[Fenn-i Münâzara]*: İstanbul Üniversitesi Türkçe El Yazmaları İbnülemin Mahmud Kemal İnal Kitapları, No: 2875.

Keçecizâde Mehmet İzzet Molla. *Islah-i Nizâm-ı Devlete Dair Risâle*: İstanbul Üniversitesi Türkçe El Yazmaları, No: 9670.

Mahmud Nedim Paşa. *Üss-i İnkılaba Ait Müdafa'anâme*: Ali Emiri Koleksiyonu Târîh El Yazmaları, No: 1032.

Mehmed Behiç Bey. *Yevmiye Kâtibi Mehmet Behiç Tarafından Tanzim Olunan İstatistik Defteri*: İstanbul Üniversitesi Türkçe El Yazmaları, No: 9075.

Primary Sources

Abdi Efendi. *Nutk-i bi-Pervâ ile Akl-i Dânâ Beyninde Muhavere*. İstanbul: Terakki Matbaası, 1287/1860–1861.

Abdurrahman Adil. 'Yeni Osmanlılar Târîhi İnkılâbât-ı Fikriyye ve Münâkaşaları.' *Hâdisât-ı Hukûkiye ve Târîhiye Mecmûası*, no. 3 (1341–1923): 9–16.

Abdurrahman Şeref. 'Fuâd Paşa Konağı Nasıl Mâliye Dâiresi Oldu?' *Târîh-i Osmanî Encümeni* 1, no. 3 (1328–1910): 129–136.

Târîh Musâhabeleri. İstanbul: Matbaa-i Amire, 1339/1923–1924.

Ahmed Agayef. 'Türk Medeniyeti Târîhi I.' *Türk Yurdu* IV, no. 40 (16 Mayıs/29 May 1329/1913): 530–540.

Ahmed Cevdet [Paşa]. *Âdâb-ı Sedad min İlmü'l-Âdâb*. İstanbul: Matbaa-i Âmire, 1294 [1877/1878].

Kısas-ı Enbiya ve Tevârih-i Hülefa. Edited by Mahir İz. 3 vols. Vol. I. Ankara: Milli Eğitim Bakanlığı Kültür Yayınları, 1972.

Ma'rûzât. Edited by Yusuf Halaçoğlu. İstanbul: Çağrı Yayınları, 1980.

Târîh-i Cevdet. 12 vols. Vol. I. İstanbul: Matbaa-i Osmaniye, 1309/1891–1892.

Târîh-i Cevdet. 12 vols. Vol. IX. İstanbul: Matbaa-i Amire, 1292/1875–1876.

Târîh-i Cevdet. 12 vols. Vol. XII. İstanbul: Matbaa-i Amire, 1309/1891–1892.

Târîh-i Cevdet. 12 vols. Vol. XII. İstanbul: Matbaa-i Osmaniye, 1301/1883–1884.

Târîh-i Cevdet. 12 vols. Vol. IV. İstanbul: Takvîmhâne-i Amire, 1275/1858–1859.

Tezâkir 1–12. Edited by Cavid Baysun. 4 vols. Vol. I. Ankara: Türk Târîh Kurumu Basımevi, 1991.

Tezâkir 13–20. Edited by Cavid Baysun. 4 vols. Vol. II. Ankara: Türk Târîh Kurumu, 1991.

Tezâkir 40–Tetimme. Edited by Cavid Baysun. 4 vols. Vol. IV. Ankara: Türk Târîh Kurumu, 1991.

Ahmed Lûtfî Efendi. *Tarîh-i Devlet-i Âliyye-i Osmaniyye*. 8 vols. Vol. VI. Dersaâdet: Mahmud Bey Matbaası, 1302/1884–1885.

Tarîh-i Devlet-i Âliyye-i Osmaniyye. 8 vols. Vol. V. Dersaâdet: Mahmud Bey Matbaası, 1302/1884–1885.

Târîh-i Lûtfî. 8 vols. Vol. V. İstanbul: Mahmud Bey Matbaası, 1302 (1884/1885).

Târîh-i Lûtfî. 8 vols. Vol. II. İstanbul: Matbaa-i Amire, 1291/1874–1875.

Târîh-i Lûtfî. 8 vols. Vol. I. İstanbul: Matbaa-i Amire, 1290/1873–1874.

Târîh-i Lûtfî. Edited by Abdurrahman Şeref. Vol. VIII. İstanbul: Sabah Matbaası, 1328/1910–1911.

Vak'a-Nüvis Ahmed Lûtfî Efendi Târîhi. Edited by Münir Aktepe. 15 vols. Vol. XII. Ankara: Türk Târîh Kurumu Basımevi, 1990.

Ahmed Midhat [Efendi]. *Fennî Bir Roman yahud Amerika Doktorları*. İstanbul: s.n., 1305/1887–1888.

'Midhat Paşa Hazretlerine Hitab.' Devir, 17 Ağustos/29 August 1288/1872, 2–4.

Üss-i İnkilab. 2 vols. Vol. I. İstanbul: Takvîmhâne-i Âmire Matbaası, 1294/1877–1878.

Ahmed Rasim. *Fuhş-i Âtîk*. İstanbul: İkdam Matbaası, 1340/1922.

İstibdaddan Hakimiyet-i Milliyeye. 2 vols. Vol. I. İstanbul: Vatan Matbaası, 1342/1923.

Matbuat Hâtıralarından: Muharrir, Şâir, Edib. İstanbul: Kanaat Kütübhânesi, 1342/1924.

Ahmed Resmî, *Hülasatü'l-İtibar*. Dersaâdet: Mühendisyan Matbaası, 1286/1869–1870.

Ahmed Saib. *Abdülhamid'in Evâil-i Saltanatı*. Kahire: s.n., 1326/1908–1909.

Târîh-i Sultan Murad Hâmis. Kahire: Hindiye Matbaası, 1326/1908–1909.

Vak'a-i Sultan Abd'ül-Aziz. Kahire: Hediye Matbaası, 1326/1908–1909.

Ahmet Refik. *Hicri On Birinci Asırda İstanbul Hayâtı (1000–1100)*. İstanbul: Devlet Matbaası, 1931.

On Altıncı Asırda İstanbul Hayâtı (1553–1591). İstanbul: Devlet Basımevi, 1935.

Ahmed Vasıf Efendi. *Mehasinü'l-âsâr ve Hakayıkü'l-ahbar*. Edited by Mücteba İlgürel. Ankara: Türk Târîh Kurumu, 1994.

Ahmed Vefik Paşa. *Lehçe-i Osmani*. 2 vols. Vol. I. İstanbul: Matbaa-i Amire, 1293/1876.

Akif Pacha. *Un diplomate ottoman en 1836: Affaire Churchill. Trad. annotée de 'l'Éclaircissement' (Tebsireh) d'Akif Pacha, Ministre des Affaires Etrangeres de Turquie*. Translated by Arthur Alric. Paris: Ernest Leroux, 1892.

Âkif Paşa. *Tabsıra-i Âkif Paşa*. İstanbul: Ebuzziyâ Matbaası, 1300/1882–1883.

Aleksandr [Alexander Karatheodori]. 'Usûl-i Te'mîniye.' *Mecmûa-ı Fünun* I, no. 16 (1280/1863): 191–195.

Ali Haydar [Bey]. 'Mecmûa-i İber-i İntibah - Mukaddime.' *Mecmûa-i İber-i İntibah* I, no. 1 (1279/1862): 2–3.

'Mecmûanın Nizâmı.' *Mecmûa-ı İber-i İntibah* I, no. 2 (1279/1863): 28–30.

Ali Haydar Midhat. *The Life of Midhat Pasha: A Record of His Services, Political Reforms, Banishment, and Judicial Murder*. London: J. Murray, 1903.

Âli Paşa. 'İltifatnâme-i Mezkûrun Sûretidir.' *Mecmûa-ı Fünun* I, no. 2 (1279/1862): 51–54.

Ali Rıza Ardahani. *Mi'yarü'l-Münâzara*. İstanbul Mahmud Bey Matbaası, 1307/1889–1890.

Ali Rıza Bey, and Mehmed Gâlib. *Geçen Asırda Devlet Adamlarımız: XIII. Asr-ı Hicride Osmanlı Ricâli*. Edited by Fahri Çetin Derin. 2 vols. Vol. I. İstanbul: Tercüman Gazetesi, 1977.

Andréossy, Antoine-François. *Constantinople et le Bosphore de Thrace*. Paris: B. Duprat, 1841.

Anonymous. '[1067 Senesinde Kâtip Çelebi Merhum].' *Basîret*, 1 Zilkade/2 February 1286/1870.

'Abdülhamid-i Sâniye Tebliğ-i Karar.' *İkdam*, 28 April 1909, 2.

'Address at the Laying the Foundation Stone of the Masonic Hall at Hassekeu.' *Freemasons' Magazine and Masonic Mirror*, no. 630 (1871): 85–86.

'Adliye Nezâretinden 11 Nisan Sene 95 Târîhiyle Vilâyet ile Müstakilen İdâre Olunanan Mutâsârrıflıklara Yazılan Telgrafnâme Sûretidir.' *Cerîde-i Mehâkim*, 12 Receb/2 July 1296/1879, 3–4.

'Adliye Nezâretinden 14 Mayıs Sene 95 Târîhiyle Umûm Vilâyete ve Ressen İdâre Olunan Mutâsârrıflıklara ve Merkez Vilâyet Ticâret Mahkemeleri Riyasetlerine Yazılan Telgrafıdır.' *Cerîde-i Mehâkim*, 12 Receb/2 July 1296/1879, 8.

'Adliye Nezâretinden 21 Nisan Sene 95 Târîhinde Vilâyete Yazılan Telgraf.' *Cerîde-i Mehâkim*, 12 Receb/2 July 1296/1879, 6–7.

'Adliye ve Mezahib Nezâretinin ve Devair-i Merbutasının Vezaifi Nizâmnâmesidir.' *Cerîde-i Mehâkim*, 19 Receb/9 July 1296/1876, 9–13.

'Al Sana Bir Merak Daha.' *Diyojen*, 11 Kanûn-i Sâni/23 January 1287/1872, 1–2.

Anonymous. *The Arabian Nights: Tales of 1,001 Nights*. Translated by Malcolm C. Lyons and Ursula Lyons. Edited by Robert Irwin. 3 vols. Vol. III. London: Penguin, 2010.

'[Astounding news come to us from Constantinople].' *The Times*, 31 May 1876, 11.

'Avrupa'da Terbiye-i Nisvâniyye.' *Hanımlara Mahsûs Gazete*, 1 Kanûn-i Sâni/13 January 1313/1898, 1–2.

'Ba'zı Âsâr-ı Hayriye.' *Takvîm-i Vekâyi*, 3 Rebiyülevvel/17 May 1255/1839, 2.

'Ba'zı Âsâr-ı Hayriye,' *Takvîm-i Vekâyi*, 4 Safer/19 April 1255/1839, 2.

'Ba'zı Âsâr-ı Hayriye.' *Takvîm-i Vekâyi*, 2 Şaban/21 October 1254/1838, 2.

'Ba'zı Zevat Tarafından Cemiyete Verilen Hedaye.' *Mecmûa-ı Fünun* II, no. 22 (1280/1864): 432–436.

'Bir Hanım İmzasıyla Aldığımız Varakadır.' *Diyojen*, 14 Kanûn-i Evvel/26 December 1288/1872, 3–4.

'Bir Zât Tarafından Gönderilen Varakadan Hulasa Edilmiştir: Kırâathânede.' *Diyojen*, 28 Kanûn-ı Sâni/9 February 1286/1871, 3–4.

'[Bu Cesim Toplar].' *İstanbul*, 14 Receb/11 November 1284/1867, 26.

'Bu Hesaba Ne Buyurursunuz?' *Diyojen*, 5 Nisan/17 April 1288/1872, 1–2.

'[Bu yakınlarda İngiltere memleketinde].' *Takvîm-i Vekâyi*, 1 Cemazeyilahir/26 October 1248/1832, 4.

'Bulletin du Jour.' *Le Temps*, 31 May 1876, 1.

'[Bundan Akdem İlan Olunduğu Üzere].' *Takvîm-i Vekâyi*, 26 Şevval/4 April 1280/1864, 2.

'[Bundan Akdem Vuku' Bulan].' *Takvîm-i Vekâyi*, 28 Cemazeyilahir/4 December 1247/1831, 3.

'Cemiyet-i İlmiye-i Osmaniye Nizâmnâmesidir.' *Mecmûa-ı Fünun* I, no. 1 (1279/1862): 2–15.

'[Cevahir-i tahmid-i hüdâ].' *Vekâyi-i Mısriye*, 25 Cemaziyelevvel (3 December) 1244/1828.

'[The Committee of British Literary Institution].' *Levant Herald*, 21 November 1860, 956.

'Constantinople, 13 Février 1857.' *Gazette Médicale d'Orient* 1, no. 1 (1857): 1.

'Constantinople, Wednes: May 13.' *Levant Herald*, 13 May 1868, 100.

'The Crisis in Turkey (From Our Special Correspondent.).' *The Times*, 20 May 1876, 8.

'The Crisis in Turkey. (From Our Special Correspondent) ' *The Times*, 26 May 1876, 8.

'[D'une pièce de Kémal bey].' *La Turquie*, 12 April 1873, 1.

'Dâire-i Maârif-i Umûmîye.' *Mecmûa-ı Fünun* I, no. 24 (1280/1864): 495–449.

'Deposition of the Sultan (By Telegraph.) (From Our Special Correspondent).' *The Times*, 31 May 1876, 7.

'The Dervishes and Masonry.' *The Freemasons Magazine and Masonic Mirror*, no. 470 (1863): 521–523.

'[Dünkü Gün Umûm Osmanlılar İçin Bir Mebdâ-i Saâdet İdi].' *Vakit*, 8 Zilhicce/25 December 1293/1876, 1.

'Dünyada Herze-Vekili Yalnız Diyojen Midir?' *Diyojen*, 25 Mart/6 April 1287/1871, 3.

'Ecel-i Kaza.' *Diyojen*, 25 Ağustos/6 September 1288/1872, 4.

'[Edirne'de ikâmete me'mûr Pertev Paşa].' *Takvîm-i Vekâyi*, 5 Ramazan/3 December 1253/1837, 3.

'Efkâr-ı Umûmîye.' *Bedir*, 27 Eylül/9 October 1288/1872, 1–2.

'Emir-Name-i Sâmî Sûreti.' *Mecmûa-ı Fünun* I, no. 5 (1279/1862): 174–176.

'Ferah Tiyatrosu Vakası.' *Mîzân*, 15 Safer/8 March 1327/1909, 367–68.

'The 'Fetva of Deposition of Sultan Abdul-Aziz.' *Levant Herald*, 5 June 1876, 161.

'Fi 20 Şevval Sene 96 ve fi 24 Eylül Sene 95 Târîhleriyle Adliye Nezâretinden Bil-Cümle Vilâyet ile Adliye Müffettişliklerine ve Müdde-i Umûmîliklere Yazılan Tahrîrât Sûretidir.' *Cerîde-i Mehâkim*, 28 Şevval/15 October 1296/1876, 115.

'[Fransa Kralı Teşrinisâni yedisinde rüesa-yı devlet ve vükela-ı milletten olan iki umûmî meşveretgahın meclisini bizzât akd edip erbâb-ı meclise hitaben ber vech-i ati takrîr eylediği makalın suretidir].' *Takvîm-i Vekâyi*, 20 Ramazan/10 February 1248/1833, 3–4.

'[Fransa Kralının verdiği cevâbın suretidir].' *Takvîm-i Vekâyi*, 25 Safer/3 July 1250/1834, 4.

'Fransızca Londra'da Basılmakta Olan İnternasyonal Nam Gazetenin 20 Teşrin-i Evvel Târîhiyle İstanbul'dan Alıp Neşr Eylediği Mektûbun Hülasasıdır.' *Hürriyet*, 2 November 1868, 7.

'Freemasonry in Turkey.' *The National Freemason* I, no. I (1863): 13.

'Freemasonry in Turkey.' The American Quarterly Review of Freemasonry and Its Kindred Sciences 1 (1858): 140.

'Gâribe der Suret-i Zuhûru Mücâzât.' *Takvîm-i Vekâyi*, 29 Şevval/1 April 1247/1832, 3.

'Fünun.' *Takvîm-i Vekâyi*, 22 Zilkade/11 May 1279/1863, 3.

'Gazetecilerin Namusu Yok Mu.' *Diyojen*, 12 Teşrin-i Sâni/24 November 1286/1870, 3.

'[Gelibolu Mutâsârrıfı Kemal Beyefendi].' *Diyojen*, 12 Eylül/24 September 1288/1872, 4.

'[Hamden li-vâhibi'l-'atâyâ].' *Takvîm-i Vekâyi*, 6 Rebiyülahir/19 June 1255/1839, 2.

'Hat Imperial.' *Journal de Constantinople*, 21 Janvier 1845, 1.

'Havâdis-i Dâhiliye (Pay-i Taht).' *Tasvîr-i Efkâr*, 4 Receb/26 December 1279/1862, 1.

'Havâdis-i Dâhiliye: Pay-i Taht.' *Tasvîr-i Efkâr*, 18 Muharrem/11 May 1285/1868, 1–2.

'Havâdis-i Dâhiliye: Pay-i Taht.' *Tasvîr-i Efkâr*, 9 Şaban/30 January 1279/1863, 1.
'İlan.' *Diyojen*, 22 Eylül/4 October 1288/1872, 4.
'İlan: [Deavi-i Vakinin Sürrati ve Serbest-i Ceryanı Emrinde].' *Cerîde-i Mehâkim*, 14 Şevval/1 October 1296/1879, 101.
'İ'lânât.' *Tasvîr-i Efkâr*, 27 Cemazeyilahir/12 November 1282/1865, 4.
'İ'lânât [Hikmet-i Tabiyye ile ilgili bir kitâbın satışı].' *Tasvîr-i Efkâr*, 14 Şaban/4 February 1279/1863, 3.
'İ'lânât [Usûl-i Kimya].' *Tasvîr-i Efkâr*, 2 Şaban/23 January 1279/1863, 3.
'İ'lânât: İstanbul'da Akçenin Raici.' *Tasvîr-i Efkâr*, 5 Muharrem/3 July 1279/1862, 3.
'Internal Commotion in Turkey. Popular Feeling Against Mahmoud Dâmâd - Softas Arrested - Revolutionary Placards.' *The New York Times*, 20 March 1876, 5.
'[İşte Bu Alâ].' *Diyojen*, 4 Eylül/16 September 1287/1871, 2.
'Kadınlarda Tahsîl ve Terbiye.' *Hanımlara Mahsûs Gazete*, 27 Teşrîn-i Sânî/9 December 1313/1897, 1–2.
'Kanûn-i Esâsi-i Memâlik-i Devlet-i Osmaniye.' *Vakit*, 8 Zilhicce/25 December 1293/1876, 2–4.
'Kısm-ı Resmi.' *Takvîm-i Vekâyi*, 23 Şaban/13 September 1293/1876, 1–2.
'Kızların Tahsili Hakkında Bir Mütâlaa II.' *Hanımlara Mahsûs Gazete*, 30 Teşrinievvel/10 November 1313/1895, 1–2.
'Knights.' *Masonic Record: A Monthly Magazine Devoted to the Interests of Fraternity and General Literature* IV (1870): 275–282.
'Le Sultan Mourad V.' *La Turquie*, 31 May 1876, 1.
'Lettres de Turquie.' *Le Temps*, 18 May 1876, 1.
'Lettres de Turquie [II].' *Le Temps*, 23 May 1876, 2.
'Lettres de Turquie [III].' *Le Temps*, 27 May 1876, 1–2.
'Lettres de Turquie [IV].' *Le Temps*, 29 May 1876, 1–2.
'Maârife Dair Bend-i Mahsûsdur.' *Tercüman-ı Ahvâl*, 2 Zilkade/3 May 1277/1861, 1–3.
'Madde-i Resmiye [I].' *Tasvîr-i Efkâr*, 18 Receb/9 January 1279/1863, 1.
'[Mâlum Ola ki].' *Takvîm-i Vekâyi*, 21 Cemazeyilahir/27 Noveber 1247/1831, 1–2.
'[Mâlum ya Fevâid Kumpanyası].' *Dijojen*, 12 Ağustos/24 August 1287/1871, 2–3.
'Meâl-i Tercüme-i Dîbâce.' *Takvîm-i Vekâyi*, 19 Şaban/1 January 1249/1834, 3–4.
'Meclis-i Umûr-i Nafi'anın Lâyıhası.' *Takvîm-i Vekâyi*, 21Zilkade/5 February 1254/1839, 1–2.

'Millet Meclisi Hakkında Bir Mütâlaa.' *Êfkar*, 18 Cemaziyelevvel/11 June 1293/1876, 2.

'Montalivet Nâm Umûr-u Dâhiliye Nâzırının Keyfiyet ve Vuku'ât-ı Hâzıraya dair Fransa Kralına Arz Eylediği Bir Kıta Takrîrir Suretidir.' *Takvîm-i Vekâyi*, 5 Rebiyülevvel/2 August 1248/1832, 4.

'[Mühendishâne- i Berri-i Hümâyun Hâcelerinden].' *Diyojen*, 3 Teşrin-i Evvel/15 October 1288/1872.

'Mukaddime.' *Cerîde-i Havâdis*, Gurre-i Cemazeyilahir/31 July 1256/1840, 1.

'[Müstağni-i Beyân Olduğu Üzere].' *Takvîm-i Vekâyi*, Gurre-i Şaban/1 June 1267/1851, 2–4.

'[Müstezil-i Saye-i Râfetvaye].' *Takvîm-i Vekâyi*, 2 Muharrem/7 November 1267/1850, 2–4.

'Mütâlaa.' *Basîret*, 27 Şevval/30 January 1286/1870.

'Nesâih-i Hükema.' *Mecmûa-ı İber-i İntibah* I, no. 1 (1279/1862): 3–8.

'Nev-Residegan-ı Maârifetten Bir Zâtın Varakasıdır.' *İbret*, 27 Rebiyülahir/4 July 1289/1872, 2.

'The New Turkish Government.' *The Times*, 23 May 1876, 8.

'[Ölüm İlânı].' *Cumhûriyet*, 27 May 1938, 4.

'[Rabbimiz Teâlâ Hazretleri].' *Takvîm-i Vekâyi*, 6 Rebiülevvel/30 May 1254/1838, 3.

'[Reîs-ül Küttab es-Seyyid Süleyman Necib Efendi Hazretleri].' *Takvîm-i Vekâyi*, 11 Şaban/15 January 1247/1832, 1.

'The Riot at Constantinople (From Our Special Correspondent).' *The Times*, 18 May 1876, 10.

'The Rulers of Turkey: Some Facts about the Softas - A Conservative Priesthood - The Governing Power of the Porte.' *The New York Times*, 10 June 1876, 5.

'[Rumelinin ba'zı mahallerinde olduğu misillü].' *Takvîm-i Vekâyi*, 3 Zilhicce/4 May 1247/1832, 2.

'[The Rustification of Kemal Bey].' *Levant Herald*, 16 April 1873, 124.

'The Salons of Vienna and Berlin.' *Bentley's Miscellany* 50, no. 1 (1861): 148–157.

'[Serasker Paşa Hazretleri].' *Takvîm-i Vekâyi*, 6 Receb/11 December 1247/1831, 1.

'Sultan Murad's First Public Visit to Mosque.' *Levant Herald*, 5 July 1876, 161.

'Sûret-i Hatt-ı Hümâyun.' *Takvîm-i Vekâyi*, 11 Cemaziyelevvel/4 Haziran 1293/1876, 1.

'Sûret-i Hatt-ı Hümâyun-ı Ma'adalet-i Nümûn-Şâhâne.' *Takvîm-i Vekâyi*, 11 Muharrem/15 March 1256/1840, 1.

'Sûret-i Hatt-ı Hümâyun-ı Şevket-Makrûn.' *Takvîm-i Vekâyi*, 12 Muharrem (21 January) 1261/1845, 1.

'Sûret-i Lâyıha.' *Takvîm-i Vekâyi*, 18 Şevval/25 December 1255/1839, 2.

'Sûret-i Münife-i Hatt-ı Hümâyun.' *Takvîm-i Vekâyi*, 27 Receb/21 June 1262/1846, 1–2.

'Tabsıra.' *Takvîm-i Vekâyi*, 1 Cemazeyilahir/26 October 1248/1832, 3.

'Tebşir-i Mânevi.' *Êfkar*, 8 Cemaziyelevvel/1 June 1293/1876, 1.

'Tefrika [Hikmet-i Târîh].' *Tasvîr-i Efkâr*, 8 Ramazan/27 February 1279/1863, 4.

'Tefrika [Târîh-i Tabi'i].' *Tasvîr-i Efkâr*, 6 Şevval/27 March 1279/1863, 4.

'Terbiye-i Nisvân.' *Hanımlara Mahsûs Gazete*, 3 Nisan/15 April 1313/1897, 5–6.

'Terbiye-i Siyâsiye.' *Hakayık*, 4 Şaban/7 October 1289/1872.

'Tercüme-i Hikâye-i Heft Peyker.' *Diyojen*, 6 Eylül/18 September 1288/1872, 4.

'Te'sir-i nüfûz-u Padişâhi,' *Takvîm-i Vekâyi*, 29 Şevval/1 April 1247/1832, 3.

'The Third Annual Ball of the Oriental Lodge.' *Levant Herald*, 9 January 1861, 1034.

'Tırnova Nâibi Müderrisin-i Kirâmdan Ahmed Şükrü Efendinin der-Âliye'ye Takdim Eylediği İbret Alınacak İlâmdır ki Aynıyla Tab Olunur.' *Takvîm-i Vekâyi*, 21 Cemaziyelevvel/6 October 1249/1833, 3–4.

'Turkey (By Telegraph.) (From Our Special Correspondent at Constantinople).' *The Times*, 15 May 1876, 7.

'Turkey, Constantinople, July 30.' *The Times*, 1 August 1881, 5.

'Turkey. (By Telegraph.) (From Our Special Correspondent at Constantinople).' *The Times* 16 May 1876, 5.

'The Turkish Revolution.' *The New York Times*, 31 May 1876, 1.

'Türkistan'da Efkâr-ı Umûmîye.' *Vakit*, May 31, 1876, 1–2.

Anonymous. 'TÜRKEI. - Adresse muselmännischer Patrioten an Lord Derby.' In *Das Staatsarchiv: Sammlung der officiellen Actenstück zur Geschichte der Gegenwart*, edited by H. V. Kremer-Auenrode and Ph. Hirsch, 213–219. Leipzig: Duncker & Humblot, 1877.

Anonymous. 'Umûr-ı Dâhiliye.' *Takvîm-i Vekâyi*, 22 Rebiülevvel/15 June 1254/1838, 1.

Anonymous. 'Umûr-ı Dâhiliye.' *Takvîm-i Vekâyi*, 10 Zilkade/11 Nisan 1247/1832, 1.

Anonymous. 'Üdebâmızın Numûne-i İmtisalleri (Ma-Bad Elli Dokuzuncu Nüshadan).' *Mîzân*, 22 Zilhicce/30 August 1305/1888, 577.

Anonymous. '[Ümrân-ı Memleketin Esâs-ı Kavisi].' *Takvîm-i Vekâyi*, 26 Zilhicce/24 June 1278/1862, 3.

Anonymous. 'Üsküdar Vapularlarından Şikayet.' *Diyojen*, 12 Haziran/24 June 1287/1871, 3.

Anonymous. 'Varaka.' *İttihâd*, 29 Ramazan/18 October 1293/1876, 2.

Anonymous. 'Variété.' *Gazette Médicale d'Orient* 1, no. 1 (1857): 16.

Anonymous. 'Vuku'ât-ı Resmiye.' *Takvîm-i Vekâyi*, 7 Receb/29 December 1279/1862, 1.

Anonymous. 'Yaşasun Sultan Murad-ı Hâmis.' *Êfkar*, 8 Cemaziyelevvel/1 June 1293/1876, 1–2.

Anonymous. '[Yeni Dünya Dediğimiz Amerika'nın].' *Takvîm-i Vekâyi*, 6 Receb/11 December 1247/1831, 4.

Anonymous. '[Zât-ı refet semat-ı zıllulahileri].' *Takvîm-i Vekâyi*, 29 Rebiyülahir/25 September 1248/1832, 1.

Arapyan, Kalost. *Rusçuk Ạyânı Mustafa Paşa'nın Hayâtı ve Kahramanlıkları*. Translated by Esat Uras. Ankara: Türk Târîh Kurumu Basımevi, 1943.

Arif. 'Urban Târîhi.' *Mecmûa-ı İber-i İntibah* İkinci Sene, no. 7 (1280/1864): 174–176.

Arif Paşa, and Hilmi Efendi. *Kanûn-ı Münâzara*. İstanbul: Muhib Matbaası, 1286/1869.

Army and Navy Chronicle. Edited by Benjamin Homans. 13 vols. Vol. VI. Washington, DC: Benjamin Homans, 1839.

Arioste, *Le premier volume de Roland furieux ... par Loys Arioste ... maintenant mys en rime françoise par Jan Fornier ... avec les arguments au commencement de chacun chant ... et avec les allégories des chants à la fin d'un chacun*. Translated by Jean Fornier. Anvers: Christofle Plantin, 1555.

Asad, Muhammad. *The Road to Mecca*. New York: Simon and Schuster, 1954.

Ayni, Mehmet Ali. *Dârülfünun Târîhi*. Edited by Aykut Kazancıgil. İstanbul: Kitâbevi, 2007.

Ayverdi, Sâmîha. *Boğaziçi'nde Târîh*. İstanbul: Kubbealtı Neşriyâtı, 2008.

Ayverdi, Sâmîha. *İbrâhim Efendi Konağı*. İstanbul: Kubbealtı Neşriyâtı, 1999.

Azzûz, Muhammed Mekkî b. 'İslâmiyet'in Bahşettiği Hûrriyet-i Âmme.' *Sırat-ı Müstakim* II, no. 27 (1327–1909): 1–2.

Balch, Thomas. *The French in America during the War of Independence of the United States, 1777–1783*. Translated by Thomas Willing Balch. Philadelphia: Porter & Coates, 1891.

[Basîretçi] Ali. *İstanbul'da Yarım Asırlık Vakayi-i Mühimme*. İstanbul: Matbaa-i Hüseyin Enver, 1325/1909.

[Basîretçi] Ali. 'Mukaddime.' *Basîret*, 20 Şevval/23 January 1286/1870, 1–2.

Bekir Efendizâde Mahmûd Efendi. *Lüccetü'l-münâzara*. İstanbul: Esad Efendi Matbaası, 1294/1877–1878.

Belin. 'De l'instruction publique et du mouvement intellectuel en Orient.' *Le Contemporain Revue d'économie Chrétienne* XI, no. Aout (1866): 214–254.

Bentham, Jeremy. *Benthamiana: or Select Extracts from the Works of Jeremy Bentham. With an Outline of His Opinions on the Principal Subjects Discussed in His Works. Edited by John Hill Burton*. Philadelphia: Lea & Blanchard, 1844.

Bereketzâde Hakkı. *Müdâvele-i Efkâr*. İstanbul: Âlem Matbaası, 1307/1890.

Bolayır, Ali Ekrem. *Ali Ekrem Bolayır'ın Hâtıraları*. Edited by Metin Kayahan Özgül, Türk Büyükleri Dizisi. Ankara: Kültür Bakanlığı, 1991.

Bolayır, Ali Ekrem. *Nâmık Kemal*, Büyük Adamlar Serisi Nr: 2: Devlet Matbaası, 1930.

Brown, John P. 'Masonry in Turkey.' *The Freemason's Monthly Magazine* 24, no. 4 (1865): 138–140.

Burgess, Richard. *Greece and the Levant, or, Diary of a Summer's Excursion in 1834*. 2 vols. Vol. I. London: Longman, 1835.

Câbi Ömer Efendi. *Câbi Târîhi: Târîh-i Sultan Selim-i Sâlis ve Mahmud-i Sâni Tahlil ve Tenkidli Metin*. Edited by Mehmet Ali Beyhan. 2 vols. Vol. I. Ankara: Türk Târîh Kurumu Basımevi, 2003.

Câbi Ömer Efendi. *Câbi Târîhi: Târîh-i Sultan Selim-i Salis ve Mahmud-i Sâni Tahlil ve Tenkidli Metin*. Edited by Mehmet Ali Beyhan. 2 vols. Vol. II. Ankara: Türk Târîh Kurumu Basımevi, 2003.

Catalogue de la bibliothèque de feu Ahmed Véfyk pacha. Constantinople: Baghdadlian, 1893.

Cemal Paşa. *Hâtırat: 1913–1922*. İstanbul: Ahmed İhsan ve Şürekası, 1922.

Challemel-Lacour, M. 'Les hommes d'état de la Turquie – Aali-Pacha et Fuâd-Pacha.' *Revue des Deux Mondes* 73, no. Février (1868): 886–925.

Chirket-I-Hairié. *Annuaire de la Société conetenant un historique de l'enterprise et une monographie du Bosphore, élaboré par la Direction*. Constantinople: Ahmed Ihsan & Cie, 1914.

Clarke, Hyde. 'On Public Instruction in Turkey.' *Journal of the Statistical Society of London* 30, no. 4 (1867): 502–534.

Clarke, Hyde. 'On the Supposed Extinction of the Turks and Increase of the Christians in Turkey.' *Journal of the Statistical Society of London* 28, no. 2 (1865): 261–293.

Clavel, F.T. B. *Histoire pittoresque de la franc-maçonnerie et des sociétés secrétes anciennes et modernes*. Paris: Pagnerre, 1843.

Defterdar Sarı Mehmet Paşa. *Devlet Adamlarına Öğütler*. Edited by Hüseyin Ragıp Uğural. Ankara: Türkiye ve Orta Doğu Âmme İdâresi Enstitüsü Yayınları, 1969.

Derin, Fahri Ç. 'Yayla İmâmı Risâlesi.' *Târîh Enstitüsü Dergisi*, no. 3 (1973): 213–272.
Devlet-i Âliye'nin Yetmiş Dokuz Senesi Muvâzene Defteridir. İstanbul: Matbaa-i Amire, 1280/1863–1864.
Dilmen, İbrahim Necmi. *Târîh-i Edebiyât Dersleri*. 2 vols. Vol. II. İstanbul: Matbaa-i Amire, 1922.
Djemal Pasha. *Memories of a Turkish Statesman 1913–1919*. New York: George H. Doran Company, 1922.
Djuvara, T.G. *Cent Projets de Partage de la Turquie (1281–1913): Avec 18 cartes hors texte*. Paris: Librarie Félix Alcan, 1914.
Dominicus Germanus. *Fabrica linguae arabicae, cum interpretatione Latina, & Italica, accomodata ad vsum linguae vulgaris, & scripturalis*. Rome: Typis. Sac. Congreg. de Prop. Fide, 1639.
Dove, John. *The Masonic Text-Book: Containing a History of Masonry and Masonic Grand Lodges from the Earliest Times: Together with the Constitution of Masonry, or Ahiman Rezon, and a Digest of the Laws, Rules and Regulations of the Grand Lodge of Virginia*. Richmond: Randolph, 1854.
Düstûr. Tertîb-i Evvel ed. 4 vols. Vol. II. İstanbul: Matbaa-i Amire, 1289/1872–1873.
Düstûr. Tertîb-i Evvel ed. 4 vols. Vol. I. İstanbul: Matbaa-i Amire, 1289/1872–1873.
Ebuzziyâ [Tevfik]. 'Farmasonluk.' *Mecmûa-i Ebuzziyâ*, no. 100 (1329/1911): 673–682.
Ebuzziyâ [Tevfik]. *Merhum Nâmık Kemal*. İstanbul: s.n., 1327/1909.
Ebuzziyâ [Tevfik]. 'Münif Paşa.' *Yeni Tasvîr-i Efkâr*, 1 Safer/12 February 1328/1910, 2.
Ebuzziyâ [Tevfik]. 'Şinâsi'nin Eyyâm-i Ahîre-i Hayâtı ve Vefâtı.' *Mecmûa-i Ebüzziyâ*, no. 105 (1911): 833–841.
Ebuzziyâ [Tevfik]. *Yeni Osmanlılar Târîhi*. Edited by Şemsettin Kutlu. 2 vols. Vol. II. İstanbul: Hürriyet Yayınları, 1973.
Ebuzziyâ [Tevfik]. *Yeni Osmanlılar Târîhi*. Edited by Şemsettin Kutlu. 2 vols. Vol. I. İstanbul: Hürriyet Yayınları, 1973.
Edhem Paşa. 'Medhal-i İlm-i Jeoloji.' *Mecmûa-ı Fünun* I, no. 2 (1279/1862): 68–75.
Elliot, Henry G. *Some Revolutions and Other Diplomatic Experiences*. London: John Murray, 1922.
Elliot, Sir H. M. *The History of India as Told by Its Own Historians: The Muhammadan Period*. Edited by Professor John Dowson. 9 vols. Vol. III. London: Trübner, 1871.
Emin Efendi. *Menâkıb-ı Kethüdâzâde el-Hac Mehmed Ârif Efendi*. İstanbul: s.n., 1305/1887.

Emin Nihad Bey. *Müsâmeretnâme: Binbaşı Rıfat Bey'in Sergüzeşti*. 12 vols. Vol. I. İstanbul: Midhat Efendi Matbaası, 1288/1872.

Emin Nihad Bey. *Müsâmeretnâme: Kapı Kethüdâsı Behçet Efendi İle Makbûle Hanım'ın Sergüzeşti*. 12 vols. Vol. II. İstanbul: s.n., 1289/1873.

Engelhardt, Ed. *La Turquie et le Tanzimat, ou Histoire des réformes dans l'Empire ottoman depuis 1826 jusqu'à nos jours*, 2 vols. Vol. I. Paris: A. Cotillon, 1882.

Erkin, Behiç. *Hâtırat 1876–1958*. İstanbul: Türk Târîh Kurumu, 2010.

Esad Efendi. *Hükümet-i Meşrûta*. İstanbul: Mihran Matbaası, 1293/1876.

Esad Efendi. 'Mukaddime-i Takvîm-i Vekâyi.' *Takvîm-i Vekâyi*, 1247/1831.

Esad Efendi. 'Umûr-ı Dâhiliye.' *Takvîm-i Vekâyi*, 25 Cemaziyelevvel/1 November 1247/1831, 1–3.

Esad Efendi. *Üss-i Zafer*. İstanbul: Matbaa-i Âmire, 1243/1828.

Eş-Şaybani, Muhammed. *Tercüme-i Şerh-i Siyer-i Kebîr*. Translated by Mehmed Münîb Ayntâbî. Edited by Muhammed es-Serahsi. İstanbul: Matbaa-i Amire, 1241/1825.

Eton, William. *A Survey of the Turkish Empire*. London: T. Cadell and W. Davies, 1798.

Evliya Çelebi. *Narrative of Travels in Europe, Asia, and Africa in the Seventeenth Century*. Translated by Joseph Von Hammer-Purgstall. 2 vols. Vol. I. London: Oriental Translation Fund, 1846.

Fatma Âliye. *Ahmed Cevdet Paşa ve Zamanı*. İstanbul: Bedir, 1995.

Fatma Âliye Hanım. *Ahmed Cevdet Paşa ve Zamanı*. İstanbul: Kanaat Matbaası, 1913.

Feridüddin Attar. *Kitâb-ı Mâ Hazar Şerh-i Alâ Pend-i Attâr*. Edited by Hâfız Mehmed Murad Nakşibendî. İstanbul: Dar üt-Tıbaat ül-Amire, 1285/1868.

Fasih Ahmed Dede. *Münâzara-i Gül-ü Mül*. İstanbul: Tasvîr-i Efkâr Matbaası, 1285/1868.

Fasih Ahmed Dede. *Münâzara-i Rūz ü Şeb*. İstanbul: Matbaa-i Dâr-üs-Saltana, 1278/1861.

Fesch, Paul. *Constantinople aux derniers jours d'Abdul-Hamid*. Paris: Librairie des Sciences Politiques et Sociales, 1907.

Fındıklılı Şemdanizâde Süleyman Efendi, Mür'i't-tevârih. Edited by M. Münir Aktepe, *3 vols. Vol. II/A*. İstanbul: İstanbul Üniversitesi Edebiyât Fakültesi, 1976.

Fındıklılı Şemdanizâde Süleyman Efendi. *Mür'i't-tevârih*. Edited by M. Münir Aktepe, 3 vols. Vol. II/B. İstanbul: İstanbul Üniversitesi Edebiyât Fakültesi, 1976.

Forbin, Comte Auguste de. *Voyage dans le Levant en 1817 et 1818*. Paris: de l'Imprimerie royale, 1819.

Foreign Office. *Treaties between Turkey and Foreign Powers 1535–1855*. London: Foreign Office, 1855.

Fontanier, Victor. *Voyages en Orient Constantinople, Grèce: Événements politiques de 1827 à 1829*. Paris: Librairie Universelle de P. Mongie Aîné, 1829.

Fontanier, Victor. *Voyages en Orient de l'année 1821 à l'année 1829 entrepris par ordre du governement français: Turquie d'Asie*. Paris: Librairie Universelle de P. Mongie Aîné, 1829.

Fontanier, Victor. *Voyages en Orient entrepris par ordre du gouvernement français de 1830 à 1833: Deuxième Voyage en Anatolie*. Paris: Librarie de Dumont, 1834.

Fuat, Ali. 'Ricâli tanzimattan Rifat Paşa.' *Türk Târîh Encümeni Mecmûası (Yeni Seri)* I, no. 2 (1929): 1–11.

Gallenga, A. *Two Years of the Eastern Question*. 2 vols. Vol. II. London: Samuel Tinsley, 1877.

Garnett, Lucy M. J. *Turkish Life in Town and Country*. New York: G. P. Putnam's Sons, 1904.

Gautier, Théophile. *Constantinople*. Nouvelle Èdition ed. Paris: Michel Lévy Frères, 1865.

[George Jones] A civilian. *Sketches of Naval Life with Notices of Men, Manners and Scenery on the Shores of the Mediterranean in a Series of Letters from the Brandywine and Constitution Frigates*. 2 vols. Vol. II. New Heaven: H. Howe, 1829.

Gibbon, Edward. *The Decline and Fall of the Roman Empire*. 6 vols. Vol. I. New York: The Modern Library, 1943.

Girardin, Saint-Marc. 'Les voyageurs en Orient: De la Moralité des finances turques.' *Revue des Deux Mondes* 31, no. Janvier/Février (1861): 471–486.

Gövsa, İbrahim Alaettin. 'Efkârı Umûmîye.' *Yedigün Dergisi* 313, no. 13 (1939): 7–8.

Hâfız Hüseyin Ayvansarayî. *Vefeyât-ı Selâtîn ve Meşâhir-i Ricâl*. İstanbul: Edebiyât Fakültesi Matbaası, 1978.

Hâfız Mehmed. *Hakayik ül-Beyân fi Hakk-ı Cennetmekân Sultan Abdül'aziz Hân*. İstanbul: s.n., 1324/1908.

Halil Bey. 'Kudemâ'-i Mülûk-i Misriyye Târîhi.' *Mecmûa-ı Fünun* I, no. 1 (1279/1862): 34–37.

Hammer-Purgstall, J. *Histoire de l'Empire ottoman, depuis son origine jusqu'à nos jours*. Translated by J.J. Hellert. 18 vols. Vol. I. Paris: Bellizard Barthès, Dufour & Lowell, 1835.

Handjéri, Alexandre. *Dictionnaire Français-Arabe-Persan et Turc*. 3 vols. Vol. II. Moscow: L'Imprimerie de l'université impériale, 1841.

Hayreddin. 'Mesâil-i Osmaniye.' *Mecmûa-ı Maârif*, 27 Receb/13 November 1285/1868, 1–3.

Hersekli Arif Hikmet. 'Levayihü'l-Hikem'den: Lâyıha.' In *Müntahabat-ı Bedayi-yi Edebiye: Mensur Kısmı / Müntehibi*, edited by Bulgurluzâde Rıza, 150–160. İstanbul: Kader Matbaası, 1327/1910.

Hilmi Emin. *Muhâkeme-i Yeis ü Emel*. İstanbul: Tasvîr-i Efkâr Matbaası, 1867.

Hisar, Abdülhak Şinâsi. *Boğaziçi Yalıları: Geçmiş Zaman Köşkleri*. İstanbul: Varlık Yayinevi, 1968.

Huneyn b. Ishak. *Kitâbu Calinus ila Tavsirun fi'n-Nabzi li'l-Müteallimin*. Edited by Muhammed Selim Salim. Kahire: El-Hey'etü'l-Mısriyyetü'l-Âmme li'l-Kitâb, 1986.

Ibn Khaldoun. *Les Prolégomènes d'Ibn Khaldoun*. Translated by M. de Slane. 3 vols. Vol. III. Paris: Imprimerie Impériale, 1868.

Ismail Kemal Bey. *The Memoirs of Ismail Kemal Bey*. Edited by Sommerwille Story. London: Constable, 1920.

İbn Haldun. *Tercüme-i Mukaddime-i İbn Haldun: Mukaddime-i İbn Haldun'un Fasl-ı Sadisi'nin Tercümesidir* Translated by Cevdet Paşa. 3 vols. Vol. III. İstanbul: Takvîmhâne-i Amire, 1277/1860–1861.

İbrahim Müteferrika. *Usûl ül-hikem fi nizâm il-ümen*. İstanbul: Dar ül-Taba'at ül-'Amire, 1144/1732.

İhsan, Ahmet. *Matbuat Hâtıralarım, 1888–1923: Meşrûtiyet İlânina Kadar*. 2 vols. Vol. I. İstanbul: Ahmet İhsan Matbaası, 1931.

III. Selim'e Sunulan Islahat Lâyıhaları. Edited by Ergin Çağman. İstanbul: Kitâbevi, 2010.

İnal, İbnülemin Mahmud Kemal. *Son Asır Türk Şâirleri*. 3 vols. Vol. III. İstanbul: Orhaniye Matbaası, 1930.

Son Asır Türk Şâirleri. 3 vols. Vol. II. İstanbul: Orhaniye Matbaası, 1930.

Son Asır Türk Şâirleri. 3 vols. Vol. I. İstanbul: Orhaniye Matbaası, 1930.

Son Sadrâzamlar. 4 vols. Vol. II. İstanbul: Dergah Yayınlar, 1982.

Son Sadrâzamlar. 4 vols. Vol. I. İstanbul: Milli Eğitim Basımevi, 1964.

[İnal], [İbnülemin] Mahmud Kemal. 'Abdülhamid-i Sâni'nin Notları.' *Türk Târîh Encümeni Mecmûası* 13, no. 90 (1926): 60–68.

[İnal], İbnülemin Mahmud Kemal. *Kemal ül-hikme*. İstanbul: Tercüman-ı Hakikat Matbaası, 1327/1909.

İrtem, Süleyman Kâni. *Abdülhamid Devrinde Hafiyelik ve Sansür: Abdülhamid'e Verilen Jurnaller*. Edited by Osman Selim Kocahanoğlu. İstanbul: Temel Yayınları, 1999.

Bilinmeyen Abdülhamid. Edited by Osman Kocahanoğlu. İstanbul: Temel Yayınları, 2003.

Sultan Abdülhamid ve Yıldız Kamarillası: Yıldız Sarayı'nda Paşalar, Beyler, Ağalar ve Şeyhler. Edited by Osman S. Kocahanoğlu. İstanbul: Temel, 2003.

İskit, Server. *Âmme Efkârımız*. İstanbul: Gazeteciler Cemiyeti, 1959.

İsmet Efendi. 'Mukaddime: Cemiyet Nizâmnâmesidir.' *Mecmûa-ı Maârif* I, no. 1 (1283/1866): 2–5.

[el]-İstanbuli, Muhammed Cemaleddin b. Bekr. *Şerhü'l-Manzumeti'z-Zahire fî Kavânîni'l-Bahs ve'l-Münâzara*. İstanbul: Mahmûd Bey Matbaası, 1904.

Kadri Bey. 'Alaim-i Semaviye.' *Mecmûa-i Fünun* I, no. 1 (1279/1862): 37–44.

Kâmil Paşa. *Târîh-i Siyâsiye-i Devleti Âliye-i Osmaniye*. 3 vols. Vol. III. İstanbul: Matbaa-i Ahmed İhsan, 1327/1909–1910.

Kant, Immanuel. *Foundations of the Metaphysics of Morals*. Edited by Lewis White Beck. London: Macmillan, 1990.

Karatay, Fehmi Edhem. *İstanbul Üniversitesi Kütüphânesi Arapça Basmalar Alfabe Kataloğu*. İstanbul: İstanbul Üniversitesi Yayınları, 1953.

Kasap, Teodor. 'Mukaddime.' *Diyojen*, 12 Teşrin-i Sâni/24 November 1286/1870, 1.

[el]-Kaşifi, Hüseyin Vaiz. *Tefsir-i Mevakib: Tercüme-i Tefsir-i Mevâhib*. Translated by İsmail Ferruh Efendi. İstanbul: s. n., 1246/1830.

Kâtip Çelebi. *Düsturü'l-Amel li-Islahi'l-Halel*. İstanbul: Tasvîr-i Efkâr Matbaası, 1280/1863–1864.

Fezleke-i Kâtib Çelebi. 2 vols. Vol. II. İstanbul: Cerîde-i Havâdis Matbaası, 1286/1869.

Mîzânü'l-Hakk Fi İhtiyari'l-Ehakk (En Doğruyu Sevmek İçin Hak Terazisi). Edited by Orhan Şaik Gökyay. İstanbul: Milli Eğitim Basımevi, 1972.

Mîzânü'l-Hakk Fi İhtiyari'l-Ehakk. İstanbul: Ebuzziyâ Matbaası, 1306/1888–1889.

The Balance of Truth. Translated by Geoffrey L. Lewis. London: George Allen and Unwin, 1957.

[Kâtip Çelebi] Haji Khalifah. *The History of the Maritime Wars of the Turks*. Translated by James Mitchell. London: Printed for the Oriental Translation Fund by A.J. Valpy, 1831.

Kay, James Ellsworth de. *Sketches of Turkey in 1831 and 1832 by an American*. New York: J. & J. Harper, 1833.

Keçecizâde İzzet Molla. *Manzumet-ül Müsemmâ be-Mihnetkeşan*. İstanbul: Cerîde-i Havâdis Matbaası, 1269/1853.

Kératry, E. de. *Mourad V, Prince Sultan, Prisonnier D'Etat: 1840–1878 (1878) d'apres des témoins de sa vie* Paris: E. Dentu, 1878.

Kesbî Mustafa Efendi, *İbretnümâ-yı Devlet: (Tahlil ve Tenkitli Metin)*. Edited by Ahmet Öğreten. Ankara: Türk Târîh Kurumu, 2002.

Kınalızâde Ali Çelebi. *Ahlâk-i-Alâî*. 3 vols. Vol. I. Kahire: Matba'a-'i Bulak, 1248/1832.

Ahlâk-ı Alâ'î: Kınalızâde'nin Ahlâk Kitâbı. Edited by Mustafa Koç. İstanbul: Türkiye Yazma Eserler Kurumu Başkanlığı, 2014.

Koca Sekbanbaşı [Ahmed Vasıf Efendi]. *Hulâsatü'l-kelâm fi reddi'l-avâm*. İstanbul: Hilal Matbaası, 1332/1916.

Koçi Bey. *Koçi Bey Risâlesi*. Edited by Ali Kemali Aksüt. İstanbul: Vakit Matbaası, 1939.

Koçi Bey Risâlesi. Edited by Zuhûri Danışman. İstanbul: Milli Eğitim Bakanlığı, 1972.

Kömürcüyan, Eremya Çelebi. *İstanbul Târîhi: XVII. Asırda İstanbul*. Edited by Hrand D. Andreasyan. İstanbul: İstanbul Üniversitesi Edebiyât Fakültesi Yayınları, 1952.

Kuntay, Mithat Cemal. *Nâmık Kemal Devrinin İnsanları ve Olayları Arasında*. 2 vols. Vol. I. İstanbul: Maârif Matbaası, 1944.

Nâmık Kemal Devrinin İnsanları ve Olayları Arasında. 2 vols. Vol. II. İstanbul: Maârif Matbaası, 1956.

Lamartine, Alphonse de la. *Œuvres complètes de Lamartine: Histoire de la Turquie*. 8 vols. Vol. VI. Paris: Chez l'auteur, 1863.

Lane, Edward William. *An Arabic-English Lexicon*, 8 vols. Vol. I. Beirut: Librarie du Liban, 1968.

An Arabic-English Lexicon. 8 vols. Vol. II. Beirut: Librarie du Liban, 1968.

An Arabic-English Lexicon. 8 vols. Vol. V. Beirut: Librarie du Liban, 1968.

Lâtîfî. *Münâzara-i Lâtîfî*. İstanbul: Asır Matbaası, 1287/1871.

Lûtfi. 'Fevâid-i Fünun.' *Mecmûa-ı İber-i İntibah* I, no. 2 (1279/1863): 51–52.

Lütfi Paşa, *Âsafnâme*. İstanbul: Matbaa-i Amedi, 1326/1908–1909.

MacFarlane, Charles. *Constantinople in 1828: A Residence of Sixteen Months in the Turkish Capital and Provinces: With an Account of the Present State of the Naval and Military Power and of the Resources of the Ottoman Empire*. 2 vols. Vol. II. London: Saunders and Otley, 1829.

Constantinople in 1828: A Residence of Sixteen Months in the Turkish Capital and Provinces: With an Account of the Present State of the Naval and Military Power and of the Resources of the Ottoman Empire. 2 vols. Vol. I. London: Saunders and Otley, 1829.

Kismet: or, The Doom of Turkey. London: Thomas Bosworth, 1853.

Turkey and Its Destiny: The Result of Journeys Made in 1847 and 1848 to Examine into the State of that Country. 2 vols. Vol. II. Philadelphia: Lea and Blanchard, 1850.

Madden, Richard Robert. *The Turkish Empire: In Its Relations with Christianity and Civilization*. 2 vols. Vol. I. London: T. Cautley Newby, 1862.

Mahmud b. Osman Bursevi Lâmî Çelebi. *Münâzara-i Sultan Bahar ba şehriyar-ı Şita*. İstanbul: İzzet Efendi Matbaası, 1290/1873–1874.

Mahmud Celâleddin Paşa. *Mir'ât-ı Hakikat*. 3 vols. Vol. III. İstanbul: Matbaa-i Osmaniye, 1326/1908.

Mir'ât-ı Hakikat. 3 vols. Vol. I. İstanbul: Matbaa-i Osmaniye, 1326/1908.

Mahmud Cevâd İbnü'ş-Şeyh Nâfi. *Maârif-i Umûmîye Nezâreti Târîhçe-i Teşkilat ve İcraatı*. Edited by Muhammed Ali bin Kemal. İstanbul: Matbaa-i Âmire, 1338/1919–1920.

Mahmud Paşa Falâki. *Mısır Ehramları: Kangı Maksada Mebni Vücuda Getirilmiş ve Ne Vakit Bina Edilmiştir?* Translated by M. Muhiddin. İstanbul: Karabet Matbaası, 1311/1893.

Mallouf, N. *Dictionnaire Turc-Français avec la pronanciation figuré*. 2 vols. Vol. I. Paris: Maisonneuve, 1863.

Marmontel, Jean-François *Oeuvres complettes de M. Marmontel, historiographe de France*. 13 vols. Vol. VI. Paris: Née de la Rochelle, 1787.

The Meaning of the Glorious Qur'an: Text and Explanatory Translation. Translated by Marmaduke William Pickthall. Beltsville, MD: Amana Publications, 1996.

Meclis-i Meb'ûsan 1293–1877 Zabıt Cerîdesi. Edited by Hakkı Tarık Us. 2 vols. Vol. I. İstanbu: Vakit Gazetesi Matbaası, 1939.

Mehmed Ata Bey. 'Memâlik-i Osmaniyede Sansürün Târîhi.' *İkdam*, 5 Kanûnuevvel/5 December 1334/1918, 2.

Mehmed Esad Efendi. *Vak'anüvis Esad Efendi Târîhi*. Edited by Ziyâ Yılmazer. İstanbul: OSAV Yayınları, 2000.

Mehmed [Faik] Memdûh Paşa. *Eser-i Memdûh*. İstanbul: Matbaa-i Âmire, 1289/1872.

Esvât-i Sudûr. İzmir: Vilâyet Matbaası, 1328/1912.

Hal'ler, İclaslar. İstanbul: Matbaa-i Hayriye ve Şürekâsı, 1329/1913.

Mir'ât-ı Şuûnât. İzmir: Ahenk Matbaası, 1328/1910–1911.

Mehmed Gâlib Bey. *Sâdullah Paşa yâhûd Mezardan Nidâ*. İstanbul: Matbaa-i Ebüzziyâ, 1327/1909.

Mehmed İzzed. 'Boğaziçi, Şirket-i Hayriye.' *Servet-i Fünun* 57, no. 1485 (1924): 169–172.

Mehmed Ramiz. 'Mebâhis-i Fennîyye ve Edebiyye, Hıfzıssıhha, Seyâhat, Terâcim-i Ahvâl ve Roman Gibi Mütenevviadan Bahseder.' *Manzara* I, no. 1 (1303/1887): 1.

Mehmed Sadık Rifat Paşa. *Müntahabât-ı Âsâr*. 11 vols. Vol. XI. İstanbul: Takvîmhâne-i Amire, 1275/1858.

Müntahabât-ı Asâr-ı Rifat Paşa: İdâre-i Hükümetin Ba'zı Kavâid-i Esâsiyesine Mutazammın Rifat Paşa Merhumun Kaleme Aldığı Risâledir. 12 vols. Vol. XII. İstanbul: Takvîmhâne-i Amire, 1275/1859.

Mehmed Salahi. *Kamûs-i Osmani*. İstanbul: Mahmud Bey Matbaası, 1313/1895.

Mehmed Süreyya. *Sicill-i Osmani yahud Tezkire-i Meşâhir-i Osmaniye*. Edited by Mustafa Keskin, Ayhan Öztürk and Ramazan Tosun. 4 vols. Vol. IV. İstanbul: Sebil Yayınevi, 1995.

Sicill-i 'Osmanî, yahud, Tezkire-i Meşâhîr-i 'Osmaniyye. 4 vols. Vol. III. İstanbul: Matba'a-i Âmire, 1308/1890.

Mehmed Tevfik. *Kâfile-i Şuarâ: Meşâhir-i Şuarâ-ı Osmaniye'nin Terâcim-i Ahvâliyle Ba'zı âsâr-ı Şi'riyyelerini Câmidir*. İstanbul: s.n., 1290/1873.

Asır: Mevâd-ı politikiyye ve mebâhis-i ilmiyye dair Osmanlı Gazetesidir 1287/1870: Sâhibi: [Çaylak] Tevfik. Edited by Ali Emre Özyıldırım. Ankara: Türk Târîh Kurumu, 2014.

Meşhûri. *Selanikli Meşhûri Efendinin Dîvânı*. Selanik: Selanik Vilâyet Matbaası, 1292/1875.

The Message of the Qur'an. Translated by Muhammad Asad. Beirut: Dar al-Andalus, 1980.

Meynard, Barbier de. *Dictionnaire turc-français: Supplément aux dictionnaires publiés jusqu'à ce jour*. 2 vols. Vol. I. Paris: Ernest Leroux, 1881.

Midhat Paşa. *Midhat Paşa: Hayât-ı Siyâsiyesi, Hidâmatı, Menfâ Hayâtı: Tabsıra-i İbret*. Edited by Ali Haydar Midhat. 2 vols. Vol. I. İstanbul: Hilal Matbaası, 1325/1908.

Mill, J. S. *Dissertations and Discussions: Political, Philosophical, and Historical*. 3 vols. Vol. II. Boston: William V. Spencer, 1864.

On Liberty and Other Writings. Edited by Stefan Collini. Cambridge: Cambridge University Press, 1989.

[Mîzâncı Murad]. 'İfâde-i Mahsûsa - İzâhat-ı Lâzıme.' *Mîzân*, 30 Receb/20 January 1312/1895, 2353–2357.

Mohammad As'ad Efendi. *Précis Historique de la destruction du corps des Janissaires par le Sultan Mahmoud: en 1826*. Translated by A. P. Caussin de Perceval. Paris: F. Didot frères, 1833.

Montesquieu. *Considérations sur les causes de la grandeur des Romains et de leur décadence: aussi Dialogue de Sylla et d'Eucrate*. Paris: Didot, 1802.

Moreau, César. *Précis sur la franc-maçonnerie: son origine, ses doctrines et opinion diverses sur cette ancienne et celebre institution*. Paris: Ledoyen, 1855.

Morris, Edward Joy. *The Turkish Empire, Embracing the Religion, Manners and Customs of the People, with a Memoir of the Reigning Sultan and Omer Pacha*. Philadelphia: Lindsay and Blakiston, 1855.

[el]-Murteza, Ebü'l-Kâsım Alemülhüdâ Ali b. Hüseyin Şerif. *Eş-Şihab fi'ş-Şeyb ve'ş-Şebâb*. İstanbul: Matbaatü'l-Cevaib, 1302/1884–1885.

Musâhipzâde Celâl. *Eski İstanbul Yaşayışı*. İstanbul: Türkiye Yayınevi, 1946.

Mustafa Naîmâ. *Târîh-i Naîmâ: Ravzâtü'l-Hüseyn fi Hulâsati Ahbari'l-Hafîkayn*. 6 vols. Vol. I. İstanbul: Matbaa-i Âmire, 1280/1863–1864.

Târîh-i Naîmâ (Ravzâtü'l-Hüseyn fi Hulâsati Ahbari'l-Hafîkayn). Edited by Mustafa İpşirli. 4 vols. Vol. II. Ankara: Türk Târîh Kurumu, 2007).

Târîh-i Naîmâ (Ravzâtü'l-Hüseyn fi Hulâsati Ahbari'l-Hafîkayn). Edited by Mustafa İpşirli. 4 vols. Vol. IV. Ankara: Türk Târîh Kurumu, 2007).

Mustafa Nuri Paşa. *Netâyic ül-Vuku'ât: Kurumları ve Örgütleriyle Osmanlı Târîhi*. Edited by Neşet Çağatay. 4 vols. Vol. III. Ankara: Türk Târîh Kurumu Yayınları, 1980.

[Mustafa Refik]. 'Esâs-ı Medeniyet.' *Mir'ât* I, no. 1 (1279/1863): 2–4.

Mustafa Refik. 'Esbab-ı Servet.' *Mir'ât* I, no. 1 (1279/1863): 5–11.

Mustafa Sâmi Efendi. *Avrupa Risâlesi*. İstanbul: Takvîm-i Vekâyi Matbaası, 1257/1840.

Münif Efendi. 'Cemiyet Merkezinde Kırâathâne Küşâdı.' *Mecmûa-ı Fünun* II, no. 22 (1280/1864): 423–427.

'Cemiyet-i İlmiye-i Osmaniye'de 1278 Senesi Zilkadesinin On Üçü Târîhinde Münif Efendinin Husûs-u Mezkûra Dair Telaffuz Eylediği Makaledir.' *Mecmûa-ı Fünun* İkinci Sene, no. 14 (1280/1863): 74–77.

'Dârülfünun Dersleri.' *Mecmûa-ı Fünun* I, no. 8 (1279/1869): 330–333.

'Dârülfünun'da Ders-i Âmm Küşâdı.' *Mecmûa-ı Fünun* I, no. 5 (1279/1862): 258–260.

'Dârülfünun'da Ders-i Âmm Vuku'-u Küşâdı.' *Mecmûa-ı Fünun* I, no. 7 (1279/1862): 301–304.

'Ehemmiyet-i Terbiye-i Sıbyan.' *Mecmûa-ı Fünun* I, no. 5 (1279/1862): 176–185.

'Mecmûa-i Fünun'un Mazhar Olduğu Hüsn-ü Kabulden Dolayı Âmmeye Teşekkür.' *Mecmûa-ı Fünun* I, no. 4 (1279/1862): 134–137.

'Mukaddime.' *Mecmûa-ı Fünun* I, no. 1 (1279/1862): 18–21.

'Mukayese-i İlm ü Cehl.' *Mecmûa-ı Fünun* I, no. 1 (1279/1862): 21–34.

'Sûret-i Hâl-i Cemiyet.' *Mecmûa-ı Fünun* İkinci Sene, no. 24 (1280/1864): 480–483.

'Zuhûr-i Tasvîr-i Efkâr.' *Mecmûa-ı Fünun* I, no. 1 (1279/1862): 46–50.

Mütercim Asım Efendi. *Asım Târîhi*. 2 vols. Vol. I. İstanbul: Cerîde-i Havâdis Matbaası, 1284/1867.

Nâmık Kemal. 'Avrupa Şarkın Asâyişini İster.' *Hürriyet*, 7 Decembre 1868, 5–8.

'Bir Muvafakkiyet.' *İbret*, 16 Muharrem/16 March 1290/1873, 1–2.

'Bizde Adem Yetişmiyor.' *Hürriyet*, 14 December 1868, 1–2.

'Cevap.' *İbret*, 27 Rebiyülahir/4 July 1289/1872, 2.

'Efkâr-ı Umûmîye.' *İbret*, 26 Şaban/28 October 1289/1872, 1–3.

'Fransa İhtilâli.' *Hürriyet*, 21 June 1869, 4–6.

'Gazeteciliğe Dair.' *İbret*, 21 Zilkade/20 January 1289/1873, 1.

'Hadd-i Sâni.' *İbret*, 30 Rebiyülahir/7 July 1289/1872.

'Hadd-i Tedib.' *İbret*, 27 Rebiyülahir/4 July 1289/1872, 3–4.

'Hâriciye Nezâreti.' *Hürriyet*, 26 April 1869, 1–6.
'Hasta Adem.' *Hürriyet*, 7 December 1868, 1–2.
'Hubbü'l-Vatan Mine'l-İman.' *Hürriyet*, 29 June 1868, 1–2.
'İbret.' *İbret*, 11 Rebiyülahir/18 June 1289/1872, 1–2.
'[İbret Gazetesi].' *İbret*, 26 Zilkade/25 January 1289/1873, 1.
'İfâde-i Meram.' *İbret*, 27 Receb/30 September 1289/1872, 1–2.
'İhtilafi ümmeti rahmetün.' *Hürriyet*, 6 July 1868, 4.
'[İngiltere Hâriciye Vekili Lord Stanley].' *Hürriyet*, 30 Novembre 1868, 1–5.
İntibah: Ali Bey'in Sergüzeştine Havidir. İstanbul: s.n., 1291/1876.
'İstikbal.' *İbret*, 7 Rebiyülahir/14 June 1289/1872, 1–2.
'Konsoloslar.' *İbret*, 15 Şevval/16 December 1289/1872, 1.
'Matbaa-i Amire.' *Hadîka*, 15 Şevval/16 December 1289/1872, 1–2.
'Matbuat-i Osmaniye.' *Hadîka*, 18 Ramazan/19 November 1289/1872, 1–2.
'Me'mûrlara Dair.' *Hürriyet*, 2 November 1868, 1–8.
'Meyelân-ı Âlem.' *İbret*, 30 Rebiyülahir/7 July 1289/1872, 2.
Mukaddime-i Celal. İstanbul: Matbaa-i Ebuzziyâ, 1305/1888.
'Mülkümüzün Servetine Dair Geçen Numerodaki Makaleye Zeyl.' *Hürriyet*, 17 August 1868, 1–4.
'Muvâzene-i Mâliye.' *Hürriyet*, 30 August 1869.
Nâmık Kemal'in Tâlim-i Edebiyât Üzerine Bir Risâlesi. Edited by Necmettin Halil Onan. Ankara: Milli Eğitim Bakanlığı, 1950.
'Romalıların Esbab-ı İkbal ve Zevâli Hakkında Mülahazat.' *Mir'ât* I, no. 2 (1279/1863): 22–25.
'Sekizinci Numaradaki Mâliye Bendine Zeyl.' *Hürriyet*, 31 August 1868, 1–3.
'Tanzimat.' *İbret*, 5 Ramazan/6 November 1289/1872, 1–2.
'Terakki.' *İbret*, 3 Ramazan/4 November 1289/1872, 1–3.
'Türkçe Matbuat.' *İbret*, 16 Zilkade/15 January 1289/1873, 1–2.
'Usûl-i Meşveret Hakkında Dördüncü Nüshamızdaki Ben Üzerine İrad olunan Ba'zı İtirazlara Cevâben Bir Zâta Yazılmış Mektûb.' *Hürriyet*, 14 September 1868, 5–8.
'Usûl-i Meşverete Dair Geçen Nümerolarda Münderic Mektûbların Altıncısı.' *Hürriyet*, 26 October 1868, 6–8.
'Usûl-i Meşverete Dair Geçen Nümerolarda Münderic Mektûbların Beşincisi.' *Hürriyet*, 19 October 1868, 6–8.
'Usûl-i Meşverete Dair Geçen Nümerolarda Münderic Mektûbların Üçüncüsü.' *Hürriyet*, 29 September 1868, 5–8.
'Veşavirhum fi'l-Emr.' *Hürriyet*, 20 July 1868, 1–4.

Neale, F. A. *Islamism: Its Rise and Its Progress, or the Present and Past Conditions of the Turks*, 2 vols. Vol. II. London: J. Madden, 1854.

Necip Asım [Yazıksız]. 'Cennet-Mekan Firdevs-Aşiyan: Sultan Abdülaziz Han Hazretleri'nin Avrupa Seyâhatnâmesidir.' *Türk Târîh Encümeni Mecmûası* VIII–XI, no. 9–62 (1335–1337 [1919–1921]): 90–102.
Kitâb. İstanbul: Matbaa-i Safa ve Enver, 1311/1894.
Nev'izâde Atai. *Münâzara-i Tuti ile Zag*. İstanbul: Terakki Matbaası, 1287/1870–1871.
Oğulukyan, Georg. *Georg Oğulukyan'ın Ruznâmesi: 1806 — 1810 İsyanları: III. Selim, IV. Mustafa, II. Mahmud ve Alemdâr Mustafa Paşa*. Translated by Hrand D. Andreasyan. Edited by Hrand D. Andreasyan. İstanbul: Edebiyât Fakültesi Basımevi, 1972.
Orpilyan, Serkiz, and Seyyid Abdulzâde Mehmed Tâhir. *Mahzen ül-Ulûm*. İstanbul: A. Asaduryan Şirket-i Mürettibiye Matbaası, 1308/1890–1891.
Osman Emin. *Hadîkat-ül Üdebâ*. İstanbul: Matbaa-ı Aramyan, 1299/1883.
Osman Hayri Mürşit Efendi. *Terbiyetü'l-Ezhân*. İstanbul: Matbaa-ı Âmire, 1289/1872.
Osman Nuri. *Abdülhamid-i Sâni Devr-i Saltanatı Hayât-ı Husûsîye ve Siyâsiyesi*. 3 vols. Vol. I. İstanbul: İbrahim Hilmi Kitâbhânesi, 1327/1909–1910.
Ozansoy, Halit Fahri. *Edebiyâtçılar Çevremde*. Ankara: Sümerbank Kültür Yayınları, 1970.
Pâkalın, Mehmet Zeki. *Osmanlı Târîh Deyimleri ve Terimleri Sözlüğü*. 3 vols. Vol. I. İstanbul: M. E. B. Devlet Kitapları, 1971.
Pardoe, Miss. *The Beauties of the Bosphorus*. London: G. Virtue, 1838.
The City of the Sultan and Domestic Manners of the Turks in 1836. 2 vols. Vol. I. London: Henry Colburn, 1837.
Paton, Andrew Archibald. *The Modern Syrians; or Native Society in Damascus, Aleppo, and the Mountains of the Druses, from Notes Made in Those Parts during the Years 1841–2–3*. London: Longman, Brown, Green, and Longmans, 1844.
Pears, Edwin. *Forty Years in Constantinople: The Recollections of Sir Edwin Pears, 1873–1915*. London: Herbert Jenkins, 1916.
Porter, Sir James, and Sir George Larpent Larpent. *Turkey; Its History and Progress: From the Journals and Correspondence of Sir James Porter, Fifteen Years Ambassador at Constantinople; Continued to the Present Time with a Memoir of Sir James Porter by His Grandson Sir George Larpent, Bart*. 2 vols. Vol. II. London: Hurst and Blackett, 1854.
Rado, Şevket. 'Tanınmış Edebiyâtçılar İstanbul'un Nerelerinde Oturdular.' *Hayât Târîh Mecmûası* I, no. I (1966): 19–20.
Recâîzâde Mahmud Ekrem. *Araba Sevdası: Musavver Milli Hikâye*. İstanbul: Âlem Matbası, 1314/1896.

Redhouse, J. W. *A Lexicon English and Turkish; Shewing, in Turkish, the Literal, Incidental, Figurative, Colloquial, and Technical Significations of the English Terms*. London: B. Quaritch, 1861.

Redhouse, James W. *An English and Turkish Dictionary in Two Parts: English and Turkish and Turkish and English*. London: Bernard Quaritch, 1856.

Rosen, Georg. *Geschichte der Türkei von dem Siege der reform im Jahre 1826 bis zum Pariser Tractat vom Jahre 1856*, 2 vols. Vol. I. Leipzig: S. Hirzel, 1866.

Rıza Tahsîn. *Mir'ât-ı Mekteb-i Tıbbiyye* 2 vols. Vol. I. Dersaâdet: Kader Matbaası, 1328/1910–1911.

Rieu, Charles. *Catalogue of the Persian Manuscripts in the British Museum*. London: British Museum, 1879.

Ruhsan Nevvare, and Tahsîn Nahid. *Jön Türk: Üç Perdelik Milli Temâşâ*. İstanbul: Kitâbhâne-i Leon Lütfi, 1325/1908.

Saçaklızâde Mehmed b. Ebubekir Mar'aşi. *Takrîr u Kavânîn fi'l-Aâab*. İstanbul: Matbaa-i Âmire, 1289/1872–1873.

Safvet Paşa. 'Suyun Mahiyet ve Enva-i ve Havass-i Hekimiye ve Kimyeviyesi.' *Mecmûa-ı Fünun* I, no. 10 (1279/1983): 419–424.

Said Halim Paşa. *Buhranlarımız*. İstanbul: Şems Matbaası, 1329/1911.

Saint-Denys, A. de Juchereau de. *Revolutions de Constantinople en 1807 et 1808: Précédées d'observations générales sur l'état actuel de l'empire ottoman, et de considérations sur la Grèce*. 2 vols. Vol. II. Paris: Brissot-Thivars, 1819.

Sakızlı Ohannes Efendi. 'İlm-i Servet-i Milel.' *Mecmûa-ı Fünun* I, no. 2 (1279/1862): 86–92.

Sâmî Paşazâde Hasan Bey. 'Ayetullah Bey ve Yeni Osmanlılar.' *Hadisat-ı Hukukiyye ve Târîhiyye* III, no. 2 (1341/1925): 1–8.

Selaniki Mustafa Efendi. *Târîh-i Selaniki*. Edited by Mehmet İpşirli. 2 vols. Vol. II. İstanbul: İstanbul Üniversitesi Edebiyât Fakültesi Yayınları, 1989.

Târîh-i Selaniki. Edited by Mehmet İpşirli. 2 vols., vol I. Ankara: Türk Târîh Kurumu, 1999.

Selanikli Şemseddin. *Makedonya: Târîhçe-i Devr-i İnkılab*. İstanbul: Artin Asaduryan Matbaası, 1324/1908.

Sertoğlu, Mithat. *Osmanlı Târîh Lügatı*. İstanbul: Enderun Kitâbevi, 1986.

Sinapian. 'Le Chirket-i-Hairié: Influence de ce service sur la santé des passagers.' *Gazette Médicale d'Orient* VII, no. 1 (1863): 1–8.

Slade, Adolphus. *Records of Travels in Turkey, Greece, etc. and of a Cruise in the Black Sea, with the Capitan Pasha, in the Years 1829, 1830, and 1831*. 2 vols. Vol. I. London: Saunders and Otley, 1833.

Records of Travels in Turkey, Greece, etc. and of a Cruise in the Black Sea, with the Capitan Pasha, in the Years 1829, 1830, and 1831. London: Saunders and Otley, 1854.

Sublime Porte Ministère des Finances. *Budget des recettes et des dépenses de l'exercice 1863–1864 et Compte-Rendu de l'emploi des ressources extraordinaires crées pour le retrait du Papier-monnaie et le remboursement de la dette flottante.* Constantinople: Imprimerie du Journal de Constantinople, 1863.

Suâvi, Ali. 'Rusya'da Dahi Efkâr-ı Umûmîyye Var Bizde Yok ' *Ulum [Muvakkaten]*, 10 Şaban/16 November 1286/1869, 139–44.

Sua[v]i'nin fi 28 Desambr 1875 (Evahir zi'lkada 1292) Târîhiyle İngiltere Hâriciye Nâzırı Lord Derbi'ye Yazmış Olduğu Mektûbun Türkçe Tercümesi Paris: Victor Goupy, 1876.

Subhi Mehmed Efendi. *Subhi Târîhi: Sâmî ve Şakir Târîhleri ile Birlikte 1730–1744 (İnceleme ve Karşılaştırma Metin).* Edited by Mesut Aydıner. İstanbul: Kitâbevi, 2007.

Suchodolska, K. C. *Souvenirs anecdotiques sur la Turquie (1820–1870) par Wanda.* Paris: Firmin-Didot, 1884.

Süheyli Efendi. *Târîh-i Misr-ı Cedîd, Târîh-i Misr-ı Kadim.* Edited by İbrahim Müteferrika. İstanbul: Dar ül-Taba'at ül-'Amire, 1142/1730.

Süleyman Nazif. *İki Dost.* İstanbul: Kanaat Kütüphânesi, 1343/1925.

Nâmık Kemal. İstanbul: İkdam Matbaası, 1340/1922.

'Nigar Hanım.' *Servet-i Fünun* 62, no. 101–1575 (1926): 354–358.

Süleyman Paşa. *Hiss-i İnkilab.* İstanbul: Tanin Matbaası 1326/1908.

Süleyman Paşazâde Sâmî. *Süleyman Paşa Muhâkemesi: 1293 Osmanlı - Rus Muharebesi [Rumeli Harb Orduları Umûm Kumandanı Merhum Süleyman Paşa'nın Muhâkemesidir].* İstanbul: Matbaa-i Ebuzziyâ, 1328/1912.

Şakir, Ziyâ. *Çırağan Sarayında 28 Sene: Beşinci Murad'ın Hayâtı.* İstanbul: Üstün Eserler Neşriyat Evi, 1943.

Şânî-zâde Mehmed 'Atâ'ullah. *Şânî-zâde Târîhi.* Edited by Ziyâ Yılmazer. 2 vols. İstanbul: Çamlıca, 2008.

Târîh-i Şânîzâde. 4 vols. Vol. I. İstanbul: Cerîde-i Havâdis 1291/1874–1875.

Târîh-i Şânîzâde. 4 vols. Vol. II. İstanbul: Cerîde-i Havâdis 1291/1874–1875.

Târîh-i Şânîzâde. 4 vols. Vol. III. İstanbul: Cerîde-i Havâdis Matbaası, 1291/1874–1875.

Târîh-i Şânîzâde. 4 vols. Vol. IV. İstanbul: Cerîde-i Havâdis Matbaası, 1291/1874–1875.

Şem'dânî-zâde Fındıklılı Süleyman Efendi. *Mür'i't-Tevârih.* Edited by Münir Aktepe. 4 vols. Vol. I. İstanbul: Edebiyât Fakültesi Yayınları, 1976.

Mür'i't-Tevârih. Edited by Münir Aktepe. 4 vols. Vol. II. İstanbul: Edebiyât Fakültesi Matbaası, 1978.

Şemseddin Sâmî. *Kamûs-ı Fransevî: Fransızca'dan Türkçe'ye Lügat*. İstanbul: Mihran Matbaası, 1299/1882.

Kamûs-ı Türki 2 vols. Vol. I. İstanbul: İkdam Matbaası, 1317/1899.

Kamus-ül Âlem. 4 vols. Vol. II. İstanbul: Mihran Matbaası, 1306/1889.

Şeyhi Mehmed Efendi. *Eş-Şekaiku'n-Nu'maniyye ve Zeyilleri: Vekâyiü'l-fudala*. Edited by Abdülkadir Özcan. İstanbul: Çağrı Yayınları, 1989.

Şeyhülislam Ebusuud Efendi Fetvâları Işığında 16. Asır Türk Hayâtı. Edited by Mehmet Ertuğrul Düzdağ. İstanbul: Enderun Kitâbevi, 1972.

Şinâsi, İbrahim. 'Bend-i Mahsûs: İstanbul Sokakları Tenvîr ve Tathîri Hakkındadır.' *Tasvîr-i Efkâr*, 28 Zilkade/5 May 1280/1864, 1–2.

'Mukaddime.' *Tasvîr-i Efkâr*, 15 Haziran/27 June 1278/1862, 1.

'Mukaddime.' *Tercüman-ı Ahvâl*, 6 Rebiyülahir/22 October 1277/1860, 1.

Müntehabât-ı Tasvîr-i Efkâr Edited by Tevfik Ebüzziyâ. Kostantiniye: Matbaa-i Ebüzziyâ, 1303/1885.

Şirket-i Hayriye. *Boğaziçi: Şirket-i Hayriye: Târîhçe, Sâl-nâme*. İstanbul: Ahmet İhsan ve Şürekası, 1914.

Tahsîn Paşa. *Abdülhamit Yıldız Hâtıraları*. İstanbul: Muallim Ahmet Halit Kitaphânesi, 1931.

Tassy, Garcin de. 'Principes de sagesse touchant l'art de gouverner par Rizwan-ben-abd'oul-mannan Ac-hissari.' *Journal Asiatique* I, no. IV (1824): 213–226, 83–90.

Taşköprüzâde Ahmed [b. Mustafa] Efendi. *Eş-Şakâiku'n-Nu'mâniyye fî ulemâi'd-Devleti'l-Osmâniyye*. Translated by Muharrem Tan. İstanbul: İz Yayıncılık, 2007.

Mevzuatü'l-Ulum. Translated by Kemaleddin Mehmed Efendi. 2 vols. Vol. I. Dersaâdet: İkdam Matbaası, 1313/1895–1896.

Risâle-i Taşköprü. İstanbul: Arif Bey Matbaası, 1313/1895–1896.

Tercüme-i Şakayık-ı Nu'maniye. Translated by Mecdi Mehmed Efendi İstanbul: Dar'üt-Tabaat ül-Amire, 1269/1852.

Thouvenel, Edouard. 'Constantinople sous Abdul-Medjid.' *Revue des Deux Mondes* XXI, no. Seris IV (1840): 68–89.

Thouvenel, Louis. *Trois années de la question d'Orient, 1856–1859: d'après les papiers inédits de M. Thouvenel*. Paris: C. Lévy, 1897.

de Tocqueville, Alexis. *The Republic of the United States of America and Its Political Institutions, Reviewed and Examined*. Translated by Henry Reeves. New York: A. S. Barnes, 1855.

Toderini, Abbé. *De la littérature des Turcs*. Translated by Abbé Cournand. 2 vols. Vol. I. Paris: Chez Poinçot Libraire, 1789.

Togan, Zeki Velidi. *Hâtıralar*. Ankara: Türkiye Diyanet Vakfı Yayınları, 2015.

Tott, François. *Mémoires du Baron de Tott sur les Turcs et les Tartares*. 4 vols. Amsterdam: s.n., 1784.

Memoires of the Baron de Tott on the Turks and the Tartars. 2 vols. London: J. Jarvis, 1785.

Ubicini, A. La *Turquie actuelle*. Paris: Librarie de L. Hachette, 1855.

Lettres sur la Turquie, ou, Tableau statistique, religieux, politique, administratif, militaire, commercial, etc. de l'Empire ottoman, depuis le khatti-cherif de Gulkhané (1839). Paris: Librarie Militaire de J. Dumaine, 1853.

Vahan Efendi. 'Fevâid-i Şirket.' *Mecmûa-ı Fünun* I, no. 8 (1279/1863): 343–353.

Verrollot, Dr. 'Hygiène Publique: Rapport sur une motion relative à l'hygiène publique, lu dans la séance du 10 Avril 1857.' *Gazette Médicale d'Orient* 1, no. 3 (1857): 33–37.

Vincent, John Martin, and Ada S. Vincent. 'Constitution of the Kingdom of Belgium.' *Annals of the American Academy of Political and Social Science* 7 (1896): 1–40.

Walsh, Rev. R. *A Residence at Constantinople during a Period Including the Commencement, Progress, and Termination of the Greek and Turkish Revolutions*. 2 vols. Vol. II. London: Frederick Westley and A. H. Davis, 1836.

A residence at Constantinople During a period Including the Commencement, Progress and Termination of the Greek and Turkish Revolutions. 2 vols. Vol. I. London: Westley & Davis, 1836.

Walsh, Rev. R., and Thomas Allom. *Constantinople and the Scenery of the Seven Churches of Asia Minor*. London: Fisher 1839.

Washburn, George. *Fifty Years in Constantinople and Recollections of Robert College*. Boston: Houghton Mifflin Company, 1909.

Wehr, Hans. *A Dictionary of Modern Written Arabic: Arabic-English*. Edited by J. M. Cowan. London: Macdonald & Evans Ltd., 1991.

Wilkinson, William. *An Account of the Principalities of Wallachia and Moldavia with Various Political Observations Relating to Them*. London: Longman, 1820.

Yazıcıoğlu Mehmed Efendi. *Muhammediye: Kitâb-ı Muhammediyye*. Edited by Amil Çelebioğlu, 4 vols. Vol. I. İstanbul: Tercüman Gazetesi, 1975.

Yusuf. 'Varaka.' *Basîret*, 2 Zilkade/3 February 1286/1870, 2.

Yusuf Kâmil Paşa. 'Mevâd-i Hikemiye-i Telemak.' *Mecmûa-ı Fünun* I, no. 12 (1279/1863): 488–495.

Ziyâ Gökalp. 'Halkçılık.' *Yeni Mecmûa*, no. 32, 14 Şubat 1918, 102.

Ziyâ Paşa. 'İhtilafü Ümmeti rahmetun.' In *Numûne-i Edebiyât-ı Osmaniye*, edited by Ebüzziyâ Mehmed Tevfik, 272–276. Kostantiniye: Matbaa-i Ebüzziyâ, 1330 (1911/1912).

ح. 'Meşrûtiyet-i İdâre – Beyân-ı Hakkiyet.' *Vakit*, 9 Şevval/28 October 1293/ 1876, 1–3.

ع ,ل. 'Jurnaller.' *Tanin*, no. 457 (27 Zilkade/10 December 1327/1909): 2.

Secondary Sources

Abdulhak Adnan [Adıvar]. *La science chez les Turcs ottomans*. Paris: G.-P. Maisonneuve, 1939.

Osmanlı Türklerinde İlim. İstanbul: Maârif Vekâleti, 1943.

Abdülhalim, Muhyiddin. *er-Re'yü'l-amm fi'l-İslâm*. Kahire: Mektebetü'l-Hanci, 1982.

Abou-El-Haj, Rifa'at 'Ali. *Formation of the Modern State: The Ottoman Empire, Sixteenth to Eighteenth Centuries*. New York: Syracuse University Press, 2005.

'The Ottoman Nâsihatnâme as a Discourse over 'Morality'.' In *Mélanges Professeur Robert Mantran*, edited by Abdeljelil Temimi, 17–30. Zaghouan: Centre d'études et de recherches ottomanes, 1988.

Abu-Manneh, Butrus. 'The Sultan and the Bureaucracy: The Anti-Tanzimat Concepts of Grand Vizier Mahmud Nedim Paşa.' *International Journal of Middle East Studies*, 22, no. 3 (1990): 257–274.

Acton, John Emerich Edward Dalberg. *Essays on Freedom and Power*. Boston, MA: Beacon Press, 1949).

Agamben, Giorgio. *The Signature of All Things On Method*. Translated by Luca D'Isanto and Kevin Attell. New York: Zone Books, 2009.

Ágoston, Gábor. *Guns for the Sultan: Military Power and the Weapons Industry in the Ottoman Empire*. Cambridge: Cambridge University Press, 2005.

'Military Transformation in the Ottoman Empire and Russia, 1500–1800.' *Kritika: Explorations in Russian and Eurasian History* 12, no. 2 (2011): 281–319.

'The Ottoman Empire and the Technological Dialogue Between Europe and Asia: The Case of Military Technology and Know-How in the Gunpowder Age.' In *Science between Europe and Asia: Historical Studies on the Transmission, Adoption and Adaptation of Knowledge*, edited by Feza Günergün and Dhruv Raina, 27–40. New York: Springer, 2011.

Ahmad, Feroz. *The Young Turks: The Committee of Union and Progress in Turkish Politics, 1908–1914*. Oxford: The Clarendon Press, 1969.

Ahmed Emin [Yalman]. *The Development of Modern Turkey as Measured by Its Press*. New York: Colombia University, 1914.

Akarlı, Engin Deniz. 'Maslaha: From Common Good' to 'Raison d'état' in the Experience of Istanbul Artisans, 1730–1840'.' In *Hoca, 'Allame, Puits De Science: Essays in Honor of Kemal Karpat*. Edited by Kaan Durukan & Robert Zens & A. Zorlu-Durukan, 63–79. İstanbul: The Isis Press, 2010.

Akdağ, Mustafa. *Büyük Celâli Karışıklıklarının Başlaması*. Erzurum: Atatürk Üniversitesi Fen-Edebiyât Fakültesi, 1963.

Akgündüz, Ahmet, and Said Öztürk. *Yedi Yüzüncü Yılında Bilinmeyen Osmanlı*. İstanbul: Osmanlı Araştırmaları Vakfı, 1999.

Akı, Niyazi. *XIX. Yüzyıl Türk Tiyatrosu Târîhi*. Ankara: Ankara Üniversitesi Basımevi, 1963.

Aksan, Virgina H. *An Ottoman Statesman in War and Peace: Ahmed Resmi Efendi, 1700–1783*. Leiden: E. J. Brill, 1995.

Aksan, Virginia. 'Breaking the Spell of the Baron de Tott: Reframing the Question of Military Reform in the Ottoman Empire, 1760–1830.' *The International History Review* 24, no. 2 (2002): 253–277.

Ottomans and Europeans: Contacts and Conflicts. İstanbul: Isis Press, 2004.

'Ottoman Military and Social Transformations, 1826–28: Engagement and Resistance in a Moment of Global Imperialism.' In *Empires and Autonomy: Moments in the History of Globalization*. Edited by Stephen M. Streeter, John C. Weaver, and William D. Coleman, 61–78. Vancouver: UBC Press, 2010).

'The One-Eyed Fighting the Blind: Mobilization, Supply, and Command in the Russo-Turkish War of 1768–1774.' In *International History Review*, 15, no. 2 (1993): 221–238.

Aktepe, Münir. *Patrona İsyanı*. İstanbul: İstanbul Üniversitesi Edebiyât Fakültesi Yayınları, 1958.

Akünal, Dündar. '[Server Tanilli'nin *Târîh ve Toplum*'un].' *Toplumsal Târîh* I, no. 11 (1984): 63.

Akyıldız, Ali. *Mümin ve Müsrif Bir Padişâh Kızı: Refia Sultan*. İstanbul: Târîh Vakfı Yurt Yayınları, 1998.

Tanzimat Dönemi Osmanlı Merkez Teşkilâtında Reform: 1836–1856. İstanbul: Eren, 1993.

Algar, Hamid. 'An Introduction to the History of Freemansonry in Iran.' *Middle Eastern Studies* 6, no. 3 (1970): 276–296.

Alkan, Mehmet Ö. 'Osmanlı'da Cemiyetler Çağı.' *Târîh ve Toplum* 40, no. 238 (2003): 4–12.

Anafarta, Nigar. *Osmanlı İmparatorluğu İle Lehistan (Polonya) Arasındaki Münasebetlerle İlgili Târîhi Belgeler*. İstanbul: Bilmen, 1979.

Anscombe, Frederick F. *State, Faith, and Nation in Ottoman and Post-Ottoman Lands*. Cambridge: Cambridge University Press, 2014.

And, Metin. *Tanzimat ve İstibdat Döneminde Türk Tiyatrosu: 1839–1908*. İstanbul: Türkiye İş Bankası Kültür Yayınları, 1972.

Anderson, Amanda. *The Powers of Distance: Cosmopolitanism and the Cultivation of Detachment*. Princeton, NJ: Princeton University Press, 2001.

Anderson, Benedict. *Imagined Communities: Reflections on the Origin and Spread of Nationalism*. London: Verso, 2006.

Andrews, Walter G. 'Singing the Alienated 'I': Guattari, Deleuze and Lyrical Decodings of the Subject in Ottoman Poetry.' *The Yale Journal of Criticism* VI, no. 2 (1993): 195–207.

Andrews, Walter G., and Mehmet Kalpaklı. *The Age of Beloveds: Love and the Beloved in Early-Modern Ottoman and European Culture and Society*. Durham, NC: Duke University Press, 2005.

Anisimov, Evgenii V. *The Reforms of Peter the Great: Progress Through Coercion in Russia*. Translated by John T. Alexander. New York: Sharpe, 1993.

Ariès, Philippe. 'Introduction.' In *A History of Private Life: Passions of the Renaissance*, edited by Roger Chartier, 1–11. Cambridge, MA: Belknap Press of Harvard University Press, 1989.

Arkun, Aram. 'Into the Modern Age: 1800–1913.' In *The Armenians: Past and Present in the Making of National Identity*, edited by Edmund Herzig and Marina Kurkchiyan. Oxford: RoutledgeCurzon, 2005.

Arrighi, Giovanni, Iftikhar Aḥmad, and Min-wen Shih. 'Western Hegemonies in World-Historical Perspective.' In *Chaos and Governance in the Modern World System*, edited by Giovanni Arrighi and Beverly J. Silver, 217–271. Minneapolis: University of Minnesota Press, 1999.

Asad, Talal. 'Muslims and European Identity: Can Europe Represent Islam?' In *The Idea of Europe: From Antiquity to the European Union*, edited by Anthony Pagden, 209–228. Cambridge: Woodrow Wilson Center Press & Cambridge University Press, 2002.

Atasoy, Nurhan. *Yıldız Fotoğraf Albümlerinden Yadigâr-ı İstanbul*. İstanbul: Akkök Yayınları, 2007.

Atsız, Nihal. 'Nâmık Kemal.' *Çınaraltı*, no. 22 (1942): 8–9.

Auerbach, Eric. *Literary Language and Its Public in Late Latin Antiquity and in the Middle Ages*. Translated by Ralph Manheim. Princeton, NJ: Princeton University Press, 1993.

Ayalon, Ami. *The Press in the Arab Middle East: A History*. Oxford: Oxford University Press, 1995.

Aydın, Bilgin, İlhami Yurdakul and İsmail Kurt. *Şeyhülislamlık (Bab-ı Meşihat) Arşivi Defter Kataloğu*. İstanbul: Türkiye Diyânet Vakfı İslâm Araştırmaları Merkezi, 2006.

Badawi, Abdurrahman. 'The Way of Hellenizers: The Transmission of Greek Philosophy to Islamic Civilization.' In *Culture and Learning in Islam*, edited by Ekmeleddin İhsanoğlu, 383–398. Paris: UNESCO Publishing, 2003.

Bağış, Ali İhsan. *Osmanlı Ticâretinde Gayrî Müslimler: Kapitülasyonlar, Avrupa Tüccarları, Beratlı Tüccarlar, Hayriye Tüccarları (1750–1839)*: Turhan Kitâbevi, 1983.

Baker, Keith Michael. *Inventing the French Revolution: Essays on French Political Culture in the Eighteenth Century*. Cambridge: Cambridge University Press, 1990.

Bakhtin, M. M. *The Dialogic Imagination: Four Essays by M. M. Bakhtin* Edited by Caryl Emerson and Michael Holquist. Austin: University of Texas Press, 2004.

Balaghi, Shiva. 'Nationalism and Cultural Production in Iran, 1848–1906.' PhD diss., The University of Michigan, 2008.

Banarlı, Nihad Sâmi. *Resimli Türk Edebiyâtı Târîhi: Destanlar Devrinden Zamânımıza Kadar*. 2 vols. Vol. II. İstanbul: M. E. B. Devlet Kitapları, 1971).

Barkan, Ömer. 'Edirne Askerî Kassamı'na Âit Tereke Defterleri (1545–1659).' *Belgeler* III, no. 5–6 (1966): 1–479.

Barker, Hannah. *Newspapers, Politics, and Public Opinion in Late Eighteenth-Century England*. Oxford: Oxford University Press, 1998.

Barker, Hannah, and Simon Burrows. 'Introduction.' In *Press, Politics and the Public Sphere in Europeand North America, 1760–1820*, edited by Hannah Barker and Simon Burrows. Cambridge: Cambridge University Press, 2002.

Barnes, John Robert. *An Introduction to Religious Foundations in the Ottoman Empire*. Leiden: Brill, 1987.

Barshay, Andrew E. *State and Intellectual in Imperial Japan: Public Man in Crisis Berkeley*, Los Angeles: University of California Press, 1988.

Barthes, Roland. *Image Music Text*. Translated by Stephen Heath. London: Harper Collins, 1977.

Bauer, Wilhelm. *Public Opinion*. Edited by Edwin R. A. Seligman. 15 vols. Vol. XII, Encylopaedia of the Social Sciences. London: Macmillan Publishers, 1934.

Bayly, C. A. *The Birth of the Modern World, 1780–1914*. Cornwall: Blackwell Publishing, 2004.

Empire and Information: Intelligence Gathering and Social Communication in India, 1780–1870. Cambridge: Cambridge University Press, 2000.

Imperial Meridian: The British Empire and the World, 1780 – 1830. London: Longman, 1997.

Origins of Nationality in South Asia: Patriotism and Ethical Government in the Making of Modern India. Oxford: Oxford University Press, 1998.

Recovering Liberties: Indian Thought in the Age of Liberalism and Empire. Cambridge: Cambridge University Press, 2012.

Baysal, Jale. *Müteferrika'dan Birinci Meşrûtiyete Kadar Osmanlı Türklerinin Bastıkları Kitaplar* İstanbul: Edebiyât Fakültesi Basımevi, 1968.

Beales, Derek. *Enlightenment and Reform in Eighteenth-Century Europe*. London: I.B. Tauris, 2005.

Behar, Cem. *Ali Ufkî ve Mezmurlar*. İstanbul: Pan Yayıncılık, 1990.

A Neighborhood in Ottoman Istanbul: Fruit Vendors and Civil Servants in the Kasap İlyas Mahalle. New York: State University of New York Press, 2003.

Beinin, Joel. *Workers and Peasants in the Modern Middle East*. Cambridge: Cambridge University Press, 2001.

Bekiroğlu, Nazan. *Şâir Nigar Hanım*. İstanbul: İletişim Yayınları, 1998.

Belanger, Terry. 'Publishers and Writers in Eighteenth-Century England.' In *Books and Their Readers in Eighteenth-Century England*, edited by Isabel Rivers, 5–26. London: St. Martin's, 1982.

Benjamin, Walter. *Reflections: Essays, Aphorisms, Autobiographical Writings*. Edited by Peter Demetz. New York: Harcourt Brace Jovanovich, 1978.

Bérenger, Jean. 'Les vicissitudes de l'alliance militaire franco-turque (1520–1800).' In *Guerres et paix en Europe centrale aux époques moderne et contemporaine: mélanges d'histoire des relations internationales offerts à Jean Bérenger*, edited by Daniel Tollet, 297–330. Paris: Presses de l'université de Paris-Sorbonne, 2003.

Berkes, Niyazi. *The Development of Secularism in Turkey*. London: Routledge, 1964.

Türkiye'de Çağdaşlaşma. Edited by Ahmet Kuyaş. İstanbul: Yapı Kredi Yayınları, 2002.

Berridge, Geoff. *British Diplomacy in Turkey, 1583 to the Present: A Study in the Evolution of the Resident Embassy*. Leiden: Brill, 2009.

Bertram, Carel. *Imagining the Turkish House: Collective Visions of Home*. Austin: University of Texas Press, 2008.

Beydilli, Kemal. 'Müteferrika ve Osmanlı Matbaası: 18. Yüzyılda İstanbul'da Kitâbiyat.' *Toplumsal Târîh*, no. 128 (2004): 44–52.

Türk Bilim ve Matbaacılık Târîhinde Mühendishâne: Mühendishâne Matbaası ve Kütüphânesi. İstanbul: Eren, 1995.

Beydilli, Kemal. Sekbanbaşı Risâlesinin Müellifi Hakkında, *Türk Kültürü İnceleme Dergisi* 12 (2005): 221–224.

Beyhan, Mehmet Ali. 'Yeniçeri Ocağının Kaldırılışı Üzerine Ba'zı Düşünceler- Vak'a-yı Hayriyye.' In *Osmanlı*, edited by Güler Eren, 258–272. Ankara: Yeni Türkiye Yayınları, 1999.

Bhabha, Homi K. *The Location of Culture*. London: Routledge, 1994.

Bilgegil, Kaya. *Ziyâ Paşa Üzerinde Bir Araştırma*. Ankara: Atatürk Üniversitesi Basımevi, 1970.

Bilgegil, M. *Kaya. Yakın Çag Türk Kültür ve Edebiyâti Üzerinde Araştırmalar I: Yeni Osmanlılar*. Ankara: Atatürk Universitesi, 1976.

Blackbourn, David. *History of Germany, 1780–1918: The Long Nineteenth Century*. Second ed. Padstow, UK: Blackwell, 2003.

Bloch, Marc. *Les rois thaumaturges*. Paris: Gallimard, 1983.

Borsay, Peter. *The English Urban Renaissance: Culture and Society in the Provincial Town 1660–1770*. Oxford: Clarendon Press, 1991.

Bossenga, Gail. 'The Financial Origins of the French Revolution.' In *From Deficit to Deluge: The Origins of the French Revolution*, edited by Thomas E. Kaiser and Dale K. Van Kley, 37–66. Palo Alto, CA: Stanford University Press, 2011.

Bouquet, Olivier. *Les Pachas du sultan: Essai sur les agents supérieurs de l'État ottoman (1839–1909)*. Leuven: Peters, 2007.

Bourdieu, Pierre. *The Rules of Art: Genesis and Structure of the Literary Field*. Stanford, CA: Stanford University Press, 1996.

Bowie, Karin. *Scottish Public Opinion and the Anglo-Scottish Union, 1699–1707*. Woodbridge, UK: Royal Historical Society, 2007.

Boyar, Ebru, and Kate Fleet. *A Social History of the Ottoman Empire*. Cambridge: Cambridge University Press, 2010.

Bradley, James E. *Religion, Revolution and English Radicalism: Nonconformity in Eighteenth-Century Politics and Society*. Cambridge: Cambridge University Press, 1990.

Bradley, John. *Voluntary Associations in Tsarist Russia: Science, Patriotism, and Civil Society*. Cambridge, MA: Harvard University Press, 2009.

Braudel, Fernand. *Civilization and Capitalism, 15th-18th Century: The Wheels of Commerce*. Los Angeles: University of California Press, 1992.

Browne, Edward Granville. *A History of Persian Literature Under Tartar Dominion*. Cambridge: Cambridge University Press, 1920.

Literary History of Persia. 4 vols. Vol. IV. London: T. Fisher Unwin, 1924.

Brummett, Palmira. *Image and Imperialism in the Ottoman Revolutionary Press: 1908–1911*. New York: State University of New York Press, 2000.

Budak, Ali. *Mecmûa-i Fünun: Osmanlının İlk Bilim Dergisi*. İstanbul: Bilge Kültür Sanat, 2011.

Burke, Peter. 'The Courtier.' In *Renaissance Characters*, edited by Eugenio Garin, 98–123. Chicago: University of Chicago Press, 1997.

Burrows, Simon. *Blackmail, Scandal and Revolution: London's French Libellistes, 1758–1792*. Manchester: Manchester University Press, 2006.

Cavallo, Guglielmo, and Roger Chartier. 'Introduction.' In *A History of Reading in the West*, edited by Guglielmo Cavallo and Roger Chartier, 1–36. Amherst: University of Massachusetts Press, 2003.

Certeau, Michel de. *The Practice of Everyday Life*. Translated by Steven Rendall. Berkeley: University of California Press, 1984.

Cezar, Mustafa. *Osmanlı Târîhinde Levendler*. İstanbul: İstanbul Güzel Sanatlar Akademisi, 1965.

Cezar, Yavuz. 'Osmanlı Mâli Târîhinde 'Eshâm' Uygulamasının İlk Dönemlerine İlişkin Ba'zı Önemli Örnek ve Belgeler.' *Toplum ve Bilim* 12 (1981): 124–43.

Osmanlı Mâliyesinde Bunalım ve Değişim Dönemi. İstanbul: Alan Yayıncılık, 1986.

Chambers, Richard L. 'The Education of a Nineteenth-Century Ottoman Alim, Ahmed Cevdet Pasa.' *International Journal of Middle East Studies* 4, no. 4 (1973): 440–64.

'The Ottoman Ulema and the Tanzimat.' In *Scholars, Saints, and Sufis: Muslim Religious Institutions in the Middle East since 1500*, edited by Nikki R. Keddie, 33–46, 1972.

Chartier, Roger. *Cultural History: Between Practices and Representations*. Translated by Lydia G. Cochrane. Ithaca, NY: Cornell University Press, 1988.

Chatterjee, Partha. 'Two Poets and Death: On Civil Society in the Non-Christian World.' In *Questions of Modernity* edited by Timothy Mitchell, 35–48. Minneapolis: University of Minnesota Press, 2000.

Chittick, William C. *The Sufi Path of Knowledge: Ibn al-'Arabi's Metaphysics of Imagination*. New York: State University of New York Press, 1989.

Clair, William St. *The Reading Nation in the Romantic Period*. Cambridge: Cambridge University Press, 2004.

Clark, Peter. *British Clubs and Societies 1580–1800: The Origins of an Associational World*. Oxford: Oxford University Press, 2002.

Cohen, Jean L., and Andrew Arato. *Civil Society and Political Theory*. Cambridge, MA: MIT Press, 1993.

Collis, Robert. *The Petrine Instauration: Religion, Esotericism and Science at the Court of Peter the Great, 1689–1725*. Leiden: Brill, 2011.

Conrad, Sebastian. 'Enlightenment in Global History: A Historiographical Critique.' *American Historical Review* 117, no. 4 (2012): 999–1027.

The Quest for the Lost Nation: Writing History in Germany and Japan in the American Century. Los Angeles: University of California Press, 2010.

Cook, Michael. *Forbidding Wrong in Islam*. Cambridge: Cambridge University Press, 2003.

Coser, Lewis A. *Men of Ideas: A Sociologist's View*. New York: Free Press, 1965.
Cowans, Jon. *To Speak for the People: Public Opinion and the Problem of Legitimacy in the French Revolution*. London: Routledge, 2001.
Cracraft, James. *The Petrine Revolution in Russian Culture*. Cambridge, MA: Harvard University Press, 2009.
Crane, Susan A. *Collecting and Historical Consciousness in Early Nineteenth-Century Germany*. Ithaca, NY: Cornell University Press, 2000.
Cunningham, Allan. 'The Sick Man and the British Physician.' *Middle Eastern Studies* 17, no. 2 (1981): 147–73.
Cust, Richard. 'News and Politics in Early Seventeenth-Century England.' *Past and Present* 112, no. 1 (1986): 60–90.
Çam, Nusret. 'Türk Sanatında Sultanların İşveren Olarak Estetik Rolleri.' *Vakıflar Dergisi*, no. XXVII (1999): 5–14.
Çamuroğlu, Reha. *Yeniçerilerin Bektaşiliği ve Vaka-i Şerriye*. İstanbul: Ant Yayınları, 1991.
Çelik, Hüseyin. *Ali Suavî ve Dönemi*. İstanbul: İletişim Yayınları, 1994.
Çelik, Zeynep. *The Remaking of Istanbul: Portrait of an Ottoman City in the Nineteenth Century*. Berkeley: University of California Press, 1986.
Çizakça, Murat. *A Comparative Evolution of Business Partnerships: The Islamic World and Europe, with Specific Reference to the Ottoman Archives*. Leiden: E.J. Brill, 1996.
Çubukçu, İbrahim Agah. *Türk Düşünce Târîhinde Felsefe Hareketleri*. Ankara: Ankara Üniversitesi Basımevi, 1986.
Dağlı, Nuran, and Belma Aktürk. *Hükümetler ve Programları*. 3 vols. Vol. I. Ankara: TBMM Basımevi, 1988.
Dalton, Susan. *Engendering the Republic of Letters: Reconnecting Public and Private Spheres in Eighteenth-Century Europe*. Montreal: McGill-Queen's University Press, 2004.
Darling, Linda T. *Revenue-Raising and Legitimacy: Tax Collection and Finance Administration in the Ottoman Empire, 1560–1660*. Leiden: E.J. Brill, 1996.
Davison, Roderic H. 'The Question of Ali Pasa's Political Testament.' *International Journal of Middle East Studies* 11, no. 2 (1980): 209–225.
Reform in the Ottoman Empire, 1856–1876. Princeton, NJ: Princeton University Press, 1963.
'Turkish Attitudes Concerning Christian-Muslim Equality in the Nineteenth Century*.' *The American Historical Review* 59, no. 4 (1954): 844–864.
Demir, Uğur. '1768 Savaşı Öncesi Osmanlı Diplomasisi (1755–1768).' PhD diss., Marmara University, 2012.

Demirel, Fatmagül. *II. Abdülhamid Döneminde Sansür*. İstanbul: Bağlam Yayıncılık, 2007.

'Osmanlı Devleti'nde Telif Hakları Sorunu.' *Bilgi ve Bellek* III, no. 5 (2006): 93–103.

Deringil, Selim. *The Well-Protected Domains: Ideology and the Legitimation of Power in the Ottoman Empire 1876–1909*. London: I. B. Tauris, 1999.

Derrida, Jacques. *Archive Fever: A Freudian Impression*. Chicago: University of Chicago Press, 1998.

Dumont, Paul. 'Freemasonry in Turkey: A By-Product of Western Penetration.' *European Review* 13, no. 03 (2005): 481–93.

'La franc-maçonnerie dans l'Empire ottoman: La loge grecque Prométhée à Jannina.' *Revue du monde musulman et de la Méditerranée*, no. 66 (1992): 105–112.

'La franc-maçonnerie ottomane et les 'idées françaises' à l'époque des Tanzimat.' *Revue du monde musulman et de la Méditerranée* (1989): 150–159.

Dunning, Chester S. L. *Russia's First Civil War: The Time of Troubles and the Founding of the Romanov Dynasty*. University Park, PA: Pennsylvania State University Press, 2001.

Eisenstadt, S.N. 'Multiple Modernities.' In *Comparative Civilizations and Multiple Modernities*, edited by S.N. Eisenstadt. Leiden: E. J. Brill, 2003.

Ekhtiar, Maryam Dorreh. 'The Dar al-Funun: Educational Reform and Cultural Development in Qajar Iran.' PhD diss., New York University, 1994.

Ekinci, Mehmet Fatih. *Türkiye'nin Mâli İntiharı: Kapitülasyonlar ve 1838 Balta Limanı Ticâret Sözleşmeleri'nden Sevres Andlaşması'na*. İstanbul: Barış Platin Kitap, 2008.

Eldem, Edhem. 'Batılılaşma, Modernleşme ve Kozmopolitizm: 19. Yüzyıl Sonu ve 20. Yüzyıl Başında İstanbul.' In *Osman Hamdi Bey ve Dönemi*, edited by Zeynep Rona, 12–26. İstanbul: Târîh Vakfı Yurt Yayınları, 1993.

French Trade in Istanbul in the Eighteenth Century. Leiden: Brill, 1999.

'Geç Osmanlı Döneminde Masonluk ve Siyaset Üzerine İzlenimler.' *Toplumsal Târîh*, no. 33 (1996): 16–28.

'Hayretü'l-Azime fi İntihalati'l-Gâribe: Voltaire ve Şânîzâde Mehmed Ataullah Efendi.' *Toplumsal Târîh*, no. 237 (2013): 18–28.

'Le commerce français d'Istanbul au XVIIIe siècle: D'une présence tolérée à une domination imposée.' *Le Négoce International XIIIe-XXe siècles*, edited by François M. Crouzet, 181–190. Paris: Economica, 1989.

Eley, Geoff. 'Nations, Publics, and Political Cultures: Placing Habermas in the Nineteenth Century.' In *Habermas and the Public Sphere*, edited by Craig Calhoun, 289–340. Cambridge, MA: MIT Press, 1992.

Ellis, Markman. 'Coffee-House Libraries in Mid-Eighteenth-Century London.' *The Library: The Transactions of the Bibliographical Society* 10, no. 1 (2009): 3–40.

Erdem, Yasemin Tümer, and Halime Yiğit. *Bacıyân-ı Rûm'dan Günümüze Türk Kadınının İktisadî Hayâttaki Yeri*. İstanbul: İstanbul Ticâret Odası 2010.

Eren, İsmail. 'Cemiyet-i İlmiye-i Osmaniye'nin Fa'âliyet ve Te'sirleri.' *Belgelerle Türk Târîhi Dergisi*, no. 45 (1971): 10–12.

Ergin, Osman. *Türk Maârif Târîhi*. 5 vols. Vol. II. İstanbul: Eser Matbaası, 1977.

Ergun, Sadettin Nüzhet. *Nâmık Kemal: Hayâtı ve Şiirleri*. İstanbul: Yeni Şark Kitaphânesi, 1933.

Ersoy, Ahmet A. 'On the Sources of the 'Ottoman Renaissance': Architectural Revival and Its Discourse During the Abdülaziz Era (1861–1876).' PhD diss., Harvard University, 2000.

Esen, Nükhet. *Modern Türk Edebiyâtı Üzerine Okumalar*. İstanbul: İletişim Yayıncılık, 2006.

Evered, Emine. *Empire and Education Under the Ottomans: Politics, Reform and Resistance from the Tanzimat to the Young Turks*. London: I. B. Tauris, 2012.

Evtuhov, Catherine. *Portrait of a Russian Province: Economy, Society, and Civilization in Nineteenth-Century Nizhnii Novgorod*. Pittsburgh: University of Pittsburgh Press, 2011.

Fahmy, Khaled. *All the Pasha's Men*. Cambridge: Cambridge University Press, 2004.

Fanon, Franz. *The Wretched of the Earth*. New York: Grove Press, 1968.

Faroqhi, Suraiya. *The Ottoman Empire and the World Around It*. London: I. B. Tauris, 2004.

Subjects of the Sultan: Culture and Daily Life in the Ottoman Empire. London: I.B. Tauris, 2005.

Feldman, Walter. *Music of the Ottoman Court: Makam, Composition and the Early Ottoman Instrumental Repertoire*. Berlin: Verlag für Wissenschaft und Bildung, 1996.

Fiala, Andrew. *The Just War Myth: The Moral Illusions of War*. Plymouth: Rowman & Littlefield, 2008.

Findley, Carter V. *Bureaucratic Reform in the Ottoman Empire: The Sublime Porte, 1789–1922*. Princeton, NJ: Princeton University Press, 1980.

Findley, Carter Vaughn. *Ottoman Civil Officialdom: A Social History*. Princeton, NJ: Princeton University Press, 1989.

Finkel, Caroline. *Osman's Dream: The Story of the Ottoman Empire 1300–1923*. New York: Basic Books, 2005.

Finkelstein, David, and Alistair McCleery. *An Introduction to Book History*. London: Taylor & Francis, 2013.

Fleischer, Cornell H. *Bureaucrat and Intellectual in the Ottoman Empire: The Historian Mustafa Âli (1541–1600)*. Princeton, NJ: Princeton University Press 1986.

'Preliminaries to the Study of the Ottoman Bureaucracy.' *Journal of Turkish Studies*, no. 10 (1986): 135–41.

Fleming, Katherine E. *The Muslim Bonaparte: Diplomacy and Orientalism in Ali Pasha's Greece*. Princeton, NJ: Princeton University Press, 1999.

Fortna, Benjamin C. 'Education and Autobiography at the End of the Ottoman Empire.' *Die Welt des Islams* 41, no. 1 (2001): 1–31.

Imperial Classroom: Islam, the State, and Education in the Late Ottoman Empire. Oxford: Oxford University Press, 2002.

Learning to Read in the Late Ottoman Empire and the Early Turkish Republic. London: Palgrave, 2011.

'Reading between Public and Private in the Late Ottoman Empire and the Early Turkish Republic.' *Comparative Studies of South Asia, Africa and the Middle East* XXX, no. 3 (2010): 563–573.

Foucault, Michel. *Archaeology of Knowledge*. Translated by Alan Sheridan. London: Routledge, 2007.

Discipline and Punish: The Birth of the Prison. Translated by Alan Sheridan. New York: Vintage Books, 1995.

'What is an Author?' In *The Foucault Reader*, edited by Paul Rabinow, 101–120. New York: Pantheon Books, 1984.

'What Is Enlightenment?' In *The Foucault Reader*, edited by Paul Rabinow, 32–50. New York: Pantheon Books, 1984.

Fox, Adam. 'Rumour, News and Popular Political Opinion in Elizabethan and Early Stuart England.' *The Historical Journal* 40, no. 3 (1997): 597–620.

Fraser, Nancy. *Justice Interruptus: Critical Reflections on the 'Postsocialist' Condition*. New York: Routledge, 1997.

'Rethinking the Public Sphere: A Contribution to the Critique of Actually Existing Democracy.' In *Habermas and the Public Sphere*, edited by Craig Calhoun, 109–143. Cambridge, MA: MIT Press, 1992.

Freud, Sigmund. *The Interpretation of Dreams*. Translated by James Strachey. New York: Basic Books, 2010.

Fyfe, Aileen. *Science and Salvation: Evangelical Popular Science Publishing in Victorian Britain*. Chicago: University of Chicago Press, 2004.

Genç, Mehmet. 'L'Économie ottomane et la guerre au XVIIIe siècle.' *Turcica* 27 (1995): 177–196.

Osmanlı İmparatorluğunda Devlet ve Ekonomi. İstanbul: Ötüken Yayınları, 2000.

Georgeon, François. *Abdülhamid II: Le sultan calife, 1876 – 1909*. Paris: Fayard, 2003.

'Les usages politiques du ramadan, de l'Empire ottoman à la république de Turquie.' In *Ramadan et politique*, edited by Fariba Adelkhan and François Georgeon, 21–39. Paris: CNRS Éditions, 2000.

'Lire et écrire à la fin de l'Empire ottoman: Quelques remarques introductives.' *Revue du monde musulman et de la Méditerranée*, no. 75–76 (1995): 169–179.

Gerber, Haim. *State, Society, and Law in Islam: Ottoman Law in Comparative Perspective*. New York: State University of New York Press, 1994.

Gershoni, Israel, and James P. Jankowski. *Egypt, Islam, and the Arabs: The Search for Egyptian Nationhood, 1900–1930*. New York: Oxford University Press, 1986.

Geyikdağı, V. *Necla. Foreign Investment in the Ottoman Empire: International Trade and Relations 1854–1914*. London: I.B. Tauris, 2011.

Gibb, E.J. W. *A History of Ottoman Poetry*. Edited by Edward G. Brown. 6 vols. Vol. IV. London: Luzac, 1905.

Gibb, H. A. R., and Harold Bowen. *Islamic Society and the West: A study of the Impact of Western Civilization on Moslem Culture in the Near East*. 2 vols. Vol. I. Oxford: Oxford University Press, 1969.

Gibb, Hamilton A. R., and Harold Bowen. *Islamic Society and the West: A Study of the Impact of Western Civilization on Moslem Culture in the Near East*. 2 vols. Vol. I. Oxford: Oxford University Press, 1950.

Gildea, Robert. *Children of the Revolution: The French, 1799–1914*. Cambridge, MA: Harvard University Press, 2008.

Gökman, Muzaffer. *Ahmet Rasim: İstanbul'u Yaşayan ve Yaşatan Adam: Hayâtı ve Eserleri*. 2 vols. Vol. II. İstanbul: Çelik Gülersoy Vakfı, 1989.

Gökyay, Orhan Şaik. *Kâtip Çelebi*. Ankara: Kültür ve Turizm Bakanlığı, 1986.

Golombek, Lisa, and Donald Wilber. *The Timurid Architecture of Iran and Turan*. 2 vols. Vol. I. Princeton, NJ: Princeton University Press, 1992.

Goodman, Dena. *The Republic of Letters: A Cultural History of the French Enlightenment*. Ithaca, NY: Cornell University Press, 1996.

Gordon, Daniel. "Public Opinion' and the Civilizing Process in France: The Example of Morellet.' *Eighteenth-Century Studies* 22, no. 3 (1989): 302–328.

Gradeva, Rossitsa. 'Osman Pazvantoğlu of Vidin: Between Old and New.' In *The Ottoman Balkans, 1750–1830*, edited by Frederick F. Anscombe, 115–163. Princeton, NJ: Markus Wiener Publishers, 2005.

Gramsci, Antonio. *Further Selections from the Prison Notebooks. Edited by Derek Boothman*. Minneapolis: University of Minnesota Press, 1995.

Green, Abigail. 'Intervening in the Public Sphere: German Governments and the Press, 1815–1870.' *The Historical Journal* 44, no. 1 (2001): 155–175.

Günergun, Feza. 'Derviş Mehmed Emin Pacha (1817–1879), serviteur de la science et de l'Etat ottoman.' In *Médecins et ingénieurs ottomans à l'âge des nationalismes*, edited by Méropi Anastassiadou-Dumont, 171–183. Paris: Maisonneuve et Larose & Institut Français d'Etudes Anatoliennes, 2003.

Güran, Tevfik. *Osmanlı Mâli İstatistikleri: Bütçeler 1841–1918*. 7 vols. Vol. VII. Ankara: Devlet İstatistik Enstitüsü, 2003.

Gürlek, Dursun. *Ayaklı Kütüphâneler*. İstanbul: Kubbealtı Neşriyâtı, 2003.

Habermas, Jürgen. *L'Espace public: Archéologie de la publicité comme dimension constitutive de la société bourgeoise*. Translated by Marc B. de Launay. Paris: Payot, 1986.

'The Public Sphere.' In *Jürgen Habermas on Society and Politics: A Reader*, edited by Steven Seidman. Boston: Beacon Press, 1989.

'The Public Sphere: An Encylopedia Article (1964).' *New German Critique*, no. 3 (1974): 45–48.

The Structural Transformation of the Public Sphere: An Inquiry into a Category of Bourgeois Society. Translated by Thomas Burger with the assistance of Frederick Lawrence, Studies in Contemporary German Social Thought. Cambridge, MA: MIT Press, 1993. Reprint, Fifth.

Strukturwandel der Öffentlichkeit; Untersuchungen zu einer Kategorie der bürgerlichen Gesellscahft. Neuwied: H. Luchterhand, 1962.

Haley, Charles D. 'The Desperate Ottoman: Enver Paşa and the German Empire - I.' *Middle Eastern Studies* 30, no. 1 (1994): 1–51.

Halman, Talat S. *Rapture and Revolution: Essays on Turkish Literature*. Syracuse, NY: Syracuse University Press, 2007.

Hamadeh, Shirine. 'Ottoman Expressions of Early Modernity and the 'Inevitable' Question of Westernization.' *Journal of the Society of Architectural Historians* 63, no. 1 (2004): 32–51.

Hämeen-Anttila, Jaakko. *Maqama: A History of a Genre*. Göttingen: Harrassowitz, 2002.

Hanioğlu, [M.] Şükrü. *A Brief History of the Late Ottoman Empire*. Princeton, NJ: Princeton University Press, 2010.

Doktor Abdullah Cevdet ve Dönemi. İstanbul: Üçdal Neşriyat, 1981.

'Notes on the Young Turks and the Freemasons, 1875–1908.' *Middle Eastern Studies* 25, no. 2 (1989): 186–197.

Hanna, Nelly. *In Praise of Books: A Cultural History of Cairo's Middle Class, Sixteenth to the Eighteenth Century*. Syracuse, NY: Syracuse University Press, 2003.

Harris, Tim. *London Crowds in the Reign of Charles II: Propaganda and Politics from the Restoration Until the Exclusion Crisis*. Cambridge: Cambridge University Press, 1990.
Harth, Erica. 'The Salon Woman Goes Public ... or Does She?' In *Going Public: Women and Publishing in Early Modern France*, edited by Erica C. Goldsmith and Dena Goodman, 179–193. Ithaca, NY: Cornell University Press, 1995.
Haskell, Francis. 'A Turk and His Pictures in Nineteenth-Century Paris.' *Oxford Art Journal* 5, no. 1, Patronage (1982): 40–47.
Hatemi, Hüseyin. *Tanzimat ve Meşrûtiyet Döneminde Derneklerin Gelişimi*. Edited by Vedat Çakmak, Murat Belge and Fahri Aral. 6 vols. Vol. I, Tanzimat'tan Cumhûriyet'e Türkiye Ansiklopedisi. İstanbul: İletişim Yayınları, 1985.
Hathaway, Jane. *The Politics of Households in Ottoman Egypt: The Rise of the Qazdaglis*. Cambridge: Cambridge University Press, 2002.
Hathaway, Jane, and Karl K. Barbir. *The Arab Lands under Ottoman Rule, 1516–1800*. Harlow: Pearson Education, 2008.
Heilbron, J. L. *Electricity in the 17th and 18th Century: A Study of Early Modern Physics*. Berkeley: University of California Press, 1979.
Elements of Early Modern Physics. Berkeley: University of California Press, 1982.
Henige, David. *Historical Evidence and Argument*. Madison: University of Wisconsin Press, 2005.
Herbst, Susan. *Politics at the Margin: Historical Studies of Public Expression Outside the Mainstream*. Cambridge: Cambridge University Press, 1994.
Hershlag, Z. Y. *Introduction to the Modern Economic History of the Middle East*. Leiden: Brill, 1964.
Heyd, Uriel. 'The Ottoman 'Ulema and Westernization in the Time of Selim III and Mahmud II.' In *Studies in Islamic History and Civilization*, edited by Uriel Heyd, 63–96. Jerusalem: Hebrew University, 1961.
Hızlı, Mefail. 'Osmanlı Medreselerinde Okutulan Dersler ve Eserler.' *Uludağ Üniversitesi İlahiyat Fakültesi Dergisi* 17, no. 1 (2008): 25–46.
Hobsbawm, Eric. *The Age of Revolution 1789–1848*. New York: Vintage Books, 2010.
Holborn, Hajo. *A History of Modern Germany: 1840–1945*. 3 vols. Vol. III. Princeton, NJ: Princeton University Press, 1982.
Hourani, Albert. *Arabic Thought in the Liberal Age 1798–1939*. Cambridge: Cambridge University Press, 1962.
The Emergence of the Modern Middle East. Berkeley: University of California Press, 1981.

Huch, Ronald K., and Paul R. Ziegler. *Joseph Hume: The People's M.P.* Ephrata, PA: American Philosophical Society, 1985.

Hupchick, Dennis P. *The Bulgarians in the Seventeenth Century: Slavic Orthodox Society and Culture Under Ottoman Rule.* Jefferson, NC: McFarland, 1993.

Imber, Colin. *The Ottoman Empire, 1300–1650: The Structure of Power.* New York: Palgrave Macmillan, 2002.

Inkster, Ian. 'The Public Lecture as an Instrument of Science Education for Adults — the Case of Great Britain, c. 1750 – 1850.' *Paedagogica Historica* 20, no. 1 (1980): 80–107.

Işın, Ekrem. 'Osmanlı Bilim Târîhi: Münif Paşa ve Mecmûa-i Fünun.' *Târîh ve Toplum* I, no. 11 (1984): 61–66.

İhsanoğlu, Ekmeleddin. *Osmanlı Devleti ve Medeniyeti Târîhi.* 2 vols. Vol. I. İstanbul: IRCICA, 1994.

Osmanlı İlmî ve Meslekî Cemiyetleri. İstanbul: Edebiyât Fakültesi Basımevi, 1987.

Science, Technology, and Learning in the Ottoman Empire: Western Influence, Local Institutions, and the Transfer of Knowledge. Aldershot, UK: Ashgate/Variorum, 2004.

İnalcık, Halil. 'Osmanlı Padişâhı.' *Ankara Üniversitesi Siyasal Bilgiler Fakültesi Dergisi* XII, no. 4 (1958): 68–79.

The Ottoman Empire: The Classical Age 1300–1600. Translated by Norman Itzkowitz and Colin Imber. London: Weidenfeld and Nicolson, 1973.

Şâir ve Patron. Ankara: Doğubatı, 2003.

'Sened-i ittifâk ve Gülhâne Hatt-i Hümâyûnu.' *Belleten* XXVIII, no. 112 (1964): 603–622.

'Şikayet Hakkı: Arz-ı Hâl ve Arz-ı Mahzar'lar.' *Osmanlı Araştırmaları,* no. VII-VIII (1988): 33–54.

Tanzimat ve Bulgar Meselesi. Ankara Türk Târîh Kurumu, 1943.

İpekten, Haluk. *Dîvân Edebiyâtında Edebi Muhitler.* İstanbul: Milli Eğitim Bakanlığı Yayınları, 1996.

İskit, Server. *Türkiye'de Matbuat İdâreleri ve Politikaları.* İstanbul: Başvekâlet Basın ve Yayın Umûm Müdürlüğü Yayınları, 1943.

İz, Fahri. 'Ottoman and Turkish.' In *Essays on Islamic civilization: Presented to Niyazi Berkes,* edited by Donald P. Little, 118–139. Leiden: Brill, 1976.

Jacob, Margaret C. *Living the Enlightenment: Freemasonry and Politics in Eighteenth-Century Europe: Freemasonry and Politics in Eighteenth-Century Europe.* New York: Oxford University Press, 1991.

Jarausch, Konrad H., and Michael Geyer. *Shattered Past: Reconstructing German Histories.* Princeton, NJ: Princeton University Press, 2003.

Jelavich, Charles, and Barbara Jelavich. *The Establishment of the Balkan National States, 1804–1920*. Seattle, WA: University of Washington Press, 1977.

Jeltyakov, A. D. *Türkiyenin Sosyo-Politik ve Kültürel hayâtında Basın (1729–1908)*. Ankara: Basın Yayın Genel Müdürlüğü, 1979.

Johns, Adrian. *The Nature of the Book: Print and Knowledge in the Making*. Chicago: University of Chicago Press, 1998.

Jr., Russell G. Kempiners. 'Vaşşâf's Tajziyât al-Amşâr wa Tazjiyat al-A'şâr as a Source for the History of the Chaghadayid Khanate.' *Journal of Asian History* 22, no. 2 (1988): 160–87.

Kabacalı, Alpay. *Başlangıçtan Günümüze Türkiye'de Basın Sansürü*. İstanbul: Gazeteciler Cemiyeti Yayınları, 1990.

Türk Kitap Târîhi: Baslangıçtan Tanzimat'a Kadar. 2 vols. Vol. I. İstanbul: Cem Yayınevi, 1989.

Kafadar, Cemal. 'The City that Rålamb Visited: The Political and Cultural Climate of Istanbul in 1650s.' In *The Sultan's Procession: The Swedish Embassy to Sultan Mehmed IV in 1657–1658 and the Rålamb Paintings*, edited by Karin Ådahl, 58–73. İstanbul: Swedish Research Institute in Istanbul, 2006.

'Janissaries and Other Riffraff of Ottoman Istanbul: Rebels without a Cause.' In *Identity and Identity Formation in the Ottoman World: A Volume of Essays in Honor of Norman Itzkowitz*, edited by Baki Tezcan and Karl. K. Barbir, 113–134. Madison: University of Wisconsin Press, 2007.

'The Myth of the Golden Age: Ottoman Historical Consciousness in the Post-Süleymânic Era.' In *Süleymân the Second and His Time*, edited by Halil İnalcık and Cemal Kafadar, 37–49. İstanbul: The Isis Press, 1993.

'On the Purity and Corruption of the Janissaries.' *Turkish Studies Association Bulletin* 15, no. 2 (1991): 273–280.

'The Question of Ottoman Decline.' *Harvard Middle Eastern and Islamic Review* 4, no. 1–2 (1997–98): 30–75.

'Self and Others: The Diary of a Dervish in Seventeenth Century Istanbul and First-Person Narratives in Ottoman Literature.' *Studia Islamica*, no. 69 (1989): 121–150.

'Yeniçeri-Esnaf Relations: Solidarity and Conflict.' MA, McGill University, 1981.

Kaiser, Thomas. 'The Evil Empire? The Debate on Turkish Despotism in Eighteenth-Century French Political Culture.' In *Early Modern Europe*, edited by James B. Collins and Karen L. Taylor, 69–81. Padstow, UK: Blackwell Publishing, 2006.

Kale, Steven. *French Salons: High Society and Political Sociability from the Old Regime to the Revolution of 1848*. Baltimore, MD: Johns Hopkins University Press, 2005.

Kamenskii, Aleksandr. *The Russian Empire in the Eighteenth Century: Searching for A Place in the World*. Translated by David Griffiths. London: Routledge, 2015.

Karal, Enver Zıyâ Karal. *Osmanlı Târîhi: Nizâm-ı ve Tanzimat Devirleri (1789–1856)*. 9 vols. Vol. V. Ankara: Türk Târîh Kurumu Basımevi, 1988.

Selim III.'ün Hatt-ı Hümâyunları. 2 vols. Vol. II. Ankara: Türk Târîh Kurumu Basımevi, 1942.

Karpat, Kemal [H]. *Ottoman Population 1890–1914: Demographic and Social Chracteristics*. Madison: University of Wisconsin Press, 1985.

'Ottoman Population Records and the Census of 1881/82–1893.' *International Journal of Middle East Studies* 9, no. 2 (1978): 237–274.

The Politicization of Islam: Reconstructing Identity, State, Faith, and Community in the Late Ottoman State. Oxford: Oxford University Press, 2001.

Studies on Ottoman Social and Political History: Selected Articles and Essays. Leiden: Brill, 2002.

Katz, David S. *The Shaping of Turkey in the British Imagination, 1776–1923*. London: Palgrave Macmillan, 2016.

Kayaoğlu, Taceddin. *Türkiye'de Tercüme Müesseseleri*. İstanbul: Kitâbevi, 1998.

Kaynar, Reşat. *Mustafa Reşit Paşa ve Tanzimat*. Ankara: Türk Târîh Kurumu, 1985.

Kemal, Mahmud [İnal], 'Sultan Abdülaziz'e Dair,' *Türk Tarihi Encümeni Mecmuası* 15, no. 9. 177–195.

Kemal, Salim. *The Philosophical Poetics of Alfarabi, Avicenna and Averroës: The Aristotelian Reception*. Oxford: RoutledgeCurzon, 2003.

Kemikli, Bilal. '19. Yüzyılda Bir Entelektüel Muhit: Şeyhülislam Arif Hikmet Beyefendi'nin Konağı.' *İlim ve Sanat*, no. 42 (1996): 92–95.

Kendall, Elizabeth. 'Between Politics and Literature: Journals in Alexandria and Istanbul at the End of the Nineteenth Century.' In *Modernity & Culture: From the Mediterranean to the Indian Ocean*, edited by Leila Tarazi Fawaz and C. A. Bayly, 330–343. New York: Columbia University Press, 2002.

Kent, E. J. 'Tyrannical Beasts: Male Witchcraft in Early Modern English Culture.' In *Emotions in the History of Witchcraft*. Edited by Laura Kounine and Michael Ostling, 77–94. London: Palgrave, 2016.

Kernan, Alvin. *Samuel Johnson & the Impact of Print*. Princeton, NJ: Princeton University Press, 1989.

Khaddūrī, Majīd *The Islamic Law of Nations: Shaybani's Siyar*. Baltimore, MD: Johns Hopkins University Press, 2002.

Khoury, Dina Rizk. *State and Provincial Society in the Ottoman Empire: Mosul, 1540–1834*. Cambridge: Cambridge University Press, 2002.

Khoury, Philip S. *Urban Notables and Arab Nationalism: The Politics of Damascus 1860–1920*. Cambridge: Cambridge University Press, 2003.

Kılıç, Selda. 'Tanzimat'ın İlanından 1864 Düzenlemesinin Uygulanmasına Kadar Geçen Dönemde Osmanlı Vâlileri ve Vâlilik Kurumu.' *Târîh Araştırmaları Dergisi* XXVIII, no. 45 (2009): 43–62.

Kırlı, Cengiz. 'Coffeehouses: Public Opinion in the Nineteenth-century Ottoman Empire.' In *Public Islam and the Common Good*. Edited by Armando Salvatore and Dale F. Eickelman, 75–97. Leiden: Brill, 2004.

'Devlet ve İstatistik: Esnaf ve Kefalet Defterleri Işığında III. Selim İktidarı.' In *Nizâm-ı Kadim'den Nizâm-ı Cedîd'de III. Selim ve Dönemi*, edited by Seyfi Kenan, 183–212. İstanbul: İslam Araştırmaları Merkezi, 2010.

'The Struggle Over Space: Coffeehouses of Ottoman Istanbul, 1780–1845.' PhD diss., State University of New York, 2000.

King, Andrew, and John Plunkett. *Victorian Print Media: A Reader*. Oxford: Oxford University Press, 2005.

Kirk, Robert W. *Paradise Past: The Transformation of the South Pacific, 1520–1920*. Jefferson, NC: McFarland & Company, 2012.

Koloğlu, Orhan. *İlk Gazete İlk Polemik: Vekâyi-i Mısriye'nin Öyküsü ve Takvîmi Vekâyi ile Tartışması*. Ankara: Çağdaş Gazeteciler Derneği, 1989.

İttihatçılar ve Masonlar. İstanbul: Gür Yayınları, 1991.

Miyop Çörçil Olayı: Cerîde-i Havâdis'in Öyküsü. Ankara: Yorum Yayıncılık, 1986.

Osmanlı'da Kamuoyu. İstanbul: İstanbul Üniversitesi İletişim Fakültesi, 2010.

Osmanlı'dan Günümüze Türkiye'de Basın. İstanbul: İletişim Yayınları, 1992.

Takvîmi Vekâyi: Türk Basınında 150 Yıl: 1831–1981. Ankara: Çağdaş Gazeteciler Derneği, [n.d.]

Kornicki, Peter. *The Book in Japan: A Cultural History from the Beginnings to the Nineteenth Century*. Honolulu: University of Hawai'i Press, 2001.

Koselleck, Reinhart. *Critique and Crisis: Enlightenment and the Pathogenesis of Modern Society*. Cambridge, MA: MIT Press, 1988.

Koz, M. Sabri. *Sarafim Kırââthânesi*. Edited by İlhan Tekeli. 8 vols. Vol. VI, Dünden Bugüne İstanbul Ansiklopedisi. İstanbul: Kültür Bakanlığı & Târîh Vakfı, 1993.

Köprülü, Mehmed Fuâd. *Edebiyât Araştırmaları*, 2 vols. Vol. I. İstanbul: Ötüken Yayınları, 1989.

Türk Dili ve Edebiyâtı Hakkında Araştırmalar İstanbul: Kanaat Kitâbevi, 1934.

Kuhn, Thomas S. *The Essential Tension: Selected Studies in Scientific Tradition and Change*. Chicago: University of Chicago Press, 1977.

The Structure of Scientific Revolutions. 3rd edn. Chicago: University of Chicago Press, 1996.

Kuntay, Mithat Cemal. *Sarıklı İhtilâlci Ali Suâvi*. İstanbul: Ahmet Halit Kitâbevi, 1946.

Kuran, Ercümend. *Avrupa'da Osmanlı İkamet Elçiliklerinin Kuruluşu ve İlk Elçilerin Siyâsi Faâliyetleri, 1793–1821*. Ankara: Türk Kültürünü Araştırma Enstitüsü, 1968.

Kuran, Ercüment. 'Derebeys et Agas d'Anatolie orientale dans le dernier siècle de l'empire ottoman.' In *Histoire économique et sociale de l'Empire ottoman et de la Turquie (1326–1960)*, edited by Daniel Panzac, 395–400. Leuven: Peeters, 1995.

Türkiye'nin Batılılaşması ve Milli Meseleler. Ankara: Diyânet Vakfı Yayınları, 1994.

Kurtoğlu, Fevzi. *Deniz Mektepleri Târîhçesi*. İstanbul: Deniz Matbaası, 1941.

Kuru, Ahmet T. *Secularism and State Policies Toward Religion: The United States, France, and Turkey*. Cambridge: Cambridge University Press, 2009.

Kut, Günay. 'Turkish Literature.' In *Culture and Learning in Islam*, edited by Ekmeleddin İhsanoğlu, 251–286. Paris: UNESCO Publishing, 2003.

Küçük, Hülya. *The Role of the Bektāshīs in Turkey's National Struggle*. Leiden: Brill, 2002.

Kütükoğlu, Bekir. *Vekâyi'nüvis Makaleler*. İstanbul: Fetih Cemiyeti Yayınları, 1994.

Laffan, Michael. *The Makings of Indonesian Islam: Orientalism and the Narration of a Sufi Past*. Princeton, NJ: Princeton University Press, 2011.

Lapidus, Ira M. *Muslim Cities in the Later Middle Ages*. Cambridge: Cambridge University Press, 1984.

Larkin, Margaret. *Al-Mutanabbi: Voice of the 'Abbasid Poetic Ideal*. London: Oneworld, 2008.

Layiktez, Celil. *Türkiye'de Masonluk Târîhi Cilt: 1 - Başlangıç 1721 – 1956*. İstanbul: Yenilik Basımevi, 1999.

Lévi-Provençal, Évariste. *Histoire de l'Espagne musulmane: Le siècle du califat de Cordoue*. 3 vols. Vol. III. Paris: Éditions G-P. Maisonneuve et Larose, 1944.

Lewis, Bernard. *The Emergence of Modern Turkey*. Oxford: Oxford University Press, 1961.

The Muslim Discovery of Europe. New York: Norton, 2001.

Political Words and Ideas in Islam. Princeton, NJ: Markus Wiener Publishers, 2007.

'Watan.' *Journal of Contemporary History* 26, no. 3/4 (1991): 523–533.

Lipson, Charles. 'International Debt and National Security: Comparing Victorian Britain and Postwar America.' In *The International Debt Crisis in Historical Perspective*, edited by Barry Eichengreen and Peter H. Lindert, 189–227. Cambridge, MA: MIT Press, 1992.

Lounsbery, Anne. "Russia! What Do You Want of Me?': The Russian Reading Public in Dead Souls.' *Slavic Review* 60, no. 2 (2001): 367–89.

Lynn, Michael R. *Popular Science and Public Opinion in Eighteenth-Century France*. Manchester: Manchester University Press, 2006.

De Madariaga, Isabel. *Politics and Culture in Eighteenth-Century Russia*. London: Routledge, 1998.

Madkour, Ibrahim. 'La logique d'Aristote chez les Mutakallimun.' In *Islamic Philosophical Theology*, edited by Parviz Morewedge, 58–68. New York: State University of New York Press, 1979.

Mango, Andrew. *From the Sultan to Ataturk: Turkey: The Peace Conferences of 1919–23 and Their Aftermath*. London: Haus Publishing, 2010.

Mantran, Robert. 'Prelude Aux Tanzimat: Presse et Enseignement, Deux Domaines de Reforme de Mahmud II.' In *Tanzimat'ın 150. Yıldönümü Uluslararası Sempozyumu, Ank., 31 Ekim-3 Kasım 1989*, 51–54. Ankara: Türk Târîh Kurumu, 1994.

Mardin, Ebü'l-Ula. *Medeni Hukuk Cephesinden Ahmed Cevdet Paşa*. İstanbul: İstanbul Üniversitesi Hukuk Fakültesi, 1946.

Mardin, Şerif. *The Genesis of Young Ottoman Thought: A Study in the Modernization of Turkish Political Ideas*. Syracuse, NY: Syracuse University Press, 2000.

'Power, Civil Society and Culture in the Ottoman Empire.' *Comparative Studies in Society and History* 11, no. 3 (1969): 258–281.

Markovits, Stefanie. 'Rushing Into Print: 'Participatory Journalism' During the Crimean War.' *Victorian Studies* 50, no. 4 (2008): 559–586.

Martin, Vanessa. 'An Evaluation of Reform and Development of the State in the Early Qājār Period.' *Die Welt des Islams* 36, no. 1 (1996): 1–24.

Marx, Karl. *Capital: A Critical Analysis of Capitalist Production*. Translated by Samuel Moore. Edited by Friedrich Engels, *Half-Guinea International Library*. London: Sonnenschein, 1897.

The Eighteenth Brumaire of Louis Bonaparte. Moscow: Progress Publisher, 1972.

Masters, Bruce. 'The Sultan's Entrepreneurs: The Avrupa tuccaris and the Hayriye tuccaris in Syria.' *International Journal of Middle East Studies* 24, no. 4 (1992): 579–597.

McGowan, Bruce. 'The Age of the Ayans, 1699–1812.' In *An Economic and Social History of the Ottoman Empire*. Edited by Halil Inalcik and Donald Quataert. 2 vols. Vol. I. Cambridge: Cambridge University Press, 1997.

McKenzie, D. F. *Bibliography and the Sociology of Texts, The Panizzi Lectures, 1985*. London: British Library, 1986.

McNair, John. 'The 'Reading Library' and the Reading Public: The Decline and Fall of 'Biblioteka dlia chteniia'.' *The Slavonic and East European Review*, 70, no. 2 (1992): 213–227.

Melton, James Van Horn. *The Rise of the Public in Enlightenment Europe*. Cambridge: Cambridge University Press, 2001.

Memişoğlu, Hüseyin. 'Bulgaristan'ın Vidin Şehrinde Halil ve İbrahim İkiz Kardeşlerin Kurdukları Kültür Vakfı ve Onun 'Şefkat' Kırââthânesi.' *Türk Dünyası Araştırmaları*, no. 169 (2007): 205–220.

Menchinger Ethan L. *The First of the Modern Ottomans: The Intellectual History of Ahmed Vasif*. Cambridge: Cambridge University Press, 2017.

Meriç, Cemil. *Sosyoloji Notları ve Konferanslar*. İstanbul: İletişim Yayınları, 1995.

Messick, Brinkley. *The Calligraphic State Textual Domination and History in a Muslim Society*. Berkeley: University of California Press, 1992.

Miller, Michael L. 'From Liberal Nationalism to Cosmopolitan Patriotism: Simon Deutsch and 1848ers in Exile.' *European Review of History: Revue europeenne d'histoire* 17, no. 3 (2010): 379–393.

Mitchell, Timothy. *Colonising Egypt*. Berkeley: University of California Press, 1988.

'Introduction.' In *Questions of Modernity*, edited by Timothy Mitchell, xi–xxvii. Minneapolis: University of Minnesota Press, 2000.

Mittler, Barbara. *A Newspaper for China?: Power, Identity, and Change in Shanghai's News Media, 1872 – 1912*. Cambridge, MA: Harvard University Press, 2004.

Miura, Toru. 'Mashriq.' In *Islamic Urban Studies*, edited by Masashi Haneda and Toru Miura, 83–184. Oxford: Routledge, 2010.

Moran, Berna. *Türk Romanına Eleştirel Bir Bakış: Ahmet Mithat'tan Ahmet Hamdi Tanpınar'a* 3 vols. Vol. I. İstanbul: İletişim Yayınları, 1995.

Murphey, Rhoads. 'An Ottoman View from the Top and Rumblings from Below: The Sultanic Writs (Hatt-i Hümâyun) of Murad IV (R. 1623–1640).' *Turcica* 28 (1996): 319–338.

Musolff, Andreas. 'The Embodiment of Europe: How do Metaphors Evolve?' In *Body, Language, and Mind: Sociocultural Situatedness*, edited by Roslyn M. Frank, Rene Dirven, Tom Ziemke, and Enrique Bernardez. Berlin: Mouton de Gruyter, 2008.

Naff, Thomas. 'Reform and the Conduct of Ottoman Diplomacy in the Reign of Selim III, 1789–1807.' *Journal of the American Oriental Society* 83, no. 3 (1963): 295–315.

Nagata, Yuzo. *Muhsin-zâde Mehmed Paşa ve Ayânlık Müessesesi*. Tokyo: Institute for the Study of Languages and Cultures of Asia and Africa, 1976.

Nejad, Masoud Kohestani. *İhtiyarat, Islahat ve Levayih-i Kanûni-i Doktor Mohammad Mosaddegh*. Tahran: Kitaphâne-i Milli-i İran, 1383/1963–1964.

Nemeth, Alexander J. *Voltaire's Tormented Soul: A Psychobiographic Inquiry*. Cranbury, NJ: Associated University Presses, 2008.

Nisbet, Robert. 'Public Opinion versus Popular Opinion,' *Public Interest* 41 (1975): 166–92.

Nord, Philip. *The Republican Moment: Struggles for Democracy in Nineteenth-Century France*. Cambridge, MA: Harvard University Press, 1995.

Nour, Rıza. *Revue de Turcologie: Nâmık Kemal* Alexandria: Imp. Hamouda, 1936.

Nüzhet, Selim. *Türk Gazeteciliği 1831–1931*. İstanbul: Devlet Matbaası, 1931.

Officer, Lawrence H., and Samuel H. Williamson. 'Purchasing Power of British Pounds from 1245 to Present.' In *MeasuringWorth*, 2016.

Okay, M. Orhan. *Batı Medeniyeti Karşısında Ahmed Midhat Efendi*. Ankara: Atatürk Üniversitesi Edebiyât Fakültesi, 1975.

İlk Türk Pozitivist ve Natüralisti Beşir Fuâd. İstanbul: Dergâh Yayınları, 1969.

Olson, Robert W. 'The Esnaf and the Patrona Halil Rebellion of 1730: A Realignment in Ottoman Politics?' *Journal of the Economic and Social History of the Orient* 17, no. 3 (1974): 329–344.

'Jews, Janissaries, Esnaf and the Revolt of 1740 in Istanbul: Social Upheaval and Political Realignment in the Ottoman Empire.' *Journal of the Economic and Social History of the Orient* 20, no. 2 (1977): 185–207.

O'Malley, Lurana Donnels. *The Dramatic Works Of Catherine The Great: Theatre And Politics In Eighteenth-Century Russia*. Burlington, VT: Ashgate, 2006.

Onaran, Burak. *Détrôner le sultan Deux conjurations à l'époque des réformes ottomanes: Kuleli (1859) et Meslek (1867)*. Paris: Peeters, 2013.

Orr, Linda. 'Outspoken Women and the Rightful Daughter of the Revolution: Madame de Staël's Considérations sur la Révolution Française.'

In *Rebel Daughters: Women and the French Revolution*. Edited by Sara E. Melzer & Leslie W. Rabine, 121–136. Oxford: Oxford University Press, 1992.

Ortaylı, İlber. *İmparatorluğun En Uzun Yüzyılı*. İstanbul: İletişim Yayınları, 2003.

Tanzimattan Sonra Mahalli İdâreler, 1840–1878. Ankara: Sevinç Matbaası, 1974.

Üç Kıtada Osmanlılar. İstanbul: Timaş Yayınları, 2007.

Osterhammel, Jürgen. *The Transformation of the World: A Global History of the Nineteenth Century*. Translated by Patrick Camiller. Princeton, NJ: Princeton University Press, 2014.

Ottoman Lyric Poetry: An Anthology. Edited by Walter G. Andrews, Najaat Black and Mehmet Kalpaklı. Seattle: University of Washington Press, 2006.

Ömer Çaha, and M. Lutfullah Karaman. 'Civil Society in The Ottoman Empire.' *Journal of Economic and Social Research* 8, no. 2 (2006): 53–81.

Öz, Tahsîn. 'Selim III Mustafa IV ve Mahmud II. Zamanlarına Ait Birkaç Vesika.' *Târîh Vesikaları* 1, no. 1 (1941–1942).

Özbilgen, Erol. *Bütün Yönleriyle Osmanlı Adab-ı Osmaniyye*. İstanbul: İz Yayınları, 2003.

Özcan, Abdülkadir. 'II. Mahmud'un Memleket Gezileri.' In *Prof. Dr. Bekir Kütükoğlu'na Armağan*, edited by Mübahat S. Kütükoğlu et al., 361–80. İstanbul: İstanbul Üniversitesi Edebiyât Fakültesi, 1991.

Özcan, Azmi. *Pan-Islamism: Indian Muslims, the Ottomans and Britain, 1877–1924*. Leiden: E. J. Brill, 1997.

Özgül, Metin Kayahan. *Hersekli Arif Hikmet*. Ankara: Kültür ve Turizm Bakanlığı, 1987.

XIX. Asrın Benzersiz Bir Politeknigi: Münif Paşa. Ankara: Elips Kitap, 2005.

Öziş, Hamdi. *Osmanlı Mizah Basınında Batılılaşma ve Siyaset: 1870–1877*. İstanbul: Libra, 2010.

Özkaya, Yücel. *18. Yüzyılda Osmanlı Toplumu*. İstanbul: Yapı Kredi Kültür Sanat Yayıncılık, 2008.

Özön, Mustafa Nihat. *Son Asır Türk Edebiyâtı Târîhi*. İstanbul: Maârif Matbaası, 1941.

Türkçede Roman. İstanbul: İletişim Yayınları, 1985.

Öztuncay, Bahattin. *Dersaâdet'in Fotoğrafçıları: 19. Yüzyıl İstanbul'unda Fotoğraf: Öncüler, Stüdyolar, Sanatçılar*. 2 vols. Vol. I. İstanbul: Aygaz, 2003.

Hâtıra-i Uhuvvet (Portre Fotoğrafların Cazibesi: 1846–1950). İstanbul: Aygaz, 2005).

Paavilainen, Helena M. *Medieval Pharmacotherapy, Continuity and Change: Case Studies from Ibn Sīnā and Some of His Late Medieval Commentators*. Leiden: Brill, 2009.

Pakalın, Mehmet Zeki. *Mahmud Nedim Paşa*. İstanbul: Ahmet Sait Matbaası, 1940.

Pamuk, Şevket. *19. Yüzyılda Osmanlı Dış Ticâreti. VII vols. Vol. I, Târîhi istatistikler Dizisi*. Ankara: TC. Başbakanlık Devlet İstatistik Enstitüsü, 1995.

'Changes in Factor Markets in the Ottoman Empire, 1500–1800.' *Continuity and Change* 24, no. Special Issue 01 (2009): 107–136.

A Monetary History of the Ottoman Empire. Cambridge: Cambridge University Press, 2000.

The Ottoman Empire and European Capitalism, 1820–1913: Trade, Investment and Production. Cambrige: Cambridge University Press, 2010.

Panzac, Daniel. 'Entre carrière et politique: Les officiers de marine ottomans a la fin de l'empire (1863–1923).' *Turcica*, no. 33 (2001): 63–83.

'International and Domestic Maritime Trade in the Ottoman Empire during the 18th Century.' *International Journal of Middle East Studies* 24, no. 2 (1992): 189–206.

Parla, Jale. *Babalar ve Oğullar: Tanzimat Romanının Epistemolojik Temelleri*. İstanbul: İletişim Yayınları, 1993.

Parolin, Christina. *Radical Spaces Venues of Popular Politics in London, 1790–c. 1845*. Canberra: Australian National University, 2010.

Peirce, Leslie P. *The Imperial Harem: Women and Sovereignty in the Ottoman Empire*. Oxford: Oxford University Press, 1993.

Perkin, Harold. *The Origins of Modern English Society: 1780–1880*. London: Routledge & Kegan Paul, 1969.

Petmezas, Socrates D. 'Christian Communities in 18th and Early 19th Century Ottoman Greece: Their Fiscal Functions.' In *Minorities in the Ottoman Empire*, edited by Molly Greene, 71–126. Princeton, NJ: Markus Wiener Publishers, 2005.

Philliou, Christine M. *Biography of An Empire: Governing Ottomans in an Age of Revolution*. Los Angeles: University of California Press, 2010.

Plumb, J. H. 'The Commercialization of Leisure in Eighteenth-Century England.' In *The Birth of a Consumer Society: The Commercialization of Eighteenth-Century England*, edited by Neil McKendrick, John Brewer and J. H. Plumb, 265–286. London: Europa Publications, 1982.

Posner, Richard A. *Public Intellectuals: A Study of Decline*. Cambridge, MA: Harvard University Press, 2001.

Prakash, Gyan. 'Introduction: After Colonialism.' In *After Colonialism: Imperial Histories and Postcolonial Displacements*, edited by Gyan Prakash, 3–20. Princeton, NJ: Princeton University Press, 1995.

Quataert, Donald. 'The Age of Reforms, 1812–1914.' In *An Economic and Social History of the Ottoman Empire*, edited by Halil İnalcık, Suraiya Faroqhi, and Donald Quataert, 759–933. Cambridge: Cambridge University Press, 1997.

'Clothing Laws, State, and Society in the Ottoman Empire, 1720–1829.' *International Journal of Middle East Studies* 29, no. 3 (1997): 403–425.

'Janissaries, Artisans and the Question of Ottoman Decline.' In *Workers, Peasants and Economic Change in the Ottoman Empire 1730–1914*, edited by Donald Quataert, 197–203. İstanbul: İsis Yayınları, 1993.

The Ottoman Empire, 1700–1922. 2nd edn. Cambridge: Cambridge University Press, 2005.

The Ottoman Empire, 1700–1922. Cambridge: Cambridge University Press, 2000.

'The Social History of Labor in the Ottoman Empire, 1800–1914.' In *The Social History of Labor in the Middle East*, edited by Ellis Goldberg, 19–36. Boulder, CO: Westview Press, 1996.

'Workers and the State during the Late Ottoman Empire.' In *The State and the Subaltern: Modernization, Society and the State in Turkey and Iran*, edited by Touraj Atabaki, 17–30. London: I. B. Tauris, 2007.

Raby, Julian. 'A Sultan of Paradox: Mehmed the Conqueror as a Patron of the Arts.' *Oxford Art Journal* 5, no. 1 (1982): 3–8.

Ralston, David B. *Importing the European Army: The Introduction of European Military Techniques and Institutions in the Extra-European World, 1600–1914*. Chicago: University of Chicago Press, 1996.

Rawski, Evelyn Sakakida. *Education and Popular Literacy in Ch'ing China*. Ann Arbor: University of Michigan Press, 1979.

Raymond, Andre. 'Soldiers in Trade: The Case of Ottoman Cairo.' *British Journal of Middle Eastern Studies* 18, no. 1 (1991): 16–37.

Redekop, Benjamin W. *Enlightenment and Community: Lessing, Abbt, Herder, and the Quest for a German Public*. Montreal: McGill-Queen's University Press, 1999.

Reed, Howard A. 'The Destruction of the Janissaries in June 1826.' PhD, Princeton University, 1951.

Reid, Donald Malcolm. *Whose Pharaohs?: Archeology, Museums, and Egyptian National Identity from Napoleon to World War I*. Berkeley: University of California Press, 2002.

Renner, Andreas. 'Defining a Russian Nation: Mikhail Katkov and the 'Invention' of National Politics.' *The Slavonic and East European Review* 81, no. 4 (2003): 659–682.

Robinson, Francis. 'Ottomans-Safavids-Mughals: Shared Knowledge and Connective Systems.' *Journal of Islamic Studies* 8, no. 2 (1997): 151–184.

Rosenthal, Franz. *Knowledge Triumphant: The Concept of Knowledge in Medieval Islam*. Leiden: Brill, 2007.

Rowe, Michael. *From Reich to State: The Rhineland in the Revolutionary Age, 1780–1830*. Cambridge: Cambridge University Press, 2003.

Rubery, Matthew. *The Novelty of Newspapers: Victorian Fiction after the Invention of the News*. Oxford: Oxford University Press, 2009.

Rubiés, Joan-Pau. *Travel and Ethnology in the Renaissance: South India Through European Eyes, 1250–1625*. Cambridge: Cambridge University Press, 2002.

Sabev, Orlin. *İbrahim Müteferrika ya da İlk Osmanlı Matbaa Serüveni (1726–1756)*. İstanbul: Yeditepe Yayınevi, 2006.

Saidah, Jean-Pierre. 'Le dandysme: continuité et rupture.' In *L'honnête homme et le dandy*, edited by Alain Montandon, 123–150. Tübingen: Narr, 1993.

Salzmann, Ariel. 'An Ancien Régime Revisited: 'Privatization' and Political Economy in the Eighteenth-Century Ottoman Empire.' *Politics & Society* 21 (1993): 393–423.

Sands, Kristin Z. *Ṣūfī Commentaries on the Qur'ān in Classical Islam*. London: Routledge, 2006.

Sands, Kristin Zahra. 'On the Popularity of Husayn Va'iz-i Kashifi's Mavāhib-i 'âliyya: A Persian Commentary on the Qur'an.' *Iranian Studies* 36, no. 4 (2003): 469–483.

Schäfer, Fabian. *Public Opinion – Propaganda – Ideology: Theories on the Press and Its Social Function in Interwar Japan, 1918–1937*. Leiden: Brill, 2012.

Schleifman, Nurit. 'A Russian Daily Newspaper and Its New Readership: 'Severnaia Pchela', 1825–1840.' *Cahiers du Monde russe et soviétique* 28, no. 2 (1987): 127–144.

Schulze, Reinhard. *A Modern History of the Islamic World*. Translated by Azizeh Azodi. London: I.B. Tauris, 2002.

Selahattin Öztürk, Abdurrahman M. Hacıismailoğlu, Muhammed Hızarcı. *Hakkı Tarık Us Kütüphânesi Kataloğu: Süreli Yayınlar*. İstanbul: İstanbul Büyükşehir Belediyesi Kültür ve Turizm Dâire Başkanlığı Kültür Müdürlüğü, 2006.

Sennett, Richard. *The Fall of Public Men*. London: Penguin Books, 2002.

Sertoğlu, Mithat. *İstanbul [1520'den Cumhûriyete Kadar]*. Edited by A. Adıvar, R. Arat, A. Ateş, İ. Kafesoğlu and T. Yazıcı. 13 vols. Vol. 5/2, İslam Ansiklopedisi: İslâm Âlemi, Târîh, Coğrafya, Etnografya ve Biyografya Lugâtı. İstanbul: Milli Eğitim Basımevi, 1988.

Sezer, Yavuz. 'The Architecture of Bibliophilia: Eighteenth-Century Ottoman Libraries.' PhD diss., Massachusetts Institute of Technology, 2016.

Shaw, Stanford J. 'The Population of Istanbul in the Nineteenth Century.' *International Journal of Middle East Studies* 10, no. 2 (1979): 265–277.

Shaw, Stanford J., and Ezel Kural Shaw. *History of the Ottoman Empire and Modern Turkey: Reform, Revolution, and Republic: The Rise of Modern Turkey, 1808–1975*. 2 vols. Vol. II. Cambridge: Cambridge University Press, 1977.

Shaw, Stanford. J. *Between Old and New: The Ottoman Empire under Sultan Selim III, 1789–1807*. Cambridge, MA: Harvard University Press, 1971.

Shaw, Wendy M. K. *Ottoman Painting: Reflections of Western Art from the Ottoman Empire to the Turkish Republic*. London: I. B. Tauris, 2011.

Shinar, Pessah. *Modern Islam in the Maghrib*. Jerusalem: Max Schloessinger Memorial Foundation & Hebrew University of Jerusalem, 2004.

Smith, Douglas. 'Freemasonry and the Public in Eighteenth-Century Russia.' In *Imperial Russia: New Histories for the Empire*, edited by Jane Burbank and David L. Ransel, 281–304. Bloomington: Indiana University Press, 1998.

Somel, Selçuk Akşin. *The Modernization of Public Education in the Ottoman Empire, 1839–1908: Islamization, Autocracy, and Discipline*. Leiden: E. J. Brill, 2001.

Sondhaus, Lawrence. *Naval Warfare 1815–1914*. London: Routledge, 2001.

Sözen, Zeynep. *Fenerli Beyler 110 Yılın Öyküsü (1711–1821)*. İstanbul: Aybay Yayıncılık, 2000.

Speier, Hans. 'Historical Development of Public Opinion.' *The American Journal of Sociology* 55, no. 4 (1950): 376–388.

Sperber, Jonathan. *The European Revolutions, 1848 – 1851*. Cambridge: Cambridge University Press, 2005.

Spivak, Gayatri Chakravorty. 'The Rani of Sirmur: An Essay in Reading the Archives.' *History and Theory* 24, no. 3 (1985): 247–272.

Spranzi, Marta. *The Art of Dialectic Between Dialogue and Rhetoric: The Aristotelian Tradition*. Amsterdam: John Benjamins Publishing Company, 2011.

Stallybrass, Peter, and Allon White. *The Politics and Poetics of Transgression*. London: Methuen, 1986.

Starr, Paul. *The Creation of the Media: Political Origins of Modern Communications*. New York: Basic Books, 2004.

Strauss, Johann. 'The Greek Connection in Nineteenth-Century Ottoman Intellectual History.' In *Greece and the Balkans: Identities, Perceptions and Cultural Encounters Since the Enlightenment*, edited by Dimitris Tziovas, 47–67. Farnham: Ashgate Publishing, 2003.

'Kütüp ve Resail-i Mevkute: Printing and Publishing in a Multi-ethnic Society.' In *Late Ottoman Society – The Intellectual Legacy*, edited by Elisabeth Özdalga, 227–256. Oxford: RoutledgeCurzon, 2005.

Sunar, Mert. 'Cauldron of Dissent: A Study of the Janissary Corps, 1807–1826.' PhD diss., State University of New York at Binghamton, 2006.

Svolopoulos, Constantin. 'L'initiation de Mourad V à la franc-maçonnerie par Cl. Scalieri: Aux origines du mouvement libéral en Turquie.' *Balkan Studies* 21, no. 2 (1980): 441–457.

Swanson, Glen W. 'The Ottoman Police.' *Journal of Contemporary History* 7, no. 1/2 (1972): 243–260.

Swift, E. Anthony. *Popular Theater and Society in Tsarist Russia*. Berkeley: University of California Press, 2002.

Şapolyo, Enver Behnan. *Türk Gazetecilik Târîhi ve Her Yönüyle Basın*. Ankara: Güven Matbaası, 1969.

Şener, Abdüllatif. *Osmanlı Mâliyesinin Şeffaflaşması: Yayımlanan İlk Bütçeler*. İstanbul: Kapı Yayınları, 2008.

Şiviloğlu, Murat R. 'Abidin Paşa.' In *Abidin Dino: Bir Dünya*, edited by Zeynep Avcı, 36–45. İstanbul: Sabancı Üniversitesi Yayınları, 2007.

Tanpınar, Ahmet Hamdi. *XIX. Asır Türk Edebiyâtı Târîhi*. Edited by Abdullah Uçman. İstanbul: Yapı Kredi Yayınları, 2006.

Tauber, Eliezer. *The Emergence of the Arab Movements*. London: Frank Cass, 1993.

Tekin, Yusuf. 'Osmanlı'da Demokrasi Tartışmalarının Miladı Olarak Meşrûtiyet Öncesi Tartışma Platformu.' *Ankara Üniversitesi SBF Dergisi* 55, no. 3 (2000): 145–173.

Ter Minassian, Anahïde. 'Une famille d'amiras arméniens: Les Dadian.' In *Histoire économique et sociale de l'Empire ottoman et de la Turquie (1326–1960): Actes du sixième congrès international tenu à Aix-en-Provence du 1er au 4 juillett 1992*, edited by Daniel Panzac, 505–519. Paris: Peeters, 1997.

Tezcan, Baki. *The Second Ottoman Empire: Political and Social Transformation in the Early Modern World*. Cambridge: Cambridge University Press, 2010.

Thomas, John Meurig. *Michael Faraday and the Royal Institution: The Genius of Man and Place*. New York: Taylor & Francis, 1991.

Tilly, Charles. *Coercion, Capital, and European States AD 990–1990*. Cambridge, MA: Basil Blackwell, 1990.

Timur, Taner. *Osmanlı Çalışmaları: İlkel Feodalizmden Yarı Sömürge Ekonomisine*. Ankara: V Yayınları, 1989.

Todd III, William Mills. *Fiction and Society in the Age of Pushkin: Ideology, Institutions, and Narrative*. Cambridge, MA: Harvard University Press, 1986.

Toprak, Zafer. 'The Financial Structure of the Stock Exchange in the Late Ottoman Empire.' In *East Meets West – Banking, Commerce and Investment in the Ottoman Empire*, edited by Philip L. Cottrell, 143–159. Farnham: Ashgate, 2008.

Türkiye'de Mili İktisat: (1908–1918). Ankara: Yurt Yayınevi, 1982.

Tugay, Âsaf *İbret: Abdülhamid'e Verilen Jurnaller ve Jurnalciler*. 2 vols. Vol. I. İstanbul: Okat Yayınevi, 1962.

Tuğlacı, Pars. *The Role of the Balian Family in Ottoman Architecture*. İstanbul: Yeni Çığır Kitâbevi, 1990.

Türer, Osman. 'Les Caractéristiques Originalles de la Pensée du Malâmat et les Transformations de Cette Pensée Avec le Temps.' In *Mélamis-Bayrâmis Etudes sur trois mouvements mystiques musulmans*, edited by Nathalie Clayer, Alexandre Popovic, and Thierry Zarcone. İstanbul: Les Edition Isis, 1998.

Unat, Faik [Reşit]. 'Osmanlı Medreselerinde İlmi Verimi ve İlim Anlayışını Etkileyen Amiller.' *Türkiye Günlügü*, no. 58 (1999): 95–105.

'Osmanlı Resmi Düşüncesinin 'İlmiye Tariki' İçindeki Etkileri: Patronaj İlişkisi.' *Türk Yurdu* 45, no. 391 (1991): 33–42.

Osmanlı Sefirleri ve Sefaretnâmaleri. Edited by Bekir Sıtkı Baykal. Ankara: Türk Târîh Kurumu, 1968.

Uyar, Mesut, and Edward J. Erickson. *A Military History of the Ottomans: From Osman to Atatürk*. Santa Barbara, CA: Praeger Security International, 2009.

Uzunçarşılı, İsmail Hakkı. 'Asâkir-i Mansure'ye Fes Giydirilmesi Hakkında Sadr-ı Âzam Takrîri ve II. Mahmud'un Hatt-ı Humayunu (2 resmle birlikte).' *Belleten* XVIII, no. 70 (1954): 223–230.

'Çapanoğulları.' *Belleten* XXXVIII, no. 150 (1974): 215–261.

'III. Selim'ün Velihat iken Fransa Kralı XVI. Louis ile Muharabeleri.' *Belleten* II, no. 5–6 (1938): 191–246.

Midhat Paşa ve Tâif Mahkûmları. Ankara: Türk Târîh Kurumu Basımevi, 1950.

'Nizâm-ı Cedit Ricâlinden Vâlide Sultan Kethüdâsı Meşhûr Yusuf Ağa ve Kethüdâzâde Mehmet Arif Efendi.' *Belleten* XX, no. 79 (1956): 485–525.

Osmanlı Devleti Teşkilâtından Kapıkulu Ocakları: Acemi Ocağı ve Yeniçeri Ocağı. Ankara: Türk Târîh Kurumu, 1988.

Osmanlı Devletinin İlmiye Teşkilatı. Ankara: Türk Târîh Kurumu, 1965.

'Sultan Abdülaziz Vak'asına Dair Vak'anüvis Lütfi Efendi'nin Bir Risâlesi.' *Belleten* VII, no. 28 (1943): 349–373.

'V. Murad'ı Tekrar Padişâh Yapmak İsteyen K. Skaliyeri-Aziz Bey Komitesi.' *Belleten* VIII, no. 30 (1944): 245–328.

Ülgener, Sabri F. *İktisadi Çözülmenin Ahlak ve Zihniyet Dünyası: Fikir ve Sanat Târîhi Boyu Akisleri İle Bir Portre Denemesi*. İstanbul: Der Yayınları, 1981.

Ünver, Süheyl. 'Yayın Hayâtımızda Önemli Bir Yeri Olan Sarafim Kırâathânesi.' *Belleten* XLIII, no. 170 (1979): 481–489.

Veinstein, Gilles. 'La voix du maître à travers les firmans de Soliman le Magnifique.' In *Soliman le Magnifique et son temps*, edited by Gilles Veinstein, 127–144. Paris: La Documentation française, 1992.

Veinstein, Gilles, and Nicolas Vatin. *Le sérail ébranlé*. Paris: Fayard, 2003.

Vernoit, Stephen. 'The Visual Arts in Nineteenth Century Muslim Thought.' In *Islamic Art in the 19th century: Tradition, Innovation, and Eclecticism*, edited by Doris Behrens-Abouseif and Stephen Vernoit, 19–35. Leiden: Brill, 2006.

Vincent, David. *The Rise of Mass Literacy: Reading and Writing in Modern Europe*. Cambridge, UK: Polity, 2000.

Vittinghoff, Natascha. 'Readers, Publishers and Officials in the Contest for a Public Voice and the Rise of a Modern Press in Late Qing China (1860–1880).' *T'oung Pao* 87, no. 4/5 (2001): 393–455.

Wedeen, Lisa. *Peripheral Visions: Publics, Power, and Performance in Yemen*. Chicago: University of Chicago Press, 2008.

Westney, D. *Eleanor. Imitation and Innovation: The Transfer of Western Organizational Patterns to Meiji Japan*. Cambridge, MA: Harvard University Press, 1987.

White, Sam. *The Climate of Rebellion in the Early Modern Ottoman Empire*. Cambridge: Cambridge University Press, 2011).

Williams, Raymond. *Marxism and Literature*. Oxford: Oxford University Press, 1977.

Wortman, Richard. 'Rule by Sentiment: Alexander II's Journeys through the Russian Empire.' *The American Historical Review* 95, no. 3 (1990): 745–771.

Wuthnow, Robert. *Communities of Discourse: Ideology and Social Structure in the Reformation, the Enlightenment, and European Socialism*. Cambridge, MA: Harvard University Press, 1989.

Yakut, Esra. *Şeyhülislâmlık: Yenileşme Döneminde Devlet ve Din*. İstanbul: Kitâbevi, 2005.

Yavuz, Yusuf Şevki. *Kur'an-ı Kerim'de Tefekkür ve Tartışma Metodu*. Bursa: İlim ve Kültür Yayınları, 1983.

Yaycioglu, Ali. *Partners of the Empire: The Crisis of the Ottoman Order in the Age of Revolutions*. Stanford, CA: Stanford University Press, 2016.

Yi, Eunjeong. *Guild Dynamics in Seventeenth-Century Istanbul: Fluidity and Leverage*. Leiden: E. J. Brill, 2004.

Yūjirō, Murata. 'Dynasty, State and Society: The Case of Modern China.' In *Imagining the People: Chinese Intellectuals and the Concept of Citizenship, 1890–1920*, edited by Joshua A. Fogel and Peter G. Zarrow, 113–142. New York: M. E. Sharpe, 1997.

Zaret, David. *Origins of Democratic Culture: Printing, Petitions, and the Public Sphere in Early-Modern England*. Princeton, NJ: Princeton University Press, 2000.

Zilfi, Madeline C. 'Elite Circulation in the Ottoman Empire: Great Mollas of the Eighteenth Century.' *Journal of the Economic and Social History of the Orient* 26, no. 3 (1983): 318–364.

Zürcher, Erik J. *Turkey: A Modern History*. London: I. B. Tauris, 2004.

Index

1856 Reform Decree, 152

â'yân, 38–40, 53, 82, 141, 191
Abdi Efendi, 100, 257
Abdülaziz, 1–2, 12, 22, 83–84, 89, 122, 146, 169, 171, 173, 193, 198, 201, 216, 222–226, 230, 232–233, 237, 240–242, 247, 251, 253, 256, 277, 291, 310
Abdülhamid I, 29, 31, 35
Abdülhamid II, 1–2, 71, 84, 87–88, 90–91, 93, 106, 137, 194, 220, 223, 225, 230, 237, 241–242, 244–248, 251, 254, 258–259, 270, 277, 290, 293, 310
Abdullah Cevdet, 151, 294
Abdüllâtîf Pasha, 196
Abdülmecid, 10, 21, 79, 90, 102, 122, 134, 140, 142, 144, 158, 200, 226, 233
Abdurrahman Adil, 84, 257
Abidin Pasha, 91
Académie française, 157
Académie Royale des Sciences, 149
Ağa Hüseyin Pasha, 44
Ahlâk-ı Alâ'î, 23, 271
Ahmed Emin Yalman, 188
Ahmed III, 216
Ahmed Lûtfî Efendi, 13, 55, 58, 76, 78, 86, 104, 106, 204, 227, 257
Ahmed Mithat Efendi, 151, 185, 224, 229
Ahmed Rasim, 104, 107, 135, 187, 191, 210, 258
Ahmed Saib Efendi, 226
Ahmed Vasıf Efendi, 66
Ahmed Vefik Pasha, 149, 210, 224, 229
Ahmet Hamdi Tanpınar, 5, 116, 129, 165, 173, 202, 220, 223, 246, 302, 309
Âkif Paşa, 179, 258
Alemdâr Mustafa Pasha, 39–40, 45, 137
Aleppo, 43, 180, 277
Alexander II, 57, 154, 311
Alexandria, 92, 167, 196, 298, 303
Alexis de Tocqueville, 35, 280
Ali Efendi, 99, 186, 228
Ali Haydar Bey, 11, 168–169, 244
Âli Pasha, 41, 85, 90, 105, 135, 138, 149, 158, 162, 182, 201, 292
Ali Pasha of Janina, 38
Ali Şefkati Bey, 93
Ali Suâvi, 108, 214, 217, 227, 248, 300
Antoine-François Andréossy, 39
Antonio Gallenga, 237
Antonio Gramsci, 85, 293
Araba Sevdası, 202, 205, 207, 277
Arabic, IV, 2, 6–8, 23, 38, 66, 72, 98, 101, 113, 118, 120, 123, 130, 137, 141, 146, 158, 162, 169, 181, 196, 203, 210, 240, 242, 272, 281, 295
Arif Hikmet Bey, 83, 106, 138
Aristotle, 98
Armand-Pierre Caussin de Perceval, 10
Armenian, 19, 107, 113, 123, 164, 183, 208
askeri, 15, 112–113
avâm, 23–24, 29, 35, 42, 50, 120, 152–153, 158, 243, 272
Ayetullah Efendi, 101, 183
Aziz Ali Bey, 2–3

Baghdad, 7–51
Balta Limanı Treaty, 61
Basîret, 186, 190, 195, 199, 248, 259, 263, 265, 281
Basîretçi Ali, 194–195, 228–229
Bektaşi, 47
Benderli Mehmed Selim Sırrı Pasha, 49

Benedict Anderson, 113, 153, 180, 219
Beşir Fuâd, 151, 303
Bosnia, 25, 245
bourgeois, 14–15, 73, 253
Britain, 29, 35, 62, 77, 111, 148, 160, 202, 227, 292, 296, 301, 304
British, 25–26, 29, 54, 74–75, 81, 110, 114, 144, 157, 160, 167, 178, 181, 185, 232, 260, 278, 285–286, 288–289, 298, 302–303, 306

C. A. Bayly, 3, 18, 26, 167, 209, 243, 298
Cairo, 2, 54, 65, 127, 163, 294, 306
Caliph, 220, 247
Çalık Ahmed, 228
Campbell Mustafa Ağa, 136
Catherine the Great, 28, 42
Cemal Pasha, 2
Cemiyet, 19, 87, 90, 98, 109, 154, 160, 164, 167–168, 170, 172, 190, 260, 271, 275, 291
Cemiyet-i Edebiye, 170
Cemiyet-i İlmiye, 19, 109, 154, 160, 164, 167, 190, 260, 275, 291
Cerîde-i Havâdis, 5, 18, 21, 46, 48, 92, 178–179, 181, 195, 263, 271, 275, 279, 299
Cevdet Pasha, V, 19, 39–40, 44, 49, 51, 54, 81, 83, 85–86, 98, 100, 105, 107, 132–133, 135, 158–159, 182, 203, 230, 246, 249–250
Charles MacFarlane, 53, 66, 137, 180
China, 58, 139, 162, 175, 181, 199, 302, 306, 311
Chitalishte, 19
Çırağan Palace, 239
coffeehouses, 24, 33, 70, 188, 190, 209
Committee of Union and Progress, 2, 93, 282
common people, 7, 23–24, 50, 152, 158, 162, 243
Comte Auguste de Forbin, 25
Constantinople, 2, 25, 39, 47, 49, 53–54, 59, 66–67, 70, 81, 110, 113, 125, 136, 140, 157, 177–178, 180, 184, 190, 207, 210, 217, 226, 229, 235, 237, 244, 259–261, 263, 266, 268, 272, 277–278, 280
Constitution, 53, 78, 199, 230, 244, 246, 250, 267, 269, 281
Constitutional Government, 242
Council of the State, 174, 217
Crimea, 29, 75, 166, 247
Crimean War, 10, 61, 77, 81, 109, 144, 154, 156, 182, 184, 196, 203, 210, 301
Cuba, 70

Dâire-i Adâlet, 17
Dâmâd Mahmud Pasha, 90, 96
Dâmâd Said Pasha, 132
Dârülfünun, 21, 109, 135, 146–147, 149, 152–154, 156, 171, 250, 265, 275
Darüşafaka, 170
Deed of Agreement, 40, 42
Delâil, 113, 115, 122, 127
ders-i âmm, 146, 153
Derviş Pasha, 54, 148–149, 154, 156
devlet sohbeti, 33
Diyojen, 183, 190, 192, 195, 207, 259–261, 263–265, 271
Dolmabahçe Palace, 144, 232

E. J. W. Gibbs, 116
Ebuzziyâ Tevfik, 84, 95, 98, 101, 106, 164, 187, 193, 196
Edhem Pasha, 147
efkâr-ı âmme, 5–6, 8–9
efkâr-ı umûmîye, 2–3, 6, 9–11, 58, 249, 251
Egypt, 3, 27, 38, 41, 75, 155, 163, 168, 203, 247, 293, 295, 302
Elias Gibb, 131
Emin Nihad, 135, 205, 268
Encümen-i Dâniş, 109, 157–158
England, 10, 14, 77, 97, 138, 147–148, 179, 184, 187, 192, 199, 203, 223, 243, 285, 289, 292, 305, 312
Enlightenment, 4, 14, 29, 37, 50, 72, 78, 87, 97, 116, 125, 151, 169, 197, 203, 218, 286, 288, 292–293, 296, 299, 302, 306, 308, 311
Enver Pasha, 2
Eric Hobsbawm, 250
Esad Efendi, 10, 50–51, 57, 65–66, 68, 80, 100, 102, 242, 256, 266, 268, 273

Esad Pasha, 103
eshâm, 31, 33, 37, 50
Eşkinci Ocağı, 48

Faruk Nafiz, 220
Fatherland or Silistra, 196, 219
Fehim Süleyman Efendi, 83
Felatun Bey ve Râkım Efendi, 202
Feyzullah Efendi, 215
France, 9, 14, 30, 37, 61, 72, 74–75, 80, 92, 101, 136, 146, 148, 151, 179, 185, 202, 225, 244–245, 248, 273, 293, 295, 300–301, 303
François de Tott, 136
Freemason, 92, 261, 266
Freemasonry, 73, 77, 81, 92–93, 169, 261, 290, 296, 308
French, 4, 6, 8–10, 14, 29–30, 37, 39, 45, 48, 51, 61–62, 72, 74, 79–80, 82, 93, 99, 101, 109, 124, 131, 133, 136, 138, 140, 144, 146, 160, 164–165, 185, 190, 196, 199–200, 203, 207, 210, 215, 226–227, 233, 241, 248, 265, 285, 287, 289–290, 293, 297, 304
Fuâd Pasha, 97, 107, 116, 146, 149, 202

Galib Pasha, 44
Georg Rosen, 49
George Jones, 53, 269
George Washburn, 229
German, 2, 4, 14, 28, 74, 87, 187, 210, 215, 230, 294, 296, 306
Germany, 2, 4, 14, 75, 160, 187, 287–288, 295
Gilles Jean Marie Barazer de Kermorvan, 136
Giuseppe Fossati, 143–144, 171
Gore Ouseley, 77
Greece, 26, 38, 41, 169, 197, 204, 266, 278, 292, 305, 308
Greek, 17, 19, 26, 41, 46, 93, 98, 125, 141, 164, 185, 190, 195–196, 208, 210, 237, 281, 285, 308

Habsburg Empire, 27
Hâfız Osman, 115
Hagia Sophia, 51
Haiti, 70
Hakayık, 215, 264
Halil Bey, 154, 156, 159, 163, 269
Halim Giray, 122
Hans Speier, 4, 185
Hariri of Basra, 120
Hawaii, 59
Hejaz, 245
Henry Elliot, 232
Hersekli Arif Hikmet Bey, 95
Hezârfen Hüseyin Efendi, 130
Homi Bhabha, 58, 126
Hüseyin Avni Pasha, 224, 232, 240
Hüseyin Vâiz Kâşifî, 120
Hyde Clarke, 26, 74, 148–149

İbni Teymiye, 122
İbnülemin Mahmud Kemal İnal, 78, 84, 102, 116, 172, 208, 210, 256
İbrahim Alâettin Gövsa, 4
İbrahim Pasha, 215
İbrahim Şinâsi, 6, 8, 85, 97, 106, 161, 170, 193, 195, 197, 202, 217, 252, 267, 270, 280
İkdam, 11, 71, 99, 135, 188, 196, 228, 258–259, 273, 279–280
İmam Birgivi, 122
Immanuel Kant, 105, 212, 271
Imperial Medical School, 137
Imperial Music School, 137
Iran, 41, 50, 58, 77, 143, 147, 283, 285, 290, 293, 306
İrfan Pasha, 97
İsmail Ferruh Efendi, 63, 73, 75–77, 80, 82–83, 87, 92, 102, 119–120, 122–126, 131, 271
Istanbul, 2, 4, 9, 11, 18–19, 24, 26, 28–30, 33, 39–40, 42–43, 47, 49, 51, 53, 57, 59–60, 62–63, 65, 67, 76–77, 79, 82, 91, 96, 99, 105, 107, 112–113, 116, 119, 122, 135, 138, 143–144, 146, 148–149, 151, 156–157, 159, 165, 167, 169–171, 175, 177–179, 181–182, 184, 188, 191–192, 196, 198, 202–203, 207, 214, 216, 227–228, 232, 235, 243, 251, 256–258, 265–268, 270–272, 276, 278–280, 283–285, 287, 289–290, 294, 297–299, 303, 308, 310–311
Izmir, 92

Jacques Necker, 37
James Ellsworth De Kay, 110
James Porter, 110, 277
James Redhouse, 6, 10, 76, 120, 141, 158, 196, 278
janissaries, 20, 25, 40, 43–51, 53–56, 60, 64, 71–72, 79–80, 82, 87, 102, 128, 133, 137, 141, 149, 155, 171, 179, 188, 200, 217, 229–230, 243, 251
Jean Antoine Nollet, 149
Jean-François Marmontel, 8, 273
Jean Pietri, 182
Jean Victor Duruy, 146
jihad, 45, 212
John P. Brown, 81, 92
John Ponsonby, 178
John Stuart Mill, 35
Joseph Hume, 185, 296
Joseph von Hammer-Purgstall, 158
Julia Pardoe, 111
Jürgen Habermas, 4, 14, 19, 25, 72–73, 75, 77, 79, 82, 86, 105, 191, 209, 251, 253, 291–292, 294
Jürgen Osterhammel, 253

Kabakçı Mustafa, 39
Kâbûsnâme, 115
Kallimaki Bey, 9
Karatheodori Pasha, 19, 161
Karl Marx, 48, 111, 147, 218, 301
Kâtip Çelebi, 17, 23, 125, 130, 190, 259, 271, 293
Keçecizâde Mehmet İzzet Molla, 115–116, 256, 271
Keith Baker, 6, 215
Kemal Paşa-zâde, 114
Kenneth Pomeranz, 25
kerâmet, 69–70
Kethüdâzâde Mehmet Arif Efendi, 76–77, 131, 310
Kınalızâde Ali, 17, 23, 119, 271
konak, 47, 83–84, 88–90, 96, 106, 108, 182
Kostaki Musurus Pasha, 10
Küçük Said Pasha, 106

La Societe Impériale de Médecine, 156
La Turquie, 26, 68, 192, 219, 237, 260, 262, 281
Le Courrier d'Orient, 182, 205
Le Temps, 229–232, 235, 260, 262
Leskofçalı Gâlib, 197
Levant Herald, 78, 157, 217, 219, 237, 240, 260, 263
Liberty, 35, 244, 250, 274
Lionel René François, marquis de Moustier, 101
Liverpool, 70
London, 2, 5–6, 11, 14, 18, 23, 26, 28–29, 34, 47, 50, 53, 55–56, 59, 61–62, 66, 70, 75–77, 105, 110–111, 113–114, 116, 119–120, 125–129, 132, 136–137, 139, 147–148, 156, 166, 180, 182, 185, 188, 190, 192, 198, 201, 203–204, 208–209, 214, 216, 222–223, 226, 232, 237, 241, 259, 266–267, 269–272, 276, 278, 281, 284–287, 289–292, 295–296, 298, 300–302, 305, 307–308, 312
Lord Acton, 37
Lord Chesterfield, 193
Lord Derby, 227, 264
Louis XV, 149
Louis XVI, 37, 45
Lucy Garnett, 207
Lyceum Movement, 160

Mahmud Celâleddin Pasha, 223, 242
Mahmud Cevad, 139, 159
Mahmud II, 1, 10, 20, 40, 42–46, 48, 50–51, 53–55, 57, 59, 64–65, 71–72, 79–80, 82, 91, 102, 116, 130–131, 137, 139, 147, 155–156, 170, 243, 251, 295, 301, 304
Mahmud Nedim Pasha, 12, 194, 216, 225–226, 228–231, 233
mâlikâne, 31
Manchester, 70, 151, 171, 226, 287, 301
maslahah, 23
Masonic, 77–78, 81, 90, 92–93, 119, 259–260, 262, 267
Masons, 77, 79, 92–93
mass education, 21, 135, 252

Mecdi Mehmed Efendi, 146, 280
meclis, 21, 72–73, 85, 97, 109, 219, 242, 251
Meclis-i Ahkam-i Adliye, 103
Meclis-i Meşveret, 39–40, 45, 102, 181
Meclis-i Vâlâ, 142, 167, 171, 255
Mecmuâ-i Fünun, 147, 160, 162, 165, 167–168, 170, 185
Mecmuâ-i İber-i İntibah, 11, 167–169
Mecmuâ-i İbretnümâ, 168
Mecmuâ-i İstatistik, 177
Mecmuâ-i Maârif, 172, 190
Medical School, 137
Mehmed Arif Efendi, 115
Mehmed Behiç Bey, 175, 257
Mehmed Emin Bey, 201, 225
Mehmed II, 125, 237
Mehmed Rüşdü Pasha, 89
Mehmed Tahir Efendi, 44
Mehmet Derviş Pasha, 147
Mehmet Kaplan, 8
Melekpaşazâde Abdülkadir Bey, 73, 76
Memduh Pasha, 229
Mexico, 160
Michael Faraday, 151, 309
Michel de Certeau, 119
Michel Foucault, 50, 63, 125, 132, 218
Middle Ages, 7, 73, 120, 284, 300
Midhat Cemal Kuntay, 84, 226
Midhat Pasha, 1, 73, 90, 93, 222, 224, 227, 237, 240–241, 244–245, 259
Mikhail Katkov, 166, 306
Mir'ât, 11, 135, 138, 172, 222, 225, 229–230, 237, 241–244, 248, 273, 275–276, 278
Mirza Abu-l-Hasan Khan Shirazi, 77
Mîzâncı Murad, 193, 274
Moldavia, 34, 62, 281
Mozart, 171
Muhammed Ali Pasha, 38–39, 65
Muhammediye, 23, 281
Muhbir, 183, 201
münâzara, 21, 73, 97–104, 106, 109, 212, 266
Münif Efendi, 138, 147, 149, 152–153, 160–161, 164–165, 190, 275
Murad IV, 24, 46
Murad V, 12, 90, 93, 225, 233, 235, 241, 248
Musa Kâzım Pasha, 208
Mustafa Fâzıl Pasha, 88, 97, 208
Mustafa II, 60
Mustafa III, 27, 29, 35
Mustafa Naili Pasha, 10, 227
Mustafa Naîmâ, 5, 17, 24, 43, 66, 114, 228, 274–275

Nâmık Kemal, 6, 21, 79, 84–85, 89, 93, 96–97, 101, 108, 114, 135, 169–170, 178, 183, 185–186, 188, 193, 195, 197–198, 201–202, 207, 210, 213–214, 216–218, 221, 226–227, 241–242, 253, 266–267, 272, 275, 279, 284, 291, 303
Napoléon III, 235, 248
New York Times, 228, 235
Nigar Hanım, 95–96, 279, 286
Niyazi Berkes, 79, 129, 139, 146, 296
Nizâm-ı Cedîd, 48, 132, 299

obshchestvo, 107
Ohannes Vahanyan, 161
Ömer Fevzi Pasha, 131
orientalism, 253
Osman Ergin, 89, 144, 148
Osman II, 27, 43
Osman Nuri, 240, 277

Paleologi, 131
Paris, 1, 4, 7, 9–10, 26, 30, 39, 42, 45–46, 48, 54, 56, 62, 65, 68, 78, 85, 88, 92, 98, 108, 110, 123, 125, 135–136, 138, 147–148, 154, 171, 177, 179, 198, 201, 215, 240, 244, 246–247, 258, 266, 268–269, 271–272, 274, 278–280, 282, 285–286, 290, 293–295, 300, 303, 309, 311
Parliament, 214, 243, 245
Pazvantoğlu, 38, 41, 293
Persian, 6, 17, 28, 58, 71, 89, 98, 113–115, 120, 123, 129, 158, 181, 196, 210, 218, 229, 278, 287, 307
Pertev Pasha, 1, 3
Peter the Great, 155–156, 284, 288
Proodos, 93

public opinion, VI, 1–4, 7–11, 13–15, 21–22, 25, 35, 37, 39, 44–45, 49–51, 53, 55, 57, 61, 71–72, 74, 82, 84, 86, 88, 91, 108–109, 124, 134, 138, 151, 165, 170, 173, 178, 180, 185, 193–194, 198–199, 202, 204, 209, 213–214, 216, 219, 222–225, 227, 229, 232–233, 237, 240, 242, 244–246, 248–249, 251–254
public reading, 19–20, 188
Pyotr Rumyantsev, 29

Qajars, 143

Râgıb Pasha, 27
Recâîzâde Ahmed Cevdet, 122
Recâîzâde Ekrem, 220
Reinhard Schulze, 59
Reinhart Koselleck, 78, 87, 251
Reşad Bey, 101, 214
Reşid Pasha, 9, 83, 85, 103, 132, 158, 200
Robert Walsh, 47, 67, 184, 188
Roger Chartier, 78, 111, 114, 122, 127, 284, 288
Russia, 27–29, 31, 42, 54, 57, 77, 107, 118, 151, 154, 156, 160, 166, 175, 179, 187, 216, 282, 284, 287, 290, 301, 303, 308
Russian Empire, 28, 57, 61, 184, 197, 215, 298, 311

Saadeddin Paşazâde Nasuh Paşa, 141
Sabah, 86, 183, 258
Sadık Rifat Pasha, 8, 11, 57, 79, 138
Sakızlı Ohannes Efendi, 161, 278
Sâlih Efendi, 116, 149
Sâmî Pasha, 145
Samuel Johnson, 191, 193, 298
Şânîzâde Mehmed 'Atâ'ulla Efendi, 5, 10, 18, 40, 46–47, 76, 102, 122, 124, 126, 133, 279, 290
Scaliari Bey, 93
School of Military Sciences, 137
schooling of the public, 21, 134–135, 142–143, 145, 147, 154, 157, 159, 161–162, 164, 171–172, 175, 220
Selim III, 24, 33, 37, 39, 42–43, 45, 48, 54, 57, 60, 63, 76, 102, 130, 132, 137, 241, 251, 295, 298, 303–304, 308
Sened-i İttifâk. See Deed of Agreement
Şerif Mardin, 9, 13, 41, 59–60, 74, 84, 168, 170, 197
Servet İskit, 5
Seven Years' War, 29
Severnaia pchela, 57
Şevket Rado, 107
Şeyh Cezuli, 114
Şeyhülislam Mekkizâde, 44
Seyyid Hasan Hoca, 137
sharia, 12, 15, 233
Shenbao, 181
Shmuel Eisenstadt, 58
sibyan mektebleri, 139
Sigmund Freud, 225
Simon Deutsch, 197, 302
Şirket-i Hayriye, 203–204, 207, 273, 280
Society for the Diffusion of Useful Knowledge, 160, 166
Society of Poets, 95–97, 138, 197
Softas, 229, 232, 244, 253, 262–263
Sublime Porte, 61–62, 83, 103, 110, 130, 142–143, 184, 200, 229, 279, 291
Süleyman İzzî, 66
Süleyman Nazif, 96, 196, 220, 227, 279
Şûrâ-ı Devlet, 104, 174
Sururi Çelebi, 119
Syllogos, 19

Ta'if, 1
Tahsîn Pasha, 91
Takvîm-i Vekâyi, 3, 25, 57, 59, 64–66, 68, 70–71, 103–105, 140, 142, 145, 149, 152–153, 158, 180–181, 184, 204, 237, 245, 260–264, 268, 275
Tanzimat, 9, 13–14, 21, 40–41, 64–65, 68, 73, 77, 83–84, 86, 88–89, 99, 102–103, 105–106, 109, 112–113, 126, 130, 133–134, 138, 143, 145, 155–156, 158, 170, 173, 178, 180, 188, 194, 202, 205, 212, 214, 217, 221, 246, 251–253, 276, 282–283, 288, 290–291, 295–298, 301, 305

Târîh-i Cevdet, 27, 40, 44–46, 48–49, 51, 54, 56, 76, 81, 102, 139, 159, 257
Târîh-i Vassaf, 114–116, 119, 127
Taşköprülü Ahmed Efendi, 99
Taşlıcalı Yahyâ, 96
Tasvîr-i Efkâr, 11, 17, 99, 106, 146, 149, 152–153, 161, 164, 167–168, 183, 186, 193, 195, 197, 217, 261–262, 264, 267–268, 270–271, 275, 280
Teodor Kasap, 195
terbiye-i âmme, 21, 134, 157–158, 160
Tercüman-ı Ahvâl, 109, 159, 195, 262, 280
The Times, 1–2, 188, 226, 229–231, 235, 247, 259–260, 263
Thomas Kuhn, 131
Topkapı Palace, 51, 102
Turkey, 2, 12, 26, 29, 40, 49–51, 59, 61, 74, 78, 92–93, 99, 110, 127, 131, 137, 139, 143–144, 146, 148–149, 168, 179, 184, 188, 201, 204, 220, 222, 228–231, 233, 235, 245, 253, 260–261, 263, 266, 269, 271–272, 277–278, 282, 286, 290, 298, 300, 306, 308, 312

ulemâ, 18, 44, 46, 54, 106, 115, 130, 186, 217, 243, 248, 251
Üss-i Zafer, 10, 51, 65, 268

Vakâyi-i Mısriye, 65, 67
Vakit, 12, 169, 233, 237, 242, 244–245, 260, 262, 264, 272–273, 282
Versailles, 40, 149
Victor Fontanier, 54
Vienna, 9, 26, 263

Wallachia, 33, 62, 204, 281
Walter Benjamin, 213
William Churchill, 178, 181
William St Clair, 165
Władysław Plater, 197

Xavier de Bianchi, 158

Yazıcıoğlu Mehmed Efendi, 23, 114, 281
Yazıcızâde Mehmed, 114
Yıldız Palace, 239, 248
Young Ottomans, 79, 87–89, 93, 101, 106, 109, 118, 172, 182, 197, 214, 217–218, 239, 241
Yusuf Kâmil Pasha, 73, 84, 97

Zafernâme, 192
Ziyâ Pasha, 95–96, 101, 183, 192, 242